The
Sixteenth
Minute

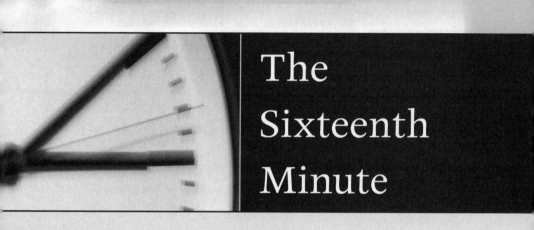

The
Sixteenth
Minute

Life in the Aftermath of Fame

Jeff Guinn
and Douglas Perry

JEREMY P. TARCHER/PENGUIN | A MEMBER OF PENGUIN GROUP (USA) INC. | NEW YORK

JEREMY P. TARCHER/PENGUIN
Published by the Penguin Group
Penguin Group (USA) Inc., 375 Hudson Street, New York, New York 10014, USA • Penguin Group (Canada),
10 Alcorn Avenue, Toronto, Ontario M4V 3B2, Canada (a division of Pearson Penguin Canada Inc.) • Penguin
Books Ltd, 80 Strand, London WC2R 0RL, England • Penguin Ireland, 25 St Stephen's Green, Dublin 2,
Ireland (a division of Penguin Books Ltd) • Penguin Group (Australia), 250 Camberwell Road, Camberwell,
Victoria 3124, Australia (a division of Pearson Australia Group Pty Ltd) • Penguin Books India Pvt Ltd,
11 Community Centre, Panchsheel Park, New Delhi–110 017, India • Penguin Group (NZ), Cnr Airborne and
Rosedale Roads, Albany, Auckland 1310, New Zealand (a division of Pearson New Zealand Ltd) • Penguin
Books (South Africa) (Pty) Ltd, 24 Sturdee Avenue, Rosebank, Johannesburg 2196, South Africa
Penguin Books Ltd, Registered Offices: 80 Strand, London WC2R 0RL, England

Library of Congress Cataloging-in-Publication Data

Guinn, Jeff.
The sixteenth minute : life in the aftermath of fame. /
Jeff Guinn and Douglas Perry.
p. cm.
Includes bibliographical references.
ISBN 1-58542-389-0
1. Celebrities—United States—Biography. 2. Fame—Social aspects—United States.
3. Interviews—United States. I. Perry, Douglas, date. II. Title.
CT220.G85   2005   2004059896
920.073—dc22
[B]

Printed in the United States of America
10 9 8 7 6 5 4 3 2 1

This book is printed on acid-free paper. ∞

Book design by Meighan Cavanaugh

Most Tarcher/Penguin books are available at special quantity discounts for bulk purchase
for sales promotions, premiums, fund-raising, and educational needs. Special books
or book excerpts also can be created to fit specific needs. For details, write
Penguin Group (USA) Inc. Special Markets, 375 Hudson Street, New York, NY 10014.

For Robert I. Fernandez, my brother
JEFF GUINN

For Deborah, my love
DOUGLAS PERRY

Contents

The
Sixteenth
Minute

Nat Finkelstein's photograph of Andy Warhol supposedly at the moment the artist predicted, "In the future, everyone will be famous for fifteen minutes." Warhol's assistant Gerard Malanga is at left beside him.

Introduction

In the future, everyone will be famous for fifteen minutes.
ANDY WARHOL

America was celebrity-obsessed long before Andy Warhol came along. In the 1920s, periodicals like the *New York Graphic* titillated readers with newsy tidbits about singers, actors, and socialites. In the '30s and '40s, gossip columnists Hedda Hopper, Walter Winchell, and Louella Parsons were competing in major newspapers to dish the best, latest dirt on celebrities (actress Joan Bennett, angered by some unflattering mention, once sent Hopper a skunk). By the early '50s, the scandal sheet *Confidential* led a flood of new "tell-all" tabloids that included *Uncensored, Exposed, Exclusive, The Lowdown,* and *Hush-Hush*. Americans were vicarious participants in the failed marriage of baseball icon Joe DiMaggio and film sex symbol Marilyn Monroe. When singer Frank Sinatra pursued, married, and split from actress Ava Gardner, their fans eagerly read about every rumored nuance of the relationship. The advent of television fed the frenzy; now you could have famous people in your own living room. In 1960, Hopper had her own network special on NBC. But it wasn't until Warhol that there was a definitive declaration of what most Americans really wanted: not only the chance to *know* everything about celebrities but also the opportunity to *become* celebrities themselves.

Warhol didn't approach the subject of fame as a detached observer. In 1965, the first year that 90 percent of all Americans owned at least one television, Warhol decided he had to have recognition beyond his limited reputation in New York City as an avant-garde artist. As part of his effort to become a national celebrity, he hooked up with a freelance photographer named Nat Finkelstein, whose photos of civil rights clashes in the South had run in almost every major newspaper and news magazine in the country. For Warhol, Finkelstein's connections to influential periodicals meant the chance for wider publicity. For Finkelstein, Warhol and his sometime collaborators—Lou Reed, Edie Sedgwick, Nico, Ultra Violet—represented "the most decadent underbelly of America for me to photograph." Finkelstein took his new subject on a photo shoot in a New York street, and during that session—with neighborhood children and a butcher in a bloody apron swarming around the odd-looking artist, trying to get into the pictures, too—Warhol apparently made a prediction: "In the future, everyone will be famous for fifteen minutes."

It proved true for Warhol, whose canvases of Campbell's soup cans and other "pop" art became a sensation for a while—almost as much so as the artist. Warhol showed up on talk shows. He made experimental movies and launched a magazine. At the height of his fame, a gun-wielding fan shot and wounded him. By then, his prediction was indelibly stamped into the collective American psyche, and his example was obvious: fame was possible for anybody who wanted it badly enough. America was rapidly becoming a tabloid nation, even if the mainstream media didn't know it yet. Education was becoming more superficial, titillation more acceptable. Digital technology would tip the balance for good. Soon, as *Life* magazine segued into *People*, as TV talk shows evolved from Edward R. Murrow's *Person to Person* to Mary Hart's *Entertainment Tonight*, "Everyone will be famous for fifteen minutes" became one of the most familiar phrases in U.S. history, right up there with "Fourscore and seven years ago" and "Give me liberty, or give me death."

Forty years after Warhol's pronouncement, there's no denying the accuracy of the notion. Thanks to cable television and the Internet, names and faces tumble into our living rooms and offices every day, every hour. We are inundated with peep-show personal websites and *Girls Gone Wild* videos and so-called reality TV, which gives ordinary people the opportunity to be watched by millions as they sing (*American Idol*) or seek a mate (*The Bachelor*) or eat live bugs (*Fear Factor*). In the 1960s, Warhol, who died in 1987, couldn't possibly have known that he was getting in on the ground floor of the greatest growth industry in human history: a celebrity boom based solely on grabbing the public's attention, for its own sake. It is an industry in which, with few exceptions, the product becomes obsolete with astonishing rapidity.

"Celebrities," declared historian Iris Chang, "are really distractions for the general public, first created, then most often destroyed—*consumed*—for our amusement."

Our need for that consumption has now become insatiable. Celebrities seem to take up ever-increasing amounts of our love and attention; they receive the validation we all want. And so, for a whole generation, the pursuit of fame has become an obsession. It doesn't matter what that fame is based on: talent or greed or sex—anything will do, as long as your face becomes even temporarily known to the rest of America. The first *American Idol* winner, Kelly Clarkson, a small-town girl from America's heartland, has never had any other ambition in her young life. Six months after achieving the spotlight in 2002, she excitedly exclaimed to a reporter: "The tabloids are the best. I think it's so cool that they think I'm cool enough to write about."

So far, they still do. But if almost everyone now seems to be getting those fifteen minutes of fame, most of them are also quickly forgotten. Left behind, they have to make sense of what happened and find a way to move on with their lives.

In a society defined by fame, how do former celebrities approach life after all the public attention has fallen away? For some, the silence that often follows fame can be devastating. For others, it can be a relief. Everyone, however, is changed by it. Sometimes, success in postcelebrity life can be as inspiring, if not more so, than whatever one did to become famous.

To explore the reality of postcelebrity life, the possibilities as well as the pitfalls, this book tracks seven men and women who in various ways came to exemplify our fifteen-minutes culture. Their stories inexorably lead us back to Kelly Clarkson and the "celebrity generation" that has never aspired to anything but fame.

Two and a half years after Nat Finkelstein snapped his first photos of Andy Warhol, the "fifteen minutes" prognostication was codified when the Pop artist put it down on paper, in the program for an exhibition of Warhol's work at the Moderna Museet in Stockholm. At about the same time, these seven Americans were in different stages of their lives. A few were already well known. The rest of them would be. All of them, eventually, would face their sixteenth minute.

In 1967, Maury Wills, at age thirty-five the best shortstop in major league baseball, had just been traded from his beloved Los Angeles Dodgers to the small-market Pittsburgh Pirates—punishment, he told friends, for defying Dodgers management. Irene Cara, barely school age, was a "Little Miss America" finalist. In another year, she would begin playing piano by ear. She believed, and was constantly told by her mother, that she was destined for fame. Jim Wright, forty-six, was a six-term member of the U.S. Congress. The future Speaker of the house was still a relatively anonymous politician whose obsessive ambition for higher office had not yet been matched by legislative accomplishment. Mick Foley, two years old, was living with his parents in East Setauket, New York, a middle-class town where his father was a well-known school administrator. Young Mick had not yet seen a professional wrestling match on TV, but already he loved showing off in front of anyone who'd watch. Susan McDougal was a twelve-year-old junior high school student in Camden, Arkansas. She was an avid churchgoer and movie buff who liked to pretend her family was "an Arkansas version of the Kennedys." Gerry Cooney, eleven, was being savagely beaten on a regular basis by his alcoholic father in their home on Long Island. The boy, big for his age and painfully insecure, spent his days hiding in the basement, praying he'd get through the day unscathed.

And in Nevada in December, a likable twenty-three-year-old loser was driving across the desert on his way to Los Angeles to try to reclaim his wife, who had run off with another man. Melvin Dummar didn't know it, but he was driving straight into the kind of future Andy Warhol had just envisioned.

Prologue

The desert outside Beatty was always black and desolate at night. Stars skated high across a wide sky, sliding away from the emptiness of the land.

Braking, Melvin Dummar let the car roll forward until it thumped onto the dirt. For a moment, he waited, listening to the chug of the car's engine, the headlights bleary against the emptiness of the night. He stared ahead at the road he'd found, what he could see of it. It disappeared almost immediately into a black hole.

Melvin sometimes felt like all he ever did was chase after Linda. It didn't used to be this way. She'd run off, and he'd simply wait for her to come back. It was a game they played. When she would disappear for a month or two, leaving their two-year-old daughter behind, Melvin would pretend she wasn't gone. And when she returned, Linda would pretend she hadn't been sleeping with other men.

Melvin let his mind roll back to the day they met in the school parking lot in California. He could picture her perfectly, checking herself in a car window, pulling her blouse tight as he started to introduce himself. She turned toward him slowly, but she was smiling, like it was about time someone approached her. Maybe it was. She was clearly waiting for something, and not just a ride home. She was fifteen years old.

Melvin liked being married to Linda. It made him feel important. If he had to go after her every few months, that was all right. He didn't mind driving long distances. Melvin erased that first image of her and created a fresher one, a view of her leaving. He had thought these same thoughts earlier in the day as he set off into the Nevada desert. He'd rolled them over and over in his brain until, finally, he had to pull over, because he was blubbering, unable to stop. That only made him feel worse, because he knew Linda always felt ashamed for him, a grown man, whenever he would cry.

That was one of the reasons, two days before he decided to go after her, Melvin had taken his motorcycle out into the desert. He'd wanted to wipe Linda out of his head; he needed to clear his mind and blow the gaskets. And just when it seemed like he could spread his arms and lift off, simply fly away, the bike squirmed out from under him. He landed face first, sliding butterfly-stroke style through the dirt. Years later he would tell the filmmaker Jonathan Demme about the accident, and he would regret opening his big mouth about it. "That's where they got the beginning of the movie," Melvin says now, shaking his head, still not able to believe it. "I was the one out there on the motorcycle, but that's not the way they did it in the movie."

Sitting in his car two days after the accident, though, Melvin Dummar couldn't possibly have conceived of someone ever making a movie about him. It wasn't even something worth fantasizing about. He flicked on the interior light in the car and checked his face in the rearview mirror. His cheeks were still pretty bad, swollen and raw and caked with little scabs. He sighed and looked out the windshield. He couldn't see much, but he knew what was out there. In the distance, the Funeral Mountains unrolled like the wound on his face, inflamed here and there, too tight against the earth's skin. Then the range dipped down into the depression that was the Amargosa Desert, which quickly beat the personality out of the landscape. Keep going west and you're in Death Valley, Melvin knew; keep going straight ahead and you hit Devil's Hole. Mostly, the open range just lay in front of Melvin like concrete, as though the highway were a miniature copy of the desert, cutting right through itself. There was nothing out there. It was just heavy, flat, dead space—ideal for a nuclear testing ground, which was exactly what it had been until a couple years before, when the government decided it had made enough craters in the desert. Many local residents still woke up at dawn, waiting for the blast, their skin prickling. If you were a regular on Highway 95 around daybreak, you knew to keep your windows rolled down, because the shock waves could suck them right out like God Himself wielding a plunger.

Melvin wasn't a regular, but he had made the trip a number of times before. It was still a ways to the next town, and he didn't think he could make it; he had to pee now. So he tapped down on the accelerator, the engine revved, and the car, a blue 1966 Chevrolet Caprice that looked cherry but didn't sound it, bumped slowly over the embankment that separated the highway from the dirt road, which he figured was probably an old, abandoned mining road. Dust filled the void outside the car, and Melvin leaned forward in his seat. Patches of scrub loomed up out of the dark like small beasts and rushed at him. Melvin squeezed his crotch with his hand to relieve the pressure; he knew it was dumb to have drunk so much beer when he was going to be driving all night. He'd hung around in Tonopah, gambling, too long. Long enough for any alcoholic buzz to wear off, but the bladder was something else. Of course, most guys would have just pulled onto the shoulder and unloaded a stream right there on the side of the highway, but Melvin could be rather prissy about such things. He didn't want some passing trucker to see him.

Appearances had always mattered to Melvin—perhaps more than they should have. He was, by his own description, a twenty-three-year-old "hillbilly at loose ends." He'd run himself out of the Air Force. He'd dropped out of junior college. His wife had left him. And he spent his days filling bags of magnesium in an old factory that seemed to be held together by stale sweat and phlegm. At the same time, though, he also knew none of that really mattered. Melvin had a picture of himself in his head that had nothing to do with any of those things, and he was determined to live up to it. That was why he didn't stop at the Cottontail Ranch to take a leak. Melvin didn't want to be seen going into a whorehouse, even by customers, even to take a leak and come right back out. So here he was a couple of miles away, on a dirt road that led nowhere. The road snaked away from the highway, nearly ending in a rut and then starting up again along the base of a low mound. Melvin continued farther than he had any need to go—he didn't know why—and when he came around a bend he finally slowed to a stop. He squinted out at what looked like a couple bags of garbage or old mining debris his headlights touched at feebly. Melvin had to pee so badly that his stomach hurt, but he waited again, looking at the dire blackness of the night as his brain repetitively turned over a new phrase he couldn't quite get right. He could hear the melody in his head being plucked simply on an acoustic guitar and the chorus kicking in with rising voices in the background. Melvin loved to sing and write songs. He knew that this was how he was going to score one day: one hit song—just one—could bring you six figures a year for a decade.

Melvin put the car into Park and climbed out. He hugged himself against the cold, searching for the right place, finding an open spot a few steps away. What happened next has varied slightly in Melvin's mind every time he's told the story over the past thirty-five years—and he's told it hundreds of times. Did he hear something or only see it? Had he taken a piss or was he about to? In this telling, he had just unzipped and let out a loud sigh of relief when he noticed movement. The breeze had caught something, and it was flapping lazily as if waving at him. He knew it wasn't garbage or old mining equipment. Melvin buttoned up, the near-freezing temperature gripping him. He became conscious of sound: the rustle of his shoes against the hard dirt, the *phhlitt* of his zipper, the disgruntled mumble of gravel at his feet. He felt suddenly small, like he had been shrunk in size and could be swept away without any warning. The blackness of the desert can do that to you, he knew—disorient you, send you spinning, the sky moving along with you as if it were stuck to your face and hands. Thinking about that, he turned, searching for the weak glow from the car's lights, and found it, seemingly moved off to his right. He stepped forward, looking for the flapping noise, until he saw the wavering mass again just beyond the headlights. He stopped. He could hear his breath rasping in his throat as he realized what he was seeing: a man, facedown, with long white hair laid out across the ground like a carpet. Melvin instinctively dropped into a defensive posture, scuttling in a half-circle as he tried to see if there was anyone else out there. No one. Nothing. The man on the ground didn't move. It was an old man, he could see now, very old, wearing a long-sleeved denim shirt and loose, stained trousers. Melvin was sure the man was dead. A drunk or an old prospector, or something worse—whatever it is that gets a man killed and dumped on a dirt road in the middle of the desert.

Melvin hugged himself again, trying to figure out what he should do. Should he drive over to the whorehouse and tell them to call the police? Should he leave some kind of marker so they could find their way back? Then, as if he were in a dream, Melvin watched as the corpse started to roll, one arm akimbo.

Melvin leaned forward in an effort to peer through the darkness that clouded his sight. What was he looking at? The old man wasn't facedown at all. He was up on elbows and knees. Melvin leapt forward and grabbed the man under the arms, and he could hear the man's breath suddenly accelerate and feel his arms become rigid. Melvin pulled him to his feet. It was like lifting a bag of groceries, he thought. The man was more than six feet tall but astonishingly thin and trembling badly. It was near freezing, and the man didn't have a coat. Another couple of hours, Melvin thought, and the geezer would've frozen to death.

"I'm all right," the man said, his voice a thin rasp, but Melvin could see that he wasn't. He was bleeding, for one thing. Melvin propped him up with an arm and his hip. The man resisted at first, but then leaned against Melvin, his legs buckling, drool running down his chin. He looked at Melvin sidelong, eyes drifting as if unmoored from any internal circuitry.

Melvin Dummar had just met the man who would change his life.

Hefting him like a duffel bag, Melvin helped the man into the Caprice and then climbed behind the wheel and turned the car around. The old man was shivering uncontrollably.

"Don't worry, I'll get you to a doctor," Melvin said. He repeated himself, but the old man didn't seem to hear him, though his fear appeared to be dissipating. The man leaned against the passenger-side door, his head lolling. It looked like he'd been living out in the desert a long time: his hair hadn't been cut in months and he had the pallor of the malnourished. "No," he finally said in a whisper. "No doctors."

"We should tell the police about this," Melvin said.

"No. No police. Just take me to Vegas." With that, the man turned away and rested his head on the passenger-side window. He wouldn't answer any more questions.

"I figured he was just some old prospector," Melvin would say more than thirty-five years later, his eyes alive with the memory, his voice rising. Melvin knew that this was his story and his alone, and he always told it with relish, building it slowly, piece by piece. "He gave me the heebie-jeebies," he continued. "He had blood on him: the hair on the side of his head was matted with blood, I couldn't tell from what. I asked him what had happened to him, but he just stared at me. I told him we should go to the doctor, that we should go to the police. He didn't say a word. He told me to take him to Vegas, and that was it. No doctor. No police. Just take me to Vegas."

Melvin could have gone into Beatty and left the old man in an emergency room or a police station, or simply dropped him off at the whorehouse that was a couple miles away; that would've been the easiest thing for him to do. But Melvin was an accommodating person by nature. He wasn't going to force the old guy to see a doctor, and he didn't mind taking him to Vegas; it was on the way. He guided the car back onto the highway and headed south again. But soon, the silence ate at him. If there was another human being in the vicinity, Melvin had to talk to him; the urge was just hardwired into his brain. And if that other person didn't hold up his end of the conversation, Melvin would do it for him.

So he told the old man he was going to Los Angeles to see his daughter, Darcy, because he couldn't work for a couple weeks thanks to a motorcycle accident that had put him in the hospital for a night. He could have added that Darcy was in L.A. because her mother had left him again and that this time, for whatever reason, Linda had wanted her daughter with her. But he decided not to mention that. Just the thought of it might make the tears come.

Melvin stared out at the empty highway, the old man silent in the seat beside him. The night and the landscape, what you could see of it, were lulling. Endless. After you came through Tonopah on the way to Las Vegas, you had better be prepared for nothing, because that was what you were going to get for mile after mile. Melvin knew that if he wasn't careful he could lose the white line in the syrupy darkness and run off the road without even realizing it. If he did that, he'd find himself right back in the hospital again, or in the morgue this time. Then how would he get Linda back?

Melvin noticed the old man was staring at him, and so he decided to talk about something positive, something that would get them the couple of hours into Vegas on the right note. "You want to hear a song?" he asked his passenger. No response. "I'm a singer," Melvin said. The old man continued to stare, but he didn't respond. Melvin said he'd always been able to hold a tune, he just had the knack. He wanted to get himself into clubs and start singing for people; he'd written some pretty good songs. You had to do your own material, he said. You're not going to get anywhere just singing covers.

That didn't get any response, either, which didn't surprise Melvin. He thought about all the great songs that never got heard, that never got recorded, whenever someone like him—someone who truly loved music down deep— had to set aside his guitar to make a living. How many hours had he sat with his friend Johnny Roman, God bless him, watching Johnny playing the guitar? Watching him attacking some difficult stretch of notes again and again and again until, finally, the notes cracked open, like a dam breaking, and music just poured out. The excitement of watching Johnny play was something he could never really talk about, could never explain, and that was okay. That's what the music was there for. For Melvin, so drawn to mournful, lonely melodies and country-and-western cheatin' songs, his musical ambition took some of the sting out of the music: he was too busy breaking down the chords and the melody to let the slap of the lyrics overwhelm him.

The old man didn't move, like he'd been paralyzed by an overdose of mournful songs himself. Melvin gazed out at the sky and the stars and decided to try another subject. "I love to fly," he told the man. "That's what I always wanted to do." The statement hung in the air between them for a moment, then the old man sat up a little, and asked him for his name. When Melvin told him, the old guy said, "You're a pilot?"

Melvin said he'd been a medic during his brief stint in the Air Force, "but I wanted to be a pilot." He'd wormed his way out of the service because he'd fallen for some girl, and he'd regretted it ever since. "I went back to the military and talked to them, and they said I could probably get back in, but I'd have to get these waivers and be examined by a psychiatrist." The old man turned to the window, breathing deeply, gazing out at the darkness. Silence again. Melvin went back to talking.

"I told him I was working at a magnesium mine in Gabbs right then, bagging magnesium," Melvin remembers. "I told him that I wanted a better job, that I'd been looking for something else, like at Hughes Aircraft in L.A., but they wouldn't hire me."

The old man turned back to Melvin, as if a bell had just gone off. Then he said, simply, "I could get you a job at Hughes Aircraft."

"Is that right?" Melvin said. "How could you do that?"

"I own the company." The old man asked Melvin for his name again, and Melvin found himself smiling at his passenger, smiling like a fool, and he decided to play along.

"You own Hughes Aircraft?"

The old man didn't say anything at first, just looked at Melvin with those tired, drifting eyes. Then he said, "I'm Howard Hughes."

Melvin turned his attention back to the road, but he couldn't take the smile off his face. Anyone who lived in Nevada knew who Howard Hughes was. He was a famous gazillionaire who pretty much owned Las Vegas, but he had disappeared from public sight years ago. Of course this old man wanted to be Howard Hughes. Why wouldn't he? Melvin shook his head. Not that he minded. Sometimes he wanted to be someone else, too. No, that wasn't quite right. Melvin wanted to be himself, but with a better shot at things. Better opportunities. He'd prefer it if the old man were a scout for a record company; then he could really be useful.

"You want to hear a song?" Melvin asked again. "I write good ones."

The old man didn't respond, but he didn't say no, so Melvin launched into his favorite, "When a Dream Can Become a Reality."

When a dream can become a reality
This is all you do
When a dream can become a reality
Work hard, have faith and courage
You can rise from a beggar to a king
With hard work, faith and courage
You can conquer anything.

He finished with a *rat-a-tat-tat* drumroll on the steering wheel. That pretty much brought the conversation to a close.

"He was just enjoying my singing; he didn't really say another word all the way in," Melvin recalls. And soon enough, the twirling lights of Las Vegas came into view, and the old man straightened himself in his seat, like he hadn't really believed they would make it to the city. It was still dark, but the first hint of dawn backlit the Strip. The casinos listed into view like distant buoys in an ocean of pavement and abandoned lots, the sidewalks ending in crumbles amid waves of wild grass. As they rolled down the Strip, the man directed Melvin, finally saying: "There. Pull in there."

The empty parking lot of the Sands casino could have been for a football stadium. Melvin's passenger pointed, and Melvin weaved around the light poles. In the back lot, just past the dumpster pen, the old bum told him to stop the car. With a grunt he heaved the passenger-side door open and climbed out. The man steadied himself, and took a step back. He seemed to give the car a good long look.

"You sure you gonna be okay?" Melvin asked him. The old man nodded and then, thinking better of it, stepped back to the car, grabbing hold of the door.

"You got any change?" he rasped.

Melvin sighed and fished a couple coins out of his pocket. He handed them over without looking at them. The man held the coins in his hand, examining them, turning them over. He gazed into the car, his eyes sticky. "Thank you, Melvin," he said. Then he turned and walked toward the back of the building.

Melvin watched him go, trying not to think about what would become of the old guy. He looked off at the still-quiet Strip beyond the parking lot, where even at this hour a few all-night gamblers wandered aimlessly. A couple of weary cocktail waitresses in short skirts and baked-on makeup exited the casino and crossed in front of him, headed for the back of the lot. Melvin knew it was at about this time of the morning that the government used to conduct its nuclear weapons tests out in the desert. For years, second-shift cocktail waitresses like these girls, giving in to an old wives' tale, put on sunglasses and slathered on sunscreen to protect themselves before leaving work every morning. There were posters all over town in the '50s to make you think about being extra-careful like that. Melvin didn't know it, but because of those posters, any cocktail waitress from back then might have thought she recognized the old man who'd just disappeared around the back of the Sands. With his matted white hair and puffy beard, Melvin's passenger was the spitting image of the hoary prospector—well, it was probably just an actor playing a prospector—who famously got his beard checked for radioactivity by a bikinied girl hefting a Geiger counter. Famous in Vegas, at least. The picture was the chamber of commerce's way of downplaying the significance of the testing site when it came on line. But Melvin had never seen the posters, or at least had never paid them any mind if he had. He took a deep breath and rubbed his face to verify that he was awake. He put the car in gear and rolled back out onto the Strip, a couple of hours behind schedule but with a story to tell Linda when he got to L.A. What he didn't know was that it was a story that was more radioactive than anything that girl with the Geiger counter—or her old prospector—had ever come across.

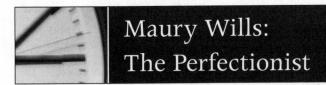

Maury Wills:
The Perfectionist

The seventy-year-old man has already been up for nearly two hours when he arrives at the church for a six forty-five A.M. meeting of his twelve-step group in Redondo Beach, an oceanside Los Angeles suburb. Immaculately dressed in a patterned silk shirt and chocolate-brown slacks, he shakes hands with old friends and makes a special point of warmly greeting shy newer acquaintances. "Good to see you. Keep on coming, and I promise you'll get it," he tells several men and women whose shaky hands and bloodshot eyes indicate that their sobriety is particularly recent. He even has a few friendly words for a smelly, unkempt bearded man who is openly drunk, sprawled in a chair outside the church and slurring "See what drinking does?" to anyone who glances in his direction.

At precisely quarter to seven on this clear October morning in 2003, he walks briskly into the smaller of two connecting rooms, takes up a clipboard with a meeting outline attached, dons elegant, gold-rimmed reading glasses, sits down in one chair among a circle of seventeen, and announces, "Good morning. My name is Maury, and I'm an alcoholic."

"Hi, Maury," sixteen voices chorus back.

For the next hour, Maury runs the meeting. He directs the brief celebration of one woman's fourteenth "birthday," or anniversary of sobriety; announces what the morning's discussion topic will be; and then makes certain that, as suggested but not mandated by the recovery program's guidelines, everyone in the room has a chance to share his or her thoughts. If someone rambles on a bit too long, Maury notes their loquaciousness with a discreet grunt or glance, and the twelve-stepper invariably concludes. In all things, Maury is friendly, firm, and unmistakably in charge. By program mandate, members take turns running meetings, and it is only by chance that on this particular day Maury serves as moderator. But that makes this meeting *his*.

After an hour, things conclude with a prayer, everyone holding hands and invoking a higher power's help in staying sober for another twenty-four

Now, at age seventy, Maury Wills gives candid speeches
about his alcoholism and drug addiction.

hours. Then, while many of the eclectic group of professionals, housewives, and retirees leave to begin their days, Maury stays behind.

"We clean this floor every morning," he notes. "I tell people, 'There's magic in the mop.'" One or two members of his group also help, but it is Maury whose eagle eye and flashing broom consign the most elusive dust bunnies and doughnut crumbs to the trash. When he finally feels the freshly swept and mopped floor is sufficiently pristine, he returns the brooms and mop to a storage shed, where he leans each implement against the wall with the same precision that an officer stacks rifles in an armory.

"Breakfast time now," Maury comments, but he isn't able to have his morning meal just yet. Outside, dozens of the twelve-steppers mill on the patio, many sipping coffee, one or two plainly putting off what they expect to be dreadful days, and more than a few just hanging around to have a word with Maury.

"I saw you on TV," one man tells him. "You looked real good."

"Ah, I always look good," Maury cracks, chuckling to make it obvious he's kidding.

Another man wants to know about a player with the Los Angeles Dodgers. A woman admires Maury's shirt. No one asks for an autograph, but it's obvious they are pleased to be kibitzing with someone so well known.

Anonymity is one of the foundations of the twelve-step program, where members are careful to address each other by first name only. But in L.A., it's impossible for Maury Wills to be anonymous: Wills, the former captain of baseball's Dodgers, one of the best shortstops in the history of the game, now just one more recovering alcoholic among many, and yet, as he must always be, someone in control. In Wills's case, the particular irony is that this control freak was a player when baseball management ruled the game, and a manager when the players gained the upper hand. His frustrations with both situations nearly destroyed him.

"I never wanted to be famous," Wills says as he shakes a final hand and walks to the gleaming, late-model BMW he's parked away from all the other cars in the church lot to prevent adjacent doors accidentally slamming into his and marring its immaculate surface. "In a basic way, fame means *you're not a part of.* I got used to it. But, see, I didn't want to be *known* as a great base stealer, I wanted to *be* a great base stealer. I loved *doing* the thing, not being known for doing the thing. Getting famous was one of the results, but not the goal itself. Do you understand the difference?"

Maury Wills's first forty-one years were spent striving for, achieving, and maintaining baseball excellence. The next fifteen included a harrowing descent into drug and alcohol addiction, when the fame he'd acquired and the records he'd set as an active athlete couldn't sustain Wills in his various post-baseball careers and relationships. The last fourteen have been a daily struggle to stay sober, to stay positive, and, mostly, to accept as much as possible that he can't control *everything*.

"The essence of my recovery program is giving up, surrendering to a higher power," Wills says over a plate of French toast in the back booth of an International House of Pancakes. "That was so hard for me. You've got to say, 'I'm not strong enough to beat this thing by myself. I'm too weak.' And you learn that, by this surrendering, you can gradually get control of your life again, because you master acceptance. When you accept whatever might happen to you, then you're content."

Wills puts down his fork, his slightly high-pitched voice gaining bass. Wills's father was a small-time preacher, and he passed the sermonizing genes down to his son. What Wills has to say next he's said countless times before, in twelve-step meetings and in keynote speeches at sports banquets and, often in his years of sobriety, in one-on-one sessions with other struggling alcoholics and addicts who might finally get clean if only Maury Wills can find just the right words to reach them—to *lead* them.

So there's a certain practiced feel to Wills's testimony, but repetition doesn't connote superficiality. Yes, he's said these words many, many times before, but, every time, he means what he's saying:

"My baseball career was always about achieving one goal and then replacing it with another, tougher one. I always despised the idea of contentment, of *settling for*, and I never, ever got contented, which was good for me as a baseball player but terrible for me as a human being. That's what I struggle for every day now, to be comfortable with contentment. I've gotten some wisdom, but there is still a great deal of wisdom for me to gain."

Wills sits back, takes a bite of now lukewarm French toast, and ponders a moment. As he does, he nods pleasantly to several people in a nearby booth who have been pointing at him and whispering. Because he looks just about the same at seventy as he did at forty, with the identical small, pinched face, whippet-lean body, and wide eyes that became so familiar to baseball fans through the then relatively new medium of television, he's constantly recognized. The years of heavy drinking and drug use scarred Wills's soul, not his features.

"You hear some people, ones who used to be celebrities, saying that fame is addictive," he muses. "For some of them, I guess that's true. But not for all of us. Fame was never my addiction. Constant striving for excellence was, and in a very selfish way. To get famous, you usually have to be selfish, putting whatever it is you are driven to do ahead of anything, anybody, else. I'm going to tell you a story. I don't tell it to show off. It just gives a good example of the way I was."

IN THE EARLY '60S, MAURY WILLS IS IN THE PRIME OF HIS CAREER. The Los Angeles Dodgers are perennial pennant contenders and also one of the most popular franchises in all of sports. Their roster is festooned with All-Stars like Don Drysdale, Tommy Davis, Frank Howard, and Sandy Koufax, but Maury Wills is team captain, the leader who gives orders on the field during games and administers locker room tongue-lashings to any teammates he believes aren't properly focused on winning pennants. Wills himself insists that his wife and children—there are five in the Wills brood at this time—stay in Spokane, Washington, during the season while he lives alone in L.A., the better to concentrate on baseball.

During this particular season, the Dodgers are in a tough fight for the National League pennant, and L.A. is about to begin a crucial series against their archrival San Francisco Giants. Back in Spokane, Gertrude Wills is approaching the final days of her latest pregnancy. Tests indicate the child will be a boy, and Wills chooses his name, Bragan Reiser, to honor Bobby Bragan and Pete Reiser, two Dodger coaches whom Wills credits with teaching him important lessons in the process of his becoming one of the best ballplayers of his era. Wills expects Gertrude to deliver Bragan Reiser Wills without her husband by her side. After all, she's given birth without him around before.

Things are just the way Wills likes them. His family, even with the birth of a new child imminent, is blocked completely out of his mind. He's focused on the San Francisco Giants, thinking about the pitchers he's going to face in the series, the way he'll move a foot this way or that in the infield when Willie Mays or Willie McCovey comes to bat, because Wills has memorized the tendencies of each Giants hitter, the pitches they swing at, where they're most likely to hit the ball. He's burning with anticipation. And then there's an interruption, an *intrusion,* on his preparation.

The first telegram informs Wills that there are medical complications up in Spokane. Gertrude went into labor, things went wrong, and now she's in a coma. Her husband needs to come home *now.* He doesn't budge from the Dodger clubhouse. The next telegram has worse news. Gertrude's doctor has determined that he can either save the mother or the baby. When will Maury be arriving in Spokane?

Lives hang in the balance, but so does the National League pennant. Wills is convinced the Dodgers can't beat the Giants without him. In a concession to family responsibilities, he picks up the phone and calls the doctor in Spokane. But he's not informing him of the flight he'll be on. Instead, he asks if the doctor can go ahead and handle the problem. What Maury Wills cares about most is on the playing field, not in a hospital bed.

The Dodgers win the series against the Giants. Wills plays particularly well.

"The doctor did take care of it," Wills recalls nearly forty years later, not sheepishly, but in matter-of-fact tones. He's telling what happened, not trying to excuse or embellish it. "So the baby was lost. I stayed with the team, and my focus was such that I could concentrate on the games one hundred percent. In that moment I just sort of pulled the shade down and was able to completely forget about my wife and the baby. Baseball was my focus. Not that I didn't love my family. Now, other players, if someone's sick in their family, they leave. That's the way they are. But that's not the way I was."

THERE WAS NOTHING IN THE FIRST TWENTY-SIX YEARS OF MAURICE Morning Wills's life to indicate he was ever going to be famous. The seventh of thirteen children, born in 1932 to the Reverend Guy and Mabel Wills, Maury grew up dirt poor in a Washington, D.C., housing project. His father made very little money from preaching. He had a second job working as a machinist and a third selling household products and cosmetics. The family diet, Wills remembers, often consisted of beans. He wasn't especially close to his siblings. The Wills kids had to share beds, and Maury was a constant bed wetter. His brothers and sisters would embarrass him in public by calling him "Pee Boy."

In those days, black kids went to segregated schools. Most of Wills's teachers, he still believes, were there to collect a paycheck rather than inspire students. He thinks maybe a half dozen of the 1,300 kids from his high school went on to college. Maury wasn't one of them. College didn't interest him.

Most of the Wills boys were hulking athletes, star players in several sports. Maury shared the talent but not the height. He eventually grew to about five feet, ten inches tall, but by family standards he was short, and by any standard he was scrawny. He compensated for lack of bulk and power with speed and smarts. If he couldn't beat opponents by knocking them over, he would outrun and outthink them.

"I studied sports," Wills says. "I never *played* baseball, I *worked* at it." Pleasure for Maury came not from participating, but from dominating. He says he was always obsessed with winning. He doesn't know where the trait came from, only that it was constantly there from the first moment he set foot on an athletic field. Being on the losing team in a pickup playground game would reduce him to absolute despair. In school he starred in football and basketball, but he believed his future involved another sport. In 1947, when Maury was still in high school, Jackie Robinson joined the Brooklyn Dodgers and broke major league baseball's so-called "color barrier." That gave Maury his goal in life.

"I started telling everybody I was going to be a Dodger, that I was going to play with Jackie," Wills says. "And I knew it was true. It sounded like some dumb kid just shooting his mouth off, but somewhere inside me I knew I could do it. I never thought that I *wouldn't* do it. And I never thought about anything else, including fame, that might come with it. My dream was strictly about what would happen on the field, not off it."

Even as he boasted he would one day be special like Robinson, Maury was proving all too typical of his ghetto environment. When he was seventeen, he had a son by sixteen-year-old Gertrude Elliott, who lived in another D.C. housing project. They eventually eloped, but didn't live together afterward. Maury stayed with his family, and Gertrude and the baby lived with hers. When he wasn't on a playing field, Maury preferred hanging out at pool halls to being with his wife and son. At those pool halls, he says now, older guys whose lives were already wasted would give him sips of cheap whiskey from the pint bottles they invariably carried in their pockets. He accepted the whiskey, but not the hopelessness. He knew he was going to play baseball for the Dodgers.

And, in 1950, it began to happen. The Dodgers were among several major league teams sponsoring a joint tryout for aspiring ballplayers in the D.C. area. Maury went, and did well enough to stand out among three hundred or so participants. He was invited to another tryout camp, then a third, and then three months passed. Finally, a Dodger scout asked to visit him at home. There, he offered the impoverished kid a bonus for signing: a sport coat, slacks, and shirt. Reverend Wills said his son needed "a few thousand." The scout offered to throw in a pair of new shoes. To emphasize this was the final offer, he turned to leave. But, as he did, he offered $500. Maury took it. He gave half to his father and the other half to his wife. Then he left her and their son behind while he moved to Hornell in upstate New York to begin his career in the lowest level of baseball's minor leagues. Maury was certain it wouldn't be long before he joined Jackie in Brooklyn.

Eight years later, Maury Wills was still in the minor leagues. He had some decent seasons and one terrible one, when he integrated a team in the Texas League and, dismayed by the overt racism he encountered, barely hit .200. He and Gertrude had several more children, but weren't together much outside the conjugal bed. Maury often spent whole seasons away from her, as much from financial necessity as anything else. The few hundred dollars he made each month as a minor leaguer couldn't fully support a family, and Maury was always more interested in baseball than in nurturing children.

During these frustrating times, Maury's baseball limitations seemed far more evident than his special talents, which were intelligence, arm strength, foot speed, and fielding ability. In particular, the right-handed hitter couldn't handle curveballs. He had no power to begin with, and major league baseball in the 1950s was all about hitting home runs, not fielding and throwing well. By 1958, when he was assigned to Spokane at the Triple-A, or "a step below the big leagues," level, it was obvious the Dodger brain trust had decided Maury Wills was a career minor leaguer, a good one but still not a major league prospect. They kept him around because he was judged just good enough to help minor league teams win. At twenty-six, Wills's dream was just about over: Jackie Robinson had already retired, and after the 1957 season the Dodgers moved from Brooklyn, New York, to Los Angeles, California. There would be no Jackie/Maury tandem in Brooklyn. But by then, Wills was nearly ready to agree with the organizational assessment of him. The only reason he hadn't quit was that he had no interests outside of baseball. He couldn't think of anything else he would want to do.

"At that point, Maury didn't have a chance to be a major leaguer," recalls former Dodger general manager Buzzie Bavasi.

Then Wills met his new manager, someone who understood what it was like when ambition failed to equal accomplishment. More than four decades later, Bobby Bragan laughs with sheer joy when he remembers his first days with Maury Wills: "He was so smart, that was the most obvious thing, and he could run and catch and throw on a major league level. What became clear, after seeing him in just a few games, was that he drove himself harder than anyone else. He expected his team to win every game and that he would be the one to make it happen. If desire was the chief qualification, Maury would have been in the majors from Day One. Except for one problem, which was he could not hit a curveball. He was afraid of the pitch. And, smart and determined as he was, he could not master that fear. My career as a major league player was a short one because I shared that same problem."

One day, Bragan saw something in pregame warm-ups that suggested only a matter of two or three feet separated Maury Wills from major league stardom.

"He was playing around in batting practice, and he swung a few times from the left side instead of the right," Bragan, now eighty-six, recalls. "He hit the ball pretty well, and I realized that, with his great speed, he could beat out many ground balls for hits. His flaw was that, batting right-handed, he couldn't hit curveballs thrown by right-handed pitchers, and most pitchers are right-handed. But in the left-handed batter's box, you can follow a right-hander's curveball better, so he didn't have to flinch anymore. I told him I thought, with practice, he could become an adept switch-hitter, which means batting right handed against left-handed pitchers and left handed against right-handers. Just step over a couple of feet from one side of home plate to the other, I told Maury. And, because he listened, he was soon making baseball history."

Bragan also taught Wills to take advantage of his speed by bunting for more hits. His pupil came out hours before games to practice switch-hitting and bunting until his hands would bleed—"No exaggeration," Bragan insists. "He would have done it twice as much if I'd allowed it." And, by the end of the 1958 season, Maury Wills was a successful switch-hitter who suddenly seemed capable of making the major leagues after all.

Just before the 1959 season, word of Wills's improvement had spread sufficiently in the insular world of baseball for the Detroit Tigers to buy his contract from the Dodgers. After watching him play in spring-training exhibition games, they returned him to Los Angeles. Bragan believes Wills should be grateful they did.

"Like most of the organizations in the late '50s, Detroit really wanted players who hit home runs," Bragan says. "Had they kept Maury, if he'd played at all they would have placed him way down in the batting order where he could not have utilized his speed and bunting ability to the fullest extent. So when he was returned to the Dodgers, they sent him back to Spokane, and I promised him that if he just kept doing what he was doing, he'd soon be a Dodger, part of one of the few teams that valued speed and baseball intelligence."

About two months into the 1959 season, the starting Los Angeles shortstop broke his foot. Bragan had the pleasure of telling Wills he'd finally been called up to the major leagues. Dodger manager Walter Alston stuck the rookie in the starting lineup. His veteran-laden club, mostly featuring aging players who'd once been stars in Brooklyn, had finished seventh (out of eight National League teams) in 1958; not much more was expected of them in 1959.

Except that, along with a few other emerging players like Don Drysdale and Sandy Koufax, Wills's determination inspired the entire team. The Los Angeles Dodgers won the National League title in 1959, and then took the World Series from the Chicago White Sox. Wills hit just .260 during the regular season and .250 in the Series, but L.A. fans loved his hustle and slick glove work.

They had no idea of what was yet to come. Even as he was adjusting to life in the major leagues, Wills was already plotting how to make the major leagues adjust to *him*.

MAURY WILLS DRIVES A CAR LIKE HE ONCE PLAYED BASEBALL: CAL-culating how to gain an inch here, a foot there, how, in some sense, to get an advantage over the other drivers. Heading from breakfast in Redondo Beach to the high-tech company in Torrance where he serves as director of public relations, Wills smoothly steers his BMW from one lane to the next, never quite cutting off other cars completely, never quite driving so much over the speed limit that he'll attract attention from cops manning speed traps.

"When I got to the Dodgers, I started carrying a major league baseball rule book with me, and I studied it every night," Wills says. "You hear other players bragging about how they study their opponents, how they maybe watch game tapes. Hey, that's easy. Me, I read that rule book over and over, looking for any little thing that would give me an edge."

Studying the rule book's official dimensions of a baseball infield, Wills discovered a useful bit of information. Like everyone else in the major leagues, he already knew bases were ninety feet apart. Like a few of his peers, he also knew each side of the base was fifteen inches wide. But he thinks he was the first to notice that, because of angles, the back inside edge of first base and the back inside edge of second base are twenty-two and a half inches closer than the presumed ninety feet.

"When I trained myself to run to that inside edge at second, that saved me nearly two feet," Wills explains. "It made a big difference. My first full year with the Dodgers, in 1960, I led the National League with fifty stolen bases. The year before, Willie Mays led with twenty-seven. I don't feel bad about saying this: right from the beginning, I changed the way baseball was played. People began realizing the stolen base was a great offensive weapon." (Bavasi, who spent half a century as a baseball executive, agrees: "Two people, and only two, could honestly say they made everybody else in baseball alter their approaches to the game. There was Babe Ruth back in 1927, when he hit sixty home runs, and Maury Wills in the '60s, with all his stolen bases. Those two. Nobody else, ever.")

As a hitter, Wills used every inch to his advantage, too.

"With time and practice, I perfected a bunt that was impossible to defense," he says, deftly swinging around a slower car and barely making it past a light in the process of changing from amber to red. Wills has no specific time to be in his office. Stopping for a red light won't make him late for anything. But beating the light means he'll get where he's going that much faster. "It's a soft bunt down the first-base line, far enough so the catcher can't come out and get it, the first baseman can't get it, but it can't be halfway down the line, forty-five feet. It's got to be just short of that, forty-three feet, so the pitcher's got to come after it at a bad angle to throw to first. You've got to get it there perfectly, just forty-three feet and no more or less. And I got so I could push that bunt exactly forty-three feet just about every time." Most years during his baseball career, Maury Wills led the league with the most bunt hits.

During games, Wills says, he was happy, confident in his ability to control the action: "Me, the little guy, the one nobody thought could play in the major leagues. I'd just get so high on that feeling." Socially, though, Wills lagged behind more sophisticated teammates. He spent many nights alone at home in his L.A. apartment, practicing on the banjo or guitar, a hobby he'd developed while riding buses in the minor leagues. While he plucked their strings, he would drink a little whiskey to relax, never so much that his play the next day might be affected. The pressure of growing stardom was gradual. In 1960 and '61, Wills's first two full years in the majors, the Dodgers didn't win pennants and Wills was overshadowed nationally by players like Roger Maris, who in 1961 broke Babe Ruth's single-season home run record. In 1962, though, everything changed. The Dodgers battled the Giants all season long, eventually losing a three-game playoff to San Francisco after finishing in a tie. Baseball was still the king of professional sports; football and basketball simply filled the winter months between baseball seasons. To be one of the best baseball players was essentially to achieve the highest possible degree of athletic celebrity. And, in 1962, the baseball star of stars was Maury Wills, who stole an amazing 104 bases to break Ty Cobb's venerable, forty-seven-year-old season record of 96. Even opposing fans chanted, "Go—go—go," whenever Wills reached first, and, most of the time, he went. Wills only failed to steal safely 13 times in 117 attempts.

"I had the same mentality Ty Cobb had as a base stealer," Wills says. "He spiked a lot of guys while he was running the bases, but they had it coming. If I spiked a guy, that was his problem, because he'd placed himself where he shouldn't be. I never felt sorry for him."

Wills had something else in common with Ty Cobb. During their respective careers, each was possibly the most unpopular player among his major league peers. Wills *liked* spiking opponents. It added a degree of intimidation to his game. Four decades later, Wills especially relishes telling about his spikes cutting into the legs of Joe Torre, then with the Milwaukee Braves, because Torre had the nerve to try and block a base Wills wanted to slide into.

OPPOSING TEAMS TRIED EVERYTHING TO SLOW WILLS DOWN ON the base paths. Baseball rules allow home teams some latitude in how they prepare their fields. Whenever the Dodgers came to town, the Pittsburgh Pirates dumped loads of sand around first base. In San Francisco, the Giants' ground crew watered the dirt around first base until it turned to sloshy muck. But it was the Milwaukee Braves who came up with the best defense against Wills.

Wills always took a long, long lead at first base. He calculated to the quarter-inch how far he could step away from the bag, trying to get as far as he could because each extra inch brought him that much closer to second base if he decided to steal. Pitchers would constantly throw to first, trying less to pick him off—he was too quick for that—than to cut down his advantage when he inevitably did take off for second.

In 1963, Joe Torre ("a big, hairy guy," Wills explains) played first base for the Braves. In a game at Milwaukee's County Stadium, Wills got to first and took his customary huge lead. Just as typically, the Braves' pitcher threw to first and Wills went diving back to the bag. But this time, Torre, instead of catching the ball in his glove hand and leaning down to try and tag Wills, simply dropped his rather large leg to the dirt between Wills and the base. Blocked by a massive thigh, Wills was tagged out. He was livid, and screamed to the umpire that Torre must be breaking some rule. But, just as Wills had studied the rule book to find some legal edge, so had Torre and the Braves. There was apparently nothing to preclude what Torre had done. Milwaukee fans cheered happily as Wills, feeling humiliated, retreated to the Dodger dugout. It was only the first game of the series. He had time to get revenge.

After the game, Wills asked the driver of the Dodger bus to drop him off in front of a hardware store near the hotel where the team was staying. He bought a file, and took it and his spiked baseball shoes back to his hotel room, and proceeded to file such sharp edges on his cleats that the metal gleamed. Then Wills smeared black shoe polish on the razor-sharp cleats so the gleam wouldn't alert the Braves to what he had done. He could have countered Torre's ploy in other ways—trying to slide around him, taking a slightly shorter lead—but Wills wanted to respond in a nastier, more intimidating way. How dare the Milwaukee Braves try a trick like this on *him*!

At the start of the next day's game, Wills wore regular spikes. He got to first base, took his lead, the Milwaukee pitcher threw over, and Torre placed his leg between Wills and the base again. The umpire called Wills out. He went back to the Dodger dugout and put on the sharpened cleats. His next time up, he reached first again, took his lead as usual, the pitcher threw over and Torre dropped his huge leg between Wills and the bag. Wills's sharpened spikes ripped deep into Torre's thigh. Blood spurted impressively. Torre writhed in the infield dirt, the fans booed, and the rest of the Milwaukee team gathered menacingly around Wills. Nobody hit him, but their intentions were obvious. Then Torre, a bandage now wrapped around his wound, pushed through his teammates, took up his position at first, patted Wills on the rear and said, "Let's go." The game resumed, and Wills knew he'd just earned the undying enmity of the Milwaukee Braves. In the next game, he recalls, Torre was the catcher instead of the first baseman. When Wills tried to slide into home plate, the massive Torre smashed him to the ground. "That was fine," Wills says now. "I played hard and he played hard. Torre understood. The rest of his team didn't, and those guys just had it in for me afterwards. And, by the way, afterwards nobody ever tried that particular trick on me again."

Other teams despised Wills, too, often because he violated unwritten baseball code by stealing bases or bunting for hits when his team was so far ahead it was obvious the game was already decided.

"I never thought about when enough was enough," he says. "Let's say we were winning by eight runs in the top of the ninth when I come up, and everybody else in our lineup has a hit and I don't. Well, I want a hit. I want to improve my performance in the game. So maybe I bunt for a hit, because their third baseman is playing back and I know I can beat it out. And the other team gets mad at me because of it. I didn't care."

Many years later, when these old resentments prevented Wills from achieving his final baseball goal, he would care very much.

AT THE END OF 1962, MAURY WILLS WAS NAMED THE NATIONAL League's Most Valuable Player. Besides stealing a record 104 bases, he also hit .299, scored 130 runs, and led the National League in triples. His performance was so exceptional that he also won the Hickok Belt, awarded annually by national writers to the best athlete in all of sports. *Sport* magazine, then the most prominent mainstream sports publication, named Wills its Man of the Year. His fame increased; Wills appeared on national television with Ed Sullivan, "playing the banjo, and playing it good," Wills recalls. There were only a few basic channels available to viewers. On any given Sunday night, as many as two-thirds of all Americans watching TV tuned in to *The Ed Sullivan Show.* Now, even if they didn't follow baseball, they still knew about Maury Wills. Afterward, along with a few teammates, Wills was invited by comedian Milton Berle to join his winter act in Las Vegas. By the next off-season, Wills was headlining at the Sahara himself.

"I got the idea that people came to see me because I was so great on the banjo," he says. "I didn't realize that, in Las Vegas, the people at a casino come to see whoever's playing there, or, if they came specifically to see me, it was because I'd stolen a lot of bases and they'd seen me on TV. Later on, when I wasn't doing as well in baseball and wasn't on TV, I guess I must have gotten worse on the banjo, because all of a sudden I couldn't get hired to play many places, and, when I did, a lot fewer people wanted to come hear me."

But for several years after his emergence in 1962 as a superstar, lots of people wanted Maury Wills—to see him play baseball, to hear him play banjo, and, he acknowledges now, to share his bed. That perk of celebrity was one he welcomed: "I hated being alone, just hated it." On the road, Wills filled his empty hours and bed with groupies, women so eager for sex with baseball players that, once Wills was through with them, they allowed him to pass them on to teammates. And, home in Los Angeles while his wife Gertrude and their children stayed in Spokane, Wills says he had a lengthy love affair with wholesome actress/singer Doris Day. This was risky business in the early '60s, and the two tried to keep their relationship secret. But somehow Dodger brass found out, and Wills was privately encouraged to break off the affair. No matter how popular an athlete he was, Wills was told, the public would never tolerate a "colored" man having sex with a famous white woman. If scandal erupted, the Dodgers would rather get rid of Wills than risk the team's wholesome public image. Wills thought he might be in love with Doris Day, but he also knew no woman could be as important to him as baseball. He ended the relationship.

But that was pretty much the only public relations risk Wills ran. In the '60s, when Wills's fame was at its height, some aspects of celebrities' private lives were still allowed to remain private, particularly in the cases of famous athletes. Teams often picked up travel and restaurant tabs for sportswriters, who, in return, kept their eyes closed to questionable off-field behavior. New York Yankee center fielder Mickey Mantle, the most famous baseball player of all, was an unabashed alcoholic for most of his career. His long home runs were regularly described in print, but not how many times he struck out because of massive hangovers, even though almost every sportswriter covering Yankee games knew what was going on. The same held true for future Hall of Famer Eddie Mathews, who, like Mantle, drank heavily and womanized with the knowledge that none of "his" writers would put anything in print about it.

Wills became recognized all over the world. After the 1963 season, he was asked to join a group of players visiting U.S. military bases overseas. Other members of the group were future Hall of Famer Robin Roberts, a pitcher for the Phillies; Jerry Lumpe, an All-Star second baseman with Kansas City; and Wills's old pal Bobby Bragan, who'd been named manager of the Milwaukee Braves.

"We were at this base outside Frankfurt, Germany, visiting the troops," Wills recalls. "It was during what they called the Cold War, you know, very tense in Germany, and they had all these rules on the base about checking I.D. no matter who it was. So there's Bobby, Robin Roberts, Jerry Lumpe, the base commander, and myself, and the guard at the main gate to the base says he has to see everybody's I.D. and he checks them all except mine, even the base commander's. He looks at me and says, 'Mr. Wills, you're okay.' That was flattering, you know?"

In Los Angeles, Wills was a huge fan favorite. After ball games, Wills would patiently sign autographs for every kid who asked. He remembered how, when he was ten, an obscure Washington Senator player named Gerry Priddy signed an autograph for little Maury, and how good that had made him feel. "I didn't mind being fan-friendly before and after games, because that was part of my job," he says. He was the toast of Los Angeles. And, through most of it, he was miserable. That misery, he believes, came from his obsession with always getting better.

"I never felt guilty about my success, or wondered whether I deserved it, because I knew I'd worked hard for everything I had," Wills says. "The problem was, my life then was always about getting to the next level. If that's the case, then you never can be happy. When I was in the minor leagues, I wanted to make it to the majors, but when Bobby Bragan helped me get there after eight and a half years of trying, I found out I wasn't satisfied just wearing that fancy uniform. I wanted to be the starting shortstop. By mid-August of that first season, '59, I had won the job. Okay, still not enough. I wanted to be a star everyday player. So I hit .295, led the league in stolen bases, and as soon as I did that I wanted more, always more. I wanted to be the National League's All-Star shortstop. In '61 I was named to the All-Star team, I'd gone up another level, and my stomach ached because people still said Pee Wee Reese was the all-time best Dodger shortstop. I wanted to be there. That was my spot, not his. When I first joined the Dodgers, Reese was a coach and I heard him tell somebody I wasn't good enough, I wasn't going to make it. I made myself remember that. It wasn't hard. By the middle '60s, when they'd have all-time Dodger lists, Reese and I would be co-shortstops, and it was still not enough. I had to have that place all to myself. And, finally, I did. And then he gets into the Hall of Fame, and I'm still not there, which makes no sense. But that's another thing, and it came later. I'll bet this is true of anybody who kills himself to succeed. People like us never settle for where we are, ever. And that's why, alone at night, we look inside and see dark places and get scared, because there's that little voice promising we're never, ever going to be satisfied and happy. I never knew where the line was, when to stop pushing myself so hard. And, eventually, it caught up with me."

But not for a while. Wills and the Dodgers won World Series titles in 1963 and '65. Though he never stole 104 bases again, in '65 he stole 94 and might have broken his own record if he hadn't hurt his leg. There was a career blip after 1966, after a dispute with team officials over whether or not he was healthy enough to play in a postseason series of exhibition games in Japan,

In 1962, Wills was the most dominant player
in baseball since Babe Ruth.

Dodgers team owner Walter O'Malley ordered Bavasi to trade Wills. He was sent to the Pittsburgh Pirates. Wills was shattered.

"To this day I ask myself how they could do that to me," Wills says, voice blurring with resentment. "I'd given myself completely to the success of that team. I was a *Dodger*. And they traded me to a team like Pittsburgh, where they didn't play smart." Still, Wills did his best to make himself an indispensable part of the Pittsburgh community, going so far as to volunteer for kids' baseball clinics on a regular basis. City staffers asked Wills to go exclusively into low-income neighborhoods, but he wanted to work with youngsters from all economic backgrounds. Just because a kid didn't go hungry, that shouldn't disqualify him from meeting Maury Wills, he insisted.

After two full years in Pittsburgh, in 1969 Wills was traded to the Montreal Expos, a terrible team that played in a cold climate he hated. For the first time in the major leagues, Wills played horribly. He'd always claimed he ignored fan reaction during games—"If you don't hear the cheers, you won't hear the jeers"—but now he heard the Canadian fans booing. He respected them for it, saying he deserved their disdain. But after forty-seven games, the Dodgers made a deal with Montreal and brought Wills back to Los Angeles.

"Of course, they hadn't won while I was gone," Wills notes. In fact, the Dodgers had two consecutive losing seasons without Wills. When they brought him back, they started winning again, and didn't have another losing season until Wills's final year in the major leagues. Wills believes that wasn't a coincidence.

Soon after he rejoined his old team, the Dodgers played in Los Angeles against the Braves, now from Atlanta, who were led by slugger Hank Aaron. Maury Wills is not someone who cries easily—showing public emotion was, and mostly still is, against his personal code—but he chokes up remembering what happened that night.

"In the fifth inning, as Hank Aaron was coming up, they put all my statistics up on the scoreboard with the line 'Welcome Home, Our Captain,'" Wills recalls, his voice quavering. "Forty-five thousand people stood and cheered. They did that for four minutes. Hank Aaron wouldn't get in the batters' box. And I felt those people weren't applauding because I'd stolen 104 bases once. They were applauding because I'd tried hard every game I'd played, because I'd signed autographs every time I was asked, because I'd just given them everything I could give. And that was the best moment in my career, when I felt like people understood what all the success had been costing me."

Among other things, it finally cost him his wife. After having a sixth child with her mostly absent husband, Gertrude Wills informed him that he shouldn't come back to Spokane anymore. Wills tried to stay in touch with his children, but they were peripheral; baseball was central, and, years later, it would be hard for Wills to establish good relationships with some of them. For the time being, he filled his empty hours with practicing guitar and with drinking. He still didn't drink so much that he couldn't play well the next day, and, though drugs were beginning to be part of the major league scene, he avoided them altogether.

Wills's commitment to baseball was endless, but his career wasn't. For three seasons during his second tenure with the Dodgers, he remained the team captain and sparkplug. Other teammates left, either through retirement or, as their skills deteriorated, trade or release. In 1971, at age thirty-nine, Wills hit .281 and, by his own unobjective estimate, was still the best short-stop in the National League. In 1972, though, he only played part time. The Dodgers, who hadn't won a National League title since 1966, wanted younger players on the field. Still, Wills was convinced the team needed him, and that he could play well enough to reestablish himself as an All-Star.

On November 4, 1972, he found out differently. The Dodgers released their captain. They didn't tell him before they announced it to the press. Maury Wills's dream was over, and his nightmare was about to begin.

THE OFFICES AND WAREHOUSE OF MAINLINE INCORPORATED ARE in a boxy, two-story building in Torrance. Wills pulls his BMW into a special spot away from all the other cars parked in the company lot. He asks his pas-

At the height of his career, Wills supplanted Ty Cobb as
the greatest base runner in his sport's history.

senger to get out before he pulls in; there's shrubbery on that side of the space, and Wills doesn't want his car door scratched.

He's eager to brag about the company. Whether he works for Mainline Inc. or the Dodgers, Wills is a loyalist who touts his organization. Mainline Inc., he says, supplies parts "to just about any satellite TV service you could name." His role in the company is to support sales personnel. When they call on purchasing managers who are sports fans, they can offer baseballs autographed by Maury Wills or even a round of golf with the former Dodger great as an inducement to place orders. Wills may say he was never quite comfortable with, or particularly interested in, his celebrity, but late in life it's the tool he uses to make a living.

"Let's go up to my office," Wills suggests, leading the way inside. He greets everyone he passes by name. One young engineer is Wills's twelve-step "pigeon," someone just learning how a recovery program can help him stop drinking. But no one, down to custodians, escapes Wills's attention.

His second-floor office is decorated with career memorabilia: in particular, four framed *Sports Illustrated* covers featuring his image are prominently displayed. Wills likes to be reminded of his baseball accomplishments by such trophies, but he doesn't have many left. Most, including the Hickok Belt, were sold off to support his massive drug habit during the 1980s.

"Actually, I'd lent the Hickok Belt to a friend to display in his hotel," Wills says. "It got stolen or lost or something and I got insurance money for it, and that went for drugs." He looks down at his fingers. "My World Series rings, well, I don't have them anymore, either. One day during my bad times, they were just gone. I don't believe I sold them. They seemed to disappear."

Wills loves Mainline Inc., he says, because he was given a job there fourteen years ago "when I was just getting into my recovery program, and I was still so weak. They gave me a chance, gave me a way to support myself. So I've been here ever since. They helped me, and I'll stay as long as I can help them."

Right after the Dodgers had no further use for his services in 1972, Wills had no idea what to do next. Still energetic at forty, he wanted to stay in baseball as a player but received no offers from other teams. He thought he'd like to be a manager, though no black man would run a major league club until Frank Robinson took over the Cleveland Indians in 1975. In the winter of 1972, though, Wills fulfilled a previous commitment to go duck hunting on the television series *The American Sportsman*. His hunting partner for the show was Curt Gowdy, the lead announcer for NBC's baseball *Game of the Week*. Gowdy was impressed with Wills's ability to ad-lib on camera. Former Dodgers pitcher Sandy Koufax had just quit the *Game of the Week*'s announcing team, Gowdy mentioned, and he wanted Wills to audition as his replacement. Not long afterward, Wills signed on with NBC for $80,000 a season, not much less than he'd been earning with the Dodgers. During the off-seasons, Wills began managing winter league teams in Mexico. During major league spring training, he served as a special baserunning coach for several teams. He hoped the experience would help sell him to major league clubs as a prospective manager.

His work in TV, spring training, and Mexican League baseball gave Wills ways to occupy his time. Still, nothing provided the same all-consuming emotional engagement as playing. He felt restless, and tried to find new hobbies. After buying a house in Playa del Rey, he learned how to make stained-glass windows and set out to completely replace all the ordinary glass windows in it. He played a lot of golf and told himself he was happy. Then in 1974, just two years after the Dodgers let Wills go, he watched in horror as St. Louis Cardinals outfielder Lou Brock broke his single-season stolen-base record, raising the bar from Wills's 104 to 118.

"That was *my* record," Wills says, still sounding upset thirty years later. "I don't buy into the shit some players throw about how, gee, records are made to be broken, and good for the guys who break theirs. Brock broke my record, and I felt my baseball legacy just melting away."

There was another bitter disappointment. Wills believed he would be an automatic selection for the Baseball Hall of Fame. Five years after retirement, players are eligible for induction if they receive 75 percent of the vote from a committee of about 300 to 350 accredited baseball writers. Usually, one or two players make it: in rare years, three; in rarer years, none. In 1978, Wills's first year of eligibility, slugging third baseman Eddie Mathews, who at the time had hit more home runs than any other third baseman in baseball history, was the only player elected. Two hundred eighty-five votes were necessary; Mathews got 301. Wills, with 115, didn't come close. He says he reacted by getting drunk. Over the years, it became his tradition after learning he'd been denied again.

When a long-term romance with a younger woman named Judy began to flounder, Wills drank because of that heartache, too. Everything he attempted now seemed to end in disaster. Trying to finally become close to his son Bump, who'd made the major leagues himself with the Texas Rangers, Wills invited Bump to stay with him and Judy whenever the Rangers played the California Angels, whose home games were in Anaheim. In 1978, Wills walked into his home and discovered Bump and Judy having sex. That ended the reconciliation. It would be twelve years before father and son spoke again. Wills got drunk over that, and, while futilely attempting to keep things going with Judy—"All I can say is that I loved her, and I had no idea what a normal relationship was"—he found plenty of excuses to drink heavily on a daily basis.

But, in the eyes of the public, he was still Maury Wills the celebrity, and he was constantly on national TV for NBC's *Game of the Week*. Hungover or not, he'd show up on camera. Wills knew the quality of his work was deteriorating, but pride was also being dissolved by alcohol. After the 1979 season, NBC informed Wills he no longer had a job. Judy was in and out of his life. A fledgling cable TV network known as Home Box Office called, asking Wills to be part of a regular baseball show called *Race for the Pennant*. In those primitive cable days, it was like going from the major to the minor leagues, but Wills took the job because he didn't feel he had many other options.

"I wasn't into drugs yet, but I was in bad, bad, emotional shape," Wills says as he fusses with papers and the nameplate on the desk in his Mainline Inc. office. "Then, in August 1980, I got a call I thought would change my life, and it did. Only, not the way I expected. See, the Seattle Mariners wanted to hire me as their manager. I was only the third black manager in major league history, right after Frank Robinson with the Indians and Larry Doby with the White Sox. Neither one of them had done very well with those teams. I thought I could be the first black manager to win pennants and the World Series. And instead the whole thing just blew up faster than I ever could have imagined. So far after leaving the Dodgers, I'd been humiliated privately but not publicly. This time, it was public."

MAURY WILLS'S CAREER AS A MAJOR LEAGUE MANAGER LASTED A grand total of eighty-two games: fifty-eight to complete the 1980 season and just twenty-four more before he was fired in 1981. His brief tenure made very little difference in Seattle's overall performance. The Mariners were in last place when Wills signed on and still in last place when he was abruptly told to leave. More than twenty years later, he partially blames himself for what happened. But only partially.

"I was irritable, very discontented," he says, looking not at his office wall but rather through it, seeing moments from the past. "My situation with Judy, the woman I loved, was bad. She was carrying on with a prominent player from another team in between the times she would be with me. I didn't work on trying to get along with the Seattle media, so from the beginning they were out to get me, which they eventually did. And my problem with the players was simple. I knew from my own experience that the only way to get better was to completely give yourself over to your manager, like I did with Bobby Bragan. Whatever Bobby told me to do, I would, and I'd never ask why because I trusted him. Those players in Seattle, and most of them weren't very good, still weren't willing to do what I told them. They didn't give me their complete trust to lead them. If they had, it all would have worked out. It would have."

But Wills didn't realize that something else about baseball had changed. The sport had entered a new era, the "free agency" era. A player was no longer legally bound to spend his entire career with one team (unless that team decided to trade or sell him). After years of being mostly middle-class working stiffs, players could now sell their services to the highest bidder, getting millions of dollars for a few seasons, then become free agents again. A big star like Nolan Ryan could leave the California Angels for more money from the Houston Astros, and then depart the Astros for better paychecks with the Texas Rangers. So players had far less organizational loyalty, even the least talented benchwarmers suddenly made a lot more money than their managers—and, with the proliferation of cable TV and other media, were now celebrities. If they didn't like the way the manager treated them, players complained to their agents, who would go directly to the team owner or general manager. Essentially, the authority of team managers and coaches was gone. They couldn't *tell* players what to do anymore. They had to *suggest*, tactfully, and tact was never one of Wills's strengths.

Wills used the last two months of the 1980 season to evaluate the players he had and start making plans for changes in 1981. As soon as the last game of 1980 was over—the Mariners won twenty and lost thirty-eight under Wills— he raced home to Los Angeles, where he believed Judy would be waiting for him. She wasn't. That night, he picked up another woman at a restaurant, using the come-on line of asking her if she was a baseball fan and telling her that he used to play for the Dodgers. It worked, and Wills's descent into hell began. His new friend had cocaine, and she was willing to share.

"I know that nobody else ever put a drink in my mouth or a drug in my hand," Wills says now, squinching his eyes shut because of the painful memory. "I was at a point in my life where I was just full of self-pity. That woman and I did some lines with a straw, and it was nice. The next night she asked if I wanted to do some more, and I said I did, and she didn't have any. But she knew some people who did. We went to their house and they were freebasing. I did that, and wow, I fell in love with it. I stayed at that house for days. I guess I spent thousands of dollars just learning about what drugs could do for me. It was the first time in my life I felt for a little while like everything was actually all right."

Initially, Wills had enough self-control to stay off drugs when he was working. The Mariners needed him to take part in a prolonged winter tour of Washington state and Canada, talking up the team and trying to sell tickets. He was unhappy without his suddenly beloved cocaine. When spring training began in March 1981, Wills was also going through another bad patch with Judy. The intense pride that once fueled his life had been replaced by anger. When his players didn't perform up to his lofty expectations, he berated them. Reporters covering the team got curt answers to their questions. The woman he loved was making a fool of him. The team whose success would have validated Wills's opinion of himself as a great manager was losing almost every game. He had no respect for his players, and many of them not only despised him but openly told the press exactly how they felt.

"I love Maury Wills, I respect him, but he just screwed that Seattle situation up," recalls Bavasi, who was friendly with the Mariners team owners. "When Maury did some things, like make a fool of himself with that girlfriend, he was never discreet. And he'd say anything to anybody in the press. He thought he was being honest, but he was being his own worst enemy."

The inevitable happened just twenty-four games into the 1981 season. The Seattle general manager called Wills and asked him to come in for a meeting. Wills replied that he knew he was going to be fired, so there was no reason to meet at all. That night, he listened on the radio as the Mariners players, thrilled to be rid of him, decisively beat the powerful New York Yankees under their new manager. For four days, Wills sat around his Seattle apartment.

"See, it was the first time in my life I didn't have anything I had to do," he says, still staring at the wall in his office. "No reason to get up in the morning. I went back home to Los Angeles, and when I tried to see Judy, she claimed I was stalking her and called the police on me. I drank for a while, but I kept thinking about cocaine. I don't think I was a drug addict before. I used it and liked it a lot. But that set me up. I went out looking for coke, and when I had it, or rather it had me, I could believe nothing that happened in Seattle or with Judy was my fault."

Wills also discovered that the old "see-no-evil" days were over for sportswriters. Newspapers and electronic media no longer allowed their reporters to accept freebies from teams. The media claimed a need for complete objectivity, which translated into an eagerness for the kind of negative stories they now believed their readers and viewers wanted. The public ate up stories about bad star behavior, many observers believed, because athletes' millions-a-season salaries completely set them apart from their fans, who now also had to pay inflated ticket prices. Sports fans still thrilled to great on-field performances. They still idolized ballplayers as heroes. But they were equally on guard for chinks in their armor, to make themselves feel better about existing on a lower plane than professional athletes.

"This was a time when the media started to write about bad things famous athletes did, not just positive stuff," Wills recalls. "And when I saw all the articles in the newspapers and magazines about how Maury Wills had screwed up, how he'd been a terrible manager, a real loser, that just made it worse. I felt like people were looking at me and laughing."

Over the years, Wills says, he's gradually come to understand the nature of an addictive personality. Compulsives like him are always obsessed with something. For a long time, Wills focused with near-insane intensity on baseball. Excelling as a player consumed him and, he says, "in some ways kept me from growing up, from learning how to just cope with the daily little problems in life." Everything else, from family to alcohol, was secondary. When he was no longer an active player, Wills's main focus turned to Judy. As things turned out badly with her, he got his long-awaited chance to manage, and, for parts of two seasons, he was so obsessed with managing perfectly that it became obvious to everyone but him that his stint running the Mariners would never be anything other than a disaster.

After being fired in Seattle and moving back to L.A., Wills needed a new addiction, and he found one in cocaine. It took the place of baseball in his life. And, as had been the case with baseball, Wills lost himself in his obsession.

"I know now I replaced one addiction with another," he says. "That's what addicts do. My disease had been present long before I used drugs. See, alcohol and drugs weren't the disease. They were the symptoms of the disease."

At first Wills had plenty of money to buy cocaine. Besides the 1981 salary the Mariners were still obligated to pay him—it came to $80,000—there were various bank accounts left over from his playing days. When that money ran out, Wills had two more sources of income: his baseball pension, which kicked in during 1982, when he turned fifty, and provided him with several thousand dollars a month, and his house, which he mortgaged. For almost three years, he hardly left that house except to buy drugs. When he had people over, it was for drug parties. He even married briefly, to a woman he later referred to as his "drug wife."

Though some of the perks of fame were still available to him, Wills was in no shape to take advantage of them. When the Dodgers would invite him to their stadium for old-timers' games or other special occasions, Wills would try to stay off drugs for a few days so he could show up able to function. Then, the day before, he'd panic, get high, and end up missing the event. Personal appearances of any sort became impossible. He couldn't leave home and his cocaine. And, in a way, he took perverse pride in that.

"I always tried to be the best at whatever I did," Wills says. "If I was going to be a drug addict, I was going to be the best one ever. Occasionally something would bother me, like when it got in the papers that I'd been arrested for stealing a car and drug possession. It was a mix-up and the case was dismissed, but people read Maury Wills was a thief and a drug addict."

In the 1980s, the Los Angeles Dodgers were among the first professional sports organizations to offer drug and alcohol counseling to their players and other employees. They did so in part because Don Newcombe, once a great Dodgers pitcher and a self-confessed alcoholic, trained as a counselor and urged his old team to give him access to anyone the organization believed had drug abuse or drinking problems. In 1983, at Newcombe's behest, the Dodgers offered to place Wills in a twenty-eight-day drug rehabilitation program. Wills agreed to give it a try, but he walked out a few days before he would have completed it. A few years after that, he finally lost his house. That scared him enough to make a semiserious attempt to straighten out his life. A friend got him a job selling telephone pagers, still a relatively new technology in 1987. His "drug wife" left him; if Wills wanted to clean up, she didn't. After she left, he fell back into using anyway.

A year later, in January 1988, Wills started attending twelve-step programs. He wasn't an instant convert to sobriety. In fact, he spent most of that spring and summer either high on cocaine or else sleeping off its effects. Food and sex no longer interested him. But he kept going back to twelve-step meetings, listening to people there tell him that most early attempts to get sober fail, that the key was to keep trying. Finally, in August, the day came when Maury Wills gave up. He hated his life. He was embarrassed by what it had come to. And he knew he would either have to get off drugs or die.

"Nothing real dramatic," he says. "Every addict just has a moment when you understand it's going to go one way or the other. Clean up or die. Very simple."

Wills wanted the sobriety he saw other members of his twelve-step program enjoying, but the critical component of the program involved admitting his failures and surrendering control to whatever form of higher power he might believe in.

That frightened Wills almost more than dying of a drug overdose. Then, too, if he got sober he would have to deal with the problems he'd created for himself. The word was out in the baseball world that Maury Wills was cocaine-addled and unemployable. His house was gone. There was no special woman in his life, though he had reconciled with his children to an extent. At age fifty-five, he had no job prospects outside of baseball.

But baseball fans still had special memories of Maury Wills. That made the difference.

GERRY COONEY, THE FORMER BOXER WHO ONCE CAME CLOSE TO winning the heavyweight championship, says he tells other athletes who've fallen on hard times through their own fault that there's a simple way to make amends with the public: "Just admit what you did, and say you're sorry. If you mean it, they'll know it and forgive you."

Despite the stories they'd read or the things they'd heard, fans in 1988 were instantly ready to forgive Maury Wills for whatever trespasses he might have committed. Within weeks of committing to sobriety, he was hired to sign autographs at a baseball card show. A cellular phone company liked the idea of a well-known former player on its sales force. While Wills had to struggle every day to avoid giving in to the temptation of drugs or alcohol, he found that earning a living, at least, wasn't going to be as hard as he'd feared.

The Dodgers welcomed him back for special events. A few major league teams even hired Wills again to come to spring training and teach their young players the finer arts of baserunning. Though most of his new employers didn't require it of him, Wills voluntarily took daily drug tests. He liked proving he was clean.

Wills switched his addiction to sobriety. As with baseball, as with drug use, he was determined to excel. He was enjoying his fans again; being able to interact with them after so many years of drug-induced reclusiveness was further proof he was recovering.

He also became an outspoken, energetic advocate of his twelve-step program. As offers began to come in for speeches at sports banquets and business events, Wills was not in any way ashamed to talk about his problems with drugs and alcohol, and how he was able to bring his disease under control. The cultural timing was right for him, he believes. Celebrity redemption was becoming a cottage industry. From former First Lady Betty Ford to Beatles drummer Ringo Starr, America had become accustomed to—and was embracing—its idols falling victim to drugs or alcohol, struggling to recover, and making the whole process public.

"The idea that even famous people can have this terrible disease of addiction seems almost comforting, I guess," Wills says. "Being able to forgive someone you think is important makes *you* feel important, is the way, maybe, it works."

After fourteen years of sobriety, Wills says he's comfortable with his life, and cognizant of how the fame he once believed didn't matter has contributed to his emotional and financial recovery. Because people love the way he played baseball, because they remember all the bases he stole and the championships he and the Dodgers won, because they want his autograph or the thrill of shaking his hand, Maury Wills can drive a BMW and wear expensive clothes. Sobriety he achieved by himself, with the help of his twelve-step program and its members. Most of the money he makes, and the personal validation he gets about his baseball achievements, come directly from sports fans.

Rummaging through his desk drawer at Mainline Inc., Wills comes up with a squarish cardboard box. Inside is a heaping stack of baseball cards.

"The card companies—Topps, Fleer, Upper Deck—send me cards to autograph that they put into the packs they sell," Wills says. "I sit here at my desk and sign them, and they pay me good money for that. I have my job here at Mainline Inc., and I go to trade shows when they need me, do whatever they ask. I work with the Dodgers, coaching on the field, before all of their home games. That's eighty-one games a year. Then for several years I've been working with a minor league team in Fargo, North Dakota. I did game broadcasts for a while; now I do appearances for them and help them have a kids' group. They built a small museum honoring me onto their ballpark, and I sent them most of the things I had left from my career, some jerseys and game bats and so forth. There are card shows where I'm paid to sign. I'm financially comfortable, and I like having the money I need. Coming out of my disease, I recall a time I was looking under the cushions of my couch, trying to find twelve more cents so I could get the cheapest Subway sandwich they had."

That's an experience Wills is unlikely to repeat. He's taking every advantage of the ongoing public demand for signed sports memorabilia. There's even a Maury Wills website that offers his signature on balls, photos, caps, jerseys, or any other items fans might want to send in to be autographed. The prices, in these days of celebrity-driven inflation, are reasonable: $8 for baseball cards, $12 for photos smaller than 11 by 14 inches, $15 for baseballs, $40 for bats and jerseys. Personalizations are $5 extra.

THERE'S AN OLD ADAGE THAT PEOPLE CAN CHANGE SOME OF THE things they do but not who they are. This is certainly true of Maury Wills. He's sober instead of stoned. He's learned how to use his fame in positive rather than self-destructive ways. But deep down, he's still the same obsessive, competitive man he's always been. It's especially evident when he talks about his current job with the Dodgers. Working with players in Los Angeles both pleases and frustrates him. He likes being back in baseball and loves teaching anyone who'll let him. The problem is, many of the highly paid youngsters won't. As far as they're concerned, Maury Wills is just some geezer who yaps about how much better baseball was in the old days.

"They don't understand how you play baseball to win," Wills grumbles. "There's one exception, an outfielder named Dave Roberts. I see a lot of myself in him. He's a little older, nearly thirty, I guess, and he was in the minors a long time before he got to the Dodgers. I'm going to be his Bobby Bragan. I'm going to give him that extra advice, that one last push, that makes him something special."

In some ways, it's working. Wills has drilled Roberts, whom the Dodgers traded to the Boston Red Sox late in the 2004 season, in the fine art of taking leads, of running from the inside corner of first to the inside corner of second to save a few feet. In 2003, Roberts, despite several injuries, finished second in the National League in stolen bases. Of course, that second-place showing didn't satisfy his mentor.

"He's good, but he could be better," Wills says. "In one bad way, Dave's thinking runs parallel to other modern players. I tell him to steal bases no matter what the score is, to use his spikes on anybody who's between him and the base, and he says, 'I don't want to make anyone mad.' I'm trying to make him more selfish as a player, because that's what you have to be, to be really good. I want him to be relentless, and he just wants to be liked. You can't be both. I never worried about being liked by the opposition. Their hatred was a sign of respect."

Yet the lingering enmity of his own old opponents is now a factor in Wills's failure to secure the only goal he has left in baseball. Without being elected to the Hall of Fame, Wills believes he will never have the ultimate affirmation that he really was one of the best players in the sport's history.

"Deep within my innermost self, I have the burning hope and prayer that I will be elected someday," Wills says. "In everyday life I push that aside. I do the things I need to do. But inside, I never stop hoping it will happen."

Back in his playing days, opponents despised him, and he reveled in it. The more they hated him, he believed, the more he gained a psychological edge.

Initially, the backlash involved the annual All-Star game. In Wills's era, the vote for starting players hadn't yet been handed over to the fans. Players in each league selected the starting lineups, and the rules prohibited them from voting for members of their own teams. This meant Dodgers players couldn't vote for Wills, and players on other teams wouldn't. So, each year, shortstops with batting and fielding statistics often far inferior to Wills's would be voted the National League starter. Wills only went as a reserve player if the Dodgers had won the National League pennant the year before. By tradition, that team's manager could select bench players, and Los Angeles's Walter Alston would pick Wills.

The antipathy that opposing players felt for him has never completely subsided. And that has kept him from fulfilling his dream of making the Hall of Fame.

When Wills first became eligible for election in 1978, it didn't seem his problems with opponents would matter. For the first fifteen years a player is up for election, sportswriters make the call. Even many of the best players—Joe DiMaggio, Roy Campanella, Whitey Ford, Harmon Killebrew—may take several years to gradually accumulate the 75 percent of sportswriters' ballots necessary for election. In 1978, Wills's 115 votes were 170 short of the necessary total, but it was a respectable showing. In 1979, his vote climbed to 166, still 158 short of the number needed that year but a significant improvement. (The number of voters varies each year.) But in 1980, his total began to drop off, and by 1991, his next-to-last year of initial eligibility, Wills got just 61 votes. Players he'd competed against, players he knew he'd been *better than*, made it instead, and it hurt. In 1992 he still fell short, and sportswriters who didn't think he deserved election said his overall offensive statistics weren't really that good, if you left out stolen bases.

Lou Brock, the man who broke Wills's single-season record and whose teams won just one World Series in his entire career compared to the three Los Angeles won with Wills, was elected. (Brock's .293 career batting average is twelve points higher.) So was Pee Wee Reese, the Dodger shortstop who'd preceded Wills and who Wills had eventually supplanted on the team's all-time lineup (Wills's .281 career average is twelve points higher than Reese's).

Reese had also failed to get sufficient votes during his first fifteen years as a candidate. He'd been selected by the so-called Veterans Committee, a group of former players and front-office personnel who met each year to elect someone who, in their collective opinion, had been unfairly snubbed by the writers. Though Reese's career numbers don't match up to Wills's, he was universally beloved during his career.

In 2003, the Hall of Fame changed its election process. A new Veterans Committee comprised of eighty-one living Hall of Fame members was designated to vote on individuals who no longer qualified for the sportswriters' ballots. To be elected, it was necessary to be named on at least sixty-one of eighty-one ballots—75 percent. The new committee failed to elect anyone. Maury Wills, the speedster who reintroduced the stolen base, got twenty-four votes and finished fifth.

He still isn't ready to give up on his final baseball goal. "I just feel I'll get elected one day," he says, looking down at his hands, where three World Series championship rings would gleam if he hadn't lost them in his drug days. "I know I belong. Maybe they'd vote for me if I asked them real nicely, but that's the one thing I won't do. I shouldn't have to ask."

Wills sighs, straightens, grins a tight little grin.

"You know," he says, "if it were the fans who voted, I'd be in already."

WILLS DOESN'T WANT TO LEAVE THE MAINLINE INC. OFFICES WITH-out a trip to the warehouse. He moves between aisles there greeting the men and women whose dusty job it is to pull components off shelves and prepare them for shipping. Some speak only Spanish, and Wills jokes with them in that language. He mastered better-than-rudimentary Spanish while managing winter league teams in Mexico.

"Some of these people are living paycheck to paycheck, never knowing when the money might run out," Wills says softly. "I remember what that's like. So I try to do little things for them whenever I can. See how many are wearing Dodger T-shirts or jackets? I buy them for them, and they pay me back whenever they can. I get them tickets to games, too. Anything to help them feel special, to remind them that somebody knows they're alive."

Wills says he gets all the companionship he needs at work, at twelve-step meetings, and at events like card signings: "What I really enjoy now is time by myself. When I was younger, I hated being alone. I couldn't stand it. My program has helped me change that. I like to go out to the golf course or the driving range and just swing the clubs. At night, I'm a movie guy. I rent a movie and watch it at home. I don't stay up late, just till around nine, because I have to get up at five the next morning for my meeting."

He's alone at home, too. Wills doesn't have a wife or girlfriend. It's not that he wouldn't like one. He just doesn't trust himself where romance is concerned.

"I've learned very gradually to value women as people and not just for sex," he says. "Baseball players don't get that chance. Locker rooms are guy places. Through my recovery program I've been able to lose some of my selfishness and learn to think about what other people might need in relationships. So I'd like to meet someone now when I could give to her as well as take for myself. I'm praying on it. If I find someone it has got to be through my higher power, because I'd make the wrong decision. That's been proven in my life. Some character defects don't go away, they just get arrested. I'm trying to grow every day. Maybe this is the next way in which I'll grow. I hope so."

He's not completely alone in life. All six of his children are in touch regularly, usually by phone or e-mail. Wills says that after years of estrangement, even Gertrude is back on guardedly friendly terms with him. And he was thrilled when a grandson named Robinson—for Jackie, of course—actually came to stay with Grandpa Maury for a few days.

"He's a champion wrestler," Wills says proudly. "I think he got to the state high school finals for California, that's how good he is. When he stayed with me, I was working for the Toronto Blue Jays, teaching some baserunning to their players, and they let Robinson suit up and get out on the field.

After watching him try to field the ball, I knew it was better for him to be a wrestler instead of trying baseball." A beat. "I never let him see that I was disappointed, a little."

WILLS TRIES TO REMEMBER SHORTCUTS ON THE RIDE BACK TO Redondo Beach. Between muttering "I should have turned there," and "Was that the street I was thinking of?" he talks about his typical day.

"It seems, mostly, like I spend my time being of service, accommodating someone," Wills says. "Maybe it's job-related, helping a salesman for my company get in to see a buyer, or at the stadium working with a player, or just going to a twelve-step meeting and encouraging someone like I was once encouraged. It's not real flashy or anything. I wouldn't call it exciting. So if you want to know what's left for Maury Wills, well, I, too, have often thought about this."

The oddest part of his life, Wills says, "is that I'm at the point where I'm running out of goals. It's a strange feeling. My hope to get into the Hall of Fame might be the only thing. But my days, my life now, is mostly about trying to be a good guy, not somebody with self-importance issues. I don't think about how I've been famous, but I like to feel I've brought joy into some people's lives."

A red light finally catches Wills. He reluctantly stops the BMW to wait for the green. It's midafternoon, and there are no more hands to shake, autographs to sign, or interviews to grant. He'll stop at a video store, rent a movie, drive home, and watch it, and be in bed by nine.

Tapping his fingers on the steering wheel, glaring impatiently at the light that won't turn from red to green as quickly as he wants it to, Maury Wills begins to say something about his fame, stops, finally starts again.

"Well, what's the bottom line? Okay, I guess this. At least I've learned that if you fall, people don't hold that against you as long as you don't stay there."

The light changes. He makes certain his car is the first to begin moving forward.

Melvin and Linda

The first television show Melvin Dummar made it on was *Truth or Consequences*. He ended up getting the consequences, which included women from the audience dousing him with a fire hose. Melvin's favorite game show was *Let's Make a Deal*, and he was surprised to learn that anyone could be in the audience and get called up on stage. All you had to do was dress up in a funny outfit, get there early to stand in line, and look entertaining. His wife liked the idea of going on a game show, too. Linda had less and less patience for the life she found herself stuck in, that of wife and mother, so she was happy that he'd finally come up with something exciting to do. But Melvin took it very seriously, far too seriously for Linda. Melvin first started going to game shows "to win stuff. We needed stuff. Then I did it because it was fun." Melvin figured it was a way to get himself noticed, and then he could show people that he had talent, too—that he could sing. So he went to costume rental shops to pick out outfits for both Linda and himself, even choosing wigs. When he didn't have money to rent costumes, he simply made them himself, even if the costumes didn't really make any sense. For one *Let's Make a Deal* episode, Melvin was, for lack of a better name, Orange Man, with orange pants, an orange sweatshirt, a string of oranges around his neck, and a hat shaped like an orange. Linda told him he looked like an idiot, but he explained to her that they needed to look silly and act silly, because that was "the kinda people who got on them game shows," she later said. On another *Let's Make a Deal* episode, Melvin wore a hat with a duck picture on it with a sign that said "Quacking up for a deal." Melvin always had good ideas for getting himself up on the stage; he believed he thought like a game-show host and wondered how he could get that kind of job.

In fact, Melvin was good at more than just getting picked to go on stage. He was good at winning. He and Linda won a piano, a weekend for two in Catalina, a toaster, and cash. They sold most of the prizes to pay bills, including the trip to Catalina, because, Linda later said in a court proceeding, she'd "been to Catalina before, and it's the pits."

"It's the what?" asked the attorney questioning her.

"A place where you don't like it is the pits," Linda said, speaking slowly because the attorney was obviously a moron. "Like a hole in the ground, see? It's bad as you go down, an' then it gets worse, an' at the very bottom it's the pits."

By late 1967, a lot of things were the pits to Linda Dummar. Her life, for one thing. Her house. Melvin most of all. Melvin never could understand her attitude. "I was out of my head; I loved her, or thought I loved her," he says. "I was going crazy."

Melvin was a nice guy, but Linda was certain there was something more out there for her. She just didn't know what that something was. She had been a sophomore in high school when Melvin first set eyes on her. He was nineteen and working construction. He was there at the school that day because a friend wanted to set him up with his sister. Melvin barely even said hello to the friend's sister, because all he saw was Linda.

"I was building houses with this guy Vance, and he kept wanting me to meet his sister, Terry," Melvin says. "We were working a job one day, just the two of us, and so I said, 'Okay, let's take off a little early, and we'll pick up your sister from school.' We went over to the high school, and we were sitting there waiting for them to come out, and this Terry Dayton and Linda West come walking across the parking lot. And when I first seen them, I said, 'That's the girl I want. Just forget Terry. Who's this other girl?'"

Melvin locked on and wouldn't let go. So, less than a year after they met in her high school parking lot, Linda married him. Not long after that, they had a baby, Darcy. That was when Linda started to get restless. Melvin worked hard, sometimes two jobs, always long hours, but it didn't seem to matter. There was never enough money to keep the repo man away. Worse, there was never enough time for him to spend with Linda. She needed someone to pay attention to her—the more the merrier. It was the only reason she went with Melvin to the game shows, where she always felt like a dope in the outfits he made her wear, until she got up on stage and people were hootin' and hollerin' at her. Her husband never made her feel like she felt at those moments.

That was why she started stepping out on him. Melvin was a nice guy, sure, but the second he walked out of a room, he was gone completely. He didn't linger in the mind. He just seemed so utterly out of place in a girl's fantasies, and Linda wasn't ready to give up her fantasies.

"She liked to spend all her time in bars," Melvin says. "There was nothing I could do about it. She didn't want me even asking her about it." With Melvin at home, Linda would stand at a bar, any bar, and smooth her dress down over her bottom and let the men gather around, buy her drinks. That made her happy. It was even better than the game shows. She'd look a man up and down with such a direct, lascivious smile that it would just freeze him in his tracks. She looked at every man that way.

Melvin watched her sometimes, when he could find her. He understood how she felt, and it only convinced him that she needed him. A woman like Linda was always popular in bars—for a few years. Then the hope in her eyes would start to show, and by then she wouldn't be so young anymore, and instead of seeing a good time, men would just see desperation. It made Melvin want to cry, and Linda hated it when he cried.

MELVIN HAD ALWAYS BEEN SENSITIVE. HE SAW PEOPLE WHO HAD it bad, and he hurt for them. He'd been like that since he was a child, always busting out in tears.

"We weren't the richest folks in Nevada," Melvin's late father, Arnold

Dummar, told the author of *Melvin and Howard: A Nevada Fairy Tale.* "When Melvin was a boy we lived in a trailer some of the time, moving around to where I could find work. . . . His momma was working in a motel for a time, and I swear even years later when we'd drive by the place, the tears would well up in his eyes and he'd think of his momma cleaning up for strangers, making almost nothing, and never seeing a tip from the rich men who could afford to stay in the rooms."

Arnold and Melvin's mother didn't know what to make of all those tears, which kept on coming even as he got into his teens. "I love my boy," Arnold said. "He grew up different from the other kids—more sensitive, I guess—and we didn't question that, just accepted it. . . . Even when he got older Melvin would cry if he saw a sad program on the television."

Melvin was never one of the popular kids in school, though that had nothing to do with his tears. In small western towns in the 1950s, sports were the only way for a boy to stand out, and Melvin was never much of an athlete. He liked to sing in the choir, which was not a ticket to many girls' hearts. It also didn't help how vulnerable he was, how obvious he was in his likes.

In high school in Gabbs, Nevada, he had such a crush on one girl that when he'd shuffle up the front walkway of her house, she'd flee out the back. "She would go out with the rest of the kids and leave him at the door," remembers the girl's mother, Shirley Mendive. "She'd just disappear. She wasn't interested, much to his chagrin. I felt sorry for him. I'd say, 'Well, Melvin, she's not interested, that's the way it goes.'"

He'd stick around anyway, talking to Mrs. Mendive, helping out with the chores. "I'd do her dishes and sweep her floors, whatever she needed done. I'd spend hours with her," Melvin says. When the girl would call the house, her mother would quietly tell her to stay the night at a friend's. Because asking Melvin Dummar to leave was out of the question. He had nowhere to go. She knew his father was a drinker, working road construction by day and knocking back his paycheck by night. Things got so bad Melvin had run away from home to live with his older brother. "He was thirteen or fourteen when he started coming to my house," says Mrs. Mendive. "He was not an intellectual by any means. But he was so sweet and nice. He liked to talk—

just a nice, nice boy. He was so sensitive—oh gosh, yes. I don't think he's ever hurt anyone's feelings in his whole life."

Melvin talked incessantly as he did her dishes and swept her floors and waited for her daughter to return. He didn't just have stories to tell. He had dreams. Big dreams. He wanted to be a pilot, he told her. He was going to go to college. Most of all, he said, he was going to be up on stage entertaining people, which surprised Mrs. Mendive. "He was not a terribly outgoing person as a boy," she remembers. "He was kind of shy. I was surprised he wanted to go on and become a singer. I never thought he'd be able to do that."

Melvin wasn't supposed to think he could do it, either. He was the sixth of ten children, and their father took pains to instill in them just one truth: you had to work hard for a living—there wasn't time for dreams. The hard work Melvin understood. It was the flip side of his father's philosophy of life he had trouble with. "My dad was a loving man, but there were a lot of things he did that I didn't agree with: drinking and smoking and things like that," Melvin says. "I know every once in a while a person might have a binge, but when it's time after time, week after week, for years, it's hard to go along with."

Melvin didn't go along with it. Sure, he worked hard at every job he ever had, no matter what it was. But he didn't drink or smoke, and he didn't give up on his dreams. After he graduated from high school in 1962, he spent nine months in the Air Force before being discharged for what his commanding officers called "emotional immaturity." He then followed his father to the Los Angeles area and went to work for a construction company his father had started, until the business went under. Then he got a job as a milkman for Rockview Dairy in the working-class suburb of Downey, and, since he was in Los Angeles, started thinking about how to get into show business. Melvin began writing songs and taking guitar lessons. He loved to sing more than anything in the world. He thought it was just a matter of time before he got noticed. This was southern California; this was where you went to become a famous performer.

But even his success getting on game shows wasn't enough to pay the rent—or to convince Linda to stay home. In 1967, Melvin took Linda and

Darcy to Gabbs, Nevada, where Melvin had gone to high school for a while, to get Linda out of the bars and also to get work in the magnesium mines there to earn some quick money. The mines in Gabbs were cranking with a newfound intensity in the late '60s, and the town's population had swelled beyond the four-hundred mark. There was decent money to be made in the mines, while it lasted. By local standards, the place was hopping, which meant the town's one diner actually did some decent business for an hour in the morning. But Linda and Gabbs didn't hit it off, not even for an hour, and it wasn't long before she started disappearing for days, and then weeks, on end. "There was just no way to stop her. She loved being around a lot of men. She was always cheating on me," Melvin says. "She would say she was going to the store, and I wouldn't see her for two or three months. And she'd come back and expect me to not even ask her where she'd been. She'd been off with some other guy. She'd just leave us and run off."

Melvin would look for her, of course. He'd find her in bars. He'd see her with her boyfriends. It made him mad, but that wasn't the only thing he felt. He felt guilty. He felt he was failing her. Some of her boyfriends even wrote Linda love letters, and Melvin found them because Linda left them lying around. Sometimes he read them before she did. He figured out how to steam letters open, and he would read them carefully, fuming, but also trying to figure out what these guys had that he didn't. Then he would seal the letters up and put them back where he found them. He didn't dare confront her.

When such provocations got her nowhere, Linda finally left for good, or Melvin thought it was for good, because for the first time she took Darcy with her, to her parents' place. That brought Melvin down to southern California on New Year's Eve in 1967. Along the way he had his encounter with that strange old man in the desert, which he told Linda and her family about when he got to California. "My father just kinda laughed at Mel," Linda said years later in court. "You know, kinda needlin' Mel, like Mel was making up the whole thing. And my father says, why didn't Mel take a picture of the man? And Mel says he didn't have no camera and didn't think it was Howard Hughes anyway, and why would he take a picture of an old bum, you know?"

LINDA KEPT RUNNING, AND MELVIN KEPT CHASING, UNTIL SHE GOT to Las Vegas. That was where Melvin drew the line. Reno was bad news—Linda had worked as a waitress at a topless bar there—but Vegas was even worse. They didn't have any morals in Vegas. Showgirls wearing big hats and almost nothing else were treated like movie stars in Las Vegas; they put pictures of them on billboards. Even in family restaurants the waitresses wore their shorts two sizes too small so their cheeks would stick out the bottom for the whole world to see. It didn't surprise Melvin at all that Linda and her new boyfriend had taken his car when they skipped town. That was the kind of thing you did when you set your sights on Las Vegas. That was when he thought about how all this was affecting Darcy, the beautiful little daughter his wife had left behind, and he realized he couldn't be married to Linda anymore. Who knew what Linda was doing in Las Vegas, what she might have gotten herself into? Just the thought of it brought tears rolling down his face. He cried all the way down to Vegas on the bus—big, heaving jags; no one would sit by him. He didn't care; he knew he had messed everything up. He knew he was better than the life he was living. He was going to divorce Linda, and he was going to get his car back, but he still didn't blame her for all the cheating. He had to make something of himself. Then he'd deserve something better from a woman.

When he arrived in the gambling mecca, Melvin found out where his wife was working and went over there to serve her with divorce papers, but he found his car in the parking lot first. Linda didn't know how to take care of a car, so he gave it a once-over, and that was when he made the first mistake he knows he'll never get over. "I found a note on the dashboard of the car," he remembers. "It was a funny note." It took him a moment to realize it wasn't from Linda. It said, "Hello, Melvin. Where have you been? Did you move to Las Vegas?"

"It told me to go to some bank in Las Vegas and ask for somebody. It gave a name," Melvin says. The note befuddled him. He thought it was a gag or a trick. There were a lot of con men in Las Vegas, but how would they know his name? "I didn't know anybody who worked in a bank, and so I thought, 'What do I want to go to some bank for?' It didn't give a bank account number or anything. It just said to ask for somebody in the bank." In interviews he gave more than two decades ago, Melvin remembered the note telling him to go to a hotel, not a bank, and to talk to the hotel's casino manager. But either way, he didn't do it. He says he just crumpled up the note and tossed it away. He was there to tell Linda their marriage was over, and he had to stay focused. He knew it wouldn't be easy to face her and to actually say the words. He still loved her desperately. But he had to do it. He had to follow through for once.

After all the papers were signed and he was given legal custody of Darcy, Melvin expected to feel relief, but he didn't. He felt lost, depressed, "just mixed up. I really broke down when I divorced her," he says. He decided every day that he'd made a terrible mistake, that he could've made it work with Linda, that Darcy needed her mother. He couldn't write any songs. He couldn't play his guitar without breaking into sobs. Melvin didn't want to be in Gabbs anymore, where Linda had been, so he and Darcy hit the road. They lived in Utah for a while, where he worked as a milkman for Cream of Weber and tried to lose himself in the wide mountain vistas and crisp white air, and then he moved back to California to give performing and school another try—and he immediately backslid. Linda, back in California, wanted to see Darcy, and so he brought her over to her mom one morning, which was a mistake. California always did wonders for Linda. She was standing there at the door, just about to crouch down and put her arms out for her daughter to rush into, and Melvin took in the shadows beneath her dress, and those bare legs and delicate ankles, and that tiny waist that insisted you put your hand around it. He decided he should at least be polite and say hello, and when all was said and done he'd remarried Linda and adopted her son, Ferrin, whom she'd had with another man. He hit the game-show circuit again, appearing on *Let's Make a Deal, The New Price Is Right,* and *Hollywood Squares,* where he won a Pontiac Astre. He started working at Rockview Dairy again, getting home from his route exhausted, just in time for Linda to be up and ready to go out to the bars. But it wasn't entirely a case of déjà vu all over again. He wasn't the same person. After the divorce, he had decided to get serious about his dreams, and so he'd got up the courage to start performing in public, taking his guitar and going to local clubs on amateur night with his friend Johnny Roman. Everybody seemed to really like his singing, so he started going out and doing it whenever he could, and especially when he'd see Linda's eyes turn dark at the sight of him. Melvin and Linda soon headed for divorce court for a second time (Melvin won custody of both Darcy and Ferrin), but this time he wasn't nearly as upset. He had regular "jam sessions" to go to, and that always made him feel good about himself. He also had a new girl, and that changed everything.

The new woman in Melvin's life, a blonde named Bonnie, was the right one. She was pretty like Linda, and she was funny, too, but not in the mean way Linda sometimes hit you with. Bonnie's laugh could strip paint, but Melvin couldn't get enough of it. When they met in 1973, she was in her mid-twenties and working at Firestone, the tire company. She'd had a number of dead-end jobs since dropping out of high school. She'd worked in a Mattel toy factory in Los Angeles and as a dental assistant trainee. Before Firestone hired her, she had worked for a company that made parts for washing machines. She was still in her teens when she became a mother for the first time. She had three kids by the time she met Melvin.

Melvin knew she was the perfect girl for him not long after they started dating. "I guess because of the situation with my first wife, I used to do a lot of cheating songs," he says. The first time he performed at a club with Bonnie there, he sang the country cuckold classic "Cold Hard Facts of Life." Bonnie has never gotten over it. "You could hear a pin drop," she says. "All the women were cryin'. Women came up afterward and told him it was the most beautiful thing they'd ever heard."

Melvin and Bonnie got married that October. Her first husband, Bonnie says, had left her every time she got pregnant, but now he was around, being a pest. So when Melvin suggested a change of scenery, she was ready to go. Melvin burned for his big break as a singer, but the amateur nights and jam sessions weren't getting him anywhere. No record people ever came to the clubs where he played. That was how he figured it worked in the record business; you waited for a talent scout to find you. Melvin had heard the stories about Rita Hayworth, or whoever it was, getting discovered at Schwab's Drugstore in Los Angeles. But that was when L.A. was smaller, more of a town than the teeming city it was now. Now it was simply too big, with too many people. There were so many bars and clubs and theaters that it took pure luck to get discovered by a talent scout. Melvin thought he could get noticed easier in a smaller place. He also thought he could spend more time working on his music if life was simpler, if he ran his own business and set his own hours. So in 1975, when he was thirty years old, he and Bonnie and the kids packed up Melvin's truck and headed for Willard, Utah, a town just north of Salt Lake City. Melvin had found a gas station on Highway 89 he could lease and run however he wanted. He wouldn't be able to appear on game shows anymore, which bothered him, but he had found a country-rock band that needed a singer, the first real band he had ever been in. They played every week, at bars and VFW gatherings and the like. He had never been happier. And against all reason, he was proven right. It was here in Mormon Utah, not in glitzy, decadent southern California, that Melvin Dummar finally got noticed.

CHUCK PAUL LEARNED HOW TO PLAY THE DRUMS AS A TWELVE-year-old in Driggs, Idaho, intent on copying a local legend there named Dean Wilkie.

"Dean Wilkie played the drums, so I played the drums," Paul says, more than sixty years later. "That was all there was to it."

Paul played them well, too. Back in those days, before rock 'n' roll, the only drummers who weren't serious musicians stuck to the bongos. If Paul was going to get a drum kit, no matter how cheap, he was going to learn how to play. He took lessons. He practiced diligently. And he learned to read music. Paul would spend most of his adult life playing country and rockabilly, but he was never more comfortable than as part of a sixteen-piece band, massaging his snare, with elegantly dressed men and women gliding across a ballroom floor in front of him.

Paul put his first band together in high school, but it wasn't much of a band. It was the Depression, and no one was hiring teenage musicians. When Pearl Harbor happened, he joined the Navy and saw enough of the war to know he believed in God and wanted a simple life. After VJ Day he settled in Utah, north of Salt Lake City. He worked hard, selling life insurance and helping his brother-in-law run a gas station. He even worked for the state liquor commission for a while as an "undercover man," as he puts it, rooting out corruption. He didn't partake in the spirits himself, didn't believe in it. He'd become a devout member of the Mormon Church. That was where he met Melvin Dummar. Melvin was a new member of the church.

Paul and Melvin had a lot in common. Melvin ran a gas station, just like the older man had once done. Paul even helped out now and again at Dummar Gas Station. Melvin worked as hard as he could, at whatever job he had, just like Paul always did. Melvin didn't like smoking or drinking or swearing. He went to church regularly. And, of course, he loved music.

That last one was actually where the two men parted, though they didn't know it then. Paul was a serious musician, and he had his own band—the Night Ryders—which played around town. But he never took performing too seriously. White guys from Utah didn't become famous pop stars, unless you were an Osmond, which Chuck Paul definitely was not. Besides, he was a grown man. By the time he met Melvin in the early 1970s, he was nearing fifty.

Melvin was not a trained musician like Paul, but he took performing very seriously and soon talked his way into the band. He played guitar just well enough to look good holding it, but now that he was with a band he was determined to get better. "Once you thought about a beat instead of playing it you were as good as dead," offered a jazz man in Ann Patchett's novel *Taft*. Melvin did nothing but think about it, day and night. He heard the beat everywhere: in the clank of the gas pump when he stuck the nozzle back in place; in the whirr of his truck's engine when it needed a tune-up; in Bonnie's voice, even when it was raised in anger. Melvin wasn't a purist in his approach to music, but he sure was in his approach to passion. He loved music as deeply and completely as he loved Bonnie, as deeply and completely as he had loved Linda.

"Mel had no musical training. The other guys did and were very good musicians," Paul says of the Knight Ryders. "The guy on bass would bump Mel in the back of the leg, to keep him on time with the beat: one-two, one-two, one-two. Some people, even though they hear it, they're not feeling it. By bumping him, Mel could feel it."

That was good enough for Paul.

"Mel played rhythm guitar and sang. He had a nice voice," the drummer says. And even though they didn't necessarily need a front man—three of the band's members had always taken turns singing—there was no resentment toward Melvin. "With his personality, who wouldn't like him?"

The Knight Ryders played every Friday and Saturday night at company parties, church dances, the American Legion, and local bars. "But not the old stinking bars where people are falling all around," Paul insists. "I arranged the jobs, paid the guys. We made, on average, about sixty dollars apiece. Remember, that was a lot of years ago."

Melvin was so inspired by it all that he began writing songs for the first time in years—a lot of them—though he didn't get a chance to show them off very often. "We'd play all over, at dances and nightclubs, here and there," says Melvin. "We played lots of covers. They didn't want me doing originals, which I think is insane. You can't go nowhere doing other people's stuff. You've got to do your own material."

One of the few originals they did let Melvin sing was a novelty tune called "Santa's Souped-up Sleigh," which Melvin wrote with Bonnie. It was a catchy little number, and perfect for the kind of family-friendly entertainment the group wanted to provide. "It was always a lot of fun; we just wanted people to have a good time," says Paul. "I'd go around and talk to people between sets, ask people, 'How's it going? How do you like it?'"

The folks in Willard and nearby towns like Ogden and Riverdale seemed to like it just fine—and Melvin liked it most of all. "I thought that was cool," his daughter, Darcy, says of the Knight Ryders. "It's what made him happy.

I remember going to churches and little gigs with him, and dancing. It was always a lot of fun. He really wanted to make it in the music industry. Music really made him happy."

Attention also made him happy, deliriously happy. All those hands clapping, all those feet stamping, all those eyes peering upward, expectantly, voices calling out song titles. For years, Melvin had felt the longing for attention as a dull ache in his gut. He felt it when he looked in the mirror in the morning and instinctively struck a pose. He felt it when he watched Sonny Bono spread his arms and try to hit a note, that tall, tan woman beside him rolling her eyes. He deserved to be on TV, Melvin thought, just as much as *that* guy. Whenever Melvin came on stage, any stage, he saw hundreds of arms reach out for him, desperate to embrace him, even if there were but a dozen people in the whole place. When a man in a nice suit and a big car stopped at the gas station one day and asked him if he was Melvin Dummar, Melvin thought, just for a moment, someone had seen him at their gig in Riverdale and word had gotten out to a record company scout. It was only natural. It was just a matter of time.

Except this man didn't want to talk about Melvin's singing. He wanted to talk about Howard Hughes.

Irene Cara:
The Prodigy

They rolled up in limousines, looking like European royalty that had been rushed out of the manor by a fire alarm. Rappers wore tuxedo tops and low-rider bottoms. Starlets wore cinched tops and no bottoms. The paparazzi hovered in anticipation, calling out the name of everyone who was stepping out of a backseat, hoping Madonna or Erykah Badu or whoever might duck forward just a little too much and accidentally allow a breast to tumble out of her décolletage. The tabs paid through the nose for money shots.

Not that that mattered to Irene Cara. She arrived with no expectations and no flashbulbs popping in her eyes. She knew she looked good—she'd lost most of the weight she put on after moving to Florida—but she didn't look *that* good. There were going to be a lot of women here tonight who looked amazing, who looked literally edible. It was February 2000, and this was Warner Brothers' Grammy Awards party, the first of the new century. For Cara, who had just put together a new band, the timing seemed perfect. She wanted a new start. She wanted to get back into the business. As she strode bare-legged through the glittery smiles and gowns, she wasn't think-ing of the circumstances that had put her in this situation, the circumstances responsible for the blank looks from most everyone as she made her way into the party. That was all ancient history.

Cara honestly expected no one would remember her, and that was the way she wanted it. They couldn't still hate you if they didn't remember you. Back in 1984—a millennium ago—she had been the queen of the Grammys. The queen, at twenty-two! Her song, "Flashdance . . . What a Feeling," had been at the top of the charts for about a million weeks before the awards show. She had just wrapped a movie with Burt Reynolds and Clint Eastwood. Industry movers and shakers stood around that night getting sloshed and talking about how Irene Cara might rule the *Billboard* charts *and* the box office for the next ten years, at least. She didn't. She didn't even last ten months. Now she was surfacing again, more than fifteen years later, like she had never even existed before this night. She saw nothing but new people, a whole new industry, new possibilities, rolling out in front of her.

It took some getting used to. The Next Big Things, her competition, were already in attendance, milling about the room, their one-of-a-kind gowns framing perfectly muscled pecs. Faces looked shellacked, limbs and torsos fitted together with wrenches. The need for physical perfection had become mandatory in the years Cara had been away; there were so many choices these days that there simply was no reason for a fan to accept less. "There are these robots now, shaking their behinds for the camera, programmed for celebrity," Cara remembers thinking. She knew what her challenge would be, trying to get back into the music industry in her thirties. This new, young generation wasn't attempting to wow you with talent. Proving you could *do* something took too long. It was all about pose, look. Cara had to be willing to be patient.

Don Engel, the entertainment lawyer and friend who had invited her to the party, stepped through the crowd of starlets who were clenching for the cameras, and Cara followed. She was still nervous about being back on the scene. She had been a child star. TV, movies, Broadway, records—she had done it all. All before her first kiss. But that was so long ago. The phone didn't ring much now, and she liked it that way. For the past year, she had lived near the shore in Tampa. She liked to walk into the water late at night

Irene Cara now.

and swim out to one of the tiny islands in the bay. Being out there alone just swept the stress away. If Jennifer Lopez tried that, there'd be helicopters hovering overhead every night, searchlights all over the place. The thought of it made Cara's stomach hurt. "As we proceeded to an empty table, [Engel] told me that he would introduce me to the new head of Warner Brothers' record division, who was his client," Cara remembers. "He spotted him by the bar and took me over there to introduce me. He was British. A tall, attractive man who appeared young, his name was Roger Ames."

Ames was one of the young bloods in the business who'd come over from Europe to save the Americans from themselves. He stood there at the bar, gazing sleepily out at the proceedings. Cara had seen that look before. This was a man who knew he was the shit. With his smooth, brown face and high forehead, with his tiny eyes appraising everything from behind designer glasses—oh, he knew. Ames had been born and raised in Trinidad, but he was British all the way. The ruling class. Cara was comforted by his cool self-assurance—no wonder he and Don got along so well. "We all ordered drinks, and the two of them chatted for a short while," Cara says. Shop talk: whose new CD was sure to make a splash, who was going to get the biggest sales boost from the awards. Cara nodded along, agreeing with everything. Then, "for some reason, Don excused himself for a minute, and I was left alone with Ames. I thought this would be a good opportunity to tell him a little about my group and the record we were working on. As I started to talk he quickly picked up his drink and left me there at the bar in midsentence."

Cara felt a wave of heat rush to her face, and for a moment she thought she might vomit. She processed the fact that this man had just walked away from her, without even saying "Excuse me." "I slowly tried to finish my drink without showing the shock and humiliation I felt," she says. She then started to get angry. Nothing had changed, nothing at all, in the last fifteen years. No one had forgotten. Here Cara was, thinking she had put all that crap behind her, that she could start fresh, and she was reliving exactly the same emotions she had felt when she was a newly minted Grammy and Oscar winner and was being turned down in auditions. By now, Cara knew what had happened to her all those years ago: she had been blacklisted. She was sure of it. All because she had dared to stand up for herself, dared to take on Al Coury, David Geffen's lackey. Dared, as it turned out, to take on the whole industry. Almost overnight, when she seemed to be on top of the world, offers stopped coming her way. Her career just fell off a cliff. "You've got to ask the question, Was that a coincidence or what?" says Cara's former attorney, Tom Nunziato.

Cara certainly didn't think so. "They can't admit that that was going on, so they had to let me be seen [at auditions]," she says of the industry's rejection of her. "Yeah, it was very ugly. And silly. The whole thing was silly. I had too much pride to just put up with it. I wasn't going to stick around for it."

So at the Warner Grammy party, after being dissed by Roger Ames, she remembered exactly why she had gotten out of town in the first place. "As the evening went on, things just got worse," she says. "Some old familiar faces I'd see here and there looked lost and miserable. Producers I used to know and work with would come to my table to make snide remarks and [share their] disgust with me. Past artists long ago discarded and forgotten were lounging around drunk, looking out of place or on the brink of a nervous breakdown. The top CEOs were huddled together at their special reserved tables with blank stares on their faces. Perhaps it was over the recent AOL Time Warner [merger] debacle, but I had never seen such a sorry lot. I left there realizing the enormous favor they had all done me."

To be sure, it had taken many years for that realization to hit home. Rage had consumed Cara for more than a decade, as she was fighting those CEOs at their special reserved tables, fighting them any way she could. And who could blame her for that rage?

Irene Cara had grown up knowing only performing and the business of performing. Her talent and drive had quickly taken her out of the rough Bronx neighborhood where she was born—to movie stardom while still a teenager in *Fame,* to the top of the *Billboard* charts with "Flashdance . . . What a Feeling." She'd never known anything but success. She'd never known anything but her own way. Which was why, she says, she hadn't been willing to put up with being cheated. Wasn't that her right as an American, to take her grievances to the courts? Music executives *lived* in courtrooms, for God's sake. Even after all these years, she still couldn't understand the response she provoked.

"My mind starts drifting, and I start to think about one of my most beloved heroes, Joni Mitchell, a giant among artists," she wrote recently, as she began to sort through her emotions. "I've often heard how she, too, was hurt and by the same mob of industry men. I begin to ponder what is it about women like us that makes these men vehemently deplore us? What is it about our breed of female artist that's so threatening? Is it that we aren't the usual brand of kiss-up whores and bitches that they love to launch? Is it that we are not so easily molded, shaped, and Svengalied into the type of 'Barbie doll' product they love to manipulate and control?"

Now, four years after that Grammy party and twenty years after she last topped the charts, Cara is still trying to make it to the top again, this time on her own—free of Svengalis. She has her own group, an all-girl group called

Hot Caramel, that she's working with in the studio. She doesn't want to tour. She doesn't want to be on *Saturday Night Live*. She just wants to make one great record. The great record she wasn't allowed to make when she was a star.

The recording is going slowly, though, because Cara is paying for it out of pocket, and because she wants it to be perfect. She has to fly in most of the singers and instrumentalists to record. Hot Caramel band members live all over the country: in Los Angeles and Atlanta and Washington, D.C. They are doing this project—coming together in Florida every three to six months to record bits and pieces of songs for a few days—despite the fact that they don't have a record deal. Cara isn't sure she wants one. If she can manage to put together distribution herself, or use the Internet, she wants to release the CD on her own, without the corrupting influence of a big corporation. She doesn't think she can trust a corporation. Not anymore.

The whole industry has proved toxic to her. She remembers watching in vain in the mid-'80s as her reputation fell apart, as "friends" and "associates" told reporters about her drug use and about supposed temper tantrums. She was powerless to stop it, even when she went straight to the press herself to clear things up. "I tried to just be as honest and open and real as possible, which was a mistake a lot of the time," she says. "I was from the no-bullshit New York environment; that didn't work in Hollywood. In Hollywood, you had to learn the art of pretentiousness in a very real and sincere way. If you didn't have that down you were easy prey. And I didn't have it down. There are times when you want to be a part of interviews that are in-depth and truthful and real and that really say something about you to your audience that is of value. And then you're sitting down with *People* magazine and it's like, 'Oh, Irene'"—she snaps her fingers as if to wake herself up—"'you don't get filet mignon from a burger joint, now do you?'"

She's thought about getting a press agent, but their philosophy has changed as well during her years in the wilderness. Cara doesn't want to be a celebrity again; she just wants to be an artist. That is what she wants to get across to people. But the publicity machinery is now set up solely for celebrity, for image-making. "Good reporting and good writing don't help my client," Pat Kingsley, Hollywood's most powerful publicist, told author Jeannette Walls in 2000. Kingsley's professional motto had become: "People don't read. The text doesn't matter."

Even though Cara believes she has been burned by the press many times, she is convinced Kingsley's vision for the future isn't a step forward. She wants her music—what she has to say—to matter. "If you're a woman and an artist, you shouldn't have to shake your ass to get attention," she says. "The talent should be enough."

No matter what, she isn't going to start compromising now, not after all those years of frustration and anger and fighting. Cara says she was lucky to find some "wonderful Indian teachers who showed me how to let go." How to deal with the rage. "Just to try to get some understanding of why I had to go through this lesson, what is it I had to learn from this. It's important. It's not just about sleepwalking through it or suffering through it. It helped me get a better understanding of who I am, what my purpose is and should be: to be at peace with anywhere I may be in life. A lot of it is about letting go and understanding your higher self."

Maybe she sounds flaky and New Agey now, and maybe she is. She doesn't care. She swears by her spiritual teachers. Whenever the world drives her crazy—and it does every day, for that is her personality—she now has something to help her put it into perspective.

"I'm no longer appalled by the pathetic state of American television," she says, by way of example. "I'm no longer shocked by what base trend passes for entertainment. I'm merely bored by it all now. I close my eyes [at the end of the day] and try to sleep, saying a silent prayer to my angels and asking for some peace of mind. I feel the presence of my animal guide and spirit protector, the Great Bear spirit. He had shown himself to me so many times before, especially at times of great duress. I sense him gently swoop me in his comforting arms and begin to coddle me to sleep."

She doesn't solely rely on the Great Bear spirit, of course. Another way to let go is to stay busy, and Cara does that, too. She periodically flies to Europe to perform, "to prostitute myself," singing her old songs for fans who don't seem to realize the eighties are long gone. She is finally getting royalties for some of those old hits, so it doesn't bother her too much anymore to sing them.

When she's back in Florida, Cara is typically manic as she organizes the flights and hotel rooms and meals for the band members who are coming into town to work on tracks. She can't help feeling like their mother, even though the instrumentalists and singers are only a few years younger than she is. Cara's mom had irretrievably bound up her maternal instincts with her daughter's performing needs when Cara was young, and now Cara, divorced and childless, is all too aware when she starts falling into those same patterns with her musicians. She tries to fight it, but you can only deny who you are so much. When she gets home every evening, she is always exhausted from running every decision through her head a million times, from second-guessing everything she does. All she wants is one great record, she reminds herself. She doesn't think that is too much to ask. She doesn't think that is beyond her.

IRENE CARA WAS A TEENAGER WHEN JIMMY CARTER CAME TO SAVE her neighborhood.

"Get a map of the whole area and show me what should be done," the president of the United States said as he stepped out of a limousine in the South Bronx in 1977. Carter had come to New York to address the United Nations about human rights; a trip to the Bronx was not on the agenda. But in recent years the borough had become famous around the world—for blight, for crime and poverty and desperation.

Carter knew all the statistics, but he probably wasn't expecting to find what he did: block after block of New York City real estate literally leveled to the ground. There were sidewalks and light poles on the streets, but where eight- and ten-story buildings had once stood, one right after the other, there was now only rubble. It reminded some older members of the president's entourage of Europe's cities at the end of World War II, cities that had been decimated by endless months of carpet bombing and combat. "Arsonists in the area," wrote the Associated Press reporter there, "have run the gamut—thrill-seeking youngsters, welfare clients seeking relocation, absentee landlords coveting insurance, and vandals intent on scavenging saleable metal from the abandoned buildings."

The *Los Angeles Times*'s writer, Robert Scheer, described what he saw that day as a "warscape dotted by garbage lakes, dunes of litter, and beached hulks of abandoned cars." The streets were empty, he wrote, "as if locusts had descended and slurped up" everything he had remembered from his own childhood in the Bronx: the "ring-a-levio and stickball games . . . the girls with fishnet stockings and stiletto heels, and the young studs with bodies some said were good for nothing but dancing."

Here, now, the young studs' bodies seemed to be good only for muggings and rapes. Some of them were on the street with the president now, lingering on the periphery behind Dumpsters and slag, the heel-to-toe gait of the gangbanger giving them the appearance of jack-in-the-box figures constantly being popped up and then pushed back down by a huge unseen hand.

Cara knew some of those studs. They lived on her block. They whistled at her as she walked to the subway. But Irene Cara didn't need to be saved, by Jimmy Carter or anyone else. She was a ghetto princess.

Who else in her neighborhood had sung for Duke Ellington and danced with Sammy Davis, Jr.? Who else had starred in the biggest African-American movie of the decade? What other black Latin girl, *anywhere*, had two Broadway shows under her belt before she even started high school? No one, that's who.

So young Irene Cara was given a wide berth in the neighborhood—out of jealousy, maybe, or respect. Or awe. "She was already known through the movie *Sparkle*," says childhood friend Jenise La Vel Super. "It was like the story of a young Diana Ross, and kids could understand that. It was a big movie in the African-American community. I saw that movie in the theater about thirty times."

She wasn't the only one. In the mid-'70s, blaxploitation queen Pam Grier was the sole black female movie star out there. And while she was impressively larger than life—pistol-whipping a crooked cop like she was burping a baby, pulling off her clothes solely to show off the utter superiority of African DNA—she wasn't exactly relatable for typical inner-city black girls. If they wanted to see someone like themselves up there on screen, they were simply out of luck.

"In those days, the child actors were Tatum O'Neal and Jodie Foster and Brooke Shields, and that was it," Cara says. "They were white, white, white. The fact that I even had the opportunity to star in a movie that was going to be seen nationally, as a person of color, was a big, big deal. I had to have those roles. At that age I was very much as intense as I am now. There are kids that way, who have a certain depth to their perception of this reality."

That alone may have caused the rough boys on the block to step back a couple paces. She would never have Grier's rangy size, but intensity positively radiated from Cara as she hustled toward the bus to get to her next audition. *Watch it, Irene is coming through!* "I don't mean to sound immodest, but I never had any doubt that I'd be successful," she told *Cosmopolitan* magazine at the time, which is exactly how her mother wanted her to feel about her place in this world.

"I was raised as a prodigy," Cara acknowledges today. "I was a little ghetto princess. I was supposed to be a star."

And so she was—a star right here in the Bronx, where no one thought it could happen anymore. Her Puerto Rican father, Gaspar Escalera, was a musician—lead horn, says Cara, for one of the bands that "brought the merengue to this country." He couldn't make a living at it, though, at least not a good enough living for a growing family. So Gaspar put away his horn and got a job in a factory. Cara's Cuban mother worked in a grocery store, stocking and bagging, and for a time at a hospital as a nurse's assistant. "It was rough," Cara says. "We were lower middle class; we didn't live on Park Avenue. We lived in a brownstone. My parents were working people."

Cara, the youngest of five children in the family, would work for a living, too, from almost the moment she could walk. She started so young that she was a star before she knew there was any other way to be. That was her job, to be a star. She made her Broadway debut in *Maggie Flynn*, a Civil War musical starring Shirley Jones, before she was old enough for school. (Cara's

Irene as an aspiring teenage actress in New York City.

parents shortened her surname to help open doors for her in the Anglo world.) As a preteen, she performed at Madison Square Garden in an all-star tribute to Duke Ellington. She spent a year on the popular children's program *The Electric Company,* singing about the alphabet and hanging out with Bill Cosby. While still in middle school, she starred in a little independent movie, *Aaron Loves Angela,* and then became a national star in the African-American community thanks to *Sparkle.*

"I'm not here to kid you. I was definitely pushed into the business," she says. "I had a very ambitious mom who saw a lot in me. But then, I was a performing child. I was always singing; I started playing piano by ear at four or five years old. So they took advantage of that."

Cara's preteen years were a blur of singing lessons, dance lessons, and auditions; it seemed like that was all she did. "Life was difficult," she says. "My parents worked two jobs each, we lived in the South Bronx, we had to travel by train or buses to get downtown to audition for anything. So my life was a bit of a contradiction. I was in special schools, private performing-arts schools in Manhattan, and that was difficult because that was way above my parents' budget. Everything went to pay for these private schools down-town. What they made and what I made they put away or it went to pay for schools."

Even in the middle of a school term, the auditions continued for Cara, and she would pile on the pressure. If the parts didn't come fast and furious, if she wasn't juggling offers and rehearsals and schoolwork, she would panic. "I didn't want to be unemployed," she says. "I wanted to work. I had to work. That's what I did."

Cara's mother had instilled in her an admirable work ethic, one that would never leave her, but it was a work ethic based as much on a need for self-validation as anything else. She worked so that her mother could tell friends that her little "Reenie" was going to be on TV next week. She worked so that her parents wouldn't be late with tuition payments. She worked so that she could prove to the next casting agent that she could do anything—*had* done anything—they could possibly want. She worked to keep the at-tention coming, day after day.

School was always an afterthought, something she did in between audi-tions or after rehearsal. When she was fourteen, she was accepted at the High School of Performing Arts, New York City's well-known public prep con-servatory, which thrilled her. It was a chance to have some structure in her life. To be normal, or at least as normal as a star could be. But after much hand-wringing, she and her parents decided she should keep working instead.

"I had been admitted there and at the last minute decided not to attend, and I regret that to this day," she says. "One of the rules was that you couldn't do professional work while you were training there. It's similar to what the Olympic athletes went through: they didn't want you turning pro till after you graduated. But my folks and I thought, 'Gosh, you've been working all these years, you want to give that up to go to high school here?' It wasn't so much something we didn't want to do as it was something we couldn't afford to do."

But only a couple of years after Cara and her parents made that decision, she would get to do both, in a way. In 1979, the young British director Alan Parker, who had just scored with the harrowing prison drama *Midnight*

Express, got the go-ahead to do a feature film about the High School of the Performing Arts. The school, so full of dreams and conflict and talent, seemed to Parker a perfect setting for an urban musical drama. It was a unique institution, with students who had compelling stories to tell.

The school was, after all, for kids just like Irene Cara: driven, ambitious young performers from the Bronx and Queens and Harlem—kids who had the talent but not the means to get ahead. The school certainly looked the part, with peeling walls and constantly stopped-up toilets to go with the students in dance shoes and leg warmers. But P.A., as students and teachers alike called it, wasn't only for kids from the outer boroughs. It was prestigious enough that the city's rich kids wanted to go there, too. Writer Hilton Als, a 1977 P.A. alumnus, recalls that the school back then was "housed in a beautiful, nearly decrepit building on West Forty-sixth Street, near Theatre Row and across the street from the Luxor Baths, a wonderful, democratic neighborhood that reflected the democratic spirit of the school itself."

However democratic it was in spirit, P.A. was as intense and competitive as Juilliard, the tonier, world-famous private arts school a few blocks away. Casting his first big musical, Alan Parker wanted to make sure his movie's auditions were more intense and competitive than both.

Cara smiles when she thinks about the endless callbacks for the movie, which would be called *Fame.* She thrived on such competition then. "I knew they had seen a lot of people from the actual school for auditions," she remembers. "The kids in the movie, for the most part, were all from Performing Arts or Juilliard." Cara, who was sixteen years old when the casting call went out, wasn't worried that those schools weren't on her résumé. She was up for Coco Hernandez, the tough-talking Latin girl with endless talent and almost as much insecurity, and she'd never been surer she was right for a role. "It was like they wrote it for me," she says. When they told her, after a handful of grueling auditions, that she had it, she wondered what took them so long.

Most of the young actors in the movie felt the same way about their casting. They were ready for *Fame* and for fame. They may have been playing dreamers struggling to make it in show business, but, finally, they were no longer dreaming themselves; with their roles in *Fame*, they were now living their big break. They had made it. They didn't quite feel like movie stars— no one recognized them on the street yet—but they were just about to burst from the anticipation of it. Parker, who shot the movie entirely on location, kept the atmosphere on the set loose. So when they weren't shooting, the actors hung around together, dawdling on the sidewalk or in coffee shops as if they were playing hooky from school, talking excitedly about the roles they wanted to play and the Hollywood mansions they wanted to live in. At the end of a day's shoot, Cara would grab a pizza slice and jump on the subway to the Bronx, still giddy and hopped-up on adrenaline. Heading into the heart of the slums on the far side of the Trans-Manhattan Expressway, she would be the only one on the subway car with a big, fat smile on her face. "It was a lot of fun. It was a blast," she says of making the movie. "All the kids bonded great. We all knew it was something special. We didn't know how special, but we thought it was cool."

They would know exactly how special when the film opened on May 16, 1980. *Fame* was in some ways a throwback to Hollywood's treacly golden age of musicals, with characters falling in love in synch with the swell of the soundtrack and then taking over a city street to belt out a song they just couldn't hold in any longer. But it was also so much more than that. Critic David Thomson would call it "as extreme a study of education as *The Wall*," Pink Floyd's rock-'n'-roll indictment of groupthink. The movie was a morality play for the TV generation, and it was as tough as the city in which it was set, with gritty language and sexuality that would make Grandma pass out, and with broken dreams as painful as a Central Park mugging.

Critics and moviegoers loved it. Riding a wave of critical huzzahs, *Fame* jumped to the top of the box office and stayed there. "By focusing on the aspirations, struggles, and personal lives of a group of talented and ambitious students at New York City's High School of the Performing Arts, [*Fame*] manages to say something about all of us and the age we live in," wrote Mick Martin and Marsha Porter. Calling the movie "a genuine treasure," Pulitzer Prize–winning critic Roger Ebert declared that "*Fame* is a perfect title for this movie. It establishes an ironic distance between where these kids are now and where they'd like to be someday, and then there's also the haunting suggestion that some of the ones who find fame will be able to handle it, and some will not."

At the time, of course, Cara wasn't thinking about such suggestions. There was too much going on. Cara was the movie's breakout star. It was Cara who sang the two songs—the title number and "Out There on My Own"—that everyone found themselves humming as they combed their hair in the morning (including Academy Award voters, who nominated both songs for the Oscar). It was also Cara—not the lithe, all-American beauty Antonia Franceschi (who played regal blue-blood Hilary)—who became the teen boys' heartthrob. "The darker the berry, the sweeter the juice," Coco growls in a signature scene in the movie, warning the haughty Hilary that no mayonnaise-white rich girl will be able to win a boy's affections over her. "Yes, but who wants diabetes?" responds Hilary.

The answer was supplied by thousands of adolescent boys across the country. Juicy-sweet Irene Cara was well worth diabetes. In fact, to a certain niche of older moviegoers, she was possibly worth even harsher penalties. As the "ambitious, albeit guileless, Coco Hernandez," Hilton Als would later write, Cara "provided a bit of seedy titillation by taking off her dress and singing the Oscar-winning theme." (Not at the same time, one hastens to add, though Als surely wasn't the first to combine the two scenes in his mind's eye.) Just as Internet-surfing middle-aged men would become obsessed with Britney Spears twenty years later, many teens in the early 1980s would have to share Irene Cara with their fathers.

With her image on billboards and movie screens, Cara suddenly found that she had to have her public face on *all the time*. Not just for press junkets and scheduled interviews but also for trips to the grocery or bus stop. "When we'd go out we'd get a lot of attention, people coming up to her, but she still remained the same," says her childhood friend, Jenise Super. "She still did normal things, still walked the streets in New York. People would come up to her, and it didn't faze her. She'd say thank you. She did expect it. She was mobbed, but she still walked the streets. She's a New York girl."

But Cara wasn't famous only in New York anymore. As *Fame* became a runaway hit, movie offers rolled in to her agent's office. She landed a key role in TV's highest-profile project, *Roots: The Next Generation*, alongside iconic stars such as Marlon Brando. She was featured in the coffee-table photography book *The Most Beautiful Women in the World*. On the Academy Awards show the following spring she would become the first singer ever to perform two nominated songs. Next up would be her debut solo album with the hottest record label in the business. She was barely old enough to vote, and she was on top of the world. That was what she thought then. It's not what she sees now.

IRENE CARA IS LEANING AGAINST THE DOOR OF HER WINE-COLORED Sentra, smoking a cigarette. It's ten thirty on a warm July night in 2003, and she is taking a break in the parking lot of a long, flat industrial building across from the highway. This nondescript building in Orlando is where Phat Planet recording studios is located, the last office suite before the building peters out into an overgrown field.

Out here in the nearly empty parking lot, Cara looks even smaller than she is. She is wearing an ornately designed gold pullover that billows around her slim trunk. Her face is tight and grim as she stares off into space. Her hair is knotted loosely at the back of her neck. As Cara inhales on the cigarette, squeezing her eyes shut in enjoyment, two men in suits come out of the Pinnacle Direct Funding office next to Phat Planet. They're big men, grossly overweight, with red faces and tiny eyes. One of them is carrying a bag of leftovers from Hot Wings, a Florida-based Hooters knockoff with waitresses in gymnastics-style tights and eruptive cleavage.

"I thought only us musicians work such late hours," Cara says to them. Her smile makes her eyes water.

"Oh, this is pretty normal for us," one of the men answers, cupping and heaving his stomach with a hand so he can turn and see who's talking to him. He takes in the thin woman smoking a cigarette, and his lips curl into an amiable smile. "Are you making a CD?" he asks pleasantly.

"Yeah, yeah."

"You an up-and-coming rock star?" the other one asks.

"Yeah." She smiles. "That's me. Up-and-coming."

"You keep at it," the first one says as he unlocks the doors of a mammoth SUV and begins to lift himself inside. "I'll look for you on MTV."

Cara drags on her cigarette and watches the SUV back out, offering a half-hearted wave. It doesn't bother her that they didn't recognize her. In fact, she likes that they saw her as a young, hungry artist looking for her first break; she likes the idea that she can still pull off a twenty-something look. The Associated Press has recently added a handful of years to her age, listing her birth date as 1959, and it drives her *crazy*. She tries to tell herself, What difference does it make if the press gets her age wrong? But it does make a difference. She feels young again, reborn, and she wants that to be acknowledged. It's been twenty years since she ruled the Oscars and the Grammys in 1984, but she's kept with the times. She's down with hip-hop and the latest street slang; she wears jeans slung so low it looks like she could step out of them with one deep breath. Sure, those two guys are probably chauvinist pigs who just want to see a pop singer shake her ass, but she doesn't blame them for that. Not anymore.

Cara drops the cigarette and grinds it into the asphalt with her shoe. She's into vitamins these days. Spiritual cleansing. But she hasn't been able to kick the cancer sticks.

"I don't even really drink anymore, but I've got a problem with tobacco," she says. "I admit it."

There's a reason for this. She's exhausted all the time. Stressed out. Nervous. It's not hard to tell. Deep bags splay out under her eyes, making her look sad, or at least wistful, even when she's smiling. She has to go to New York next week for a radio show, and it's weighing on her. "I couldn't live in New York again," she says to no one in particular. "Hellhole. No, it's not. It's my hometown. I love it, but I couldn't live there. Running around, jumping on the subway, grabbing taxis. I could do it when I was a teen. Not now."

It's not surprising that Cara first made a name for herself as an actress. Her face is so expressive it seems as if you can read every thought in her head. Right now she's thinking about all the things she has to do over the next year—or two, or three—to finish this Hot Caramel album and make it a success. She started putting the band together in 1999 and has been slowly recording ever since, flying in her musicians and vocalists when she has the material and the money.

"That's why we ran over to Europe a little while ago," she says. "I have to prostitute myself. It's not playing with my band, Caramel. It's the old stuff."

At least she has been able to take some of her Caramel band mates with her, to sing backup. On the last trip overseas, which was mainly for a performance in Amsterdam, Caramel members Chanda Bailey and Reina Poindexter went along. "It wasn't an arena, but it could seat maybe ten thousand," Bailey says of the Amsterdam gig, as she lounges in Phat Planet's waiting room. "About five thousand people were there. They were mainly old fans; they wanted to hear the old stuff they knew, not new stuff. Which you can understand. But some of the fans were younger than me. That was good to see. Everybody was into it."

Cara used to resent having to sing those old hits all the time but not anymore. She respects the nostalgic power a song can have—how hearing the ballad "You Were Made for Me" might bring back for a fan the sweet pang she felt twenty years ago, as she sat in her bedroom waiting for a call from the boy she hoped would ask her out. To be sure, Cara understands that this does not actually mean anything about the quality of the song. Depending on your experience, the old Almond Joy jingle can have the same effect. Like TV commercials, pop music—the music created specifically with adolescents in mind, the music that made Cara a star—is tops at squeezing universal, often trite emotional responses out of us.

Of course, there's "alone" pop music like "You Were Made for Me," and then there's "out in the world" pop music. And Cara got famous—serious famous—with her out-in-the-world pop. "Flashdance . . . What a Feeling" was a strutting-through-the-neighborhood pop song. You put that one on the Walkman and you not only had a bounce in your step, you were looking around for someone to give it form. It's probably not an exaggeration to say that hundreds of girls fell in love in the mid-'80s because they were listening to "What a Feeling." The object of desire may have been just passing by on the street, or sitting across the room at a coffeehouse, and the smitten may not have ever said a word to him, but that didn't make it any less real.

"Everybody remembers 'Flashdance,'" Cara says. "It still is difficult to sing my old hits, and now when I'm forced to for money gigs, I usually lip-synch them and sing live only my current material. But people still like those old songs. They still respond to them, and that is nice."

One of the reasons those old songs sometimes grate on her is that Cara doesn't define herself simply as a "pop singer." That was supposed to be a phase that she would grow out of on her way to a more mature, sophisticated sound. She can close her eyes and picture herself in the 1985 Clint Eastwood gangster movie *City Heat,* in which she played a Depression-era chanteuse crooning "Embraceable You" in a glorious red gown, and she likes what she

Irene with mom Louise and dad Gaspar at the
1984 Oscars, the year "Flashdance" won
for best original song.

sees. But she knows that's not how most people see her. She remembers clearly the day she met her idol, Joni Mitchell, a few months before *City Heat* was released and when her *What a Feeling* album, with five chart hits to its name, was still going strong.

"I was the typical gushing fan towards her and Marvin Gaye," she says. "It was during the 1985 Grammy Awards afterparty. I couldn't resist coming up to both of them for an autograph and to express my awe in having the brief opportunity to say hello. They both condescendingly referred to me as the '*Fame* girl' as they proceeded through the crowd. I realized then that it takes a lot more than a commercial hit to garnish any real respect from people who are truly artists. The kind of artists whose body of work clearly defines what they're about to the public. I always knew this was something I was capable of. I never anticipated how hard, as the years rolled by, I would have to fight for it."

Slumping backward in a straight-back chair in Phat Planet's control room, as if she has released the memory only with effort, Cara looks like she still can't believe how hard a road it's been these past two decades. After all, through the first nineteen years of her life, Cara didn't have to fight for much of anything. She worked hard throughout childhood—endless voice, dance, piano, and acting lessons, wave upon wave of auditions—but that's not the same thing. That all came naturally to her, and she loved almost every minute of it.

"I was the wide-eyed artist so happy to please, searching for everybody's affection and attention and love through my talent," she says. "I saw how I set all that up subconsciously."

In 1984, that love and attention multiplied, time and again, more than she had ever imagined it could. That year, Cara won a Grammy Award for "What a Feeling." She also won a Golden Globe and an Oscar for the same song. She won a lot of other awards, too. So many she can't remember any of their names.

"What a Feeling," which she had cowritten and recorded on short notice for the soundtrack of the movie *Flashdance*, wasn't just an award-winning hit song, it was a phenomenon. Throughout 1983, it spilled out of bedrooms, gas stations, and dentists' offices, and no one seemed to get tired of it. Teenagers, parents, and even grandparents would be getting ready for school or driving to work or pulling a package of toilet paper off the shelf at the grocery store, and they'd find themselves singing the chorus under their breath, over and over, unable to stop.

Cara, the street-smart *Fame* star, the serious actress of *Roots: The Next Generation* and *The Medgar Evers Story*, had to sacrifice some of her cool quotient for that multi-demographic popularity. The kids listening to The Police's *Synchronicity* simply wouldn't be caught dead with the *Flashdance* soundtrack or Cara's spin-off *What a Feeling* album. But still, the song's success was a bracing tonic for her. It made her realize not just that people liked her work but that she could do so much better. Her disappointing first album, *Anyone Can See*, released in 1981, had largely been dictated to her: she would sing this song and then this one and then this one. Most of the songs were mediocre. Now she was ready to take control in the recording studio, and that meant doing a lot more than singing, which she didn't even consider her strong suit. "I have a pleasant voice, but I have no great range," she told *TV Week* when "What a Feeling" was at the zenith of its popularity. "I will say that I know how to make a song come alive, and I guess I do have a sincerity that comes across. But I do a lot of things better than I sing. I play piano and write better than I can sing. Songwriting is therapy for me. If I've gone through a particular experience that I have to get out, then I'll write a song about it, just to get it out so it doesn't eat me up inside."

The question was, would anyone want to listen to "The Record Label Blues"? About a year or so before *Flashdance*, Cara had "caught wind of something peculiar going on" at her record company. RSO, established and run by Robert Stigwood, was one of the most high-profile companies in the music business, thanks to the success of the soundtrack albums for *Grease* and *Saturday Night Fever*. "So you can imagine how shocked I was [when I] heard that the Bee Gees were suing the label and Robert Stigwood, who just happened to also be their manager," Cara says. "Suddenly, all of the executives and their assistants working at the company were tense and nervous."

The only person in the company who seemed calm, she remembers, was Al Coury.

Coury, the company's president, was calm not because he was naïve (RSO would soon fold), but because he was a survivor. With her success as both an actress and a singer, Cara could have written her own ticket at any record label in the world after RSO closed up shop. Instead, she signed with Coury. When RSO shut down, its former president decided to launch his own label. "He called it Network Records and led us to believe it would be just like RSO and that nothing would change," Cara says.

She didn't see this grandiose statement as a warning sign, or the fact that she was for some time the only artist on the new label. She trusted Coury, sought his advice on acting offers as well as their recording projects. Besides, at the time, she wasn't paying very close attention to much of anything. For one thing, she was barely out of her teens and she was one of the biggest entertainment stars in the world, so there was some navel gazing to indulge in. For another, she had discovered cocaine. It was introduced into the mix, she says, when she was struggling to get through long recording sessions for her first album. Soon, rumors were circulating in the industry and in supermarket tabloids about Cara's "drug problem." (A headline in *The Star* blared: "*Fame* Beauty's Shocking Claim: Music Bosses Turned Me into a Coke Addict.")

"I got over it as soon as I got over a lot of the people at the record company who were putting it in my face," she says of her drug abuse. "Everybody had a drug problem. It was the eighties. You never think about what you're doing; you want to be with the in crowd. What I do find rather despicable is that the people who were putting it in my face were so quick to talk about the problem like they had no responsibility in it. Meanwhile it's their drugs, it's their money, it's their environment, and it's them putting it in your face. My lawyer felt later that they were out to poison me to control me. I don't know; it's a possibility. I take full responsibility for being dumb enough to fall into that. I also take full responsibility for getting well. I got into a lot of holistic things. I learned a lot about nutrition, about vitamins."

Her head was certainly clear enough to realize that there was something fundamentally wrong when you have the biggest song in the world and you're not seeing a dime in royalties. Contracts for unknown or emerging performers are notoriously one-sided in the music business, but Cara found she not only wasn't getting paid, she was supposedly in *debt* to Coury. Record stores couldn't stock "What a Feeling" fast enough in 1983, and yet her ledger sheet with Network Records stayed stubbornly in the red.

"It was a lousy contract; it was a first-time artist's contract," Cara says. "He was already getting half of everything I made [by the terms of the contract], why did he have to steal my half, too? Maybe he was using a lot of my money to build his company. There was a lot of deceit involved, a lot of fraud. He was playing poppa; in a lot of ways he was acting like a manager, which he shouldn't have been doing."

When Cara finally realized she wasn't getting paid for her first album or for the *Flashdance* soundtrack, or even for some of the movies she acted in, she decided to speak up. She demanded explanations. She demanded to see the books.

Coury, who declined requests from the authors to be interviewed for this book, tried to appease her with gifts and promises. Cara was having none of it. "Maybe it was my thespian snobbery, but I had never heard of such unorthodox horseshit in all my life," she says. "I knew then that I had to go through with suing him and regain my freedom."

Cara consulted her agent and hired a team of entertainment lawyers. Her goals were simple and straightforward: She wanted her share of the record-sales profits that were stipulated in her contract with Coury, and she wanted to leave Network Records. The results, however, would be neither simple nor straightforward. "I never realized that what seemed so logical a decision at the time would cost me so much," she says now.

On February 27, 1985, United Press International reported that "Grammy- and Oscar-winning singer Irene Cara filed a $10 million suit against a record company executive. . . . The suit claims [Al] Coury took advantage of Cara's trust in him to get her to sign agreements that were 'patently one-sided, unfair, unjust and oppressive.'"

Irene Cara, the reigning Grammy champ, the winner of the songwriting

Oscar, costar with Clint Eastwood and Burt Reynolds in the upcoming major Hollywood release *City Heat*, was nearly broke. The phalanx of entertainment lawyers she hired decided not to make a case for fraud, arguing instead that Network was not a functioning label. They seemed confident Cara would get all the royalties she was owed, but they warned her she was in for a long fight. As it turned out, they didn't know the half of it. The fight would take eight years. And, Cara contends, it wasn't just a long fight, it was a dirty one.

"This was a street business; this was not the legitimate [theater] business I grew up in," Cara says of the recording industry. "And that's where I went wrong. If I had realized that, I would have played the game differently. But I thought I had every right to sue this man and fight for my money, with no consequences. He—they—made sure that there were consequences. Big time. Coury and all his mogul buddies. He basically made sure I'd never record again. They blacklisted me. They sent out letters to all the labels saying they were in a legal battle with me and don't dare sign her," she insists, charges that were never proven in court. "They did all that—very ugly stuff. Everything changed, just like that," Cara says, snapping her fingers. "As soon as I brought the lawsuit, everything changed."

Rage boiled up inside Cara, a rage that she still carries with her. "I really felt [Coury] was someone in my corner at first. How do you work for someone who's involved in slave labor? You don't," Cara says. "That's not what I thought then. I'm sure there's a lot of racism involved in all this. 'I don't need to pay the little black Latin from the Bronx. She doesn't need her money. We need her money.' Racism was a factor. I'm still wondering why we don't hear about a singer like Pink talking about how she went bankrupt. I'm sure she's getting her money. And she's on the same label as TLC [the black hip-hop/pop group that sold more than 13 million albums in the early '90s but declared bankruptcy in 1995]. What is it about black female artists that make people feel they are entitled to rob and rape them? All of that, you hate to bring it up, because you get accused of playing the race card. But you know what? It's not a card. People love to dismiss it: 'Oh, she's playing the race card.' But this is not a game. It's what we live through. It's our reality. When you live on this side of the fence, then you talk to me about playing the race card."

Racism or not, record executives wouldn't meet with Cara after she filed the lawsuit. Film producers wouldn't return her calls. Rumors swirled mercilessly about rampant drug use, spreading the notion that, in her early twenties, this great talent already had been hollowed out. Less than a year after she was the toast of the Academy Awards, less than a year after Quincy Jones had excitedly embraced her at a Grammys afterparty, Cara couldn't get a job. "Casting people who once adored me now quickly escorted me out of their offices," she says. "Restaurants and hangout spots I frequented and felt comfortable in now looked at me with disdain. The glares and sneers of other L.A. celebrities had become so vicious that I knew I could not tolerate living there any longer."

In the spring of 1985, with her acting and recording careers going nowhere, Cara decided to get out of town. Tense and high-strung by nature, she recognized that she had to get her mind off her legal woes, and figured going out on a nightclub tour was the best way to do that. Preparation, for the first time in her life, was an afterthought. It never dawned on her that she might get bad reviews.

"Surely, somebody is being paid to produce Irene Cara's nightclub act, but she's being ripped off," began a typical review, this one in *Variety* on April 3. "The hour staggers along with little concept and great awkwardness, despite the obvious vocal talents of Cara herself.... Cara can cause fireworks, but will have to do so with better programming and more audience contact; as it is, she has to beg the audience to stand or clap along with her biggest hits."

The shaky concert tour was only the beginning of Cara's abrupt and, to most observers, inexplicable collapse, a career free fall so precipitous that by the end of 1985 she was starring in a cheap exploitation film called *Certain Fury*. The nearly straight-to-video movie included an extended scene of Cara, naked, taking a shower (just taking a shower: soaping up and rinsing, and soaping up again and rinsing, and still more rinsing . . .), a scene that finally concluded with her—still naked—fighting off a would-be rapist. Cara, the star of one of the biggest movies of 1980, didn't think twice about accepting the role. It was the only job she could get, and she had bills to pay.

"She had stood up and complained about [not receiving her royalties], and apparently—I don't know this for a fact—but apparently that pretty much ended her career," says Tom Nunziato, the attorney who took over Cara's case in the early nineties after it had sat fallow for years. "Nobody wanted to deal with her. If she had played the game, this probably wouldn't have happened. But she didn't play the game. She saw all this money coming in, and she demanded they renegotiate her contract. I guess the industry viewed her as a fungible: we'll just go find someone else to sell with."

After his Network Records began to founder, Coury went to work for the record label owned by David Geffen, one of the most powerful people in the entertainment business, and Cara became convinced that Coury had enlisted Geffen in his vendetta against her. At every turn, she felt she was being attacked. She tried to step away from the business; she moved out of Los Angeles and got married after a brief courtship, but nothing seemed to help her state of mind.

"By the end of the eighties, I found myself broke, alone, and out of work," Cara says. "To the Hollywood establishment, I had managed to piss off David Geffen, who by all accounts is a tyrannical mogul whose insatiable appetite for destroying people is legendary. I had alienated an industry giant, Warner Brothers, for whom I had done some of my best work as a young actress in films like *Roots: The Next Generation*, *City Heat*, and *Sparkle*. My marriage suffered under the financial and emotional strain, and we got divorced. I was in a state of rage over the fact that neither my husband nor anyone else had protected me or come to my defense."

Cara was consumed by anger at Coury and at the industry, and often on the brink of emotional overload, but she made a "valiant effort to go on with my life during the lawsuit years." As the lawsuit ground on, she continued writing music and searching for a label. She went to Latin America, Europe, and Asia to perform in concert, singing her old hits to appreciative audiences. The overseas concerts were small potatoes compared to those few heady years between *Fame* and *Flashdance*, but they were something, and Cara tried to appreciate them.

She was trying to let go of the anger—she was exploring various mystical beliefs and reading voraciously—but the anger still bubbled up, and she sometimes let it out on friends. "Blackballing her wasn't fair," says Jenise Super, who kept in close touch with Cara. "Here's a girl who is just trying to make a living. The [record companies] made tons of money off her, and now they won't let her make a living. Mariah Carey, Whitney Houston—she was as big as any of them. She'd get upset about what was going on, with her lawyers or whatever. I wouldn't say dire, but times were rough. She had rough times. She didn't talk about the legal problems, not with anybody. Not even her family."

She would not, however, give up the fight. Yes, she was angry that in four years with Coury, a period that included the recording of *Anyone Can See* and *What a Feeling*, she had been paid a total of $183 in royalties. But the fight with Coury, to her mind, had become about much more than money. It was a battle to clear her name, and she was a proud and stubborn woman. She was determined to fight to the very end, even if it broke her emotionally as well as financially. Finally, after burning through a series of law firms over a period of a half-dozen years, Cara showed up at Tom Nunziato's offices.

There had been "a lot of hostility" between Cara and her previous attorney, Nunziato remembers, and "the lawsuit itself had been stayed or somehow stopped for many, many years." Nunziato saw little reason to expect success at this point, but he believed her. "She was obviously strung out and upset, but she was very credible," he says. "She was impressive. I'm a contingency lawyer, and ninety percent of a contingency case is the believability of your client, assuming the facts are there."

Nunziato took the case and successfully fast-tracked it. Finally, Cara was going to be heard before a jury. "It was a complicated accounting case, the case we took to trial," Nunziato says. "I don't think that was really her beef. I think she was just ripped off and defrauded, but that's a different issue. We weren't allowed to try that; the statute of limitations had run on being able to go back and rename as fraud in the lawsuit. We had to take an accounting case. Essentially what happened was, on any song the artist gets a certain percentage, but out of that percentage that the artist gets, she has to pay back the money used to sell her song—the promotional costs. And her production costs. So if she goes to an opening and spends five thousand dollars on a limousine and dinner and whatever, that five thousand dollars comes out of her share of the royalties. Same thing for production costs. So that's very onerous on young artists. Irene was very young, she was in these shows, she had a wonderful, skyrocketing career, and she was making virtually no money. Literally no money. Whereas everyone around her was packing it in. And she had the audacity to stand up and say, 'Look, I may be a young black girl, but dammit, what's going on here?' That's when they basically—we weren't allowed to argue this to the jury, it's my perception—that's when they basically said, 'Fuck you. You want to be that way? You don't want to play the game? We're just not going to deal with you anymore.' That started the downfall of her career—when she stood up for her rights. We couldn't prove that; I'm telling you my gut instinct, from what I saw at the time."

Their big break in court, Nunziato remembers, came from a simple slip of the tongue by one of the defendant's expert witnesses. "The defense just threw up huge accounting issues, showing there was this expense here and that expense there and they had to remaster this and they had to hire an extra drummer and Irene wanted an extra limousine. Hour after hour of detail. Fortunately, on cross-examination, their expert witness slipped up and characterized the whole mess as 'Hollywood accounting,' and you could hear a sigh from that side, sort of an admission. So that was their defense: that she hadn't earned all this money, that she wasn't really all that successful, that this is how the industry is. And the truth of the matter is, it *is* how the industry is. They rip off—at least they used to, I'm no expert—they rip off young singers, and it's not until the artists play the game for a while and get to the point where they can renegotiate their contracts that they can start making a lot of money. Irene just wasn't willing to wait for that."

On February 18, 1993, eight years after the original lawsuit was filed, Cara was awarded $1.5 million by a Los Angeles County Superior Court, which found that "the conduct of Al Coury Inc. and Network Records has severely damaged her career." It was a triumphant moment for Cara, but in the end a largely symbolic one.

"We established that they had misaccounted for $1.5 million, and this is $1.5 million in a relatively short time frame, at a time when $1.5 million meant a bit more than it does now," says Nunziato. "There were no punitive damages. No fraud damages. We weren't even allowed to go into those arenas. Now here's the sad part. Because only the corporations [Al Coury Inc. and Network Records] were sued back in the beginning and not the individuals, the corporations just declared bankruptcy; supposedly they used all the money to pay attorneys. I think we found money being transferred, a couple hundred thousand dollars, and stopped it. But that was it. In my view the companies were drained after the litigation started, well after the trial started. We just couldn't get at the individuals who really pocketed all the money. Irene was vindicated by the jury, but the legal system kind of fell down, and there was no way to compensate her."

IRENE CARA WAS ONLY THREE OR FOUR YEARS OLD WHEN SHE first felt it. It started in her chest and radiated outward until her whole body was tingling and pulsing. As the years went on, the rush only got more intense. It was a wonderful feeling—the reason she worked so hard, the reason she got out of bed in the morning. Standing up there in the spotlight, she could sense them out there, her audience, nodding along with her voice, not just in agreement but in exaltation—in love. They actually *loved* her. They *wanted* her. She could feel it as a prickle on the back of her neck. The desperation. She looked forward to the crush of fans at the stage door almost as much as she did to getting a song just right.

Cara's problem was that she was too smart for her own good. The cheers and praise and pampering she got for performing were thrilling when she was four years old—and even when she was nine and ten—in a puppyish sort of way. It was different when she was seventeen. She still enjoyed it and craved it, but she was old enough and self-aware enough to know that the attention wasn't normal—and she was starting to suspect that it wasn't honest, either.

By the time she was starring in *Fame,* Cara had begun to think of herself as a woman, and she wanted the attention a woman could get, the kind of attention that had nothing to do with getting up on stage and belting out a song. She was a remarkable beauty by then, with cheekbones cut from marble and those piercing eyes coming at you and at you, like high beams approaching out of a perfect, copper-colored night. But when she looked in the mirror in the morning, Cara didn't see a stunning beauty. She only saw that she was skinny. Shapeless. Flat. She didn't see anything special at all. And she was sure no one else did, either. She certainly couldn't strut through the neighborhood in a tight miniskirt and get hooting come-ons from the brownstone steps, the guys nudging each other and looking up to the heavens—the kind of attention that could make a nervous teenager feel assaulted and powerful at the same time. Not unless the guys knew it was Irene *Cara* strutting past them, not just some girl from the block.

Cara was beginning to figure out that guys weren't paying attention to her for the right reasons, that maybe they just wanted to be with "the *Fame* girl" but not with her. Terror would lodge in her throat when she saw boys approaching, even if they only wanted an autograph, because what if that wasn't *really* what they wanted? "The first two years [after *Fame*] were rough. I would be rejected by men for what I was instead of who I was, and it made me angry and bitter," Cara said in 1984. "If I had been introduced to guys as a sweet, pretty girl who worked in an Automat, I would have been married ten times over. But because I'm a famous, successful woman, I can't even get a phone call on a Saturday night. I find that men pursue me and then flee. Maybe it's a conquest thing, a feather in their cap, like 'Irene Cara's in love with me.' There are times when I've felt like a freak."

These personal traumas had an indelible effect on Cara. To anyone who flipped through paparazzi photos of her at this time, it would be clear that she had no talent for acting when she was offstage. Her beauty was rapidly becoming not just mature but melancholic, her eyes heartbreakingly inconsolable. As Cara slowly reached the conclusion that she couldn't trust anyone, her open-faced response to the world gave way to something brooding, distant. Inevitably, that look carried over into her actions as well, so that in her late teens and early twenties, when she should have been knocking down doors to get out and explore the world, she began to retreat inside herself. "I didn't have affairs, I didn't really go out to the clubs all that much," she says. "I was concentrating on my career. That was what I decided to do. That was my focus. My only focus."

The problem was, an important part of her career was presenting a pleasing persona to the world, and she was finding that increasingly difficult to do. Cara had been giving interviews since she was four years old, and she always had been open with the press. Now she began to look on reporters with suspicion, and for good reason. Faced with diminishing attention spans in the burgeoning video-game era and the rapid growth of cable-TV franchising, the mainstream press was suddenly going downscale. The *Saturday Evening Post* and *Look* were gone by the early '70s, and even venerable *Life* magazine had gone bankrupt. CBS's stentorian icon, Eric Sevareid, retired, while a young, flamboyant hotshot named Geraldo Rivera was drawing millions of viewers. *People* magazine, a controversial experiment launched by Time Inc. in 1974, was derided as "fluff" and mockingly called "Peephole" by veteran journalists, but everyone was reading it—and soon every media company was trying to copy it. When Cara gave interviews for *Fame,* she was surprised to be asked, over and over, about her social life and whether there had been any conflict between her and her costars. She read, with gut-twisting anger, about how she was staying out late into the night and drinking to excess, at places she had never even heard of. She didn't know what was happening to her.

"I was never really comfortable talking to the media after that," she says now. "Things were taken out of context, things have been written that hurt. I just always feel that there's some kind of ulterior motive [with the press], some other agenda going on. I never feel like there's ever any naked, honest, true approach to someone who's in my field. I always feel there's some unspoken intention, from whomever you're talking to, to expose something, or spin something, or delve into something that they feel is there that may not be."

Cara's inherent reticence did not help keep the gossip hounds at bay; in fact, it only made them yelp louder. Rumors circulated in celebrity magazines that she was "stuck up" and difficult to work with. Cara began to feel besieged and increasingly angry. The ego-boosting attention and pampering of celebritydom, in Cara's view, could hardly compete with having a life that belonged only to herself and her family. It was a battle, looking back over the past twenty-five years, she knows she lost.

"That double-edged sword, that is a very rooted part of having to learn to manage in this field as an artist," she says. "If you don't manage that properly, it leads to all kinds of hell: self-destruction, drugs, low self-esteem, all kinds of aberrant behavior and illnesses. It's one thing that I have a lot of rage about. I do, man. It bothers me; it always has. You're exalted and persecuted at the same time. The celebrity aspect of being an artist goes so far beyond the art. And that's just it. I don't want to be a celebrity. I'm not interested. Especially at this point in my life. I just want to be an artist. I think any people who choose the limelight or are thrust into it, they are exalted and put down because of the power they have over people from being in that limelight. But a great artist up there on the stage is not up there saying, 'I'm so much better than the audience.' That's not what you're meant to communicate. It's give and take. For the great ones, it's always give and take. People should be able to recognize that."

Cara has always recognized it because she has never known anything but a performer's life. She never graduated from high school. Never had any job that didn't require singing, dancing, or acting. Despite all her doubts about the industry and the media and celebrity, when she was shut out of her career in her early twenties, she went into shock. She didn't know what to do but fight and keep on fighting. It took her years of spiritual searching and self-discovery to come to terms with what happened to her.

"I think upon what I've learned from my various Indian teachers: some native by blood, some white. Some Hispanic. Some black. All indigenous in philosophy and spirit," she says. "Their teachings of letting go, of releasing abuse and victimization, of knowing that I alone am the author of my life, are all ingrained in me now like another aspect of my anatomy. I've come to understand that purging is a sacred form of purification. My teachers have been generous in giving me the gift of that knowledge."

That knowledge, Cara says, allowed her finally to move forward and set new goals. And with the trickle of royalties that began arriving post-lawsuit in the mid-'90s, a new life, full of ghost memories of the past but separate from it, started to come together. She started writing again. She got herself in shape, physically and emotionally. For the first time in her life, she expected nothing and gratefully took opportunities as they presented themselves, seeing even the smallest ones as blessings.

"The nineties were a kind of renaissance for me," she says. "I kept busy creating roles for myself by writing screenplays as well as music. I was dancing again and succeeded in having some one-off hits abroad. I even did some musical theater tours across the U.S. and Canada and appeared in a few television guest spots. My health was improving, and I had begun to get control over some of the psychosomatic illnesses I had suffered from during my ordeal."

Next up was her own band, Hot Caramel, put together and managed by her, not anyone else, not a record label. They have been together for five years now, slowly building a sound they can call theirs and theirs alone. She believes she and her bandmates are creating a brand of music that isn't getting air time today but that the world is ready for—a fusion of pop, jazz, hip-hop, and soul that has been bubbling up out of her ever since she put herself on this new course in life.

Cara is inspired by Britney Spears and Christina Aguilera. She hates them that much. Whatever her Indian teachers have to say on the subject, anger and hatred still have a place in her life, if properly directed. She wants to know how the self-affirming idea of "girl power" mutated into such self-righteous sluttiness. She wants to know how today's successful female pop singers got brainwashed into desperately needing the respect of misogynistic rappers who act like thugs and chant tunelessly about "ho's" and "bitches."

"Sexism [in the music industry] is so prevalent," she says. "Women are supposed to be cute and that's it. Seen and not heard. That's everybody's attitude in the music industry. The minute you have any kind of artistic contribution it's an immediate threat. People have to hack at you and mold you and control you, or they are not happy. Or else you're difficult. I wish that the men who rule this industry, when they come across a young girl who has more to offer than being cute and shaking her little rump, that they'd develop that. They'd embrace that, instead of stifling it."

This is the new passion in Irene Cara's life: the role of women in music and, by extension, in our culture. "People have to know that there are women out there in music who are really about music," she says. "And who are beautiful and sexy, but they are about music. Not about anything else but music. All the other connotations associated with women and music, you know, are about everything but music, in my opinion. With this record I want to say to the public, women can be about music, not tits and ass, dyed hair, bleached skin and the belly button and the gyrating and all the other stuff that really has very little to do with great music. That's all I want to say with this record."

Her Caramel bandmates are with her on that, and they enthusiastically come to Orlando to make her record happen. Chanda Bailey picks up the subject in the car on the way to the recording studio. "I've got a bone to pick with Beyoncé and Christina Aguilera," she says. "They've got talent. They have voices; they can write. Why do they have to take their clothes off? Let the talent be larger than life instead of your breasts. If all you've got is your look, I can understand it. But they have more than that. Makes it harder for people like me."

Bailey, who studied jazz piano at Spelman College in Atlanta, has a perfect, brown, oval face, and a head full of tiny cornrows, as if tufts of hair have been screwed into her skull. She's wearing a T-shirt and jeans that she has smarted up with a little green corduroy hat. She doesn't believe she's beautiful, not pop-star beautiful anyway, but that's not what she means by Beyoncé and Christina Aguilera making it harder for her. Music is a calling for Chanda Bailey, not a get-rich-quick scheme. Not background noise for an MTV striptease. It's one of the things that drew Cara to her: to each of the young women she recruited for the band.

On this day at Phat Planet studios they are working on the background vocals for a ballad called "Don't Know How to Make You Love Me." Cara has told the singers she is looking for "something kind of boy-band stupid" for the harmony, but it hasn't been working.

"Maybe it's my note, but something doesn't sound right in there," Reina Poindexter offers after one attempt.

"The climb up is still a little messy," agrees Audrey Martell, who has sung backup on recordings for Céline Dion, Anastasia, and Mary J. Blige.

"Yeah, we'll get it," Cara says, but they're not going to get it just yet. She's decided they need a break so she can consult with her producer.

Bailey, Martell, and Poindexter head into Phat Planet's waiting room. Bailey and Martell hover around the table, picking at the remains of the lunch they ordered a few hours before. Poindexter plops down on the couch across the room and opens a Nora Roberts novel. Back home in Washington, D.C., Poindexter sings in a couple of wedding bands and dances with a modern dance company that doesn't perform very often. She waitresses, she adds. She is twenty-seven years old. ("That's her résumé age," says Martell with a laugh.) Poindexter puts her feet up on an end table and sinks into the back of the couch. She is wearing tight blue jeans that end at the calves and a tighter, low-cut blouse that makes the tops of her breasts bulge out. Unlike Bailey, she doesn't seem to have a bone to pick with Beyoncé, even though she considers herself a good Christian girl. She doesn't mind men looking at her if that's all they're doing. She owns more than one pair of "booty shorts." But she says she passed up playing the lesbian girlfriend role in a national tour of *Rent* because of what her mother might think.

The one thing she's sure about in her life is that she wants to be famous. At least she used to be sure, before a photo of Hot Caramel made it into *People* magazine a little while back.

"When that magazine came out, all these people, people I knew, were whispering about me, like I was a star," Poindexter says. "Guys going, 'Hey, I saw you in *People*.' Girls wouldn't talk to me. It made me think, 'Do I want this?' You have to be overly nice to everyone to make them feel comfortable. That's the hard part. And these are people I *knew*. I want to make my friends now. Before I become known. So I know they like me for me."

"They might not even know themselves, if they like you or the persona," says Martell, who has two young children. "I love the arts, I just hate the business, what comes with it."

Cara, who's just arrived in the waiting room, agrees with Martell with a mighty nod of her head. The music should be at the top of the pyramid, not down at the bottom, she says.

How would she describe the music they're making for this CD? she's asked.

"Over most people's heads," Cara says, launching into her signature stuttering chuckle: *Heh-heh, heh-heh-heh.*

During the drive home that night, Cara admits that the CD, for her, is about forgiveness as much as anything else. Forgiving herself and moving on. "I was so young when so much of this was going down," she says. "Sometimes I forget how young I was."

She comes back to that thought later. "One thing I know is certain: You can't move forward and claim your future until you make peace with the past. . . . This is something my teachers have been drilling into me for years. But I never fully understood it until now. More important is being able to forgive yourself. I look back on that young child that was me and I forgive all her naiveté, her youthful ignorance and immaturity. I forgive that young girl who so foolishly trusted and wanted to belong and be loved."

Just like the song that made her famous boldly stated, she sought fame because she wanted to live forever—and to be worshipped in the here and now. She believed it was her destiny before she was old enough to read and write. But now that fame is everybody's obsession—whether or not they have any talent or anything to say—she has her doubts. Now she realizes it's not anyone's destiny; it's just another business.

"As for my advice to future generations of *Fame* hopefuls," she says, warming to her theme, "I wish I could assure them that they will be loved and cherished for the human beings they are and not merely for the talent they may possess. I wish I could say that they will be protected from hateful journalists [who criticize out of envy] and not out of any honest judgment of the work. I wish I could tell them that they will be shielded from people with the power to tear them down and display them to the world in any light they choose. I wish I could assure them that they face a fair and just industry that does not enable evil and wickedness by turning a blind eye to it. But that would be untrue. I wish I could say that they will never suffer the shame and humiliation of being robbed and exploited for somebody else's financial gain, but I can't. I can only hope and pray that they will find the inner strength to persevere and never allow other people to define them or write their story. I can only pray that God will bless them with a true sense of their spirit and their self value. I can only wish that they will always find the will to sing their song another day."

Having more or less made peace with the men who exploited and cheated her, Cara gets up every morning and presses forward. She still has songs she wants to sing. She's still obsessed with music, with the art of expressing her thoughts and feelings in music. And yet there are still times when, instead of envisioning herself once again at the top of the charts, she imagines an entirely different future for herself. In this dream, her past is different, too, but not the way even she would've expected. In this version of her life, she doesn't sing a song while a preteen for a delighted Duke Ellington. She doesn't star in a movie that's a modern classic or record a song that's an anthem for a generation. In this version of her life, she has never signed a single autograph. She lives in the Bronx, or maybe Queens or Long Island. She works in an Automat—do they still have Automats?—or maybe an office of some kind, like her friend Jenise. Nobody but her family and friends ever recognize her on the street. She does have a family, by the way. She's married and has kids, and they all love her very much.

Cara doesn't bother with this fantasy much anymore, certainly not nearly as much as she did ten or twelve years ago, because it's slowly come true, or at least parts of it have. After another night of only a few hours of sleep, she steps over to the mirror and looks at herself: she's still the same, to her eyes, as that famous girl from all those years ago. She has a Christmas tour with Sheena Easton and Christopher Cross coming up in a few months, one of those nostalgia tours that are so popular, now that the teenagers of the eighties are all grown up and have discretionary income to throw around. She'll be ready for it. First, though, there's more recording to do.

She arrives at the hotel at ten to pick up her singers. This is prime tourist season in Orlando, and the lobby is packed with vacationers, mostly British, who are loitering or wandering through, the women in snug, off-the-shoulder tops and micro shorts, the men shirtless and wearing drawstring pants. Most of them are already sunburned. None recognizes Cara; only the few African-Americans in the lobby turn to follow her as she crosses the room to where her singers are sitting with cups of coffee. Two middle-aged men, hotel employees, talk the hotel's manager into asking Cara if she would mind signing autographs for them. They stand there nervously as Cara signs, not quite able to make eye contact or engage her in conversation, even though she does her best to smile at them.

To be fair to the two men, Cara is a little distracted this morning. She knows she's forgotten something, and so, rummaging through her brain, she seems to be concentrating too hard on signing her name. When the light bulb finally goes on, she hands over the second autograph and hurries off to the car. Bailey, Martell, and Poindexter don't move. They know Cara has to work through her morning manic phase before they can go to the studio and get down to productive work for the day. Bailey gets up and heads over to the lobby convenience store for a doughnut. A fortyish African-American woman in a tank top, shorts, and plastic sandals, with a preteen girl in tow, hustles up to her, as if this is her last chance to speak up. "Excuse me, excuse me. Was that Irene Cara?"

"Yes, it was," Bailey says.

The woman turns to the girl with a sigh. "I *told* you. I *told* you that was Irene Cara."

The girl offers an exaggerated shrug and responds, pleadingly, "I said I don't know who that is."

The woman waves a hand. "Aw, girl, then you don't know anything."

 # Melvin and Howard

April 27, 1976

D arcy Dummar knew that her father was up to something, and she didn't like it.

She was coming around the stove at the back of the service station's office when she saw him. Her father, his back to her, was hunched over the table in the center of the little room and was slowly easing open an envelope. Darcy held her breath.

At first glance, there wasn't anything happening that was alarming. Her father had always liked to open the mail. He found it exciting, the possibility that his luck could change, just like that, with a letter. He couldn't even guess what the letter would say. It could be an important job offer—to be the supervisor of, say, all of Cream of Weber's drivers—or it could be from a record producer who'd heard one of his songs. Melvin didn't know, but he figured when you flipped through the mail it was kind of like pulling the lever on a slot machine: you do it long enough, and sooner or later it's gonna come up aces, just because it's your time and you deserve it.

Darcy was only ten years old, but already she was more cynical than her dad ever would be. Besides, she could tell he wasn't simply opening the mail. This was something different. "We had this store area in the front, and behind was this little stove," Darcy says now. "I remember going back there, and he was steaming open a letter. You know, I was a little kid, so I was thinking, 'Oh, he's opening a love letter someone wrote to Bonnie.' I just kind of watched him. I thought, 'Oh, he's going to be mad at Bonnie.' I didn't know what he was doing. I just knew he was being sneaky. He was being sneaky about something."

Darcy had good reason to suspect it was a love letter for her stepmom. Her mother had gotten love letters all the time when she and her dad lived together, and Melvin, heartsick and desperate, had learned how to steam them open and reseal them. Darcy figured it was just a matter of time before the same thing happened with Bonnie, which was fine with her. Bonnie could be pretty bossy, acting like she was her mother. But Darcy still didn't like the way love letters made her father act.

Melvin didn't like it, either. Sometimes you did things because you had to; you didn't think about whether you should or shouldn't. A voice inside your head just tells you to do it. This was one of those times, Melvin says. Twenty-five years later, he says he remembers the moment clearly. He had been messing around in the office, "sweeping up, cleaning up," waiting for the next customer, when he found the envelope. It was just lying there on the counter where customers paid for their gas. He remembers staring at the envelope for a good five minutes, turning it over and over in his hands. He didn't know if it was a joke or a mistake or what, but he finally decided he had to find out. He went around the stove to the kitchenette in the small, private room behind the office, pulled out an electric frying pan, filled it with water, and plugged it in. He says his motivation for opening a letter that wasn't addressed to him—a letter that had probably been left on the service counter by accident—was a simple one: "I just said to myself, I got to see what this is all about." But after he'd steamed it open, he says he knew he'd made a mistake right away. "I read it. God, I put it back in the envelope and took it out again two or three times and read it again and again. And I just kept getting scareder and scareder."

Now all he wanted to do was get rid of it, but he didn't know how to do that. First he made himself calm down, enough so that Darcy got bored watching and went back outside; her father never knew she was there. Pulling himself out of the chair, Melvin rummaged through the drawers in the office desk until he found a handful of unused envelopes. He started to work the inside flaps with his finger, slowly bringing up small amounts of glue and balling it on his fingers. He wetted the glue and spread it carefully onto the back flap of the steamed-open envelope. Then he put the envelope in the oven, turned it on, and let it bake until he figured the envelope was good and sealed again. When Bonnie returned from running her errands, Melvin rushed out, barely saying a word.

It wasn't what Darcy was thinking. Bonnie didn't have a boyfriend, and Melvin wasn't snooping into her secret love letters. When Melvin eventually told everybody what he knew about that letter, after it had made him famous all over the world, Darcy never doubted it. She never believed for a moment all the conspiracy theories that insisted he was behind all the trouble. "I don't think he'd be bright enough," she says now, "you know, smart enough or clever enough, or could ever be so scheming, to do that kind of thing."

THE SCHEME, IF THERE WAS A SCHEME, WAS EITHER INFINITELY complex or astonishingly simple. Even now, more than twenty-five years after the fact, no one is quite sure which it was. But whichever it was, there was no doubt that its execution left a lot to be desired. If there was a plan in place that sent Melvin Earl Dummar rushing out of his service station in Willard, Utah, that day, it was undeniably a stupid one. The letter itself could probably solve everything now, thanks to the advent of DNA technology. But it's long gone, destroyed according to court procedures for the elimination of evidence in old cases. So all we have are Melvin's words and the words of all those around him at the time: the handwriting experts and the lawyers, the con men and the reporters and the media whores. There are a lot of facts and semifacts, and lies and semilies, in those words. The truth is in there, too.

From Melvin's point of view, the truth was simply an unfair burden to put on his shoulders. He would eventually testify, after telling an entirely different story for nine months, that at about ten in the morning on April 27, 1976, a man he had never seen before stepped out of the backseat of a blue Mercedes-Benz at his service station in Willard. He was a short man with a grimacing face and a rolling, gnarled walk, like one of those squirrely gunslingers in a John Wayne movie who gets his in the first reel. "He asked me if I was Melvin Dummar," Melvin testified nearly a year after the fact. The stranger was wearing an expensive suit, and Melvin said the man told him "he had been looking for me for some time." Melvin didn't find that strange. Maybe bill collectors were making house calls now; he didn't know. It was busy at the station, so Melvin went about his business, pumping gas and cleaning windshields and making change. The man followed and kept up a running commentary of sorts. He mostly talked about ordinary things—the weather and whatnot—and that included the subject of Howard Hughes, who had died three weeks before. It had been all over the news, and everybody was talking about it. Hughes was, after all, perhaps the richest man in America, a famous multibillionaire. It also turned out that Hughes was one strange fellow, a recluse, and that no will for his massive estate had been discovered. Melvin testified that the man said something about a will being found a few years before in Joseph Smith's house. Smith had been the president of the Mormon Church from 1970 until he died in 1972, though Melvin says he'd never heard of Smith. Melvin remembered the man saying "somethin' like, wouldn't it be nice if someone like me was in a will of Howard Hughes?"

Melvin says now that he wasn't thinking about his encounter all those years before with the old bum in the desert who had said he was Hughes. And he wasn't thinking about the note he'd found on his car dashboard in Vegas that had told him to go to some bank in town. The reclusive billionaire was a normal topic of conversation right then; the man in the Mercedes surely hadn't been the first customer to mention him in the past couple of weeks. So Melvin didn't even notice when the stranger got back in his Merdeces-Benz and left, without buying any gas or even a pack of cigarettes. He says it could have been a half hour later when he found the envelope lying on the counter, where a customer waiting for his change might have accidentally left it. Except, he says, he knew instantly that it wasn't something that had been left by accident. The envelope had a scrawl across the front that read: "Dear Mr. McKay, please see that this Will is delivered after my death to Clark County Court House, Las Vagas [*sic*], Nevada. Howard R. Hughes." David O. McKay had been president of the Mormon Church in 1968, not that Melvin knew that, either.

MELVIN REMEMBERS HIS STOMACH PLUMMETING AS HE READ THE words scrawled on the outside of the envelope. He thought his wife was playing a joke on him. He thought he was reading it wrong, even though he kept staring right at it. He stepped into the small room adjacent to the office and set to work. Using the methods he had perfected ten years earlier to open his first wife's love letters, he steamed open the envelope. Inside were three sheets of yellow legal paper, each page covered with a morass of messy, smeared handwriting. He says he was alone in the room. He began to read:

LAST WILL AND TESTAMENT

I, Howard R. Hughes, being of sound and disposing mind and memory, not acting under duress, fraud or the undue influence of any person whomsoever, and being a resident of Las Vegas, Nevada, declare that this is to be my last Will and revolk [*sic*] all other Wills previously made by me—

After my death my estate is to be devided [*sic*] as follows—

first: one forth [*sic*] of all my assets to go to Hughes Medical Institute in Miami—

second: one eight [*sic*] of assets to be devided [*sic*] among the University of Texas—Rice Institute of Technology of Houston—the University of Nevada—and the University of Calif.

third: one sixteenth to Church of Jesus Christ of Latterday [*sic*] Saints—David O Makay [*sic*]—Pre

Forth [*sic*]: one sixteenth to establish a home for Orphan cildren [*sic*]—

Fifth: one sixteenth of assets to go to Boy Scouts of America.

sixth: one sixteenth to be devided [*sic*] among Jean Peters of Los Angeles and Ella Rice of Houston—

seventh: one sixteenth of assets to William R. Lommis [*sic*] of Houston, Texas—

eighth: one sixteenth to go to Melvin Du Mar of Gabbs, Nevada—

ninth: one sixteenth to be devided [*sic*] amoung [*sic*] my personal aids [*sic*] at the time of my death—

tenth: one sixteenth to be used as school scholarship fund for entire Country—

the spruce goose is to be given to the City of Long Beach, Calif.

the remainder of My estate is to be devided [*sic*] among the key men of the company's [*sic*] I own at the time of my death.

I appoint Noah Dietrich as the executer [*sic*] of this Will—

signed the 19 day [*sic*] of March 1968

Howard R. Hughes

Melvin read the will through time and again, each time stopping on his name and just staring at it to make sure it wasn't a mirage. For a moment he wondered if he was actually awake and tried to figure out how he could identify a dream and then wake himself up. His thoughts returned to Bonnie, that she must be pulling a trick on him. He had told her about picking up the bum in the desert—it was the kind of story that impressed a certain kind of girl on a date (Bonnie wasn't that kind of girl, as it turned out), and ever since she had kidded him about it. "One of these days," she liked to tell Melvin, "Uncle Howie is going to leave us money in his will." The kidding had picked up since Hughes had actually died.

Melvin reread the contents of the envelope. There was no sense of elation or pleasure in the experience, no matter how many times he read the cramped cursive handwriting. More than twenty-five years later, there is only resignation as he recalls what he felt that day. "I just knew from the situation, the first time I seen the will, without knowing anything about it, I knew somebody somewhere was going to accuse me of writing it, and it scared the hell out of me," he says. "I knew there was something wrong here. Why was it brought to me? Why didn't they take it to the court in the first place? I thought somebody was trying to pull a joke on me, and I didn't know who or why. I thought it would be unfair to throw it away, in case it was real. I was afraid to do anything with it."

But he knew he had to do *something*. He never even considered showing it to Bonnie, and to this day it irks her that he didn't. "Why not show it to the one person in the family with some sense?" she exclaims, bursting into a pained guffaw. That morning in April 1976, she took the car to run errands. When she returned home, Melvin told her to watch the station and he jumped into the car and drove off. Bonnie assumed he was going to school—Melvin was taking some business classes at Weber State College in Ogden.

Instead, Melvin drove into Salt Lake City, thirty-five miles to the south. Heading into the city on Highway 89 (the interstate that would soon make 89 a back road was still under construction), Melvin decided what he was going to do. He had become a practicing Mormon since moving to Utah, and he was devout. He had even toyed with the idea of becoming a priest. So he would take the will, or whatever it was, to the president of the church. The president—Melvin didn't know the man's name—would be able to tell him what he should do. It was around four P.M. when Melvin hurried up the steps in search of guidance. No one would remember seeing him, not a secretary, not a guard, even when it was the president of the church himself, Spencer W. Kimball, asking people to come forward.

But there's no doubting that somebody left an envelope that day on the desk of a public relations staffer in the headquarters building. The envelope was new, from the Mormon Visitors Center on the first floor. Written across the top in bold, mashed-together letters was: "President Spencer W. Kimball, Church of Jesus Christ, Salt Lake City, Utah." No one had ever mistaken this cramped, cluttered little room on the twenty-fifth floor for the president's suite before, but the staffer didn't think anything about it. He simply delivered it to its rightful place down the hall, where it was opened by Kimball's secretary. Inside was another sealed envelope, this one older, crisp and brittle seemingly from age. A note, also written on stationery from the visitors' center, came with it. The note said: "This was found by Joseph F. Smith's house in 1972—thought you would be interested." The second, older envelope had another address, in handwriting different from the note and the newer envelope. It announced the contents: the last will and testament of Howard R. Hughes. The secretary took it immediately to President Kimball.

Within an hour, the church had launched an internal investigation. Employees were told not to go home. Almost everybody working in the building was quizzed by the church's general counsel and his assistant; President Kimball himself questioned employees. But no one could recall anything out of the ordinary; no one had seen anybody who seemed strange or who was carrying a large, old envelope.

Until they got to Inez Stanton, who manned the information desk in the lobby. Stanton vaguely remembered a tall, well-dressed woman in her forties who had stopped at the information desk. The woman had had an air of sophistication about her and was dressed all in black—somewhat unusual for unpretentious, down-home Salt Lake City. She had asked for directions to President Kimball's office, and she was carrying a large envelope.

It was a recollection that would cost Melvin dearly.

ON APRIL 29, 1976, TWO DAYS AFTER IT HAD MYSTERIOUSLY SHOWED up at headquarters in Salt Lake City, the Church of Jesus Christ of Latter-day Saints delivered what would become known as the "Mormon will" to the probate court in Las Vegas, Nevada. The previous day, the church had received authentication of the will from a Salt Lake City handwriting examiner who had once testified in court as an expert on Howard Hughes's handwriting. After nearly two hours examining the will against samples known to be Hughes's handwriting, the woman told the church's general counsel, simply, "It was written by Howard Hughes." When the reaction to her statement was shock, she shrugged and reiterated that there was not a doubt in her mind. She pointed out that it was one thing to fake a man's signature, but it was nearly impossible to fake three full pages of writing.

Despite such a definitive declaration, the church, since it was named as a beneficiary, decided to take no position on the will's validity. "How the envelope containing the papers was delivered to the headquarters of the church and who delivered it, we do not know," declared Wendell Ashton, the church's public-relations director. "Circumstances surrounding delivery of the envelope frankly puzzle us after a day of extensive checking. Whether or not the will is the actual will of Mr. Hughes or is a hoax, we do not know."

Which is exactly what the reporters gathered around Ashton wanted to hear. Details of Hughes's strange, reclusive last years had begun to leak out of the billionaire's empire since his death three weeks before, and the bizarre discovery of the will was all they needed to bust loose. Reporters from around the United States descended on Las Vegas and Salt Lake City. Since there was no hard evidence of anything at this point, they latched on to the sexiest angle: the Mystery Woman. "Howard Hughes 'will' left by mystery woman at Mormon Church," the *Los Angeles Times* declared on its front page, sparking an orgy of speculation among the Hollywood tastemakers and gossip hounds whose tittering reached around the world. Was the mystery woman Hughes's movie-star ex-wife, Jean Peters, whose name had a prominent place in the will? Could it have been Jane Russell, the actress for whose thirty-eight-inch bust the famous jet maker and film producer had personally designed a missile-like truss? How about a secret Mormon mistress? By the time a reporter thought of tracking down this Melvin Du Mar to tell him he was on the verge of collecting a hundred and fifty million dollars, the story of the mystery woman had been widely reported, discussed, and dissected. It would be hard to trump a story that had such intrigue and shadowy, sexy possibilities. But then Melvin told that intrepid reporter about picking up an "old bum" in the desert.

"I was the one who took that first call, from a TV reporter or whoever it was," Melvin's daughter, Darcy, remembers. "He said, 'Did you know your dad's in Howard Hughes's will?' I had no idea what they were talking about. After that it was mayhem and chaos. Reporters were following us everywhere. I remember them taking pictures of girls at school they thought were me. It was a girl in my class, and those pictures showed up in a magazine."

Over the next few days, dozens of TV and newspaper reporters put in calls to Melvin. Still more showed up at the service station and at his home above the station. "They camped out on the lawn," Melvin says. "They peeked in the windows all the time, in the middle of the night." The momentum became unstoppable when Noah Dietrich, Hughes's chief executive for more than thirty years and the man listed as executor in the will, examined the document and seconded the handwriting expert, reversing his initial judgment after having had the will read to him over the phone. "This morning I said it was a goddam fake. But I hadn't seen a copy of it," the eighty-seven-year-old businessman told reporters. Now he knew the truth: "It's his handwriting and his signature. It's the real thing." Reporters asked him about Melvin Du Mar of Gabbs, Nevada, who was named in the will, and Dietrich admitted he had never heard of him. Which, again, was exactly what the media wanted to hear. Soon Universal Studios was contacting Melvin about making a movie based on his story of finding Hughes in the desert. And reporters continued to arrive at his house, not just from Las Vegas and Salt Lake City and Los Angeles, but from New York and London and New Delhi. Melvin didn't have anything new to say, but no matter who was asking the same handful of questions, Melvin could be counted on to recount with enthusiasm how he found the old bum in the desert and took him into Vegas. On the rare occasion when it came up, he also insisted he knew nothing about the will until he saw it mentioned on TV.

"Of course, I knew what happened and that I'd taken the will to the church," Melvin says today. "But the first thing I heard was that a mysterious woman delivered the Howard Hughes will to the Mormon Church headquarters. And I just thought, 'Well, if they think a mysterious woman delivered it to the Mormon Church, I'm just gonna let them believe that.' Because I didn't want any part of it. I didn't want to be accused of touching it or seeing it or anything. So when they contacted me about it, I denied ever seeing it or touching it."

"In the end, that was the fatal mistake," says Gary Magnesen, a retired FBI agent who has recently investigated the origins of the will.

But Melvin didn't know that yet. He didn't even know there would be a probate trial. He was too busy dealing with his public. "Everywhere I go, people would be whispering about me: '*That's him. That's him,*' " he remembers. "We had a lot of people coming by the station, stealing everything. I guess as souvenirs. They'd take calculators, pens. Anything. Everything just started walking off."

Melvin's credibility, however, was not one of the items that went missing. Was his story about Howard Hughes true? Had he really picked up the richest man in America in the middle of the Nevada desert in December of 1967? Did he really know nothing about this strange will that had shown up just a handful of miles from where he lived? Most Americans weren't even asking those questions. People wanted to believe that good things happened to good people, and Melvin certainly looked the part. There was just something about his story, and about his pudgy, wet-eyed face, that Americans liked. For the two-year-old *People* magazine, as well as newspapers and TV stations across the country, that was enough. "Overnight," journalists James R. Phelan and Lewis Chester later wrote, Melvin was elevated "into national prominence as a unique pop hero—a male Cinderella with a billionaire as his wand-waving fairy godmother, a desert Samaritan whose good deed was about to reap huge rewards on earth."

Like the pens and calculators in his station, Melvin himself had become a kind of souvenir. People stopped for gas at his station, but really they were there to shake his hand and take his picture—and maybe stand around in the background while a TV interview was going on. Ronald Brown, a distant relative by marriage, flew from his home in California to Willard and latched on to Melvin, becoming his de facto press spokesman. This was the 1970s, after all—the Age of Television had reached full maturity. Of course Melvin needed a press spokesman.

Melvin didn't know anything about such things, except on the most basic, instinctual level. He felt very natural talking into a camera, even happy; it was the slick men in suits who made him uncomfortable. Ronald Brown thought he was a slick man himself, but Melvin knew better. Brown worked for a living, just like Melvin, and he was a relative. Melvin may have been a little suspicious of him—he'd only met the guy a couple times in his life—

but if Brown wanted to set up interviews for him and shoo away the people who stood around in his yard, that was fine with him. "My uncle married his mother, so I guess he's sort of a cousin," Melvin says of Brown. "Right when everybody heard about the will, a lot of people like that—my uncle, him, my aunt—all of them came running. They all wanted a piece of the action. Maybe they thought, 'Oh, he's gonna be rich.' I don't know. [Brown] just showed up. What they didn't know is that we didn't have any money at all, because now we had to pay lawyers."

Those lawyers had come running, too. Like Brown, they wanted Melvin to speak to the media—they knew a believable face when they saw one—but they wanted to control what he said. A group of Hughes's cousins, supported by Hughes's parent company, planned to contest the will, and so Melvin's lawyers didn't want him doing or saying anything that could be used against him at a probate trial. Brown, however, proved harder to control. He and Melvin's father planned to produce merchandise that traded on Melvin's name, and Brown insisted he was in serious talks with book publishers about an authorized biography. Bonnie, always fiercely protective of her husband, didn't like all the plans that were swirling around. "His dad and I went around and around," she says. "I didn't want Mel to be exploited, and they thought I was a busybody."

Melvin didn't care much about selling T-shirts or books. He saw the attention as an opportunity to show off his true passion—his music. When given half a chance in interviews, he would mention that he was in a band and suggest that he sing a little something. Of all the offers that poured in, he only bothered to read the ones that had something to do with music. "I had a contract to cut a record," he recalls of those heady days. "This guy who played the keyboards with Steppenwolf, he and his producer came to see me and had me sign a contract. They were going to pay all my expenses, fly me to Los Angeles, and either do some of my own songs or I could pick out whatever I wanted to do. They had it all arranged, percentage and up-front money and everything. I was all ready to go—and then I never heard from them. I kept waiting and waiting to go to L.A., and finally I went in to see my attorney, Roger Dutson, and I said, 'What happened to that record deal? Did you ever hear from those guys again?' And he said, 'Oh, yeah, we heard from them a month or so ago, and we decided to just squash the deal.' They never even told me. Never had the courtesy to tell me or ask my opinion. They just said, 'Oh, we think it would cause adverse opinion, so we just canceled that for you.'"

Melvin didn't understand the reasoning—how could his singing bring adverse opinion?—but he found attorneys intimidating, so he accepted it. Still, it made him mad. Music was his passion; it was more important to him even than that will. He wanted nothing more from life than to get up in front of people and sing. The lawyers stopped him from cutting a record, but they let all the other craziness swirling around him go on. He didn't get it. When reporters interviewed him after that, he stopped mentioning he was a singer. He just told his story, over and over. It was starting to make him unhappy.

It didn't help that he was having doubts, doubts that kept him awake night after night. He wasn't a hundred percent convinced that the will was legit, he says. A little niggle in the back of his brain wouldn't let go of the notion that maybe his wife was behind all this.

Even now, Bonnie willingly accepts the blame for that. "That was my fault," she admits. "Let's see, Hughes died on April 5, and we got the newspaper every day, and we'd sit in the station office, and I'd say, 'Well, Uncle Howie wouldn't forget us, not to worry.' And by golly, Uncle Howie didn't forget us. And yes, at one time, I sat there and said, 'Was it you? Did you write the will?' And he said, 'No, did you?'"

"I really thought that maybe she did write it, for a while," Melvin says. "But I didn't know what to think. I was going crazy. I was going nuts."

As it turned out, he wasn't the only one.

THE GROUPIES BEGAN TO GATHER SOON AFTER MELVIN'S FIRST appearance on TV. They stood on the side of the road across from the little service station, staring, plotting, mumbling amongst themselves, sometimes for hours. Throughout the day, they would periodically pull their cars and trucks up to one of the two pumps, watching Melvin, waiting to see if he would come over.

The first attack came on a day when Melvin's attorney, Roger Dutson, had stopped by to bring Melvin up to date on possible court action concerning the will. The two men were talking outside the office when they heard what sounded like a Rebel war cry.

"I turn," Melvin recalls, "and a guy's running at me, screaming, 'I was with you! You must remember! I was with you!' He jumped right at me, clawing at my face. Literally clawing at me. Roger Dutson had to drag him off me. The police took him away, but they just released him. Not long after that, I had the radio on as I parked the car for church, and this kid, the one who attacked me, came on saying he and his cousin picked me up cuz I was hitchhiking and then they picked Hughes up. And I just sat there laughing. People walking by must have thought I was crazy."

Letters began to arrive, hundreds of them. Most asked for help, thinking Melvin already had Hughes's money in hand. A woman pleaded on behalf of orphans in South Africa. A man in India asked, "May I tell you about some of my difficulty and request for your kind help?" His three-year-old daughter, he wrote, had a congenital heart condition.

But there was another kind of letter, too.

"I remember a couple letters that said, 'Don't be surprised if someone takes a shot at you,'" Melvin says. One time, after Melvin had taken a second job delivering beer to help pay his legal bills, a man approached him in a bar when Melvin was making a delivery, pulled out a switchblade, and said, "Give me fifty thousand dollars right now or I'll cut your heart out." Melvin didn't even have five dollars on him, so he said, "Well, you better start cutting." He laughs at that now, all these years later—it was a pretty good response, he thought—but just for a moment. Then his face bunches up like a child's, the tears launching themselves in a sudden kamikaze burst.

Melvin admits he got paranoid. Every morning he would stand, shakily, outside his car and reach through the open window to turn the ignition, so if it were rigged with a bomb, "maybe it would just blow my arm off and not kill me."

"He's never really been able to get over it," says Gary Magnesen. "The media attention was so sudden and overwhelming, from the day after the will was discovered. He was under constant pressure. And not just from the media. People started asking for money. People called and threatened him: 'Better tell them I was with you.' That sort of thing. He really almost went insane, literally, from the whole ordeal."

"He was afraid of us being kidnapped," remembers Darcy. "Sometimes we would stay at a friend's house, the whole family, when he would get scared. He would watch TV and just be real quiet. I think he didn't know what to do or think. He was scared."

As Melvin brooded over his family's physical safety, Bonnie, who was paying closer attention to the cases that were being built both for and against the Mormon will, knew there was something else they had to worry about— a fraud charge.

"I saw what was happening," she says. "I was sure scared Mel was gonna go to jail for something he didn't do."

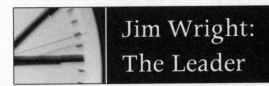

Jim Wright:
The Leader

For two years after he resigned as Speaker of the U.S. House of Representatives, Jim Wright thought Newt Gingrich was the worst thing that would ever happen to him. When he gave up in 1989 after months of fighting ethics investigations instigated by the Republican congressman from Georgia—investigations that received international media coverage and resulted in several of America's most prominent newspapers' demanding his ouster as Speaker—Wright went home to Fort Worth, Texas, humiliated and angry. After sacrificing so much during thirty-five years in Washington, D.C.—financial security, time with his children, his first marriage—to gain and wield political power, he'd been beaten by an opponent he mistakenly believed was nothing more than a loudmouthed lightweight. That he'd been brought down on charges he considered frivolous, even nonsensical, was maddening. That his vanquisher was Newt Gingrich—well, nothing could be worse than that.

Then, in 1991, Wright was diagnosed with cancer. It was the legacy of a three-pack-a-day habit he'd indulged over more than three decades. Wright quit smoking in 1978, but thirteen years later a BB-sized lump in his mouth was found to be malignant. Surgery saved his life but cost him a fifth of his tongue. The man who loved above all else to speak had to learn to talk all over again, and now there were letters he couldn't quite pronounce, sounds he wasn't able to make anymore. But he kept working at it until he could be understood by people willing to listen hard.

In 1999, the cancer was back. Now Wright's jaw was riddled with the disease. "Mr. Wright," cautioned the doctor who broke the news, "if you think the last time was difficult, that, compared to this, will seem like a piece of cake." The right half of Wright's lower jaw was sawed off and replaced with bone from his leg, making him appear, from that side, to have the same right-angle profile as cartoon character Dick Tracy. Once again, Wright had to teach himself to talk—and how to chew with just four lower teeth and a new dental bridge that never seemed to stay in place.

Gradually, it dawned on him. Had he not resigned as Speaker, had he still been back in Washington, D.C., working eighteen-hour days brokering legislative deals, why, he would surely have ignored that first lump under his tongue, being too busy helping run the country. By the time he finally couldn't ignore it anymore, it would have been too late. When he thought about it that way, the case could be made that Newt Gingrich saved his life.

"That still doesn't make me like the man," Wright, now eighty-one, observes. "To borrow a phrase someone used in another situation, I hold Gingrich in minimal high regard. But time and events have helped me see things that have happened in a somewhat different light. What I'd considered a coup de grâce turned out to be a blessing. Cancer has given me perspective. And perspective is exactly what most people who seek office, who gain power and fame, lack. I like to believe I finally have it, now."

THE TWO-STORY HOUSE WHERE JIM AND BETTY WRIGHT LIVE IS virtually indistinguishable from the other homes in their upper-middle-class Fort Worth neighborhood, except for the flowers that adorn its front and back yards. These, during the spring and summer, explode with color, overwhelming by far most of the blooms cultivated by neighbors. That's exactly how Wright, ever competitive, likes it. When he's not giving a talk some-

The former Speaker and Mrs. Wright at home in
Fort Worth with family pets Maggie and Gigi.

where or teaching a college class or writing an opinion column for the local paper, he's probably in his backyard with pruning shears and a watering can. Maybe he doesn't obliterate opponents in elections anymore, but Jim Wright's roses will still be better than yours.

"He's just got to win," says Ben Procter, laughing. Proctor is a retired professor of history at Fort Worth's Texas Christian University, where Wright teaches a history class each year. "A while ago we went out on a fishing trip. Jim caught the biggest, a six-and-a-half-pounder, and that made him happy. I've never known him not to be competitive in anything he does, even if it's just who caught the best fish."

Back home in Fort Worth after resigning as Speaker, Wright had to compete against himself. He wanted to show the whole damned world, particularly the political opponents who'd brought him down, that Jim Wright's life was far from ruined. By God, he'd be happier than he ever was, and to do that he first had to eradicate from his psyche any vestiges of self-pity or bitterness.

"I had political power for some time, the ability to make decisions that affected many others," Wright muses. "That was taken away. The only person left for me to command was myself, and so I turned all my energy to this. I controlled my own attitude. That was all the power I had left. I made myself put aside bitterness by acknowledging the immutable fact that being constantly angry is like taking poison. My anger at Gingrich, at my political enemies, wasn't going to hurt *them*. But a lack of anger on my part might frustrate those who wished me harm. I don't deny their potential frustration was a factor in my determination to become happy. 'See?' this would say to them. 'You couldn't ruin my life. Only I can do that, and I won't. Your worst wasn't good enough.'"

It took Wright a while to get to that emotional place. But after a year or two, he gradually realized that spending more time with his wife, children, and grandchildren, teaching at Texas Christian University and making speeches to every area organization that invited him, filled not only hours but also the holes in his ego. Keeping busy was the key, he decided, especially when he did so by using his undeniable gift for gab in every positive way imaginable.

Then came the cancer and the loss of his ability to speak clearly. Talking had always been the basis of his political prowess as well as his favorite avocation. His first local campaigns in the 1940s—for state legislature and then for mayor of his small Texas hometown—required him to constantly give stump speeches, climbing up on makeshift stages or the beds of pickup trucks to extol his virtues at some length. Wright even taught himself to play harmonica so he could leaven the politicking with a tune or two. Folks in that TV-less era wanted an afternoon's or evening's entertainment from their candidates, he recalls. Then came the U.S. Congress and reelection campaigns every two years for seventeen consecutive terms. A man who wanted to stay in office had to come home on weekends and talk his way around the district. As the years passed, Wright developed a particularly mellifluous, ornate pattern of speech. He spoke in rhythms as much as in sentences, instinctively choosing words for the way they sounded and blended together as much as for their individual meanings. During the sound-bite 1980s, when his political star imploded, this habit served him far less well. Wright never fully understood that as television became the public's primary means of getting information, politicians were required to say more with fewer words. By the time Newt Gingrich was hounding him out of office, Wright was too set in his talkative ways to respond concisely to the charges against him. Gingrich, better attuned to the needs of modern media, just shouted "Crook!" over and over until that was the one word the public remembered.

Back home in Fort Worth, talking remained precious to Jim Wright, and this was what cancer threatened to steal from him. He feared that would be a blow he couldn't take. Before each operation, Betty Wright remembers, her husband stayed awake all night, chattering to nurses and orderlies and anyone else who came into his room, just in case, postsurgery, he wouldn't be able to speak intelligibly again. And, afterward, he constantly practiced moving what was left of his tongue against what remained of his jaw until he could make specific sounds. Wright never did adopt less flowery speech. He'd talk the way he always had, damn it, because Newt Gingrich hadn't crushed Jim Wright, and cancer wouldn't, either.

"I would *not* feel sorry for myself," Wright says. "I made it a point after both surgeries to begin accepting speaking engagements as soon as possible. Rotary, Lions clubs, that sort of thing. I got up in front of people and I spoke to them." Driving to these events, Wright practiced in his car. Words including *gl* and *gr* gave him particular trouble, so he developed a chant of "glitter-glow-grow-green-greet-glean-glossary" that he'd repeat over and over, faster and faster, until he'd stretched the muscles in his mouth a little and could talk a bit more intelligibly. Wright made it clear to his audiences that if he said something they didn't understand, he'd gladly repeat himself. He never apologized for his mangled pronunciation and didn't want anyone to feel embarrassed for him. They'd all just keep trying until communication was accomplished.

"While I breathe, I must talk," Wright chuckles as he lounges in his den.

"If I'd lost my ability to speak completely, well, that might have been the thing to have done me in. But it didn't happen that way."

JIM WRIGHT DIDN'T SET OUT TO BE A POLITICIAN. THE SON OF A salesman who moved his family on a regular basis, young Jim Jr. lived in several different towns before he started high school in Dallas. He learned to handle always being the new kid in town in two ways: by instantly making friends with everyone he could and by training as a boxer so he could deal with anyone else. Above all, Jim loved playing football and dreamed of becoming a coach, but during his junior year in 1937 he suffered a serious knee injury. Trying to give the energetic, bored youngster an alternative to standing on the sidelines, wistfully watching healthier teammates practice, Wright's football coach suggested he join the school debate team.

"It soon appeared that I had a talent for debate," Wright recalls. It was a chance for the teenager to compete one-on-one with an opponent. Plus, he could be the center of attention, and how the youngster liked that! Wright stopped wanting to be a football coach. One day, while prepping for a debate, he began reading transcripts of speeches by Woodrow Wilson. These bemoaned isolationism as practiced by many members of the U.S. Senate following World War I. "I thought, how wonderful to be in a position where it might be possible to change people's minds, like those of the senators after World War I who rejected the concept of the League of Nations," Wright recalls. He decided to go into politics, and he immediately had a goal. He wanted, even expected, to become president of the United States. Where Woodrow Wilson had failed to bend others to his will, President Wright would make such effective cases for his policies that everyone would support them.

"That came, really, from my mother and dad," Wright says. "My parents told us kids we could do anything in the world so long as we were willing to pay the price, and they emphasized that there was definitely a price for anything worth attaining. So it never did occur to me that I couldn't be president if I was willing to learn what was involved in the process and then work harder than anyone else to achieve it."

While still in high school, Wright began learning the electoral ropes by forming a club to influence class elections. He also organized a "Young Democrats" group. The Democratic Party was then the dominant one in Texas, and from the beginning Wright passionately believed Democrats stood up for the little people while Republicans tried to help the rich get richer. Even during his years in Congress, when he became friends with members of the opposing party, Wright never wavered in that basic belief. He wanted to be a politician for two reasons: to help "the little guy" and to be the center of attention. Both of these things made him happy.

Wright attended the University of Texas in Austin, but his collegiate days ended forever on December 7, 1941, when the Japanese attacked Pearl Harbor. Wright, nineteen, immediately dropped out of college and enlisted in the army as a private. This was, he says, a decision that had nothing to do with future political ambition: "I am of the generation that believes you serve your country in time of war. Later in life I saw a limited number of other World War II veterans-turned-politicians emphasize their time of service as though the fate of the nation had rested on whether or not they were in uniform. I simply enlisted for the chance to fight for my country." And fight he did. After earning a commission as second lieutenant, Wright ended up flying bombing missions in the Pacific. He was awarded the Distinguished Flying Cross for his service.

At war's end, Wright came home. He didn't go back to college. Having survived combat and married his girlfriend, Mab Lemons, he was anxious to get on with what he saw as his life's work. Wright worked as a salesman in Weatherford, a small town just west of Fort Worth, to pay his family's bills, but most of his free time was devoted to politics, an interest the new Mrs. Wright definitely did not share. Her husband paid little attention. His focus was already on running for office. Wright was active in the Young Democrats of Texas, and, as he'd hoped, he impressed enough people to be urged to run for the state legislature. He won that race in 1946, but his tenure in Austin was controversial.

"I did not have at that time the patience to watch a while before I began inserting myself in the important debates of the day," Wright says, chuckling at his youthful exuberance. "I advocated radical concepts like abolishing the poll tax and letting women serve on juries, and even letting black students into the University of Texas law school. I certainly enjoyed the attention I received when I spoke out on these topics. But back home, more conservative folks were somewhat appalled by my temerity." In 1948, he lost his bid for reelection.

Undaunted, a year later, when he was still only twenty-six years old, Wright was elected mayor of Weatherford. He immediately began to build a wider political base by helping in the campaigns of Democratic candidates throughout Texas. This brought him to the attention of U.S. Senator Lyndon Johnson, who mightily impressed the young mayor.

"There was about him a sense of power and of destiny," Wright says. "Naturally, I had some hope of growing into that sort of person myself." Urged on by Johnson and other state Democratic leaders, Wright was elected president of the League of Texas Municipalities, effectively becoming the spokesman for all the mayors in the state. But this was still only the equivalent of batting practice before the real game. Jim Wright intended, *burned,* to go to Washington.

In 1954, Wright ran for U.S. Congress in Texas's 12th District, which included Weatherford and Fort Worth. He won easily and went to Washington convinced he would someday occupy the White House.

"THERE IS SOMETHING IN ME, I THINK IN EACH OF US WHO SEEKS public office, that craves recognition," Jim Wright says, unself-consciously using a napkin to blot drops of soup that have dripped down his chin. Sitting in a small Mexican restaurant, dining on *caldo de pescado,* Wright can't help having some of his meal dribble out his mouth as he tries to spoon and swallow. He doesn't have quite enough control of his lower facial muscles and jaw to be tidy when he eats. But he doesn't order less difficult food. He likes soup and won't give up eating it just because it's now a messy process. Obstacles are there to be dealt with, not avoided.

"All of us want to be loved," Wright continues after swallowing, then dabbing again with his napkin. "But it's more powerful in those who run for office, I believe. For our peace of mind, we convince ourselves we're seeking power for the benefit of others. But it is true, always, that we seek power to help others at least in part so they will be grateful to us, so they will appreciate us. Thus, any young congressman wants as soon as possible to gain power and exercise it on behalf of his constituents. That way, the love and gratitude will wash over us. People will know who we are."

In January 1955, Wright's first session in Congress, he had very little influence. Fellow Texan Sam Rayburn, beginning his seventh two-year term as Speaker of the House, presided over a 435-member body that rewarded longevity rather than talent or ambition. Congressional committees, the bodies that shaped legislation, were chaired by their most senior members. Newly elected members were expected to keep quiet, vote as their party elders directed, and, after a few terms, gradually begin to insert their own ideas into the process. Rayburn had stern advice for first-termers: "To get along, go along."

That was against Wright's nature, but he tried. He meant his stay in the House of Representatives to be just a rung on the political ladder, since U.S. senators were much better positioned to run for president. In particular, Lyndon Johnson was an intriguing role model. He, too, had been elected to Congress from a small Texas district before becoming a senator.

"So I accepted there must be a term of apprenticeship and set out to be pleasing to my elders in Congress," Wright remembers. "That must have lasted upwards of almost one whole two-year term. I was returned to Congress by my district voters in 1956 and assumed I would now be given the opportunity to demonstrate my abilities."

Wright thought he saw his chance in 1957, when Russia successfully launched its Sputnik spacecraft and panicky Americans cringed at the prospect of Soviet-dominated space. "Lyndon Johnson is said to have immediately declared he did not want to sleep under the light of a Russian moon, and no doubt he did say that," Wright says. "But many, many others in Congress and the Senate said pretty much the same thing, including me. Lyndon was able to claim credit for the phrase. He became president. I did not. Perhaps there is some clue there why one did and the other didn't."

Wright decided a sound step would be for Congress to fund "better, more intensive science classes" in public schools and to mandate the formation of Future Scientists of America, modeled on the then popular Future Farmers of America. He put it all into standard legislative language and introduced the bill to the House in 1958. Congressional rules required that it then be referred to the Subcommittee on Education and Labor for discussion; committee members could then send the bill back to the full House with a recommendation for passage, suggest the House not vote in favor of it, or else tinker with the plan however they liked. In this case, the National Education Defense Act eventually was voted into law, and it included most of what Wright had originally written into it. But the congressman publicly credited with conceiving the bill was Alabama's Carl Elliott, a mossbacked multitermer who happened to chair the subcommittee. As a sop, the Future Scientists of America provision was credited to Jim Wright.

"There was no personal momentum for the furthering of my ambitions, and this frustrated me," Wright says. "I wanted to influence policy. You may call it arrogance. I felt I had leadership to offer to Congress and to my country. But these experiences during my second term impressed upon me as nothing had before that if I wanted to make an impact, I had to get myself in a better position to do so. Only two things would accomplish this: getting reelected to the point where I had sufficient seniority, and by demonstrating meanwhile that I would work hard, study issues, and be a dependable member of the Democratic fold."

Wright still dreamed of being president, and to do that he believed he needed the prestige of a seat in the Senate. Opportunity arrived in November 1960 when Lyndon Johnson was elected vice president on the Democratic national ticket with John F. Kennedy. Just to be safe, Johnson also ran for his old place in the Senate and beat Republican John Tower in that race. When the Kennedy–Johnson ticket won, Johnson's seat in the Senate was declared vacant, and three-term Congressman Jim Wright entered the special election that was set for April 1961. Wright hoped his presence would scare off other entrants. It didn't. Eventually, seventy other candidates were listed on the ballot, including Tower and William Blakely, who'd been appointed by the Texas governor to fill Johnson's seat until the election. To his dismay, Wright finished third behind Tower and Blakely. Only the top two went on to the runoff, which Tower won. He became the first Republican senator from Texas since 1870.

Forty-three years later, Jim Wright still glowers at the memory of losing. "It was purely because I had an inability to raise enough money," he insists. Wright will talk for hours about how he felt after resigning under pressure in 1989, but that was different. He believes he was routed from the speakership by nasty political enemies dedicated to his personal destruction. That he can accept, if not forget. In 1961, *voters* spurned him because they preferred someone else, and that hurt in a way that stepping down as Speaker never could.

There was financial pain involved in the Senate loss, too. Wright discovered his campaign had finished $90,000 in debt. It was, and still is, traditional for candidates whose campaigns end in debt to schedule fund-raisers to make up the deficit. But Wright personally borrowed the $90,000 to pay off creditors, and spent the next sixteen years paying off the loans.

"My pride required this of me," he says now. "Those debts cast a certain pall over my personal finances for so long, and, to some extent, had a negative impact on my marriage. Mab really didn't like Washington, anyway, and I know it seemed to her that my dedication to our family's financial well-being was being sublimated in favor of my desire to square those campaign debts myself. Well, I said I was motivated by pride. I can't deny that there may have also been a degree of outright stupidity." The Wrights' marriage, already strained by his devotion to politics over family, never recovered.

ALL OLD MEN LIVE AT LEAST PARTIALLY IN THE PAST, AND JIM Wright is no exception. Sitting in a restaurant or in the living room of his home, he beams when he's asked to talk about the days when he walked with the mighty and, eventually, became one of them. As he tells these stories, as he tosses out names that proliferate in history books, it's possible to get a sense of just how much power and influence this bent, white-haired codger once had.

The earliest stories he relates, about Dwight Eisenhower and John Kennedy, are from the perspective of an observer. As a very young congressman, he had no real relationship with Eisenhower. The JFK stories are more detailed, especially those involving Kennedy's assassination. Wright helped host a rally for Kennedy in Fort Worth on the morning of November 22, 1963, then headed with the president and Lyndon Johnson to Dallas to be part of a motorcade through its downtown streets. Wright rode a few cars behind the presidential limousine in that procession and clearly heard three shots ring out. The motorcade detoured frantically to Dallas's Parkland Hospital, and Wright describes seeing bright gouts of Kennedy's blood on the upholstery of the presidential car. When LBJ took the oath of office on Air Force One at Love Field a few hours later, Wright was standing near his side.

It's with recollections of the Johnson administration that Wright begins including himself more often. This was due not only to his friendship with LBJ, which dated back to the early '50s in Texas. Slowly, surely, Wright was moving up in the Democratic congressional hierarchy. His lips widen into a huge smile when he tells of his role in helping Johnson get many of his Great Society programs through Congress. Wright's was now an influential voice on the House Public Works Committee, which was charged with considering many of the Great Society bills. The Highway Beautification Act, the Economic Development Act, the Job Corps—Wright knows these names mean little or nothing to most Americans now, and he's eager to explain just how important they were, what social barriers they struck down.

The Vietnam War drove Johnson from office. Richard Nixon became president, and Wright had his doubts about the man. But Nixon faced near-unsolvable problems with the Vietnam conflict, and Wright was sympathetic. In the fall of 1969 Wright passed the biggest leadership test of his career when he organized a bipartisan House resolution supporting Nixon's overtures to the North Vietnamese for peace talks designed to lead to free elec-

Wright with Senator John F. Kennedy in 1960, as Kennedy
campaigned for the presidency in Fort Worth.

tions in Vietnam. The president was immensely grateful, and, on top of that,
Wright had the satisfaction of making national headlines. He truly loved attention from the media. It reinforced his opinion of himself as a man of great
destiny.

About the same time, there were changes in Wright's personal life. He
and Mab hadn't been close for years, ever since she realized her husband
wasn't going to leave Congress after a few terms and head back home to
Texas. He'd stayed married, in part, because it was taken as political gospel
that voters wouldn't support a divorced candidate for president. That ambition still lived on in Wright. In 1966, he briefly considered challenging John
Tower for his seat in the Senate, but didn't because he still owed so much
money from his failed campaign in 1961. In 1972, he thought about running
against Tower again, but now he had to factor in how much time he would
lose from his duties in Congress. He was a leader among the Democrats. If
he devoted the year necessary to face off against a two-term Senate incum-

bent like Tower, he might lose the standing he'd spent so many years impatiently accumulating in the House. So he didn't challenge Tower, but he did divorce his wife. On his fiftieth birthday, he wrote in his diary that he'd finally accepted the fact he'd never be president.

He was, however, becoming a congressman of considerable influence. When Vice President Spiro Agnew resigned under legal duress for accepting bribes while governor of Maryland, Wright was one of the Democrats Nixon called to ask advice about who he should name as the new vice president. Wright knew House Minority Leader Gerald Ford very well, and liked him. In those less politically partisan days, one of Wright's daughters had even worked in Ford's congressional office. He was glad to tell Nixon good things about Ford, and, when Nixon resigned, Wright had another close friend as president. What he didn't realize was that the Watergate scandal that brought down Nixon ushered in a new, meaner era of political reporting. Post-Nixon, members of the media would always be on the lookout for possible corruption, and the more prominent their targets, the better. And Jim Wright's prominence would continue to increase.

Not long before Ford took office, two momentous events occurred that would shape much of Wright's future. The first was personal. He married Betty Hay, whom he'd met in Fort Worth in the mid-'60s and who subsequently was employed in Washington, first by Wright, then by the congressional Committee for Public Works—a committee on which Wright served. The marriage, then and now, can be objectively described as blissful. Unlike Mab, Betty Wright understood and supported her husband's political ambition. At approximately the same time as their marriage, that ambition came much closer to fruition.

In January 1973, Tip O'Neill of Massachusetts was elected majority leader, the number two position in the House of Representatives, by his fellow Democratic colleagues. O'Neill, in turn, appointed new whips. One of them was Wright, who was now officially part of the House leadership.

The Speaker of the House, Carl Albert, made it clear he didn't envision staying in Congress after 1976. O'Neill, a bulky, white-haired Boston pol, was going to be Speaker after Albert left, since it was apparent the Democrats would continue to enjoy a solid congressional majority. That would leave a vacancy as majority leader. Several House members began to sound out support for the post. Wright wasn't among them. He wasn't convinced he'd built a sufficient power base to run for majority leader when O'Neill moved up. Oh, Wright *wanted* the majority leader's job—"a natural escalation from that office, without modern exception, was the speakership, and I did want to become Speaker"—but several other Democrats had already declared their own intentions to run. Phillip Burton of California was the early favorite, though he and O'Neill didn't get along. Missouri's Richard Bolling was as ambitious as Wright, and, at least by reputation, a whole lot meaner. He fully intended to be majority leader, then Speaker. A third candidate was John McFall of California. Everybody liked him, but liberals in the party found him too conservative.

All three men began politicking among the Democratic membership. Wright thought his wisest course would be to wait until the next time his party would elect a majority leader, even though he was convinced he would be far better at the job than the trio of current candidates. But as months of backroom coaxing and coercing went on, neither Bolling nor Burton, the two favorites, were able to come up with enough pledged votes. Too many of their fellow Democrats just didn't envision either one as the right choice.

Jim Wright simply glows when he gets to the next part of the story.

"Some colleagues in Congress began to privately approach me," he says, still made proud by the memory. "I'd considered Phil Burton to be the favorite. He'd already run for every other office we had, including jobs like caucus leader that, previously, were given to members who foolishly stepped out of nominating meetings for phone calls or something of that nature. I couldn't fault him for that. Fate doesn't tap you on the shoulder. I saw so many other members, some almost as talented as they believed themselves to be, simply wait modestly for others to come and plead with them to step forward, to lead. If I hadn't put myself forward yet as a candidate for majority leader, it was because I wasn't sure I could get the votes. Then, out of our three hundred or so Democrats, perhaps eight or a dozen came to me to say 'Jim, these other candidates won't do, and we need you.' No doubt many other potential candidates were receiving similar visits, but to me, it seemed I was the focus of a popular groundswell."

Wright then approached other members. To his pleasure, some declared that he had their votes—enough, in fact, so that when Wright counted, it seemed none of his rivals would be able to get a majority on the first ballot. Under House rules, the lowest vote getter was eliminated after each round. If Wright could pick up the support of each eliminated candidate without being eliminated himself, then just maybe . . .

He announced he was also a candidate for majority leader. The vote would be held in December 1976, when old and newly elected members who would make up the Democratic majority of the 95th Congress in 1977 convened for the first time at the Capitol.

In the fall of 1976, Wright crossed the country offering his assistance to several Democrats trying to win their first terms in Congress. "He told me he was just happy to help," remembers David Bonior of Michigan. "Of course, he hoped his help would get him my vote." And, after winning his first Congressional term, Bonior did vote for Wright, "because, of the four, he was the one who seemed to take the most interest in everybody else. He had better people skills, I felt."

On December 6, the Democrats caucused. On the first ballot, the count was 106 for Burton, 81 for Bolling, 77 for Wright, and 31 for McFall, who was eliminated. The second ballot ended with Burton receiving 107 votes, Wright 95, and Bolling 93. By the barest of margins, Wright's strategy was working. More of McFall's supporters chose him than Bolling. Burton's total had remained almost exactly the same, meaning, Wright figured, that Burton wouldn't pick up any of Bolling's backers at all in the final round.

"I expected to win quite comfortably," Wright recalls, "only to find that the result was 148 for Jim Wright, 147 for Phillip Burton. So I was elected majority leader by one vote, probably from someone who considered me the least of four evils." It was even closer than that. It could have been a tie. Besides the ballots for Wright and Burton, there was also one marked "Neither."

But the closeness of the contest didn't matter. At age fifty-three, Jim

Wright was majority leader of the U.S. House of Representatives, still young enough to feel certain he would one day succeed Tip O'Neill as Speaker.

Finally, Wright had power. Not the ultimate power in the legislative branch, yet—that was reserved for the Speaker of the House. But at least Wright had enough now to make his opinions not only heard but acted upon.

JIM WRIGHT STILL LIKES TO KEEP BUSY. DURING THE WEEK, HE spends most mornings and many afternoons in his office on the second floor of the Texas Christian University library. For several years after he resigned as Speaker, the government paid for an office for him in downtown Fort Worth's Lanham Federal Building. When that perk expired, TCU was glad to give space to Wright, who has taught one class for the school each year. In that office, Wright spends time grading student papers, working on the opinion columns he contributes regularly to the *Fort Worth Star-Telegram*, and, very occasionally, offering political advice to incumbent Democratic congressmen.

Now Wright has lots of time to spend with Betty and his children and grandchildren. There are dinner parties at the Wright home where politics aren't discussed at all. Betty Wright enjoys dance classes and lunches with friends. Sometimes her husband is invited along, and lots of times he isn't, which is fine with him—his flower beds won't water themselves. There's even time for Wright to watch television, something he never did during his years as majority leader and Speaker. His favorite program, the one he refuses to miss, is *The West Wing*.

"Leisure time is a relatively new experience for me," Wright says. "During my early and middle years in Congress, any time away from the floor of the House was usually devoted either to answering constituent mail, making visits back home to my district, or studying the piles of printed materials relating to pending legislation. Even so, after my marriage to Betty I tried to make myself find time for personal things. For instance, we would enjoy bicycle rides together. Then I became majority leader, and this changed. From that point, I had no real hobbies or other recreation. If I played golf, it was with members whose votes were required on something. When Betty and I had dinner parties, the guest list was chosen in token of some issue needing to be resolved. Everything—*everything*—was job related."

As soon as he assumed his new role in January 1977, Wright remembers, he was treated differently. Reporters from national magazines and TV news programs pleaded for a few moments of his valuable time. Colleagues who wanted certain legislation passed went out of their way to be pleasant. As majority leader, Wright's was the key voice in determining which members served on what committees, and he made it clear he was ready to reward the faithful and punish the independent-minded.

"In the course of any legislative year, there would be twelve to eighteen really key votes where wholehearted party support was needed," Wright explains. "As majority leader I had not only the right but the responsibility to do what I could within the rules of the House to muster that majority vote, including a policy of awarding assignments to certain prestigious committees like Rules, Appropriations, and Ways and Means solely to those colleagues who demonstrated support on those key votes. Among the other two hundred or so votes cast each year, members could vote as they liked, reflecting their own constituencies and ideological bents. But on the big ones, I expected every Democratic member to play on the team, and I rewarded those who did so."

Wright didn't let his new job distract him from responsibilities to his home district and state. In fact, whenever it came to bills in any way favorable to Texas, Wright was enthusiastically bipartisan.

"There weren't, around this time, too many Republican congressmen from Texas," recalls former congressman Tom Loeffler. "But the few of us there were always knew that, if we had something working that was good for Texas, any district in Texas, Jim Wright would be there to help in any way he could. His word was absolutely good, every time." Years later, the solid friendship forged between Wright and Loeffler would have impact far beyond the Texas state borders.

Meanwhile, Speaker O'Neill devoted much of his attention to working with the new president, Jimmy Carter, a fellow Democrat. Even before

Majority Leader Wright consults President Jimmy Carter over legislative
initiatives in the White House cabinet room, 1979.

Carter took office in January 1977, Wright was one of eight Democrats invited to meet with the president-elect at his home in Plains, Georgia. There
was more: Carter intended to broker peace in the Middle East, and one of his
frequent emissaries to Anwar Sadat of Egypt and Menachem Begin of Israel
would be the majority leader of the U.S. Congress. Wright relished the opportunity. He and Sadat became friends. When Sadat made his historic visit to
Israel to address that nation's Knesset, it was at least partially at Wright's suggestion. Wright was an honored guest that evening at the invitation of Begin.

The media took notice of his influence. He wasn't personally surprised at
his effectiveness at international deal brokering, but he was pleased that his
successes were being publicized. Wielding power was wonderful, and the
celebrity that came with power was equally gratifying.

Back in Washington, Wright also was involved in drafting new legislation
that effectively limited outside income for members of Congress. There had
been recent scandals where members had been accused of taking substantial,
but legal gifts from shady influence peddlers. Tip O'Neill wanted to end any
public perception that their congressional representatives were for sale. He
appointed a bipartisan committee to develop a strict set of internal rules gov-

erning what members could and couldn't do to make money. The committee's main recommendation, endorsed by O'Neill and acceptable to Wright, his chief lieutenant, was that members could no longer accept outside income amounting to more than one-third of their annual congressional salary. Fees for speeches could never exceed $2,000. Individuals could not contribute more than $1,000 to any congressional campaign. Contributions from political action committees were limited to $5,000 each. Income derived from outside work, no matter how minuscule, had to be reported. Income from business investments, stocks, and family inheritances was exempted. So were royalties from books. This was an important exemption for Wright and many other members. They frequently published books, often collections of their speeches. There was a certain personal satisfaction in being an author. Also, such books made handy purchases for political groups that wanted to distribute the volumes to their memberships. About ten years later, these rules—or interpretations of them—would claim their most prominent victim, Jim Wright.

As he spent his first years as majority leader, Wright couldn't help noticing how Congress was changing. The obvious traditions remained in place—two-year terms as opposed to the Senate's six, parliamentary control held by the majority party over the minority—but the attitudes of many new members were different.

"After Watergate, it became fashionable to run for Congress or the Senate or even the presidency as an outsider, someone who wasn't all caught up in the supposed political intrigue in Washington," Wright says. "People campaigned on the basis of coming to town and cutting through the red tape, pushing aside old-timers who had no idea what the real world was like. When they were elected, their tactics were to insert themselves into every issue whether they understood it or not. Public, overly partisan comments became common, and I believe they were encouraged by the media, which for the first time devoted great attention to such remarks. So many of the newly elected set out to blow things up. That's what they'd promised voters and the press they'd do, and, to the detriment of courtesy and compromise, they kept their word."

Newt Gingrich, a professor of history at West Georgia College, was elected to Congress in 1978 after failing in two previous campaigns. He was one of a number of new Republican members who immediately irritated O'Neill and Wright. Gingrich, Wright recalls, had barely been sworn in before he stood up in the well of the House and demanded a longtime Democratic member not be allowed to serve as chairman of the Committee on the District of Columbia. House rules required any member indicted for a felony to give up a chairmanship, and Charles Diggs of Michigan was currently being investigated for taking kickbacks. Though it later would be, no indictment had been issued at the time of Gingrich's demand. The subsequent House vote allowed Diggs to remain as chairman. Wright says Gingrich didn't seem to care; he'd taken the floor and gotten attention, which was what he'd wanted. "One day I'm going to be as good as you are," Wright recalls Gingrich crowing to him after the vote. Wright just grinned politely, certain there was no chance of that ever happening.

For a while, name-calling was done more in private than in public. In House cloakrooms, at parties, members of both parties began saying things about each other, and especially about House leadership, that would have been unthinkable during the '50s and '60s, when Wright had slowly earned his congressional spurs. To an extent, Wright felt baffled; Congress wasn't supposed to be this way. He'd frequently tell his favorite story about Speaker Sam Rayburn. Once, two members engaged in a nasty argument about whether one of them was eligible to cast his vote on a key issue. One claimed the other member hadn't been on the floor of the House in time to vote; that member swore he was there. Rayburn said gently but firmly to the accuser, "The chair *always* takes the word of a member," and the accuser, suddenly aware of his awful gaffe, cried as he apologized. Nobody was apologizing in 1978.

Compounding the problem for Wright was his sensitivity to any form of criticism. "I gained a reputation over the years for being thin-skinned," he says. "People knew all about it, especially the new young Republican members. Looking back, I consider this being thin-skinned to be my worst public weakness. It would, eventually, prove very costly to me."

IN 1979, O'NEILL AND WRIGHT INADVERTENTLY HANDED THEIR Republican foes a powerful weapon. House proceedings had never been televised. In early 1979, C-SPAN, a small start-up cable network, wanted to have cameras in Congress daily to broadcast every debate, resolution, and roll call. The Speaker and the majority leader had the votes to deny such unprecedented access, but Wright in particular thought it might be a good idea.

"I voted, I fought for C-SPAN," Wright says, shaking his head ruefully. "Let the American people watch their House at work, I believed. I will frankly add that I thought being constantly on television would improve the performances of some members. They could never be sure when the folks back home who elected them might be watching, and so they would have to be always on the top of their games."

O'Neill set limits. The C-SPAN cameras would focus only on the podium in front of the House, where the Speaker presided and members who had something to say came to stand. The well, or floor of the House, could only be shown during actual votes. Otherwise, all viewers would see would be whoever stood up front to speak.

"Long before C-SPAN arrived, we had a rule in the House that if any member had something additional he wanted to say, at the conclusion of the day's business he could, by unanimous consent—which was never denied, as a courtesy—address the House for no more than one hour," Wright says. "The presumption was that a good many colleagues might stay to listen. In fact, that was never the case. People were tired, wanted to go home, had legislation to study or meetings to attend; the place would empty out pretty quickly, leaving just the member who probably wanted to read certain statements or newspaper stories into the official record to please the home folks. And nobody did it too often."

C-SPAN televised everything, including whatever any member had to say at the end of the day to a virtually empty House chamber, though the single angle of the camera gave the impression that whoever was speaking was addressing a significant congressional audience. Some of the young, aggressive Republicans like Gingrich and Bob Walker of Pennsylvania, Wright says, began using that specific TV time "to rant and rave about Democratic treachery, one taking up his full hour and then yielding to the next. Walker or Gingrich would attack a Democrat, just making outrageous remarks, and then add, 'Let my colleague rise and say so if he feels I have misrepresented him and his views.' Of course, they were careful to attack someone who wasn't there."

It was a while before O'Neill and Wright took the problem seriously—after all, who was watching C-SPAN? In fact, the number of viewers rapidly multiplied—swelled, Wright insists, by "right-wingers from all over the country who got the word Democrats were being bashed every day" in Congress. Wright, the old political pro who says he believes politicians should take advantages where they find them, simply can't give the Republicans credit for finding a way, within the rules of the House, to use the C-SPAN broadcasts for considerable political advantage. The Speaker and the majority leader had been outfoxed by younger, more media-savvy opponents. It wouldn't be the last time.

"That was the true moment of arrival of what I would call 'mindless cannibalism' in my final remarks as Speaker a half-dozen years later," Wright says. "Previously, unwritten House etiquette required all members be courteous to each other in public. I know, there have been instances of insults, even a few physical attacks. But there had never been anything as calculated as this. The cannibalism had commenced."

AS RONALD REAGAN'S SECOND FOUR-YEAR TERM AS PRESIDENT GOT underway, Tip O'Neill began talking about retirement. At the end of 1986, he would be Speaker for ten years, and the increasingly rancorous atmosphere in the House had drained him. It was time, he thought, to step aside, especially since the current majority leader was eager to accept the challenges of being Speaker. Though he was frequently frustrated and often angry at the changing political atmosphere, overall Jim Wright enjoyed being in the middle of things.

"I had watched Sam Rayburn closely, and his successors John McCormack and Carl Albert and Tip," Wright says. "Even with the new, less amicable attitude on the part of the minority party, I had an exalted view of what the Speaker should be able to accomplish. I was certain I could bring a sort of legislative common sense to bear, and that I could reason enough with members of both parties to bring about better, more *sensible* days."

O'Neill announced he would retire at the conclusion of the 99th Congress in late 1986. The elections that November returned another Democratic majority to Congress. Wright would be Speaker of the 100th Congress in January 1987. Then, less than two months before he was sworn in, a scandal broke in Washington that ended any chance Wright could ease into the Speaker's job.

Since 1979, a new coalition Nicaraguan government had been an irritant to Republicans. Some, though not all, of its leaders were Marxists, known as Sandinistas. When Ronald Reagan succeeded Jimmy Carter, he began making frequent public references to "Marxist governments" in Central America.

Then leftist rebels began operating in neighboring El Salvador, and the CIA warned Reagan that the Nicaraguan government was supporting them, with the encouragement of Cuba. On three occasions, Wright as majority leader mustered enough House votes to defeat White House–driven bills directing financial aid to the Nicaraguan rebels, who were known as Contras. A year earlier the House had also banned the sale of any U.S. weapons to Iran. But in October and November 1986, news reports established that some U.S. government operatives, acting either with or without the president's knowledge, had sold arms to Iran and used the money to fund the Contras.

Still six weeks away from officially becoming Speaker, Wright took Senate Majority Leader Robert Byrd to meet with Republicans Robert Dole and Robert Michel, minority leaders in the Senate and House, respectively. They agreed that, instead of many congressional and Senate committee investigations, there would be one joint panel composed of members of the House and Senate, with both parties proportionately represented.

"I had no desire to embarrass the president in any way," Wright says now, leaning back on the couch in his den. "In January, when I was sworn in as Speaker, I hoped I had demonstrated by my actions that I truly believed in bipartisanship. I had an opportunity to take political advantage of events and chose instead a course designed to serve the country rather than pure party interests. From the very beginning as Speaker, I was placing my trust, the public's trust, in the ability of elected men and women of good faith to put aside partisan differences. What more could I have done?"

WRIGHT'S TENURE AS SPEAKER GOT OFF TO A SUCCESSFUL START. In all, the 100th Congress of 1987–88 developed and passed the most significant appropriations bills in more than forty years. Only on the Reagan-proposed tax bills that the new Speaker believed aided the rich and further impoverished working Americans did Wright fail to get his way, mostly, he says, "because the right-wingers among the Republicans had reduced the word *tax* to practically an obscenity in the minds of voters."

Even so, Wright had become an undeniable force, a man whose cooperation or opposition impacted every major act of the American government. But it wasn't enough. Not every Democratic congressman was voting the way Wright wanted. Some bills he opposed got through anyway. It ate at him. Wright always had a fierce temper. Now there were too many moments when he was consumed with rage. "As I grew in political power, I grew in anger," he says. In his private office at the Capitol, in meeting rooms and in cars and on the phone, even admirers like Bonior remember, he would often tell other Democrats in hard, salty terms exactly what he expected them to do, and what would happen if they didn't. Once, Betty Wright, not entirely joking, asked her husband, "Do you want to be a leader or a dictator?" When he hurt his colleagues' feelings, he usually tried to make amends afterward. Sometimes he forgot, or was distracted by more pressing issues.

"It was just that some issues were so obviously crucial for the well-being of our country that I *had* to have cooperation," Wright says now. "Whatever I did as Speaker, even if it hurt some others, I told myself the action was necessary for the greater good. I was always very convincing to myself."

In July 1987, Jim Wright had been Speaker for about six months, and the Iran-Contra hearings were still lurching along. (It would take almost a year for the committee to rule that President Reagan was unaware of the illegal activities of subordinates. It also concluded that Reagan still bore "ultimate responsibility.") Loeffler, a Republican who'd left Congress earlier to make an unsuccessful run for governor of Texas, privately approached his old pal Jim. President Reagan, Loeffler said, desperately wanted the fighting to end in Central America. Would Wright consider a joint, bipartisan resolution from the Republican president and Democratic Speaker that called for governments and rebels in El Salvador and Nicaragua and their immediate neighbors to cease hostilities immediately and enter into negotiations for peace? Sandinistas, Contras, it didn't matter who, would be politely required to sit down and work things out, at pain of losing all forms of U.S. aid.

"I'd gotten a call from Howard Baker, President Reagan's chief of staff," Loeffler recalls. "He asked if I'd help them work with Congress, somehow break up the logjam about what to do in Central America. I went in and, when they asked what they had to do, I told them, 'There's only one way to work with this Congress. You have to go through Jim Wright. He's got the expertise, he's got the control over votes. I know you've been fighting him. But if you deal with him honestly and he tells you he'll do something, you can absolutely count on his word.' I got the go-ahead, and I then met with Jim."

Wright pondered the proposition. It was certainly tempting. Leaders of five Central American governments, including El Salvador and Nicaragua, were scheduled to meet August 6 and 7 in Guatemala. If this "Reagan-Wright" initiative could be made public before then, if the five Central American leaders all embraced it, then there could be peace. It would prove that the president and the Speaker, who'd clashed for so long, could put political differences aside. Despite misgivings on the part of some Democratic colleagues, Wright agreed. As developed by Wright and Reagan's staff, the final plan called for immediate cease-fires, suspension of U.S. military aid to the Contras, no more aid to the Sandinistas from Cuba or the Soviet Union, restoration of civil rights in countries where they had been suspended, and democratic elections in Nicaragua that would be supervised by some objective, international body. On August 7, the leaders meeting in Guatemala accepted the plan. Jim Wright's dream of bringing peace to Central America had apparently come true.

"The day I received that news was, without exaggeration, the greatest day of my life," he says now. "I had always believed in the power of the Speaker's office to bring about great good, and in the concept of a president and a Speaker being able to work together for the common good even if they represented opposing parties. To think, so many people would live instead of die, have the chance for happy lives instead of the certain fate of painful ones, because of something I had helped bring about."

Yet, after initial celebration, the peace process slowed. In Nicaragua, the Sandinistas would not meet directly with the Contras. The Reagan administration would not deal directly with the Sandinistas. The conflict continued. In November, Wright met privately with Cardinal Miguel Obando y Bravo, the Catholic prelate of Nicaragua who had been proposed as a mediator. White House sources immediately claimed Wright was negotiating critical foreign policy without the administration's knowledge or permission. Wright fired back, testily reminding the president through the media that Reagan requested Wright's cooperation on the peace plan, not vice versa. A private meeting with Reagan went badly. The president accused Wright of overstepping, Wright snarled that he was supposed to be an equal partner, and afterward Wright was convinced Reagan and his advisors didn't actually *want* peace in Nicaragua.

"I think there was complete sincerity on the part of the president and those members of his staff who'd worked with Jim," Loeffler says. "That didn't mean that others who weren't directly involved felt the same way. They were the ones who, as sources, told the press that Jim Wright was overreaching. Well, that wasn't true. We reached out to him. Any suggestion that he was putting himself ahead of the president was hogwash."

Still, in February 1988, the administration brought a new bill to the House authorizing more military aid for the Contras. Wright led a floor fight to defeat it, then passed a substitute measure providing the Contras with humanitarian aid instead: medicine rather than bullets. Soon afterward, there was another, longer-lasting cease-fire and, in 1990, the long-promised national elections that resulted in a new, democratic government. Whether Reagan had really intended it or not, the proposal he and Wright crafted together did bring about peace.

But by then, Jim Wright was back in Fort Worth, trying to be happy so Newt Gingrich wouldn't have the satisfaction of having ruined the former Speaker's life.

"I FORGOT FOR A TIME THAT I WAS NOT THE ONLY MEMBER OF Congress with the desire for power," Jim Wright says, poking in his backyard at the roots of some flowers he feels aren't blooming to their full potential. It's a hot summer day. The former Speaker is wearing a huge, floppy straw hat that would look more appropriate on the head of a horse pulling a wagon. So what? It provides plenty of shade, and these days Wright doesn't have to care what people think about how he looks.

"One distinct difference between being Speaker and majority leader was that, after I became Speaker, my focus had to be on the big things, the major legislation, instead of on day-to-day doings in the House," Wright continues. "I had wonderful help there—Tom Foley as majority leader, Tony Coelho as whip, David Bonior as deputy whip—but I still lost a certain connection to what was happening. That allowed my opponents, or at least one of them, to begin certain operations that were well underway before I fully realized their intentions and the potential danger."

Newt Gingrich had been a professor of history and a student of politics. He understood the various functions of government very well, and in the first months that Wright was Speaker, Gingrich recognized how brilliantly Wright was succeeding at thwarting Ronald Reagan and passing his own legislation instead. *How* Wright was accomplishing this was particularly impressive. In an era of increasingly uncivil relations between Democrats and Republicans, he was actually building bipartisan coalitions and overriding presidential vetoes by bargaining for Republican votes in the Senate. If Wright continued to consolidate his power, Gingrich told colleagues, he was going to become such a force that it would be impossible to stop him in any way. He was just too good a deal maker, too shrewd at figuring out how to give enough people part of what they wanted to get most of what *he* wanted. So, to keep him from becoming too powerful to oppose, Wright would have to be taken out of the picture soon. If this could be done in a way that elevated Gingrich at the same time, so much the better.

There was never any secret plot on Gingrich's part. From the beginning, he was always open about what he was doing, which was to take advantage of the media's increasingly desperate obsession with ferreting out political corruption. At the end of 1989, investigative journalist John M. Barry published an excellent book, *The Ambition and the Power: The Fall of Jim Wright.* In devastating detail over 768 pages, Barry delineated everything Gingrich did to destroy Wright and everything Wright did to try and stop him. Astonishingly, both men granted Barry complete access, including to staff meetings where they'd plot how to foil each other. After the book was published (and it didn't depict either in an especially good light) neither Gingrich nor Wright denied its accuracy. So those seeking a detailed description of Jim Wright's political downfall can find it there.

Here are the basics: in the spring of 1987 Gingrich began contacting every media outlet and government watchdog group, asking for investigations into Wright's personal finances and business dealings. Gingrich assigned an aide to investigate these things herself. He had no idea if there was anything to find. He simply assumed that if the search went on long enough, something would turn up. At one point Barry quoted Gingrich as saying, "I'll just keep pounding and pounding on his ethics. There comes a point where it comes together and the media takes off on it, or it dies . . . He's from Texas. He's been in politics over thirty years. An aggressive investigator with subpoena powers might find something." Barry noted that Gingrich, "with an odd tone of respect in his voice," added, "If Wright survives this ethics thing, he may become the greatest Speaker since Henry Clay."

All through 1987 and on into 1988 Gingrich persisted. He contacted journalists at the *Washington Post, 60 Minutes, Time.* His research began to result in some specific suggestions: why didn't somebody look into Wright's relationship with a Fort Worth businessman named George Mallick? What about a sweetheart book deal Wright arranged for a collection of his speeches titled *Reflections of a Public Man?* In September 1987, the *Washington Post* did write about Wright's book. The newspaper revealed he received a 55 percent royalty, about five times the publishing norm. The book was printed by a Fort Worth company owned by a friend of Wright's. Nothing immediately came of it, but Gingrich felt it was a start. He kept trying.

For much of this time, Central America occupied Wright's attention. If there were now ongoing rumors that Gingrich thought he had enough on Wright to file charges with the House Ethics Committee, well, a man fighting dragons didn't have time to worry about mosquitoes. Ronald Reagan's second term as president was just about up. When the vice president, George H. W. Bush, was elected to succeed Reagan, it meant Wright would have to work with yet another Republican president. At least it would be someone he'd known for years, a man he thought would be more reasonable, more *aware*, than Reagan.

"God, I would have loved to be Speaker during a Democratic administration," Wright says. "In that situation, I would have been a partner to the president, I believe. I would not have been the lightning rod for the Republicans. At least George Bush, I thought, would welcome a cooperative spirit. It did not turn out that way, to my disappointment. Another blow to me was the loss of Bob Byrd as Senate majority leader. Before he stepped down from that post, I knew I had an ally who would work with me to build coalitions and, when necessary, stand up to the president. But when I wanted us to balance the budget even before Bush got to the White House, when it might have been possible for us to reduce the deficit by canceling some of Reagan's top-heavy tax cuts for the wealthy, George Mitchell was the new Senate majority leader, and he would tell me, 'Jim, I just can't sell this on the Senate floor.' He could have! He just didn't try. He thought he might fail and look bad. You have to be bold to succeed."

Unfortunately for Wright, Newt Gingrich was very, very bold. By May 1988, he'd managed to create enough doubt about Wright's business dealings for the *Wall Street Journal* to call for an Ethics Committee investigation. Two weeks later, seventy-one other Republicans joined Gingrich in submitting a written request for such an investigation, and in June the committee hired Illinois attorney Richard Phelan as an independent counsel to delve into the matter.

Jim and Betty Wright had formed a company back in Fort Worth with developer George Mallick and his wife, Marlene. The two couples were the best of friends. They called the company Mallightco, combining their last names. Mallightco was an investment business. Betty Wright's job, according to Mallick when he testified before the Ethics Committee, was to search out potential investments. Wright recalls his wife, "a very smart businesswoman," made some good decisions about when to buy and sell stocks. But Phelan found a lot to question about her role in the company. There was her annual salary of $18,000, but no record that she spent many hours on the job. Betty Wright drove a Cadillac that belonged to Mallightco, and this might be classified as a gift rather than a perk if she wasn't really a full-time employee. Plus, when the Wrights were in Fort Worth they lived in an apartment owned by Mallick, paying rent only for the days on which they occupied it; yet many of their personal belongings were stored there. Shouldn't that make the apartment their permanent residence, requiring them to pay Mallick rent on a full-time basis? Why was George Mallick doing Jim Wright and his wife all these favors? Mallick was, after all, a Fort Worth developer who conceivably could be gaining financially from some of the government funds Wright regularly funneled back into Texas's 12th District.

Taken separately, these things seemed minor, but Gingrich kept agitating and Phelan kept looking. While they did, Wright tried to carry on as Speaker. His efforts to maintain at least some degree of cordiality between the parties completely collapsed that spring, thanks to his Democratic colleagues in the Senate. Newly inaugurated President Bush had nominated former Texas Senator John Tower, the same man who had defeated Wright in 1961, to be secretary of defense. Cabinet nominations must be confirmed by a Senate vote. In March 1989, the majority of senators were Democrats. Former colleagues of both parties knew Tower drank a lot. There were rumors he was beholden to military contractors who had been campaign contributors in the past. Tower was an extremely intelligent, shrewd individual, well-versed in everything on which secretaries of defense are supposed to be expert. Bush expected Tower's confirmation to be automatic, but after days of rancorous debate, the Senate rejected his nomination by a vote of 53 to 47. Tower's supporters were livid, and, Wright says now, it was only hours after the Tower rejection that word spread fast through the Capitol that the Republican leadership was determined to bring a Democrat down to even the score. Who better than the leading Democrat, the Speaker of the House who'd upstaged Ronald Reagan on foreign policy and ruled Congress with an iron hand?

Today, Wright is certain Gingrich wouldn't have been able to unseat him if Tower's rejection hadn't united moderate Republicans with the right-wingers. But the Ethics Committee's investigation of Wright had already been in full swing for eight months. If no single item uncovered was incriminating enough to drive Wright from office, small, troubling things kept cropping up. On April 13, Wright felt compelled to come before the press and essentially plead for a chance to give his side of the story. Though the Ethics Committee had yet to announce what, if any, charges it would pursue against Wright, he'd picked up enough information to make educated guesses. It was going to come down to Mallightco and Betty's role in it, plus questions about the income he received from *Reflections of a Public Man*. Wright swore that he was completely innocent of wrongdoing. Betty had done a lot of work for Mallightco. The company car in question was nine years old, he said. By congressional fiat, income from books was exempt from House control. Hell, if the committee did bring charges, except for Gingrich and the right-wingers nobody was going to vote against the Speaker of the House on such frivolous accusations!

On April 17, 1989, the House Ethics Committee charged Wright with sixty-nine separate violations of House rules. Most involved Betty Wright and Mallightco. A few were about *Reflections of a Public Man*. The committee believed it had proof Wright deliberately circumvented House limits on speech honorariums by having his staff suggest to groups that they buy a few hundred copies of *Reflections* in lieu of paying him to speak.

"I have never denied my judgment is sometimes imperfect," Wright says now, choosing his words carefully. "I never, ever, asked any group to buy a certain number of copies of my book to specifically pay me for speaking. Neither did my staff. But I was enthusiastic about selling the book, of course. I should have realized certain sales instances would give the impression, perhaps, of wrongdoing."

There's something more Wright wants to make clear.

"George Mallick died in 1999," he adds. "It pains me when I think of how he was held up for public contempt, for ridicule, during the process of my destruction. He was maligned as a wrongdoer, someone who did me financial favors and requested much in return. Listen, and believe me: George Mallick was my good friend, and he never asked me for anything."

The April 1989 announcement of the charges didn't mean there would be an instant floor vote on whether Wright should be censured. Phelan intended to keep digging; already, he and his staff had spent $2 million on their investigations. Wright spent full days with attorneys who billed hundreds of dollars for each hour of their time. He was shocked that things had gone so far, but he was also completely convinced of his innocence. Betty did work for Mallightco! Book income wasn't regulated! It was a *nine-year-old car*! These were stupid little charges, quibbles rather than serious accusations. Surely people would realize what was going on.

But Wright's congressional career was doomed. Public reaction to the charges was overwhelmingly against him, except back home in the 12th District, where polls indicated 78 percent of all voters still supported him. *Time* magazine called on Wright to resign. The editorial page of the *Washington Post* declared his days as an effective Speaker were over. As the days went on, the outcry against Wright intensified rather than died down. It was obvious that, when the charges against Wright came up for consideration on the House floor, there would be enough votes—all of the Republicans, of course, and sufficient Democrats—for a majority to censure him for his conduct. That edict would be Wright's political death knell. Even if he didn't resign in disgrace, the Democrats would have to depose him and elect a new Speaker, because they wouldn't want their Republican counterparts and every conser-

vative media commentator charging they *condoned* questionable activities
when the next elections rolled around.

"I was very disappointed in many of our [Democratic] members," David
Bonior says. "Jim Wright deserved better. Not enough of us came forward to
support him in recognition of his great leadership."

Wright says now that even before the Ethics Committee publicized its
charges, he was ready to go home to Fort Worth, although he would have
waited until his two-year term was up. "I finally realized that, as Speaker, I
was not going to please everybody, which to some degree I had once thought
I could do," he says. "I thought, 'Well, what else is there? I'm making people
so angry, though I'm trying my damnedest to do the right things.' It sickened
me then, still sickens me now, to see Congress, which I love, reduced to
name-calling and posturing. And of course I look back and wish I had done
some things differently, from not allowing certain book situations to holding
my temper better with colleagues. But there was no way to undo what had
been done, and the investigation was clearly going to carry on much longer.
I already had half a million dollars in legal fees. I couldn't afford any more.
That's why I resigned. And I felt that, if I was resigning, I should do so in a
spirit that might help heal some of the wounds that so obviously festered on
our political landscape."

On May 31, Wright asked for permission to address the House. He spoke
for about an hour, first addressing the charges against him. He'd been waiting almost a year to tell his side, Wright said, and now, point by point, he
maintained his complete innocence. Once those remarks were part of the official record, though, he turned to the subject he really wanted to discuss.

Sweating profusely, abandoning for this one time his usual florid, ornate
speechifying, Wright asked that the partisan bloodletting finally stop: "Let us
not try to get even with each other. Republicans, please do not get it into your
heads you need to get somebody else because of John Tower. Democrats,
please do not feel that you need to get somebody on the other side because of
me. We ought to be more mature than that."

As he spoke, Wright could feel the power draining from him. He was giving up what he had obsessively pursued, gained, and wielded over thirty-five

years, and he was losing it under the most humiliating circumstances. The calculating politician who never left anything to chance had no prepared text. The words he spoke were drawn directly from his heart and his conscience.

"When vilification becomes an accepted form of political debate, when negative campaigning becomes a full-time occupation, when members of each party become self-appointed vigilantes, carrying out personal vendettas against members of the other party, in God's name that is not what this institution is supposed to be about!" Wright said. Trying not to appear he was accusing Republicans and excusing Democrats, he added, "All of us in both political parties must resolve to bring this period of mindless cannibalism to an end. There has been enough of it."

He eventually came to the final, plain words he wanted to say.

"Have I made mistakes? Oh, boy. How many. If I have offended anybody in the other party, I'm sorry. Are there things I would do differently if I had them to do over again? How many may I name for you? Well, I tell you what. I am going to make you a proposition. Let me give you back this job you gave me as propitiation for all of this season of bad will that has grown up among us. I will resign as Speaker of the House . . ."

There was just a little more. Ever conscious of House schedules, Wright suggested a Democratic caucus the following Tuesday to choose a new Speaker. He closed by asking that his resignation "be a total payment for the anger and hostility we feel toward each other." He asked God's blessings on Congress and the United States, and then Jim Wright walked out.

Twelve years later, John Barry, asked to sum up everything he'd written about in *The Ambition and the Power,* replied, "When it was all over, I thought Jim Wright had been treated more unfairly than any other figure in American political history. No one ever lost more political power for less reason."

SO JIM AND BETTY WRIGHT MOVED BACK TO FORT WORTH. THEY bought a house near Texas Christian University, where Wright would do some teaching. The important thing, he believed, was to immediately have things to do. He wouldn't allow anyone to get the impression that Jim Wright, devastated by what had happened, was spending his days sitting at home brooding. For years, Wright had maintained an office in downtown Fort Worth's Lanham Federal Building, and now every weekday morning he put on a suit and went to work. Suddenly bereft of legislation to craft or study, of deals to broker and press conferences to hold and private meetings with presidents to prepare for, he had to create things to do, and he did. Wright began a book about his thirty-five years as a congressman, though not a sad, defensive tome about how mean, unprincipled Newt Gingrich had unfairly brought him down. Only losers dwelled on defeat, after all, and Jim Wright was not a loser. He also devoted hours to planning the college class he would teach on the last half of the twentieth century.

"Work is the best antidote to self-pity," Wright says. "I don't deny that had I given myself the opportunity, I might very well have descended into bitterness. But when I was tempted to do so, I would remind myself that this would be the ultimate satisfaction to those who had pitted themselves against me. How they would love to see Jim Wright broken in spirit! So I kept busy during the day, and then went home to Betty, who understandably was still quite shaken over all that had occurred. Remember, she had been attacked in all this, too. One of Phelan's arguments was, this intelligent, capable woman was not deserving of a fifteen-hundred-dollar monthly salary from our business with the Mallicks!"

Wright was able to see his grown children often, and his grandchildren, though some of them were grown, too. On weekends he cultivated flowers, went on fishing trips, and even watched television. He and Betty were able to live comfortably on his government pension, and he began investing in various businesses and stocks. He assiduously avoided the most obvious opportunities to become wealthy. Wright was inundated by job offers from lobbyist groups and businesses seeking government contracts. Having the former Speaker as a spokesman would have been a coup for any of them, and they offered Wright six-figure annual salaries. He turned them all down.

"I just don't feel it's appropriate for someone who has been Speaker to afterwards approach former colleagues on behalf of someone who would benefit from certain legislation," Wright says. "I don't fault other former members of the House who have done that, but none of them had been Speaker. That's a special honor and responsibility."

And always, Wright followed the news. What he saw, heard, and read often appalled him. He had hoped his final address to Congress might have mitigated the atmosphere of nasty, name-calling partisanship, but it only got worse. As a reward for ridding them of Wright, Newt Gingrich was promoted by Republicans to minority whip. That hurt Wright, though he wouldn't admit it even to close friends. There was further electoral pain: eventually, even Wright's beloved 12th District elected a Republican as its congressional representative.

Two years into his Gingrich-imposed retirement, Wright noticed that small lump under his tongue. In Washington, Wright always considered himself too busy to pay attention to potential ailments. But Wright's Fort Worth schedule allowed time for a visit to the doctor. Cancer was diagnosed, and about a fifth of his tongue was surgically removed. Postoperative radiation treatments followed, then speech therapy. Wright approached the ordeal the same way he'd guided legislation through Congress. He studied each step, determined what had to be done, and did it. In an odd way, he found the process comforting. Cancer, like political opponents, offered the chance for a spirited fight. This was a big battle, and Wright's competitive instincts were fully aroused. It was even a way to somewhat restore his reputation. For the first time since he'd left Washington, there were national news reports about Jim Wright, and he was quoted in them as being optimistic about beating cancer. Here, the media reported, was a man who had every right to be despondent, and, instead, he was courageously, even cheerfully, getting on with his life. Take that, Gingrich! Jim Wright was back in control of his own story.

Still, in private Wright had to battle not to obsess over political might-have-beens, especially in 1992, when Democrat Bill Clinton defeated Republican incumbent George H. W. Bush. Wright watched enviously as Tom Foley, his successor as Speaker, got the chance Wright had wanted to work with a Democratic president. It didn't last long. In November 1994, the near-unthinkable happened. The Republicans won control of the House for the first time since 1952, and Gingrich was selected as Speaker. Wright, who so revered the office, had to adjust to it being occupied by someone he felt was totally unworthy. Worse, Gingrich immediately dominated the political and legislative scene even more than Wright once had, dictating to a president of the opposing party what Congress would and wouldn't approve. He crafted the headline-grabbing "Contract with America," a list of campaign promises endorsed by Republican congressional candidates. Clinton felt threatened enough to declare, "The president is still relevant," when Gingrich crowed that only legislation acceptable to the Republican majority would ever pass in Congress.

"I had to remind myself then that thinking about Gingrich would just be wasting my time," Wright says. "I could not allow that man the power to disrupt my serenity." Wright distracted himself by working on his book. *Balance of Power: Presidents and Congress from the Era of McCarthy to the Age of Gingrich* was published in 1996. In it, Wright combined personal anecdotes with special sections devoted to each president who'd served during his Washington tenure. He did not get around to the Gingrich-instigated investigation that led to his own downfall until page 481 of the 514-page book, and even then he limited the topic to ten pages, reserving the final two dozen for a sweeping essay on the ideal approaches to democratic government. "Politics is not a four-letter word," this section began. "It is not the name of a process inherently venal and corrupt. Politics is the art of living together, the science of operating a common country for the benefit of all." The book didn't sell particularly well, but Wright believed he'd at least offered common sense instead of partisanship and placed his own achievements and defeats in proper perspective.

WHEN NEWT GINGRICH'S OWN POLITICAL DOWNFALL CAME, IT eerily paralleled Jim Wright's. The problems started in 1994 with a book, *To Renew America,* a political manifesto proselytizing conservative philosophies. Amid great fanfare, HarperCollins announced it would publish the book and pay the new Speaker a whopping $4.5 million advance. But HarperCollins, Democrats pointed out, was owned by Australian business mogul Rupert Murdoch, who was pursuing new legislation in Congress to ease restrictions on the American media empire he was building. Stung, Gingrich negotiated a new contract: a $1 advance, plus an industry-standard 15-percent royalty on sales. Democrats in Congress, still smarting from the pain of suddenly becoming the minority party, realized that Gingrich, too, was vulnerable to accusations of improper behavior.

They started looking hard for more questionable actions by Gingrich and soon found something. By the end of 1996, the House Ethics Committee ruled that Gingrich had improperly used public money to fund partisan political activities and had provided false information to the committee during its investigation. Democrats, led by Bonior, clamored for a floor trial and subsequent censure. Gingrich avoided that by admitting he'd misled the committee. He paid a $300,000 fine.

About the same time, Gingrich twice led highly publicized temporary shutdowns of most government operations during long battles with the Clinton administration over budgetary issues. In 1998, he predicted huge gains for Republicans in the Senate and Congress as a result of President Clinton's sex scandal involving a White House intern, but Republicans came close to losing their House majority instead. Under pressure from his own party, Gingrich resigned as Speaker and from his seat in Congress.

"I fell back on my religious beliefs to avoid hating Gingrich, and I took no personal pleasure from his troubles," Wright claims now, though he smiles when he says it. "I was sad instead that, once again, the public perception of Congress and the office of Speaker were tainted by scandal. Let's say I love Congress far more than I dislike Newt Gingrich. My experiences since leaving office myself, the cancer mainly, offer me the perspective of appreciating my own blessings rather than begrudging happiness to others. All right, I may not wish Gingrich unlimited happiness, but I also do not wish him particular ill."

Driven from the Speaker's grandeur that he, too, loved, Gingrich has made a good living since. He's written more books, including a history-based novel in which the South wins the critical Civil War battle of Gettysburg instead of losing. He's also spent lots of on-camera time as a political commentator on cable television. Glib, quick-witted Jim Wright would have been a prime candidate for cable TV commentary, but his surgery-twisted visage and slurred speech mean he'll never get that opportunity. "I'm not much of a fan of those television and radio political talk shows, anyway," he says. "They're not meant to allow audiences to share thoughtful, informed debate. It's all shouting and name-calling. I'm glad not to be a part of that."

In the fifteen years since Gingrich drove Wright from power, the two have had only one instance of direct contact. While Gingrich was still Speaker, he was asked on a television broadcast why his issues before the ethics committee were any different from Wright's. He replied that Jim Wright was a crook.

Wright was livid. Though he never acknowledged it publicly, he wrote Gingrich a letter demanding an apology. Angry as he was, Wright couldn't help complimenting Gingrich in the same missive for rallying Republicans to finally take away the House majority from the Democrats: "That's leadership!" he wrote. Still, he wanted Gingrich to take back what he'd said.

Gingrich eventually replied. Wright kept the letter. On rare occasions, he'll show it to someone. Gingrich said that he had prayerfully considered how to respond, and he'd finally decided to promise Wright he would no longer make any public comments about him. That wasn't quite an apology, but Wright hadn't really expected one.

"So far as they can be, the issues between us are settled," he says. "We're done with each other."

AT EIGHTY-ONE, JIM WRIGHT STILL SPENDS WEEKDAYS IN HIS office, always wearing a suit to work. When he writes opinion pieces for the Fort Worth newspaper, he keeps his tone statesmanlike even when he's being critical of elected officials. One column suggesting President George W.

Bush should not have ordered the invasion of Iraq postulated that Bush was "not a knave, but naïve." Wright reads voraciously, sometimes three or four books at a time, mostly nonfiction. He's writing a children's book about his experiences in World War II. After that, he hopes to team with some former Republican colleague from Congress to coauthor an examination of campaign finance laws. "The public still doesn't realize the extent to which donors control candidates," Wright says. "This is the current greatest danger in politics. I want to address it, and if I write this book with a Republican it may be accepted by reasonable readers as bipartisan."

Wright hasn't become tranquil in his twilight years. The most innocuous question about the amount of his congressional pension (it's about $7,600 a month) elicits a hot-tempered response: Why ask such a thing? Who cares about an old man's finances? Where exactly is this question leading? The emotional scars from 1989 haven't entirely healed, and, despite Wright's best efforts, they never will. He's managed to suppress the memories, but he can't completely free himself of them.

Wright still gives speeches as often as possible. It's usually just a Lions club or a Sunday school class, but it's still a chance to be the center of attention. He's pragmatic enough about himself to realize he can't do without that. On increasingly rare occasions, there's an opportunity to speak to a wider audience. In late 2003 he was invited to address a national symposium on the history of Speakers of the House. His carefully prepared remarks focused on four major policy challenges he faced during his brief two-and-a-half-year tenure. Wright made no mention at all of the circumstances under which he resigned.

At his church on Sundays, in diners where he drops in for breakfast or lunch, Wright still retains his old politician's habit of treating everyone like a potential voter. Meeting Jim Wright today, you'll get the same treatment he gave new acquaintances when he was running for reelection to Congress: a handshake that's just firm enough, eyes locked on yours, questions about where you're from and what you're interested in until the perpetual candidate locks onto something you and he have in common. It might be a friend, a book you've both read, or simply delight in the current weather. But Wright will find *something* to forge a connection. The habit's too ingrained to break.

If he's changed at all from the man who was driven out as Speaker of the House, Wright says, it's in finally not obsessing over whether people *like* him. "I used to believe that if I worked hard enough, I could win anyone over," he says. "Now I realize that if someone wants to believe ill of me, there isn't anything I can do about it, though I would like ideally for them to at least respect me and recognize my sincerity of purpose. But that's impossible, and, after all that has happened, I've concluded it's futile to worry about it."

His main regret, Wright says, "is that when I was Speaker, when I was powerful and famous, call it what you like, I never let myself enjoy it. And so I regret that, though regret is useless. Friends would say, 'You're at the top of the heap. Go out and enjoy it. Just walk around the Capitol grounds. Smile.' But I had that conquer-the-entire-world-or-else, Alexander-the-Great syndrome, as so many so-called important people do. I always had to get up every day and do more than the day before, at peril of being bitterly unhappy with myself. And now, in some part because of that, here I am."

Had he remained Speaker, Wright believes, subsequent history would have been very different. "For instance, the impeachment of President Clinton," he muses. "Were I still Speaker then, I believe we would have avoided that." Of course, by the time Clinton was impeached, the Republicans had taken over as the majority party in Congress. Wright would have been minority leader rather than Speaker. "Well," he says, his surgically scarred face twisting into something approximating a disdainful grin, "had they not been able to remove me so publicly, thus gaining political momentum, if I had still been in place to keep them from passing certain of their legislation, perhaps they wouldn't have become the majority party after all and I would have been Speaker at that critical juncture. I will not speculate further. These are idle thoughts."

It would be wrong to assume Jim Wright views his life and career as a disappointment. "I try to be candid about my weaknesses and my mistakes, and that may be possible because I also recognize I did, in fact, try to use the power I attained for good," Wright says. "In the end, that is all anyone can do." His two last great challenges were to beat cancer, which he did, and to finally become happy, which might confound and frustrate his enemies. He did that, too.

In the twilight of his life, the man who so desperately wanted the approval of others has to let history say what it will about him. In the years since his exile from Washington and political power, Wright has thought about this a lot, what it was that drove him, what drives anyone whose success depends on making voters or audiences approve.

"People will remember me however they want to," Wright says. "I was a guy who wanted everyone to love me. I believe most politicians, most celebrities of any stripe, share that trait whether they acknowledge it or not. The more someone once well-known insists, 'I never cared about being famous,' well, that's the clue indicating just how much he did. To have fame or power and then to lose it is the equivalent of losing the approbation to which we have become addicted. It's a hard, hard thing to overcome. How well I know it! That constant seeking of approval—that's the essence of politics, and of fame."

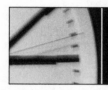

"The Gas Station Attendant"

The reasons to embrace the "Mormon will" were always romantic ones, which was why the media were quick to turn Melvin Dummar into a pop hero. People liked the idea of a "good deed" being rewarded. Plus, most of the other beneficiaries in the will were good causes. The list of problems with the will, however, was daunting. There were fifteen spelling errors in it, errors that were rarely duplicated in reams of memos written by Hughes at or near the same time the will was supposedly written in 1968. His aunt's family, with whom Hughes had lived as an adolescent, was incorrectly spelled "Lommis" instead of "Lummis." In life Hughes had shown little or no affinity for the universities listed in the will, or for the Boy Scouts, for that matter. Hughes hated the nickname The Spruce Goose and never used it; he didn't even own the famous military transport plane in 1968—the government did. (He would buy it from the government six years later.) And perhaps most significant, after thirty-two years as Hughes's right-hand man, Noah Dietrich had left Hughes's employment in 1957 on bad terms and never spoke with Hughes again. Why would Hughes name Dietrich, of all people, to be the will's executor?

"To those with more than a cursory knowledge of the world of Howard

Hughes, the will was shot through with incongruities," wrote James R. Phelan and Lewis Chester in *The Money: The Battle for Howard Hughes's Billions.* "Whatever his other oddities, Hughes in 1968 had a meticulous writing style and an expert grasp of legal terminology. He could recite dense passages of the tax laws and was not likely to bequeath a portion of his estate to such imprecise beneficiaries as 'the key men of the company's [*sic*] I own.'"

There were, on the other hand, those "oddities." Like spending literally days at a time sitting naked in a leather chair, watching the same movie over and over and over, not getting up even to move his bowels. Like writing pages and pages of memos to his aides, directing them in minute and preposterous detail on how to conduct their duties without bringing him into contact with germs. Like the ratty, crusty, unwashed beard obscuring his chin, mouth, and neck. Like the fact that when he had to urinate, he did so in jars, which were carefully labeled and stored on shelves, like they were a precious book collection.

Howard Hughes had been a dashing ladies' man, a fearless aviator and movie producer, and a businessman of unusual success. But in his later years, he was also barking mad—and insulated from proper medical treatment by his wealth and secretiveness. When the "Mormon will" was read to Noah Dietrich over the phone, Hughes's former right-hand man had dismissed it as a fraud. But when Dietrich saw a photocopy of the document, he immediately changed his mind; he knew Hughes's handwriting better than his own. As to why Hughes would turn to Dietrich in death when in life he had banished him, Dietrich speculated that Hughes had become sentimental as he saw his life inexorably slipping away. Hughes had been a teenager who had just inherited his father's tool company when he hired Dietrich, telling the then thirty-six-year-old CPA that his job description was simply to make him the richest man in the world. And Dietrich did it, making Hughes a multibillionaire, in large part—to Dietrich's way of thinking—in spite of Hughes, who squandered money making planes that didn't fly and movies no one wanted to see. Hughes, Dietrich believed, knew that the best days of his life, the most carefree and happy, were the ones where he relied so thoroughly on one Noah Dietrich for almost everything. Hughes, Dietrich said, "knew that I knew more about his business than anyone else did—a hell of a lot more than he did. He trusted me. He never trusted anyone else. He always respected my expertise in financial matters. He respected my ability and my integrity."

Besides, knowing Hughes as he had, it just made sense to Dietrich. "He came to hate those he depended on most, and he often taunted them by telling them he'd written a will out by hand, and that they would never find it. Two weeks before he died he told one of his aides, 'Don't bother to look for my will, you're never going to find it. It's safe. I've given it to someone I can trust.' But he never said who. He once mentioned the will in a memo, using almost the exact same words that appeared in the Mormon will."

From the very beginning, Dietrich recognized the obstacles to getting the will admitted into probate, chiefly the legal fight that was certain to come from the potential heirs in Hughes's family. But Dietrich was eighty-seven years old, and he viewed the will as his legacy. If it were declared valid, his reputation as the man who made Howard Hughes into one of the most powerful industrialists in history would be indisputable. For Dietrich, a cocky, fiercely competitive man down to his marrow, the risks in money and time were worth the potential payoff in recognition.

Dietrich's lawyer, however, wasn't so sure. Harold Rhoden was equally cocky and brilliant, but he had more practical concerns: avoiding professional humiliation. Rhoden later admitted that when Dietrich called to tell him the handwriting was legit, he wondered if his client had slipped the bonds of sanity just as Hughes had. This "will" was clearly a fake, he thought. It was handwritten "in chicken scratch," it left millions of dollars to a gas station operator named Melvin Du Mar, and it was found at the Mormon Church headquarters in Salt Lake City, not far from where this Du Mar fellow, a Mormon, lived. "Gee, do you think there was any connection?" he remembered thinking. But then Rhoden—the professional cynic, the hard case, the guy who looked for all the angles—saw Melvin in action.

In his memoir, *High Stakes,* Rhoden recalled that a day after Dietrich asked him to take on what promised to be a spirited probate fight with an opponent that had nearly unlimited resources, he and colleague Stanley Fairfield turned on the TV in his office and happened upon Melvin on the six-o'clock news. Rhoden felt the air in the room bunch up in his lungs as he got his first look at the flat, featureless face of Melvin Dummar, a plain workshirt open at the collar, bulbous gut hanging over his belt. "The gas station attendant," as Rhoden always thought of him, was thirty-one years old but looked like a baby. In a nasal drawl Melvin announced to the camera that he was "awful upset" about everything that was happening.

How did he know Hughes? Melvin was asked.

"Well, I was drivin' down from Tonopah to L.A. an' I seen this old man. I thought he was a bum or somethin'. I gave him a ride an' dropped him off in Las Vegas. An' when he got out, he asked me if I could loan him any money, an' I gave him a quarter. He said his name was Howard Hughes. I din't believe him at the time. But I guess it really musta been him."

The reporter asked, "That was your only connection with Howard Hughes?"

"Uh-huh."

Fairfield, who Rhoden had just recruited to join the cause, stared at the TV as if he were about to throw up. "What the fuck was that?" he blanched.

Rhoden told him not to panic, but Fairfield was already rethinking joining the case. "Hughes left a hundred and fifty million bucks to this kid? For having done *what*?" Fairfield moaned. "Oh, no!"

But for Rhoden, the performance he'd just seen was strangely comforting. He would later explain that it was while watching that scene—silly, fat Melvin, skittish and excited and overwrought, surrounded by reporters and local rubes, a rusting old gas pump behind him—that he realized why he was right to take on this case.

"The reporters had flocked to his gas station in little Willard, Utah, to ask him how he knew Hughes, and I sat and watched Melvin tell the preposterous story," he recalled in *Melvin and Howard: A Nevada Fairy Tale*. "I watched his little eyes drip tears down his chubby cheeks as he told of tossing Hughes a quarter—Melvin's investment in his first hundred and fifty million—and I told a colleague that if the Mormon will were a forgery, Melvin Dummar would have had to have been in on it and that that would have been simply impossible. Why? I was asked. Because Melvin Dummar, I said, is just too dumb. Too dumb to have forged the will, and too dumb for any self-respecting forger to use as a frontman. It was, as I think back now, at that moment that the most frequent and convincing defense of the Mormon will was launched. It was so unbelievable, it had to be true."

This did, in fact, become the cornerstone of Rhoden's defense of the will, which the opposing lawyers sneeringly referred to as the "Rhoden doctrine of immaculate conception." In short, this doctrine held that whatever evidence there was of the will being a fraud only made the will more likely to be authentic. To wit, the ridiculous spelling and factual mistakes in the will. Though each side ultimately found plenty of handwriting experts willing to do their heavy lifting on whether Hughes wrote the Mormon will, there was no denying that the handwriting was strikingly similar to that of documents known to have been written by Hughes. So if the will were forged, went Rhoden's reasoning, it would have taken a great deal of study and talent to capture Hughes's writing quirks so well, especially over three pages. Wouldn't any forger that careful and thorough also have taken the time to check his spelling ("revolk") and some basic facts (such as whether Hughes owned The Spruce Goose in 1968)?

Rhoden, who died in a private plane crash in 1989, quickly bolstered the skeleton of his case by digging up a possible medical reason for Hughes misspelling simple words: a long-term kidney ailment. Hughes's kidneys, he argued, didn't properly dispose of wastes. The resulting uremic poisoning, which would eventually cause Hughes's death, could seriously damage the mind as well as the body and could affect basic mental and motor skills, such as writing and spelling. With such an ailment, some neurologists agreed, it was reasonable to believe that one might spell a simple word correctly in one place and incorrectly just a few sentences later (such as "among/amoung," among other examples, in the Mormon will).

But Rhoden would come upon much more compelling evidence than that. In fact, what Rhoden had initially thought was an unwinnable case was, after a few months' work, looking surprisingly strong. For starters, the FBI established that the will was written with a type of Paper Mate ink that had been discontinued in 1972. Rhoden discovered that Hughes, obsessive in everything he did, used only Paper Mate pens in 1968. Specifically, Paper Mate's formula 307 with PAGO dye. In 1968, there were some three *thousand* different types of ink in the marketplace, but the ink used for the will was exactly the kind Hughes exclusively used: Paper Mate's formula 307 with PAGO dye. "It turns out Hughes's aides bought him Paper Mate pens by the box load; it's all he ever used," Rhoden argued. "In a market that had three thousand pen inks in use, the odds of a forger picking precisely the right ink for 1968 seemed staggering."

Furthermore, there was a Pitney Bowes postal-machine imprint on the envelope that contained the will. It showed LAS VEGAS NEV and MAR for March. The day and the year were not visible, nor the serial number of the machine, but the envelope showed a stamp charge of six cents, the price of a first-class stamp in 1968. In 1976, it was thirteen cents.

The team contesting the will argued that Melvin forged the will in April 1976, after news reports that Hughes might have died intestate. But Melvin, busy running his gas station and taking evening college classes, never left Utah that month. "How would he have gotten the six-cent Nevada postmark?" asks Gary Magnesen, whose private investigation into the case in 2001 led him to believe that Melvin had nothing to do with the creation of the will. "I think it's impossible. I don't think there's any way he could have done it."

Then there was the basic storyline question: If Melvin was telling the truth, what was Hughes doing out in the desert? Melvin maintained that the old man in his car never answered when asked what he was doing out there. The lawyers opposing the will jumped on that claim as proof of Melvin's ineptitude as a criminal. On top of that, Hughes's personal aides would argue that Hughes didn't answer Melvin because Hughes wasn't there. They said they monitored their boss twenty-four hours a day, and that in December 1967, Hughes never left the Desert Inn in Las Vegas, which he owned.

Except Rhoden didn't believe that. Yes, Hughes was a sick, crazy old man who entered the Desert Inn hotel and casino on a stretcher when he took up residence there in 1966 and who left the same way four years later. But if

Hughes's life history proved anything, it was that as much as he hated germs, he loved intrigue. Rhoden had discovered memos written by Hughes, among other evidence, that he believed proved that Hughes often sneaked out of the Desert Inn, usually with the help of an aide named Howard Eckersley. "I feel better doing something highly secret like this when Howard is on and it is at night," Hughes wrote in one memo. Rhoden believed he could prove that the "something highly secret" to which Hughes referred was in fact a field trip to the western Nevada desert.

There was just one problem with all this, a problem that Rhoden was about to discover he had significantly underestimated. It was time for him to meet "the gas station attendant."

THE LAWYERS REPRESENTING THE POTENTIAL HUGHES FAMILY heirs planned to take Melvin's sworn deposition on December 7, 1976. Rhoden recognized the possible disaster such a deposition could be and decided to preempt it. He couldn't imagine how this sad, simple gas station attendant could forge a will that would fool Noah Dietrich, but he couldn't outright dismiss it as a possibility. And if anyone was going to catch Melvin Dummar out in a lie, Rhoden wanted it to be him. After all, few had more at stake than he had. The lawyer had already put aside his private law practice and taken on large-scale personal debt to devote himself exclusively to investigating the will over the past nine months. Now, before it went any further, he wanted to make sure this Dummar character wasn't going to be the weak link.

Rhoden had no doubt he was up to the task—or any task, for that matter. The Chicago native had been a B-24 tail gunner in World War II and spent a year as a POW in Nazi Germany. Anyone who knew Rhoden, or had looked down the gun sights of his contemptuous stare, could be easily convinced that the Nazis had quit the war simply to get away from him. At fifty-four years of age, the former Los Angeles deputy district attorney had a head full of heavy, gray-black hair that almost seemed to clank when he walked. He had deep, crisscrossing creases in his cheeks, like he folded up his face and put it away each night, and he stood stock straight, his barrel chest heaving with each breath. Meeting Melvin for the first time a couple days before the deposition, he was not impressed. In his 1980 memoir, Rhoden wrote: "Melvin sat back tensed in the center chair in front of my desk, and as I lit my pipe, I looked at this boyish blob of blubber and thought, 'If this hick thinks he can lie to me, he's crazy.'"

Rhoden's plan was simple: using his skills as an interrogator, he would intimidate and pressure Melvin until he was certain that his witness was telling all he knew—and *only* what he knew. Having warned Roger Dutson what he was going to do, he lit into Melvin almost as soon as he walked in the door with his lawyer. "Now, listen carefully!" he recalled telling Melvin, snapping him upright in his seat. "If this will is a fake and you tell us today when and where and how it was written, and by whom, so that this case can end without the waste of any more time or money or energy, especially mine, I'll inform the court that you've repented, and I promise you'll get straight probation. What about it?"

Rhoden sucked on his pipe, allowing that to sink in. "What's your answer?" he demanded.

Melvin blinked at him. "To what?"

"Are you ready to confess?"

"To what?"

Rhoden began to realize what he was dealing with. Melvin Dummar might be even more of a dumb bunny than he'd thought, which he found encouraging. He slowly walked Melvin through his—and everyone else's—doubts. In the end, he said, it came down to this: If Melvin Dummar, gas station attendant in Bumbleweeds, Utah, never met billionaire industrialist Howard Hughes, the will had to be a forgery. "Did you pick up Howard Hughes in the desert and give him a ride to Las Vegas?"

"The old man I picked up said his name was Howard Hughes, but I didn't think it was him," Melvin said.

"You never had any other contact in your life with Howard Hughes?"

"No."

"If Howard Hughes wasn't the old man you picked up in the desert, Howard Hughes would never have known your name, would he?"

"I don't see how he could've. Who would've told him my name?"

Melvin asked the question as if he really thought Rhoden might know, and the dumb act was starting to bother the lawyer. He stepped up his interrogation, telling Melvin he didn't believe his story and pressing him on every detail, telling him he would rot in jail if he was lying.

Through all of it, the dumb act never wavered, and Rhoden went home that night confident that the gas station attendant's story was ridiculous but was going to hold up.

He was wrong. The opposing lawyers knew something that Melvin, and Rhoden, did not know: Melvin's thumbprint had been found on the envelope that contained the will. Without tipping their hand, they eased into their questioning at the deposition on December 7.

> Q: Do you, as of today, Mr. Dummar, have any idea how this purported will ended up on the desk of one of the Mormon Church employees on the twenty-fifth floor of the church office building headquarters?
>
> A: No.
>
> Q: You had nothing to do with getting the will there?
>
> A: No.
>
> Q: You never had your hand on this outside envelope?
>
> A: No.

They had him, and they knew it—and soon everyone else would know it. (They had also discovered that Melvin's fingerprints were on a Utah library book that included a photograph of a letter written by Hughes, which was how they believed Melvin learned to mimic Hughes's handwriting.)

Finally, faced with the evidence, he broke down and confessed to Rhoden in early January that he'd been lying all along. He had found the will at his gas station and took it to the Mormon Church himself. He said he hadn't told the truth because, quite simply, he didn't think anyone would believe him.

Rhoden seethed with anger at the "miserable, sniveling liar." He hadn't had the resources to do the kind of digging the other side had done. He counted instead on his ability to judge character and had been humiliated. He now told Melvin it was over; he wasn't getting a dime of Hughes's money. In fact, there would be a court hearing on January 25, and this time Melvin was sure to be arrested for forgery and perjury. If he wanted any chance at leniency he had better own up to everything right now. Rhoden leaned in to Melvin and jabbed at him with a stubby finger. It was time to spit it out, he said. He wanted a full confession; getting it might save Melvin from jail time, and it would also help repair Rhoden's reputation and, just maybe, lead to good-faith fees from the court that would help him recoup some of his expenses. At this point, with Melvin distraught, he fully expected him to confess all, including giving up his accomplices. But Melvin had nothing more to add. Someone left the will at his gas station, and he had taken it to the church headquarters—that was what he had lied about, he said. He started to insist again that everything else he had said over the past nine months was true, that he had just done an old man a good turn and now look where he was, when Rhoden erupted in frustration. With spittle flying, he demanded that Melvin fess up. Instead, Melvin came apart. He tried to deny again that he was a forger, but his voice broke and the tears came. He wept openly, uncontrollably, "scared to death," Melvin admits, scared he was going to prison for the rest of his life.

And the strangest thing happened: Rhoden believed him. This simple man—this "gentle dunce," as the lawyer would later describe Melvin to a jury—had no more defenses. He'd been found out and he knew it. He would have confessed all, Rhoden believed, all there was to tell and then more. Instead, he just bawled, not from guilt and despair but from self-pity. "With that kind of anguish," Rhoden thought, "how could he be lying?"

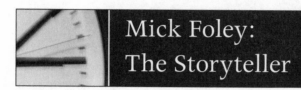

Mick Foley:
The Storyteller

In late May 2003, organizers convened a press conference in Glen Cove, New York, to promote the "Summer of 2004 Long Island Festival of Books." Local media were invited to meet some area authors who'd be participating. Three camera crews from Long Island TV stations were on hand, as well as a half-dozen print and radio reporters. The event, for some unexplained reason, was being held at Glen Cove's Marquis Care Center, a rehabilitation facility for upscale clients. The press conference was in the center's expansive recreation room. A few patients in robes lolled on overstuffed chairs. Some high school students, invited to cover the program for their school papers, clustered in a corner with handheld video games and cell phones.

Then there were the authors, gathered loosely near the podium where they would be asked to speak. The eight men and women represented an interesting literary mix. Nelson DeMille could legitimately be described as well known. His shoot-'em-up novels regularly made national best-seller lists. All but one of the others were crafters of decent fiction and nonfiction whose fame was mostly limited to family and just enough readers to justify publishers continuing to print their books on a regular basis. (Publishing-industry insiders doubt more than a few hundred American authors actually generate enough income from book sales to fully support themselves. Most need day jobs.)

Then there was a bulky man in his late thirties who wore black jeans, a blue shirt, and a wide tie decorated with snowmen and, in one corner, a carrot-chomping Bugs Bunny. His tentlike black suit jacket was baggy, an amazing thing since his upper body was so thick. His lower body—thighs and seat—was even thicker. But he moved with a near-nimbleness that belied his bulk. The fellow wore a scraggly moustache and goatee; his dark, curly hair almost touched his collar and hung long on the sides, though sometimes when he moved, his hair swung just enough to reveal he had only a lumpy stump where his right ear should have been. There was about him the same sense of gentle power found in any big man who is acting nice even though he could clearly beat up anyone in the room.

Finally, a grinning middle-aged man walked to the podium, fiddled with the microphone, and asked for everyone's attention. The reporters dutifully got out their notebooks, the TV cameramen focused, and the authors formed a crooked line. Master of ceremonies Larry Davidson ("local radio and cable television host," according to the press handout) identified Walt Whitman and F. Scott Fitzgerald as "Long Island writers," and then segued into introducing the authors in attendance by suggesting they were Whitman's and Fitzgerald's logical literary heirs. Then Davidson asked each of the authors to make brief comments. All of them, he emphasized, would take part in festival programs during 2004. Meanwhile—Nelson DeMille!

DeMille, a veteran of such events, managed to seem charming and emotionally removed at the same time. The next few authors were clearly nervous, stumbling over words, awkward in making any kind of public appearance.

Davidson, though, introduced each as though he were announcing the winner of the Pulitzer Prize. His tone of grandiose awe flagged only when it was time to introduce the bearded, bulky man, who'd offered his complete attention to each of the other writers as they'd bumbled at the microphone before resuming their original places in the line of authors to the right of the podium.

"Okay," Davidson said, waving his arm at the authors. "Guess which one is the wrestler? Writers come from the strangest places, including the wrestling ring. Mick Foley."

The thirty-eight-year-old Foley, whose first two full-length books, both autobiographies, had reached number one on the *New York Times* best-seller list, flashed a warm smile as he stepped forward. As he smiled, it was obvious to the suddenly interested crowd that, besides an ear, he was missing two front teeth. And there *was* crowd interest. The TV crews maneuvered for better camera angles, the radio reporters thrust microphones forward, the print journalists opened the notepads they'd closed after jotting down De-Mille's innocuous remarks. Even the high school kids put down their cell phones and Game Boys.

"I'm really flattered to be here with so many great writers like Nelson DeMille," Foley began. "I was a wrestler who took too many shots to the head, so don't take anything I say seriously. I really didn't know so many writers of this magnitude were going to be here. I'm flattered to be asked to join them."

Foley could have pointed out that his first two books probably sold more copies (almost two million) than all the other authors' books put together, with the exception of DeMille's. He could have snarled at Davidson for his condescending introduction. But he genuinely *was* honored to participate, having retired from wrestling to concentrate full time on writing. "I hope people start seeing me more as a writer than a wrestler," he'd said on the drive over to the Marquis Center. "I know it'll take a while." And though he really wanted everyone's focus to be on his first novel, *Tietam Brown*, which would be published in two more months, Foley was also happy to be remembered for his sixteen years in wrestling rings. "I worked hard to become a well-known wrestler," he pointed out during the drive. "It wouldn't make sense for me to have done it if, all of a sudden, I wanted people to forget I had."

So Foley, looking remarkably youthful for someone who'd spent sixteen

Mick Foley and his family at one of their
favorite vacation spots, Disney World.

years launching his body from great heights onto opponents and, often and deliberately, unforgiving steel and concrete, spent the first of his limited moments at the press conference joshing a little about his wrestling background and emphasizing his pleasure at being in the company of authors Foley and everyone else present realized were much less famous than he. As a rookie wrestler, Foley gladly gave pride of place to older veterans whose time on the job, if nothing else, convinced him they deserved his respect and even deference. He was bringing the same attitude to writing.

Still, he was also proud of his novel *Tietam Brown*, an often violent, sometimes tender tale of a teenaged boy struggling to grow up under horrifying circumstances, and the press conference was one more way, albeit a minor one, to publicize it. Again, his wrestling background helped. Working his way up the professional wrestling ladder, Foley earned an early reputation as someone who tried just as hard to provide entertaining matches for crowds of twenty-five as he did for audiences numbering in the thousands. No matter what the wrestling or writing circumstances, anyone who comes out to see him is entitled, in Foley's mind, to the best he can do.

So, having given proper credit to others, he moved on at the press conference to himself and his new book. "I've done a couple of autobiographies," he noted, and, as he did, one of the high school kids muttered, "Mankind! Yeah!" just loud enough for everyone to hear, and Foley, who during his previous career *had* been known as Mankind—and as Cactus Jack and as Dude Love before finally wrestling his last few matches in 2000 under his real name—nodded in appreciation rather than, as many Speakers would have, glaring or becoming disconcerted because of the interruption.

"Anyway, I woke up one morning and decided I wanted to become America's best-loved author of children's books," Foley continued, not adding that *Mick Foley's Christmas Chaos* and *Mick Foley's Halloween Hijinx*, his two ventures into the genre, were also best sellers in that literary category. "My first two autobiography books had pretty much, I think, exhausted everyone's interest in my own story. I'm going to have a new book, a novel for adults, coming out soon. It's called *Tietam Brown*. I'm hoping with the new book, readers will get past the guy who for sixteen years pretended to beat people up for a living."

Before he could say more Davidson moved toward the podium, a signal that Foley needed to conclude his remarks even though, for the first time in the thirty-minute program, everyone there finally seemed to be interested in one of the Speakers. So Foley good-naturedly waved, said, "Thanks for inviting me," and took his place back with the other writers. Davidson then invited the press to interview "these wonderful, talented, Long Island writers whose books please us all so much." Two reporters briefly spoke to De-Mille before joining the rest of their media peers clustered around Foley. He said over and over that it was nice, for a change, to do something that didn't hurt his body. Yes, he believed reading was important, and he was pleased to be a part of the book festival. Sure, he missed wrestling a little. In his new novel, *Tietam Brown*— No, he didn't think wrestling was terrible for kids to watch. And if teenagers read his new book, they'd see— Yes, he missed wrestling sometimes, but he was a full-time writer now. No, he wasn't sure if he'd do anything in wrestling again. And about *Tietam Brown* . . .

At that point all the reporters had their sound bites about the writing wrestler, emphasis on *wrestler*, and began to drift away. One did begin asking Foley specific questions about his new book, but she was interrupted by a middle-aged woman from the Marquis Center staff who rushed up and blurted, "You were Mankind! I've seen you on TV! My God!" The woman had a Polaroid camera. She asked Foley to pose for a picture with her, so she could prove to her son ("He's nuts about wrestling; he watches your crazy stuff all the time") she'd met him. Without a glimmer of reluctance, Foley put his arm around her, smiled, and waited while someone else pressed the camera's button, and the flash didn't go off, so he had to wait while another shot was taken, and, since the flash worked this time, he had to wait another minute while the picture was developed, so he could autograph the photo. After that, a wave of about twenty nurses and janitors who worked at the center descended on Foley. They had cameras, too, more Polaroids in one place than at a camera factory, and everybody wanted a picture with Mankind, several of the men asking Foley to adopt fighting stances with them, faking headlocks or jabs. He accommodated them all, telling each one it was nice to meet him or her, never seeming upset that nobody was talking about his new novel anymore, and it was surprising to realize that at some point, smiling and posing all the while, Foley had begun moving slowly but steadily toward the main door, not giving the impression that he was eager to leave but still gradually freeing himself. Finally he made it outside, hustling to his car, but before he got in one more staffer from the center came galloping up, explaining she'd wanted to go to the press conference but she'd been busy with a patient, and it was her husband's birthday that weekend. Could Mr. Foley pose for a Polaroid? "Sure." Could he sign it to her husband? "Happy to. What's his name?" And, well, if Mr. Foley really did live on Long Island and he wasn't doing anything on Saturday afternoon, would he come to the birthday party? Because her husband would just be thrilled. "I wish I could. I've got this thing with my family. But tell him I wish him a happy birthday." By the time Foley drove away, he'd spent thirty minutes as part of the press conference and forty-five more making his way out of the center after it. During that time, he'd been able to mention *Tietam Brown* perhaps half a dozen times and never for more than a moment or two.

"Well, that's sort of what I expected," Foley said, driving cautiously out of Glen Cove, heading for his home in a nearby suburb. "Look, if I think people are idiots for only thinking of me as a wrestler, then I'm an idiot for spending sixteen years trying to make them recognize me as one. What I'm hoping is that people who never watch wrestling, who never heard of Mankind or Cactus Jack or read my first two books, will read this one and love it because of the story it tells. If they'll keep open minds, not have a prejudice against it because some wrestler wrote it, I think they'll say, hey, this guy can tell a really good story.

"And I can, because in that way wrestling and writing novels are exactly the same. You tell a story that pulls in the audience so they forget something's made up instead of real. I expect critics to say I don't have any credentials to write novels, that I somehow haven't paid any dues. Listen, I spent sixteen years in wrestling trying to become a good storyteller, and I did. I know how to communicate. I hate people thinking I only got a chance to write this book because I'm a famous wrestler instead of a real writer. I *earned* this contract to write a novel."

For the first time, he sounds resentful.

IN THE BACK ROOM OF AN ITALIAN RESTAURANT, SEATED THERE AT the suggestion of the owner "so won't nobody bother you" (right after he asked for an autograph for his father), Mick Foley is talking about the first time he felt a little like a celebrity.

"It was, I guess, in '89, when I wrestled for a promotion based in Dallas, Texas, and after I'd been a wrestler for about three years," Foley says, pausing to be certain about the dates while he bites into a kite-sized wedge of pizza. He always takes an extra moment to get times and places and people's names right. Toward the end of his wrestling career, after all the dives from the ring onto concrete gymnasium and auditorium floors that resulted in countless concussions, plus literally thousands of "chair shots"—metal folding chairs smacked by opponents against his head as part of match histrionics—Foley began having some trouble remembering little details. The problem has cleared up since he retired, but he's still in the habit of double-checking himself.

"Anyway, there had been a video of me that had aired on that promotion's regional TV stations for a few weeks before I got there," Foley continues. "I got to Dallas, had my first couple of matches, and then I'd drive down the street and people would look and point. It was the first time I'd gotten recognized and I felt fairly famous. I liked it. As a wrestler in those days when there were dozens of little territories for individual promotions, unlike the way it is now with just one big organization—World Wrestling Entertainment that puts all its wrestlers on national TV and makes them instant stars—you'd come into a new territory and start judging the level of your success there by how often local people noticed you. My big thing in those early days of my career was to go to a Waffle House—that's where I'd eat, because it was cheap and I wasn't making much money—and see if anybody there knew who I was."

Usually, the response from fans in the Waffle House was enjoyable. They'd ask for autographs from the man who was then calling himself Cactus Jack. Once in a while, it got scary.

"I remember going into a Waffle House later on when I was working for World Championship Wrestling in Atlanta," Foley says. "I was making a little more money then, but I still ate at Waffle Houses because I had a very justified reputation as one of the cheapest wrestlers ever. Anyway, I went in and this guy came up and said, 'I want you to *kill* Vader [a gargantuan 400-pounder whom Foley was wrestling in a series of matches],' and he meant it. He really hoped Cactus Jack would kill Vader. And I thought to myself, 'This is not the reaction I want to be getting.'"

But a drawback of celebrity is that it is the fans rather than the famous who determine the nature of their reactions. Foley, of course, knew he and Vader (real name Leon White, a former college football player) were simply providing a bit of rough-and-tumble entertainment for people who liked to temporarily forget their problems by indulging in what some scholar once called "willing suspension of disbelief." But the Waffle House fan was certain Vader deserved to die and Cactus Jack might really kill him. And he believed it because, as Cactus Jack, Mick Foley did such a good job pretending to hurt people and be hurt by them, though in the latter instance he often wasn't pretending. Common sense on the part of everyone he tried to entertain was something Foley couldn't guarantee. Common sense, too often, is the missing element on one or both sides in the star/fan give-and-take known as fame.

Still, up until June 1998, when he'd been a wrestler for twelve years, Mick Foley's fame was of modest proportions. Dedicated wrestling fans—the ones who watched all the free shows on TV and who often paid about thirty dollars for monthly pay-per-views that actually showed the much-anticipated matches that were teased, but not delivered, by free TV—knew that Cactus Jack of World Class Wrestling had morphed into Mankind of the World Wrestling Federation. Cactus Jack/Mankind had never really been more than an "upper midcard heel," wrestling jargon for a bad guy who wasn't quite popular enough to participate in many main events. That severely limited Foley's income; main eventers like Hulk Hogan, Ric Flair, Stone Cold Steve Austin, and the Rock were the only ones who might eventually retire from wrestling as millionaires. Upper midcard heels could earn $150,000 a year, but that figure is deceptive. Wrestlers must pay most of their own travel expenses when they crisscross the country for shows. Few are provided with health insurance. All of them need frequent time off to heal from injuries, and many aren't paid by promoters when they physically can't wrestle.

But in June 1998, Foley reluctantly participated in a pay-per-view match that became one of the most talked-about in wrestling history. A year later, executives of the World Wrestling Federation decided they'd try to capitalize on an upswing in public interest by publishing ghost-written autobiographies of three of the promotion's wrestlers, two featuring unquestioned superstars and one "written" by a popular, but clearly second-rung, grappler.

And on these two things Mick Foley's life turned. Five years later, he was still trying to gain some control over the unexpected fame they brought him.

MICK FOLEY USUALLY LOOKED FORWARD TO HIS MATCHES, GET-
ting out in front of fans and making them cheer or boo but always react to the
story he and his opponent were telling with their bodies and facial expressions. But one night in June 1998 he wished he never had to leave the dressing room.

In a cultural era when evermore extreme violence was accepted, even expected, as part of mainstream entertainment, professional wrestling had
moved far beyond its early days on TV in the '50s, when announcers would
snap matchsticks to make it sound like bones were cracking in the ring. Almost any 1998 video game featured characters that would fly through the air,
pound opponents, and make blood splatter. Movies routinely contained the
sort of graphic, special-effects-driven carnage that would have been unthinkable just decades earlier. That sort of gory spectacle was what pro
wrestling was now competing against, so wrestlers ramped up their blood
spilling accordingly, especially in monthly shows when viewers were expected to pay as much as thirty-five to fifty dollars to watch the programs in
the comfort of their living rooms.

King of the Ring was one of the World Wrestling Federation's premier
annual pay-per-view events. Earlier, Foley—wrestling as Mankind, a de-
ranged killer who wears a leather-and-metal face mask modeled after Hannibal Lecter's in *The Silence of the Lambs* (pro-wrestling "characters" often
mimic current pop culture)—had been told he would headline 1998's *King of
the Ring* against Stone Cold Steve Austin, the current WWF champion and
its most popular wrestler. In every way, that was a good thing for Foley. He'd
be paid more for headlining the card; because he was wrestling Austin, the
crowd would be even more excited by what it witnessed than usual; and the
match would be a showcase that would help reignite fan interest in the character of Mankind.

After two years of wrestling in the WWF as Mankind, Foley felt audiences were getting tired of the character. Try as he might, throwing his body
off ring ropes onto concrete floors, deliberately cutting himself so the result-

ing blood would help "sell" the fans that the action they were seeing might be real, using all the violent tricks he'd learned over twelve long years, appearing for a few months as Cactus Jack (a shaggy brawler) and Dude Love (a cowardly hippie) instead, there just didn't seem to be any way Foley could keep his current masked-man gimmick fresh. And, if WWF owner Vince McMahon decided fans had lost interest in Foley, he wouldn't hesitate to get rid of him. Foley had a family to support, and being fired from the WWF would mean a dramatic drop in income. So he was prepared to do anything—anything—in the Austin match to thrill fans and regain enough popularity to ensure his place in the WWF.

Except that, a few weeks before *King of the Ring*, WWF executives informed Foley he wouldn't be wrestling Steve Austin after all. They'd decided a main event between Austin and a wrestler called Kane, a fresher villain to tangle with the fans' ultimate hero, would draw a bigger pay-per-view audience. Foley was informed he'd wrestle instead a longtime WWF icon known as the Undertaker. There had already been a long series of Mankind/Undertaker matches, and Foley's stomach lurched. He believed fans had already seen too many of those. They'd be bored by the match at *King of the Ring*, and their resulting apathy might cost Foley his job.

The WWF "booking committee"—staff who met in advance to plan who would win and would lose each match and how—tried to spice up Undertaker/Mankind by designating it as a "Hell in a Cell" contest, a concept used only once before in the promotion's history. A sixteen-foot-high cage would be placed around the ring. It would extend its hard wire mesh frame over the top of the ring, too. In theory, the gigantic roofed cage would prevent either wrestler from fleeing if his opponent began getting the upper hand. As the designated heel, Mankind would be deprived of cowardly retreat, a routine villain's strategy in the world of professional wrestling.

Foley started thinking: What could he and his opponent bring to the match that would utilize the "cell" in some unexpected way to thrill fans? The Undertaker, a hulking Texan named Mark Callaway, had participated in the first "Hell" match, throwing his opponent repeatedly into the steel mesh. Blood spurted everywhere. Foley couldn't use his traditional techniques of "blading" (wrestling jargon for deliberately cutting yourself) and "bumping" (allowing yourself to be thrown around the ring) to unique effect because it had been done before. As always, Mick Foley wanted to take what pro wrestling fans expected and turn it into something much more extreme, much more entertaining.

Then, a new problem emerged. The Undertaker had a broken foot. This would have put any fan and most athletes completely out of action, but among pro wrestlers such an injury was simply something to be endured until it eventually healed. But for *King of the Ring*, the Undertaker wouldn't be able to move around much. Whatever wild action took place would have to be supplied by Mick Foley, and, inside that steel cage, what he could do with an immobile opponent was so limited that it would be impossible to deliver an entertaining match.

Except, Foley thought, there was no rule that said the action had to take place *inside* the cage. What if he and the Undertaker fought on top of it, some twenty feet above the concrete floor below, counting both the height of the cage and the elevation of the ring itself? And what if, for the first time in wrestling history, one of them "took a bump" that involved falling all the way from the top of the cage to the concrete? That action would, of course, guarantee injury, possibly severe, and between the two only Foley would even consider risking it. He'd deliberately fallen from lesser heights before, but had never attempted anything this dangerous and dramatic.

So, before the match, Foley sold the Undertaker on his risky plan. (Though the booking committee had mandated a win for the Undertaker, its members allowed the two veteran wrestlers to work out between themselves just how the match would play out.) They wouldn't start battling in the cell. They'd start on top of it, and fight there to a quick, spectacular conclusion that would leave the Undertaker victorious and Mankind popular—if he was able to wrestle again afterward.

"Before the match, fans were only interested in the gimmick rather than the wrestlers who'd be in it," recalls Rick Scaia, a longtime Internet wrestling writer whose popular *Online Onslaught* opinion columns appear three times each week on www.onlineonslaught.com. "But Mick was smart enough

By the time his name was familiar to wrestling fans
around the world, Foley had participated in every
imaginable form of bloodletting in the ring.

to realize two or three impossible spots [stunts] could leave those fans amazed,
wondering, 'God, is he dead?' and give them a sense there was a real guy out
there doing that, not a cartoon character called Mankind. Of course, he'd
have to live through it to enjoy that kind of response afterwards."

ON THE NIGHT OF KING OF THE RING, *MANKIND IS INTRODUCED
first. Foley, in keeping with the creepy nature of the character he is playing, scut-
tles out to the ring. He is greeted with a smattering of boos, and the lack of response indicates to him he's right; after two years, fans are bored with Mankind.*

*Instead of entering the ring through a door in the cage that is to be chained shut
after both participants are inside, Foley first tosses a metal folding chair up on top
of the cage, then begins to clamber up the side of the mesh himself. This is un-*

expected; the fans begin to buzz. Even the climb is tough on Foley. He weighs well over three hundred pounds, and hauling his bulk up chain link isn't easy. One of his fingers, pulling so hard against the metal, is numb for weeks afterward.

Foley makes it to the top. The mesh sags alarmingly under his weight, and this is before the six-foot-ten, three-hundred-pound Undertaker joins him up there. That doesn't take long. The house lights dim, the Undertaker's music plays, and there he is, climbing the cage quite nimbly for a behemoth with a broken foot, and for about two minutes he and Foley exchange "shots," some with fists and some with the chair, all with enough steam to flatten anyone without pro wrestling training in how to accept blows and return them. Then, as planned, the Undertaker grabs Foley's shirt—part of Mankind's unique look is to wrestle in white shirt and tie as well as the brown, sweat-stained mask—and throws him off of the top of the cage.

The idea is for Foley to half-flip in midair so he can land flat on his back and butt—the wide area of contact will cushion the overall blow. A complication is that, for spectacular visual purposes, he is to crash through one of the tables being used by announcers describing the action. This table has been "tricked" in advance to collapse when he hits it, somewhat lessening the still-dreadful impact. But Foley—flying through the air, trying to remember to turn his body to just the right angle—also has to somehow adjust his fall to avoid the TV monitors that rest on the table. These, being metal and glass, won't give.

Foley does miss them. The table smashes into pieces. The crowd gives a collective shriek. No one has ever seen such a thing, even in the colorful annals of pro wrestling. The WWF announcer describing the match on pay-per-view screams, "With God as my witness, he's been broken in half."

Not quite, but there is still considerable damage. Foley's left shoulder is dislocated on impact. A kidney is severely bruised—afterward there will be blood in his urine. The Undertaker balances on the top of the cage far above the carnage, staring down. As scripted, WWF staff race to ringside with a stretcher. Foley is gently rolled onto it. The fans, their lust for violent entertainment sated beyond any expectation, stand and gape as one. Afterward, Foley will remember them not making much noise and assume they weren't as impressed as he'd hoped, but Foley is wrong. For a few moments, the fans have been shocked into near-total silence. Then they begin to cheer. In just about 150 seconds, Mick Foley has pulled it off, a victory for the Undertaker that still makes the fans fall in love with Mankind all over again.

And then Foley takes it further. To the amazement of the fans, announcers, and even some fellow wrestlers who were in on the first part of the scripted action, Foley rolls off the stretcher and, dislocated shoulder and all, climbs the cage again to get back at the Undertaker. This is the "extra" the two combatants have planned. Having stunned the crowd already, they will combine to sacrifice more of Foley's physical well-being to extend an already amazing match into one wrestling fans will talk about forever.

Back on top of the cage, the two exchange punches. But the mesh is sagging, and they can't do much more on their precarious perch. So the Undertaker wraps one massive hand around Foley's throat, lifts him a few inches in the air, and slams him on his back against the mesh over the ring. The mesh tears through, and Foley falls sixteen feet straight down into the ring, crashing against the slightly springy canvas floor. The impact stuns him.

The metal folding chair had been discarded on top of the cage after the early moments of the match. Now, lying too close to where the mesh has given way, it tumbles down into the ring, landing squarely on Mick Foley's face as he lies flat on his back. The fall through the mesh has been planned; the fall of the chair hasn't. It crashes directly into Foley's mouth, knocking out some teeth, dislocating his jaw, and tearing a huge hole in his lower lip. Reflexively, he sticks his tongue in the hole, and his tongue extends right through to waggle in plain sight under his lip.

And still the match isn't over; Foley and the Undertaker have planned more. While Foley lies helpless, WWF staffers rush to the ring to minister to him. This gives the broken-footed Undertaker the chance to slowly climb down the side of the cage. He spends a few moments throwing staffers aside before finally turning his attention to his fallen opponent, who, suddenly, isn't fallen.

Foley knows the plan now involves a little more fighting before the Undertaker finally pins Mankind's shoulders for the traditional one-two-three referee count that ends matches. But his head has banged off the canvas, and he can't quite remember what is supposed to happen next. Worried, the Undertaker whis-

pers, "Let's go home," wrestle-speak for ending the match. But Foley vaguely re-calls what he is supposed to do, and hisses that he's okay.

Fans are astonished as Mankind staggers up and actually attacks the Under-taker, knocking him to the canvas. He writhes there for a few moments, giving Fo-ley extra time to clear his head as he, too, drops to the canvas. The camera crew focuses on Foley, and two odd things are apparent. One, he is smiling. Two, some-thing white is protruding from his nostril. A camera close-up reveals the near-impossible: it's a tooth. Foley has crashed down into the ring so hard that the force broke off one of his teeth and propelled it up and out his nasal cavity. And he is still wrestling.

Somehow, both men make it to their feet and spend a few minutes taking turns pounding each other. At one point, the Undertaker picks up the massive metal steps that lead to the ring and crashes them repeatedly into Foley's dislocated shoulder. His left arm dangles almost uselessly at his side. But he fights back, rak-

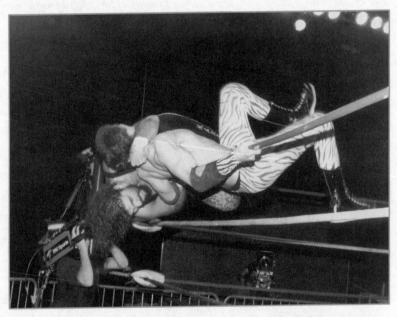

From the first bouts in his career, Foley gladly took
great physical risks to entertain his audiences.

ing the Undertaker's head against the steel mesh, and the Undertaker "blades,"
deliberately cutting his own forehead. Now Foley reaches under the ring and ex-
tracts a large bag, which he opens with a dramatic flourish before emptying its
shiny contents on the ring canvas. Thousands of thumbtacks scatter in a wide pool.
Earlier in his career, Foley had participated in so-called "thumbtack" matches,
where wrestlers were actually body-slammed onto the sharply pointed things.
Much of wrestling is, of course, pretend, but Foley has always heightened drama
by introducing "real" elements. Now he's doing it again.

The King of the Ring *plan, of course, never included the Undertaker being*
slammed into the thumbtacks. That kind of suffering is reserved for Mick Foley,
the man who has built his career on enduring such things for the entertainment of
the paying customers. Arm dislocated, jaw dislocated, kidney bruised, lower lip
torn, teeth knocked out, tooth sticking out his nostril, Mick Foley is picked up
twice and violently slammed into hundreds of tacks, which stick into his back and
neck and arms and face. The Undertaker picks him up, delivers a "tombstone pile-
driver," and pins him. It is finally over.

Except it isn't, quite. A stretcher is brought back out for Foley, but he chooses
not to climb onto it. Instead, he slowly limps up the aisle to the dressing room.
Many fans who, fifteen minutes earlier, couldn't be bothered to boo during his en-
trance, now stand and chant "Foley! Foley!" because they know his real name
(there are few secrets left in pro wrestling), and realize what suffering he's just en-
dured for their pleasure. Though he doesn't immediately realize it, the gamble has
paid off. Mick Foley is now a wrestling legend, and his future with the WWF
is secure.

"IT WASN'T MY BEST MATCH EVER," MICK FOLEY SAYS, CHEWING
pizza and looking thoughtful. "But it's the one everybody remembers. Some
people use it as an example of how I must love pain, which is stupid. Nobody
loves pain. I was just willing to accept a lot of it as part of the price of success, is all. And, afterwards, I told people in the back that I didn't think the
crowd ever really got into it. In retrospect, I guess they did. I'd taken some
pretty good shots. I wasn't real alert."

The first result of Hell in a Cell was that fans gradually began responding to Mankind as a "babyface" (good guy) instead of as a heel. Over the next few months, the WWF booking committee scripted a gradual "heel turn" for the Rock that culminated in him cheating to beat Mankind in November 1998's *Survivor Series* pay-per-view. Foley began to add a comic element to his bouts. Instead of thumbtacks or metal folding chairs, his new prop was a sweatsock nicknamed "Socko." At some crucial moment, Foley would pull the long white cotton sock out of his wrestling tights, push it over his right hand, and apply Mankind's dreaded "Mandible Claw," where Foley's fingers were jammed under his opponent's tongue, supposedly deadening nerves there and swiftly rendering the other wrestler unconscious.

Foley was now being cheered as much or more than any of the other top-echelon WWF stars. This resulted in what wrestlers refer to as a "push," lots of high-profile matches that often doubled and occasionally tripled Foley's income (the more a wrestler's match is featured on pay-per-view events and nontelevised "house shows," the more he is paid). When fans continued to respond, WWF bookers even scripted three temporary Mankind ascensions to the promotion's world championship, though the longest of these lasted only a matter of weeks. He had moved as high up the promotion's ladder as he could without displacing either the Rock or Steve Austin, and that, Foley says now, was never going to happen. The WWF had invested too much time and too many marketing dollars on behalf of Austin and the Rock. They *looked* like superheroes, with photogenic faces and body-builder physiques. Mick Foley, his pleasant but ordinary facial features mostly obscured by the Mankind mask, also had the body of the Pillsbury Doughboy.

Still, it was clear the fans loved him, and in 1998–99 pro wrestling was at the zenith of its popularity. In particular, the Internet had spawned thousands of websites designed by computer-literate wrestling buffs who enjoyed posting endless columns presenting their opinions on industry "news," which could range from which wrestler was moving to what promotion to offering their own opinions on the best and worst entertainers among the grapplers. Pay-per-views would be reviewed on many of these sites the morning after they'd taken place; the reviewers critique each match and assign star ratings in much the same way film critics might grade movies. Among this computer set, Mick Foley was perhaps the most popular wrestler. His all-out efforts that wreaked havoc on his body endeared him to the new wave of Internet commentators.

"The first times I saw Mick Foley on TV in the 1980s, my impressions of him were not particularly good," says Scaia, who first began writing about wrestling on the Internet in the 1990s. "He was this fat, scruffy guy calling himself Cactus Jack. But gradually I realized, and I think most wrestling fans realized, that this guy would just do anything to put on a good show."

Many details about Foley's personal life surfaced on the Web. Fans perusing the sites could learn the names of his wife and children, facts about his latest injuries, and guesses about who he'd "feud" with next, along with predictions for that feud.

Having recently become a publicly traded company, the WWF was particularly on the lookout for ways to expand its product line. Besides the wrestling events themselves, the promotion had always raked in extra profits from sales of licensed items like T-shirts, posters, plastic wrestler action figures, and videos. The wrestlers whose images appeared on these products received a small royalty; the promotion took the bulk of the profits. Then, in the spring of 1999, the WWF brain trust came up with another way it might earn shareholders additional dividends.

"Somebody came up to me and said, 'Hey, the WWF's going to put out three autobiographies,'" Foley recalls. "One was going to be the Rock's, one was going to be Steve Austin's, and the third would be mine. And mine was going to go first in case the idea of these books didn't work, because Austin and the Rock were the very biggest stars and I wasn't at that level. The WWF wanted it to be that if somebody's book failed, it would be mine and not theirs. I went first not because I was most important but because I was least important. I realized that, and I accepted it. It wasn't personal."

Foley was informed that the WWF would publish the three titles through ReganBooks, a division of the prestigious publisher HarperCollins. He was surprised to learn he'd be teamed with ghostwriter Larry Nahani: "If it was my book, wasn't I supposed to be writing it?" Foley wasn't being entirely disingenuous. He'd graduated with honors in radio and television production from Cortland State in New York and was an avid reader. But Nahani assured him that the book—which would be titled *Have a Nice Day!* after a catchphrase Foley occasionally used while playing Mankind in interviews—would be mostly the wrestler's own: "He said he'd ask me questions, record my answers, then go off and write everything. So he did that, asking me all about my childhood, and a few days later he was back with the first chapters, which I hated, because they were all wrong."

The Nahani version of Mick Foley's life had teenaged Mick unable to get dates because girls in his Irish-Catholic neighborhood refused to socialize with a boy who never took communion. Foley's father, in real life an articulate, sometimes gabby man, was presented as a taciturn disciplinarian.

Foley's wife, Colette, recalls that even though her husband was disgusted by what Nahani wrote, "he wondered whether he should just go ahead and be a good guy and let him write what he wanted. That's how nice he is. It took a while, but finally with the support of me, of his family, he put his foot down and said it wasn't going to work."

The WWF offered to get Foley another ghostwriter, but he had his own plan.

"Just to see, I started writing myself. I wrote on legal pads because I was what they call computer illiterate. I told the WWF I really, really wanted to write the book myself. Finally, they agreed to let me try."

"And the WWF was smart to do that, because Mick could have gone to Harvard and not gotten a better writing education than he did from wrestling," says Terry Funk, who was winning pro wrestling championships while Foley was still in junior high and who eventually became one of Foley's best friends, traveling companion, and frequent in-ring opponent. "As far as telling a story goes, that's the essence of wrestling. Each full wrestling show is a book, each individual match is a chapter. Everything has to add up at the end for the audience to be happy."

From May 7 through July 1, working on planes and in cars and in dressing rooms, filling legal pads with scrawl, Mick Foley wrote his book. There was so much he wanted to tell, about himself and the unique world of professional wrestling and all of the engaging oddballs he'd met there. Thanks to both the Internet and the public pronouncements of wrestling moguls trying to avoid state taxes for staging "sports events," few wrestling fans still believed their sweaty entertainment was anything other than just that: staged action that was just as difficult to perform and just as rigorously scripted as movie stunts, but without the luxury of second takes. So Foley wasn't giving away professional secrets when he revealed how matches were planned and how wrestlers learned to pull punches and take falls.

The surprise of Foley's book was the engaging way in which he was able to write about his own life and career. If there was a good deal of sophomoric humor, there were also articulate explanations of why wrestlers in general, and Mick Foley in particular, were so willing to risk physical well-being. Response from the fans, being the center of attention, made it all worthwhile, Foley wrote. In particular, Foley's account of his early years as a wrestler resonated, how he slept in the back of his car and subsisted on peanut butter while often earning as little as twenty dollars for an evening's work, if promoters even paid what they'd promised.

Foley sparkled as a storyteller. He had a better sense of himself and his violent craft than any ghostwriter could have brought into print, and Foley brilliantly segued between accounts of matches and moments outside the ring, moving along briskly, never getting so caught up in his own memories that he risked boring readers. And on the basis of what he'd learned about story pace in the ring, he offered just the right ebb and flow to keep readers interested.

Mick Foley began *Have a Nice Day! A Tale of Blood and Sweatsocks* with a vivid description of a March 1994 match against Vader when, while attempting a "hangman" maneuver that involved twisting his own neck between the ring ropes, Foley's right ear was torn off right in front of everyone. He kept on wrestling to the bout's planned conclusion; the lost ear was retrieved, but couldn't be reattached to Foley's head.

"Welcome to my world," Foley wrote, "the world of professional wrestling, where fact is often stranger than fiction, and the line between the two keeps getting tougher and tougher to distinguish."

Have a Nice Day! was published in late September 1999. To the surprise of everyone, especially its author, the book shot to the top of the *New York Times* best-seller list.

MICK AND COLETTE FOLEY AND THEIR FOUR CHILDREN—DEWEY, Noelle, Mickey, and Hughey—live at least for now in a beautiful home in a tony Long Island suburb. Their house is set back from the road on a broad, expansive lawn; the backyard has plenty of room for Foley to pitch batting practice to the kids. The nearest neighbors are hundreds of yards away. The Foleys bought the house after King of the Ring 1998 and *Have a Nice Day!*— when it was obvious Mankind would stay in the wrestling spotlight for a while.

"One of the things I regret is that we moved into a house where there was a whole lot of work to do, a lot of money needed just to keep it up," Foley says, walking down the hall to the kitchen with two-year-old Mickey lurching along behind him. Mickey has his father's physical exuberance; he's a child who seems to enjoy bouncing off furniture and walls. "If *Tietam Brown* doesn't work, if it and the next novel I've written don't sell well, I'll gladly move to a smaller house. My wife loves me being retired from wrestling, but she's noticed those big pay-per-view checks don't come in anymore. I was always careful with my money, and we've got some investments, though I got hurt in the stock market recently like everybody else."

Foley leads the way to his favorite room, one dedicated to a holiday he enjoys celebrating year-round. In Foley family jargon it's "The Ho-Ho Room," with Christmas decorations—mostly Santa Claus figurines—that stay on permanent display. There are some other adornments, too, notably the framed dust cover of a book featuring Colette Foley during her modeling days.

"I know she didn't marry me for my money, because when we met I wasn't making any," Foley says, chuckling. "Colette had really been a very successful model, working for Avon, Revlon, companies like that. Why she decided she loved me is something I can't figure out, but I'm glad she did."

It was in 1990, Colette Foley recalls, that she met her husband at the Riverhead Raceway in Long Island. She was there visiting relatives; he was publicizing a small independent wrestling card on which he'd be appearing. Foley's sweetness appealed to her, she says, and his obvious enjoyment of life even though, financially, he was struggling: "God, I think he maybe had five hundred dollars to his name. But he cared so much for what he did; he considered it a craft, really. I think my experience in modeling helped me understand him, how you had to seem to be something in public that was different than you were in private."

The walls of the Ho-Ho Room also feature original pencil sketches from classic Disney movies including *Pinocchio* and *Snow White*. "These are what mean the most to me," Foley says proudly. "You may notice I don't have many things up from my wrestling career. I kept a few, but most of it—photos, posters, things like that—I gave away. Why hang on to stuff I'd just keep in drawers, when owning it would make other people really happy? I did keep my championship belt from the WWF, but it's just in a bag in the closet. I've got videos of some of my big matches, too. I guess I'll feel like looking at them someday, but for now, I don't."

Foley inserts a cassette into a VCR deck atop a wide-screen TV, and an animated musical blares into colorful life. Little Mickey Foley immediately breaks into a maniacal dance. "I taught him how to do that," his father says, and hops happily with his son for a few moments before leaving Mickey to dance on alone. "For a while, I overcompensated with my kids for being gone so much while I was wrestling," Foley says, grinning fondly at his gy-rating child. "It's so tough; you're gone ten days on a tour, back two, gone eight, back three. So whenever I was home I'd try to take them everywhere, and it interrupted their own routines, the things they wanted to do. Now, my oldest kids, Dewey and Noelle, remember me wrestling, but Mickey and Hughey, who was born about a month ago, won't have any memories of it. For a while, Dewey was so much into wrestling he had all the plastic figures and watched all the videos, but he burned out on it by the time he was ten. He and my daughter are both into sports, but if either one wanted to be a wrestler, I'd try to talk them out of it. It's so hard—on you, on your body, on your family."

In *Have a Nice Day!* Foley addressed these issues, but he also found many positives to a career in wrestling. It was, he emphasized, a satisfying profession for someone who enjoyed attention enough to make ongoing physical and financial sacrifices to get it.

"I hate it when people say wrestlers aren't athletes, because we have to be," he says, settling down on a couch. Mickey stops dancing and leaps, panting, onto his father's lap. Foley strokes the child's hair as he continues talking. "If you call golfers, guys who just stand there and swing a stick at a ball, athletes, then wrestlers are *really* athletes. The difference for us is, if, say, you play baseball, fans don't have to love you for you to succeed. You hit .300 all the time, you win twenty games every season, and you've got a job, you make the big money. For wrestlers, it's all about whether the fans love you or not. We call it "being over" with them. If you don't get over with the character you're playing, then you're not going to succeed, you're not going to make money. Some of the best wrestlers in the world can't make a full-time living because they can't make the fans *care*. And some guys who can't do more than two or three moves make millions in main events because, for whatever reason, they got the fans on their side."

One reason *Have a Nice Day!* was so popular, Foley believes, is that he respected wrestling fans enough to tell his life story conversationally: "Just me talking to them, not pretending to be anybody I wasn't. Writing that book was the only pure writing experience I've ever had. Now, I write books with the hope lots of people will buy them. I didn't even think about that the first time. The thought then was 'Hey, I'm writing a book, isn't this great?' I had no expectations other than that my mom would be pleased because she always told me she thought I could write books. And I've learned that it takes more guts to write than to wrestle. With books, you're putting your real heart out there for people to make judgments about. In wrestling, if people hate you they're probably hating the character you're pretending to be.

Luckily, nobody who read *Have a Nice Day!* seemed to end up hating me, maybe because I just told my simple, true story."

AFTER OPENING *HAVE A NICE DAY!* WITH HIS LOSS OF AN EAR AT the hands of Vader, Mick Foley took his simple, true story back to the beginning, a pleasant childhood in East Setauket, New York. His father was the public schools' director of health, physical education, and recreation; his mother, a retired teacher. Jack Foley was, his son recalls, "sort of a local legend. That was my first encounter with any type of fame. I grew up being referred to as 'Jack Foley's son.' It was hard sometimes with the other kids because my dad was somebody who disciplined them."

Born in 1965, Mick—never Mike or Michael, please—was a decent high school athlete, a member of his school's wrestling and lacrosse teams. He made good, if not excellent, grades and had a creative streak that sometimes expressed itself in crafting alternative, obscene lyrics to popular songs. After high school Mick moved on to Cortland State, studying hard enough to make good grades, and, if his first book is to be believed, striking out with every pretty girl on campus. In 1983, though, he found his eventual calling. Mick had always loved watching pro wrestling on television—he gradually made his dad a convert, too—and, now in college, he hitchhiked to New York City to watch an epic match between Superfly Jimmy Snuka and Don Muraco at Madison Square Garden. The two "fought" in a cage, the match ending when Snuka, bleeding heavily, dived from the top of the cage onto Muraco, who was plastered on the canvas.

"That was it, definitely," Mick Foley says twenty years later in the Ho-Ho Room. "Right there, I knew what I wanted to do. I was standing up and cheering and I wanted to be a wrestler and make other people feel the way I just felt." Now he needed a way to get into the profession. At first, he had to be satisfied with producing homemade wrestling "films," casting himself as an oddball grappler named Dude Love who emerged from pratfalls from roofs onto mattresses with fake blood (food coloring) streaming from his mouth. Eventually, he got a job helping a small-time promoter set up the ring for local matches. Doing that, Foley met a wrestler named Dominic DeNucci who ran a school for wannabe grapplers in Freedom, Pennsylvania, a town just outside of Pittsburgh. To train there, Foley had to make 800-mile round trips each weekend from Cortland State. DeNucci charged him $25 per session. The perpetually broke kid spent those nights sleeping in his car. He learned immediately not only that pro wrestling was tough to master but also that Mick Foley lacked the most basic skills to succeed in it.

"I wasn't acrobatic; I couldn't do all these complicated flips off the ropes to impress fans," he says, smiling a little at the memory. "And I didn't have a great, muscular body, either. Genetically, I just look kind of lumpy. I did even back then when I was younger. And those were really the two categories: be acrobatic, or else at least look like a big, strong guy. I got in the ring for the first couple times, and I couldn't even do some of the simplest things."

The canvas floors of wrestling rings are like stiffer versions of trampolines: there's enough bounce to sap leg strength quickly. But the springiness is necessary to provide impetus for leaps and to cushion crashing falls. Ring ropes can be used to generate momentum, but hitting them at a wrong angle results in nasty scrapes and bruising. In mimicking violence, wrestlers have to work together, with the one being thrown putting in just as much effort as the one doing the throwing. Newbie grappler Mick Foley was abysmal at all these things. In his early training days, he exhibited only one talent.

"I could take what they call *bumps*," Foley says, with the same truculent pride as someone claiming he can at least sing loud if not necessarily on key. "This body of mine, this wide load, turned out to be perfect for landing. It would look kind of spectacular. So other people liked to throw me around."

Foley discovered another attribute: his lifelong penchant for broad facial expressions and flamboyant physical gestures was perfect for the unsubtle stage of professional wrestling. That, combined with a kamikaze-like willingness to risk every body part in every match, gradually convinced Mick Foley that he just might be able to earn a living in his chosen profession after all.

"What I had to offer was entertaining by doing the crazy things nobody else would even think of doing," he says. "It was a matter of using what I had, which was accepting risks and working hard. I learned gradually to be a storyteller, too. Every wrestling match is, in its way, a story that two people are trying to make interesting to an audience. You do it for the response, especially at first, rather than the money. Because, at the grassroots level of pro wrestling and pretty much all the way up to the top promotion, the WWF, there is no money."

In June 1986, Foley wrestled his first pro bout, which he lost. Soon afterward, he was paid ten dollars "to get beaten up in front of about twenty-five people in some little town in West Virginia." For the first two years he wrestled, Foley felt lucky to be paid twenty dollars a night, and he had to cover his own expenses. After buying gas and an occasional sandwich, he frequently didn't break even. To support himself, he worked as a landscaper and moonlighted as a combination bartender/bouncer.

In 1988, Foley hooked on full time with a territory based in Memphis. He made about $300 a week. To survive, he and several other wrestlers shared a room. They drove to towns for each evening's matches, opponents in the ring who carpooled before and afterward. But Foley made the most out of his first regional chance, testing different ring techniques to see what pleased fans most. He called himself Cactus Jack; wore loose shirts to disguise some of his bulk; let his beard, moustache, and hair grow long; and threw himself into being a heel, since he didn't have the right look for a babyface. Soon, Cactus Jack was making a particular impression with his signature move, a dive off the ring to land elbow-first on an opponent sprawled on the concrete floor. This always hurt him far more than the opponent, though fans didn't know it.

"For Mick, the problem was that at that early point in his career the only way he could succeed was by damn near killing himself," veteran wrestler Terry Funk recalls. "To make an impression on the crowd, to be popular enough to keep his job, the only thing he knew how to do was torture himself by jumping off high places and legitimately getting hurt."

Eventually the Memphis promotion fell on hard times, and Foley's weekly paychecks dropped to around $200. His work, though, had been impressive enough to attract interest from a promotion in Dallas. Foley had some film of his body-bashing feats put together by the Memphis TV crew.

He sent it ahead to Texas, where it aired before Cactus Jack made his first appearance in the ring. Lots of Dallas fans still watched local wrestling on television, and Foley's reckless antics went over well. For the first time, he was often recognized on the street or in the Waffle House. His body was already aching during every waking moment, but this initial taste of fame was sweet.

"FAME IS A DIFFERENT THING FROM BEING FAMOUS," MICK FOLEY says, shifting his two-year-old son on his lap. "One is temporary, and the other lasts just about forever. I've got the first, and I'm not the second. I know that. The height of my fame came in a roller-coaster line. The Wrestlemania in 2001 was at the Houston Astrodome, and I'd retired from active wrestling, but I was refereeing a match on that card. The Astrodome is by a theme park called Astroworld, and I love parks like that with roller coasters. So I go to the park, and I'm led right to the front of the roller-coaster line, being put ahead of people who've been waiting two hours to ride on it, and the people I'm cutting in front of are cheering and chanting my name. That's fame."

It helped, Foley adds, that he didn't acquire extensive fame all at once. His national reputation with wrestling fans came only after a dozen years of relative obscurity: "That meant I had some control of my ego when it finally happened. I think it also means I'm going to have the ability to deal with it when I don't have fame anymore, when nobody's running up to get my autograph or yelling, 'Hey, is it really you?' A good example came at a sports show I did recently, signing autographs. There were also some retired New York Mets baseball players, and somebody mentioned that I drew a bigger crowd than Bud Harrelson, who was the Mets shortstop when they won the World Series out of nowhere in 1969. I said, 'Hey, 1969 was something like thirty-five years ago. We'll see how much of a crowd I draw in 2038.' Bud Harrelson is famous; I just have some fame."

Still, Foley admits, "I have an ego, and the whole purpose of being a wrestler was to get as much fame as I could. So, when I got to Dallas and got some attention, I was still telling myself not to settle for what I'd accomplished so far. The next step was to get to one of the two big promotions, the WCW (World Championship Wrestling, based in Atlanta) or the WWF (World Wrestling Federation, headquartered in Connecticut), and the step after that was to become one of its top stars. Other people kept telling me it wouldn't happen, that I didn't have the right look, but I was very confident from the beginning in thinking what I had to offer as a wrestler was unique and valuable, as long as my body held up."

IN 1989, A TRYOUT MATCH EARNED FOLEY A ROSTER SPOT WITH World Class Wrestling. For about eight months, he made the kingly salary of $1,000 a week, though the costs of commuting to events all over the country instead of within a small, restricted region ate up a lot of the extra money. There were other problems. National TV exposure meant Cactus Jack became familiar to many more fans, but it also meant Foley's in-ring character was constantly on display. If WCW officials decided his appeal was wearing off, he could be dropped anytime, and it was also true those officials didn't believe a galumphing performer like Foley could ever become a top-echelon star.

"After a while my pay went up to $1,500 a week, but it was obvious I was just buried in the midcard," Foley recalls. "I decided I'd try working as an independent."

Foley quit WCW and began hiring himself out to any promoter who'd pay $250 for a Cactus Jack match. Besides promotions in the United States, he traveled to Japan, where fans loved his willingness to shed blood and risk debilitating injuries. In tandem with Terry Funk, who himself had long been known for hurting his body to entertain fans, Foley began to participate in brutal "specialty" matches, including contests where ring ropes were replaced by barbed wire. He acquired countless scars and occasional second-degree burns from being struck by flaming objects. (His front teeth, however, were lost in a car wreck.) Yet Foley rarely questioned whether the pain or the near-poverty-level income was worth it. He still loved being a professional wrestler, entertaining fans and being recognized in the Waffle House. And he still dreamed of wrestling superstardom, even at the cost of his own physical well-being.

"My look and physique limited me, but I was competitive in wanting to have the best match every night no matter who I was wrestling," Foley says. He returned to the WCW for a while, lured by a steady paycheck and the eventual chance to headline one pay-per-view, though he lost this high-profile match. In fall 1994 he went back to the independent wrestling circuit, charging $500 for weekday matches and $750 to work on weekends. Needing steady income to support his growing family, Foley began accepting spots in bizarre, highly dangerous matches that frequently involved such props as broken glass, tacks, baseball bats wrapped in barbed wire, and, a few times, even a flaming branding iron. He may not have enjoyed pain, but he never avoided it, either.

Tours of Japan often culminated with Foley flying home in battered condition. In the United States things weren't much better. Foley caught on with a fledgling promotion based in Philadelphia that eventually called itself Extreme Championship Wrestling, and the name was apt. Its entire roster was dedicated to Foley-like stunts. Once, wielding a flaming chair, Foley accidentally set Terry Funk on fire. The ECW crowds were small, but vocal, and their appreciation of Foley's efforts was reflected in dozens of signs proclaiming "Foley Is God" at every event. These fans knew the matches were scripted, but they also knew that the wrestlers they cheered or jeered were deliberately hurting themselves in their efforts to entertain.

"WCW hadn't let Mick show a lot, except for a series of matches with Vader," Scaia says. "It was in ECW that he really started to stand out as a unique character. He got a chance to give long interviews; he got showcased, really, against some other great wrestlers like Terry Funk. When he finally got this chance to be the headliner, he grabbed it."

But Foley wasn't satisfied. His family, he says, lived in a small house without air conditioning. Colette Foley focused on mothering rather than modeling, so it was Dad's responsibility to make money. The ECW only put on a few events each month, leaving Foley to scrounge the rest of the time for independent bookings. If Foley was ever going to make big money as a wrestler, he had to do it soon, and the only place left to do that was the WWF. Owner Vince McMahon was open about presenting "sports entertainment" rather than actual competition, and his vision of pay-per-view telecasts and national rather than regional promotion had kicked off the modern pro-wrestling era in the mid-'80s. The WWF kept a close eye on ECW, occasionally raiding its roster for prime talent. In December 1995, Foley finally got the call he'd been waiting for. Vince McMahon wanted to see him. Though he wasn't pleased with the character McMahon wanted him to portray—a psychopath called "Mason the Mutilator" whose face was obscured by a leather mask—Foley agreed to give it a try, after getting McMahon to agree he'd be called "Mankind" instead.

Foley made his WWF debut in March 1996, and to his pleasure became a favorite heel as he battled the Undertaker in a series of pay-per-view events. By the fall, he even headlined a pay-per-view against the WWF champion. Though he lost, he thought the match itself might have been the best in his whole career. In 1997, McMahon let him extend his ring identity by having Foley wrestle for a while as Dude Love, the character he'd first invented back in college. Cactus Jack made a few reappearances, too. Foley enjoyed portraying both but realized he was only doing so because fan reaction to Mankind was lessening. With the WWF's half-dozen cable shows, its wrestlers were constantly visible. That made overexposure all too easy; fans constantly required new "storylines" and wrestlers to participate in them. Almost all WWF wrestlers occasionally switched between babyface and heel just to keep themselves interesting to fans who probably watched them three or four times every week. Mankind and his mask had become too familiar, and reaction to the character waned. By the time Foley made his hesitant way out for the King of the Ring match against the Undertaker, the fans at that event couldn't even be bothered to boo very much. Then the Undertaker threw him off the top of a sixteen-foot-high cage.

Six months after that, Mick Foley as Mankind temporarily held the WWF championship. He appeared—as Mankind—in a Chef Boyardee TV commercial on national TV. Five months after *that*, the WWF decided to have three of its superstars "write" their autobiographies. In October 1999, *Have a Nice Day!* was published, and for about the next three months Mick Foley sold more nonfiction books than any other author in America. *Have a Nice Day!* eventually shipped 750,000 copies in hardcover and 700,000 in paperback. Under the usual royalty arrangements for authors, Foley might have expected to clear at least $800,000 to $1 million from the book's hardcover sales alone, giving him the financial wherewithal to get out of wrestling entirely if that was his wish. But there was a catch to Foley's literary success.

"That first book and my next one, *Foley Is Good,* were owned by the WWF," Foley explains, his scarred eyebrows knitting together in frustration. "I didn't own my own best-selling books. I had to fight to get the name 'Mick Foley' on the cover of *Have a Nice Day!* at all. If you look at it, you'll see it's got 'Mankind' in big letters and 'Mick Foley' in much, much smaller ones. I think I was given five percent of what the WWF made on my books. After *Have a Nice Day!* sold so well, the advance from ReganBooks for *Foley Is Good* was in the six figures, and I didn't get any of it. I knew how the deal had been drawn up in the beginning, but then the WWF and I never expected it was going to be a big best seller. So, particularly with the advance on *Foley Is Good,* when I didn't get anything, I thought that was very disrespectful. I mean, unlike the other wrestlers who did autobiographies after mine that were really written by ghostwriters, I wrote every word of my books."

Still, Foley enjoyed his newfound literary celebrity. He appeared on TV as a featured guest of Conan O'Brien, Larry King, Roseanne Barr, and Howard Stern, among others. (He didn't think much of King, who he says "pretended he knew a lot but really didn't," and he loathed Barr, who kept interrupting him.) Foley set several records for most books signed at various stores: 750 at the Virgin MegaStore in New York City's Times Square, 1,100 copies at a Wal-Mart in St. Louis. Wrestling fans, it turned out, liked to read about wrestling as well as go to bouts or watch them on TV. The success of *Have a Nice Day!* encouraged WWF management to churn out more "autobiographies" of their stars, though none of these were actually written by the wrestlers. Some made brief appearances on the best-seller lists, but none were as engaging, or sold as well or as long, as Foley's.

Unfortunately for Foley, his body began to break down rapidly just as his unexpected status as a best-selling author bloomed. He's quite specific about when he realized his wrestling days were about to be over: "November 2, 1999. I was in Philadelphia feuding with a guy named Val Venis, whose character was a porn star. If you knew him in real life you'd realize he's exactly the opposite, way to the right of Pat Buchanan. Anyway, we filmed this earlier scene of me chasing him through the scary underbelly of Philadelphia. Then I had to wrestle in a match after that. It was the first time I felt embarrassed by the way I looked out there. I couldn't move because my body was so sore. My knees could not support my weight, which was way up. I actually fell down twice during the match, just fell down."

Colette Foley says that after every pay-per-view match she would tell him, "You can't keep doing this. We can't live this way. I asked him to think what would happen to us if he was paralyzed or something even worse. And he'd promise me he wouldn't do some of those dangerous things anymore."

But Foley was simply unable to rein in his risk-taking instincts. Always ready to acquiesce to his wife's wishes when he dragged home bruised and broken, after a few weeks of healing he'd start thinking about what top-the-last-one stunt he might try next.

"This is what drove Mick Foley," Terry Funk explains. "I know this because I have been with him so many times before and after matches, and, hell, even in them with him hundreds of times. He loved the whole thing of going out in front of people, 30 of 'em or 30,000, gassing himself, coming back to the locker room, sitting in a puddle of his own sweat and probably blood, and saying out loud, knowing it was true, 'God, I gave 'em their money's worth.' He wanted to have that moment more than anything else. It's what satisfied him right up to the moment he started thinking about how he could work out the next match to get the same feeling again."

But Foley wasn't a fool. His knees throbbed, his balance was off, his short-term memory was causing him problems. Finally in late 1999, he and WWF owner Vince McMahon decided he'd simply shut down as an active grappler and instead become an on-air personality for the promotion. But a series of injuries to other top stars made Foley feel obligated to keep wrestling a while longer. With Austin and the Rock out for some time, Foley dragged his battered body into a series of high-profile pay-per-view matches and actually won the WWF title one last time, though he lost it on cable TV the next night.

"My body just was falling apart, and I accepted it," Foley says. "Except for my last couple of big pay-per-view appearances, one a "Street Fight," one another "Hell in a Cell." I lost that one and was supposed to have to retire as a result. And I thought I *was* retired, but then the WWF insisted I have one more match as part of the main event at Wrestlemania. I regret that I didn't perform in that match at the level that I wanted people to remember about me. I admit that was and is a big thing with me, the way people who paid their money remember me."

Foley found himself being remembered for something else that troubled him. During the latter part of 1998 and early 1999, when Foley's popularity was at its highest, a filmmaker named Barry Blaustein received Vince McMahon's permission to film some WWF matches and backstage interactions as part of a big-screen wrestling documentary. When the film was released McMahon disassociated himself from the project, which he believed made his promotion look bad. That was probably true, especially since the most talked-about scenes of *Beyond the Mat* involved footage of Mankind defending his WWF title in a *Royal Rumble* pay-per-view against the Rock. The match took place in Anaheim, and the Foleys had decided to take Dewey and Noelle to Disneyland afterward. Foley's wife and two children were seated right at ringside when, as part of the match, the Rock smashed seventeen consecutive chairshots to Mankind's unprotected head (earlier, Foley's hands had been handcuffed behind him). Foley had always tried to explain to his kids that wrestling was really pretend, but these blows opened an old cut on his head, which bled profusely, and Blaustein's cameras captured Dewey and Noelle wailing with fright and Colette, looking horrified, too, rushing them out of the arena.

"I'd taken the children to some of Mick's matches before, but we always sat way up high, far from the ring," she says. "This time we were in the front row, and we could hear the guys breathing and moaning, we could hear those chairs smashing against Mick's head. It was a mistake to sit there, obviously."

Afterward, Blaustein recorded Noelle holding Daddy's hand while his wound was stitched backstage. Foley's final scene in the film came when he and Colette sat in their living room, watching the Royal Rumble footage Blaustein had recorded. "I don't feel like a very good father," Foley commented. He also said he knew that someday it would be time for him to start doing something other than wrestling, but he had no idea what. Then *Have a Nice Day!* came out, and he did. He would be a writer, and in this second career he wouldn't have to work his way up from the bottom. After all, it took Cactus Jack twelve years to make it to the WWF. Mick Foley was a number-one best-selling author right out of the gate. This time, he thought, there would be few dues to pay.

He soon learned he was wrong. Vince McMahon was unhappy with what Foley says he perceived as *his* WWF employee speaking out on behalf of Blaustein's film when McMahon himself hated it. The WWF owned the non-fiction books Foley wrote, including *Foley Is Good*, published in 2001. Written on legal pads again, this book described his last days as an active wrestler. In contrast to *Have a Nice Day!*, though, easily half of this second book proselytized on behalf of the profession he loved so much: the book's subtitle was *And the Real World Is Faker Than Wrestling*, a heartfelt but ungrammatical message that did little to change critics' assumptions that a wrestler couldn't write intelligently. There were also innumerable "top-ten" lists of Foley favorites: movies, amusement parks, matches in which he competed. Most critics who noticed *Foley Is Good* at all panned the book. Wrestling fans still supported Foley as an author. The final numbers on *Foley Is Good* were 250,000 copies shipped in hardback and 130,000 in paperback, still good enough to make the book a brief number-one best-seller, though a big drop from the sales performance of *Have a Nice Day!* Foley was offended that the WWF didn't voluntarily share more of his second book's revenues with him, and even angrier with how his company treated an illustrator for *Mick Foley's Halloween Hijinx*, his second children's book.

The first, *Mick Foley's Christmas Chaos*, was published in December 2000, after *Have a Nice Day!* and before *Foley Is Good*. The funny, sometimes rude (an elf moons Santa) rhyming tale shipped 115,000 copies—excellent for a children's book—and was illustrated by Jerry "the King" Lawler, another WWF wrestler. In September 2001, not long after *Foley Is Good* was published, he brought out *Mick Foley's Halloween Hijinx*, another holiday-themed children's book that involved scared kids feeling braver when they dressed for the holiday as WWF wrestlers. Foley used an outside illustrator this time, and says that the WWF never paid her for her work: "That really made me mad." *Hijinx* shipped 80,000 copies, still very respectable, but now Foley constantly felt resentful over WWF control of his books.

And there were more disagreements. Though he hadn't wrestled a match since 2000, Foley was still a frequent on-air performer for the WWF, often acting as the promotion's "commissioner" who would adjudicate disagreements and thrill fans by making heels fight opponents they clearly didn't want to face. Wrestling fans still loved Foley: in arenas, he'd get louder cheers than the wrestlers who actually had to grapple in the ring. But he wanted to use his celebrity for more than eliciting those cheers. He'd always been keenly interested in the world around him. Even during his busiest days as a wrestler, Foley particularly made himself available to groups assisting terminally ill children. Now, newly free of the torturous schedule of a working wrestler, he began to read and think more about how he could have some impact on real, rather than scripted, events. In particular, Foley became a strong advocate of an international campaign to ban land mines: "I wanted to go to Angola on this publicity event to point out how terrible they are, but the WWF wouldn't let me go. They didn't think their fans would support anything that might be seen as antiwar."

Mick Foley, wrestler-turned-commissioner, advocated "pretend" violence. Mick Foley, father and prominent author, wanted to use his combined wrestling and literary celebrity to help eliminate one form of very real violence. And his bosses wouldn't let him. As a result of that, and of not getting money he felt he deserved from his books, so far as Foley and the WWF were concerned, he says, "The relationship became strained."

Mick Foley wanted to keep writing and, perhaps as much, wanted complete control of his life and his work. He got an idea of how to accomplish both in early 2001 after reading Stephen King's *On Writing*, which explained the longtime best-selling author's approach to fiction and storytelling. "Until I read that book, I was sure writing a novel was beyond my grasp," Foley says. "After reading him I thought, 'I can do this.'" Lots of people reading *On Writing* probably felt the same way, but none of them had Foley's track record of best sellers. He felt certain he could get a contract to write a novel, and, he made clear to the WWF, they might own what he wrote about his real wrestling experiences, but they had no claim on characters and stories he created in his own mind.

After he mentioned to a *New York Times* reporter that he might attempt a novel, publishers contacted Foley wanting to talk. He had "a very good idea in my head of what I wanted to write about, a novel about revenge by a manipulated kid." Knopf, a respected imprint whose author stable includes Toni Morrison and John Updike, was willing to offer a contract, and, though the money was less than Foley's six-figure WWF pay-per-view paychecks, he wanted to take it. The WWE—the company had just changed its name from World Wrestling Federation to World Wrestling Entertainment after losing a lawsuit to the World Wildlife Federation over identical abbreviation—was not going to support any book it didn't profit from. Foley quit. For the first time in sixteen years, he was no longer part of professional wrestling, except through past reputation. Now he could stay at home, play with his kids during the day, and write his book at night.

"I was supposed to start *Tietam Brown* on September 1, 2001," Foley says. "I got a little behind, and then 9/11 happened and I finally got going on the book a month after that. I'm sure the tone of the book was affected. I was writing about this kid, Andy Brown, and then I started writing about Tietam, his dad, and he was a much more compelling character. It made for an odd story flow. It was much different, much more challenging than writing about my own life and career and opinions, which just involved remembering things or saying what I already felt."

There was another challenge. For sixteen years, Mick Foley had constant attention from fans, and, mostly, he thrived on it. The only time he didn't enjoy being recognized, he says, is "when a group of teenagers, probably boys, would know me and come over while I was with my family, because the kids would be trying to show off for each other and say things they shouldn't. But mostly, it was a pleasure."

Colette Foley enjoyed her husband's fame less than he did. "It's cooled down a little, but for a while it was just unbearable," she says. "We couldn't go out to restaurants, really. Some people were nice, but others were rude and would talk badly, even curse, right in front of the children. One reason we moved from Florida up to New York was that too many people knew where we lived in Florida. They came right up to the house. I'd come home from shopping and there would be these greasy nose prints and fingerprints on the windows from people trying to look inside."

Fame, Foley insists, "is mostly nice. Everybody should know what it's like to be in an arena and have 20,000 people chanting your name. The first time it happens, it's the greatest thing, the greatest experience, and if it keeps happening you get used to it, and then it's taken away and it's very difficult to do without. They say fame is addictive and they're right. After I left the WWF and started writing full time, I'd still get the individual fans coming up and wanting autographs or to take pictures, but the big moments were gone, and I can't deny I wanted them back sometimes. I still do."

He filled some of the empty moments with appearances for just about any charity that wanted his help. "I'm trying to make good use of this temporary fame," he says. "I try to do all the things I can, and sometimes I don't even wait to be called. I found out the other day our post office is going to have a Breast Cancer Awareness day, so I volunteered to do something for that. I'm very lucky to be able to do these things. Doing them gives me some pride, helps me feel good about myself. I'm getting while I'm giving. People think I'd just say that to sound modest or something, but it's true. At some point my name won't mean anything anymore, but while it does, I want to use it. Even then, I know I'll still end up being like the guy at the end of *Schindler's List*, wondering if I could have done more."

Foley thinks he was particularly lucky to have a good perspective during his early postwrestling months: "When I was Mankind, when I was Cactus Jack, away from the ring I was always Mick Foley, the normal guy. A lot of wrestlers start believing they are the characters they play for fans. You think you're that character, you get used to getting attention as him, and then when the attention is gone you have trouble settling for being your real self. I had a good marriage, my kids, my parents, the writing, all that to fall back on after the wrestling. And I still miss it. So how bad must it be for the guys who bought into their own reputations?"

KNOPF SIGNED MICK FOLEY TO WRITE HIS FIRST NOVEL BECAUSE editors there believed in his ability to sell books as well as to write them. Foley's reputation as a wrestler was a handy marketing tool. If enough wrestling fans bought *Tietam Brown,* the book would make a profit regardless of whether critics liked it or if readers who weren't wrestling fans mostly ignored it. But that possibility didn't sit entirely well with Foley. He was proud of his wrestling past, he embraced it, but he now saw himself as a serious author whose novel ought to be appreciated on its own merits. The storyline of the novel, as he wrote it, reflected the contradiction of being simultaneously proud of his past career and wanting to move beyond it. Andy Brown became a multifaceted protagonist whose social and private sufferings were movingly described, but he was also missing an ear. Tietam Brown, Andy's father, was an outrageous, over-the-top character who drank and chased women and, in his odd way, loved his son. He was also a former wrestler whose life was still marked by past experiences in the ring. Foley even wrote his novel sitting in a folding chair from an arena in Worcester, Massachusetts, that was given to him by a fan as a memento of the night he won his first WWF championship there. "I want readers to get past the fact that an ex-wrestler wrote *Tietam Brown,*" Foley kept saying, but he put enough personal wrestling elements into his story to make it impossible for readers to forget.

"I think *Tietam Brown* will do okay based on what my other books have done," Foley says in late May 2003, driving through his Long Island hometown on a warm, sunny afternoon. "I'm hoping to sell 75,000 copies and I don't think that's too unrealistic." Told that first novels generally don't sell 5,000 copies, he's momentarily nonplussed. "Well," he finally says, "maybe as a writer it's my good fortune to be naïve. I feel like I have my own style, and that will eventually be the basis for my success. Now, as the wrestling reputation wears off, the fame as a writer might turn out to be smaller than I'd like. But that's going to happen the way it happens."

Mick Foley didn't finally succeed as a wrestler because he was shy about taking advantage of every opportunity. Thinking about his book, worried that his main audience might still be wrestling fans rather than general readers, he began to consider reconciling with the WWE. During the last week of May 2003, he had someone make a call to the promotion on his behalf.

"I didn't entirely walk away from the WWE with bad feelings," Foley says, driving slowly through the main street of his Long Island hometown. "It wasn't like I hated them and they hated me and we could never get back together. In fact, they've called me a couple of times since I left, suggesting how I might get involved in some storylines they had going, but I didn't see anything interesting. It just happens that right now, I do. They've got a pay-per-view coming up in the middle of June that nobody really cares about. Steve Austin can't wrestle anymore because of an injury, the Rock is gone making movies, I've retired—they're having trouble keeping people interested. The main event at the pay-per-view is going to be a Hell in a Cell match; the two guys in it just aren't drawing any heat. Well, nobody's more associated in the minds of wrestling fans with Hell in a Cell than me. I'm proposing that the WWE bring me in as a special referee to get in the cage with the guys. I wouldn't have to do much, just take a bump or two, but my being there would get them lots of extra cable buys. I've been away two years; the fans would want to see me. I might get a nice paycheck, which my wife would like." He pauses. "And, of course, it would be good publicity for the book."

The WWE loved the idea. Within a week, Foley was introduced on its Monday-night cable show *RAW* as the Hell in a Cell special referee. Right after the announcement he walked down to the ring to tumultuous applause.

The crowd stood as one and chanted "Foley! Foley!" Triple H, the heel in the pay-per-view match that would be held in six more days, first threatened Foley, then bashed him. Foley took the bump well and landed a few punches of his own. For the Hell in a Cell contest itself, he bled along with both participants. The buy rate for the pay-per-view increased dramatically in the few days before the event when it was known Foley would be on hand. In return, the WWE let Foley appear on their cable programs promoting *Tietam Brown* just before its publication in July. On Foley's final pre–*Tietam Brown* WWE TV appearance, he came out to the ring and told fans he would leave them with the immortal words of Frosty the Snowman: "Now I'll say goodbye, but don't you cry, I'll be back again someday." Then, as the cameras kept filming, Foley went backstage and was promptly tossed down a steep flight of stairs by an up-and-coming young heel named Randy Orton, which set up the potential for a future grudge match between the two, even though Foley said afterward that he didn't know if he'd have a *real* wrestling match again.

TIETAM BROWN WAS PUBLISHED IN LATE JULY 2003, AND BOOK CRITics pounced. A few commented on Foley's good sense of story pace. Most reviews, though, were barbed, and the knocks showed that the reviewers had factored in Foley's wrestling background: "Hardly a literary body slam" (*Entertainment Weekly*); "You've got a book as specious as a World Wrestling Entertainment bout, an event manufactured to look much more serious than it actually is" (*New York Daily News*). Even the positive comments took shots at Foley the wrestler: "Like the WWF itself, this frighteningly readable novel is a cartoonish meditation on the clash of good and evil, innocence and experience" (*Los Angeles Times*).

Foley had long bemoaned the failure of the *New York Times* to make any mention of his earlier books. Now he learned the lesson about being careful what you wish for. The *Times* reviewer concluded his very succinct, biting review of *Tietam Brown* with, "What the book lacks isn't action, though, but a character, a scene, or even a scrap of dialogue that feels fresh or unexpected."

Foley's publicist at Knopf suggested that he not read the *Tietam Brown* reviews, but he did anyway. Afterward, he tried to look on the bright side, noting some of them weren't *that* bad. And, immediately after the novel's publication, he took off on a month-long promotional tour. It was originally supposed to last about ten days, but Foley told the Knopf publicist that he was happy to drive all around the country himself rather than costing his publisher money for plane fare, and that he knew all the inexpensive motels from his days on the wrestling circuits. And, once on the road, Foley gladly signed books at any store and spoke to audiences at any library or community center that would host him.

The results were mixed. Foley was still able to draw reasonably substantial crowds—200, say, where three or four times that number might have shown up for *Have a Nice Day!* appearances when Mankind was still the darling of the WWF—but most of the people showing up wanted to talk about wrestling, not *Tietam Brown*. Foley said a few months earlier that he'd rather have "fifty people come to see me because they'd read and loved my book than five hundred who wanted to ask me about Undertaker and Hell in a Cell," but on the *Tietam Brown* tour practicality won out. Foley would answer every wrestling question he was asked and look for opportunities to start talking about his novel, too. He was also stymied by hosts on whatever local media appearances he made: after a polite question or two about his current book, they all wanted to ask Foley why he thought public interest in pro wrestling seemed to be in decline. That, and would Mick tell them what the Rock and Steve Austin were *really* like?

Even Scaia, who has such great appreciation for Foley, hasn't read *Tietam Brown:* "My mom works at a library. The book is something I'd love to check out sometime. But I haven't, yet."

In the end, Foley's efforts on behalf of *Tietam Brown* weren't entirely in vain. Some people who came out to see him or who heard him on the radio did buy the book. By late fall, Knopf had shipped 65,000 copies, below Foley's goal of 75,000 sold but still much, much better than almost any other first-time novelist could have hoped for. Of that 65,000, some certainly were returned, unsold, to the publisher. But *Tietam Brown* had at least done well enough for Knopf to consider working with Foley on his second novel, the baseball-themed book.

"No decision has been made, but Mick is ready to go elsewhere if he has to," Colette Foley says in early 2004. "He's learned a lot about how the publishing business works, and he's definitely a gifted writer. Mick doesn't give up."

BACK HOME AFTER THE CONCLUSION OF HIS *TIETAM BROWN* TOUR, Foley was mostly philosophical.

"I guess the sales were okay, but I didn't realize that until I got back from the trip Knopf sent me on to England," he said. "The book did all right over there, and combined with sales in the States I wasn't too far off when I guessed we'd sell 75,000. More people have told me I did great for a first-time novel, and I'm going to assume they know what they were talking about."

Foley, who'd said so much about wanting potential *Tietam Brown* readers to look past its author's wrestling background, admitted that, upon reflection, he thinks his short return to the WWE might have worked against him with mainstream audiences.

"I'd hoped, in terms of who read the book, of who came out to see me on the tour, that I would get a fifty-fifty split between wrestling fans and non-wrestling people," he said. "It obviously didn't turn out that way. I had not talked about wrestling, I had not been even a little part of it, for about a year and a half, and so the wrestling fans really responded to seeing me again. I knew what I was doing would sort of reinforce the negative picture some critics already had of me, but just before I did the WWF stuff there were a couple of advance reviews of *Tietam Brown* that leaned so heavily against wrestling that it brought out the rebellious nature in me. I figured, 'Well, fine, I'll just show them.' If there was any backlash, I agree I may have brought it on myself. But, to be honest, I may do something like it again if I get the chance."

Mick Foley was in no way ready, or perhaps even able, to turn away from wrestling altogether. Part of the reason was financial: "I look at all I put into *Tietam Brown*, how many hundreds of hours I spent writing and rewriting it, all the weeks I was on the road for it, the hundreds more hours I spent on the phone doing extra interviews, and I could have made more money from wrestling just one WWF match than I'll make from all the time I spent on the book." Foley's family likes living in the big, expensive-to-keep-up house. He decided he wouldn't be willing to move after all.

Then, too, he believes there will be a second Foley novel out soon, the one he promises will be completely about life and baseball, not life and baseball and wrestling.

"I just sent in my revised manuscript [to Knopf], and the editor's had several more comments," he said. "I think I'm meeting her a little more than halfway, so we'll have to see. I know, though, that this one's not as dark as *Tietam Brown*. And, of course, I'm hoping that when this one comes out the critics will have gotten their little puns out of the way, their jokes about wrestling."

Still, Foley wasn't kidding himself. Most of the people who bought *Tietam Brown* were wrestling fans. Without them, Foley's beloved book might not have sold any more copies than the 5,000 or so of the typical first novel. So hooking up again with the WWE to simultaneously beef up the promotion's TV and pay-per-view numbers and promote novel number two to wrestling fans is something he knew he would probably do.

But there's another reason he'd consider it. In May 2003, Foley had been doubtful he'd ever try to actually wrestle a match again, as opposed to refereeing one: "I'd have to know ahead of time that I was in decent shape, that I could perform at the high level the fans would expect of me and I'd expect of myself." But his June and July WWE appearances pleased him for reasons other than promoting his book. He loved being in the ring again, hearing 20,000 people chant his name. Foley always agreed fame was an addiction, and now he'd been reintroduced to wrestling celebrity, his longtime drug of choice.

"I tend to write in bursts, use the writing energy when I have it and then taking time off to do other things," he says in October 2003. "You know,

Wrestlemania XX is coming up in March 2004, the twentieth-anniversary pay-per-view, and it's already being advertised as the biggest wrestling card in history. It'll be at Madison Square Garden just about four years to the day from my last match. If I were part of that, if I had my one-time comeback match, well, I could make a lot of money. And the people might cheer like you've never heard before."

Terry Funk, still wrestling occasional matches in his late fifties, says he knew his close friend would eventually have to get back in the ring. "Hell," Funk says, laughing, "nobody who truly loves it like Mick does can ever get out of this goddamned business. It's got some kind of horrible emotional hook that it sinks in you. He'll never walk away from it completely."

IN NOVEMBER 2003, MICK FOLEY MADE AN UNEXPECTED APPEARANCE on a live Monday night broadcast of WWE's *RAW* national telecast. He announced he'd once again accepted a job as *RAW*'s "commissioner." Fans in attendance and those watching on TV erupted with joy. Over the next couple of weeks, the show's ratings climbed. Then, through a series of scripted events, Foley accepted an invitation to wrestle for the first time in nearly four years against, naturally, Randy Orton, the young heel who'd tossed Foley down a flight of stairs months earlier when he'd briefly rejoined the WWE to promote *Tietam Brown*. Their match was to be the last on one evening's show, but it never took place. Instead, Foley "changed his mind" about wrestling Orton and walked out of the building, though not before his erstwhile foe spit in his face and mocked him for being a coward. It was all obviously planned as a buildup for a big Foley-Orton match on pay-per-view; physical health and author reputation be damned, Mick Foley wanted to get back into the ring as a headliner on a major card.

And wrestling fans were thrilled because of it. "In the end, people who love wrestling and Mick Foley don't see his missing ear," Rick Scaia says. "We see an amazing man who goes all out to entertain us at great cost to himself. And so we love him. What we, I, want really more than anything would be two or three big moments a year. He wouldn't have to wrestle full time or anything. We realize that physically he couldn't do it. We just want to be able to see Mick Foley wrestling every once in a while, entertaining us."

Colette Foley, who'd welcomed her husband's retirement from the ring in 2000, said that after Foley made the decision to return "you could just see his brain brewing up all these ways to have exciting matches. If things work as he hopes, there'll be mostly things where he doesn't have to actually wrestle and maybe two or three matches a year. He's so happy. He needs to do that."

In March 2004, Foley returned to the ring when he teamed with The Rock at *Wrestlemania XX* in a tag-team match against three wrestlers, including Randy Orton. After about twenty minutes of bruising action, Orton pinned Foley. A week later, Foley was back on TV challenging Orton to a one-on-one match at the WWE's April pay-per-view. This one, Foley declared, would be a "No Holds Barred" match. He lost that one, too, and finished the bout with his face streaming blood. It was as though he'd never retired.

On the December 2003 *RAW*, just before Foley walked off without wrestling Orton, the TV cameras panned fans at ringside. Wrestling fans are renowned for bringing handmade signs to televised matches, waving them on high in hopes of getting a fleeting on-camera moment, the closest most of them will ever come to fame. On this night, one bulky woman in a front-row seat waved a large, square, cardboard poster, its succinct message crudely scrawled but obviously heartfelt:

<pre>
      F
  G   O   D
      L
      E
      Y
</pre>

Melvin and Harold

Most Americans didn't really care if Melvin Dummar was lying. It was fun simply to speculate about *something*. The Vietnam War was over. Watergate was over. The presidential election was over. Feminists had stopped burning their bras when the Equal Rights Amendment faltered. The energy crisis was still around, but it wasn't exactly the kind of thing you could put on your television set each night to take your mind off your problems. But there was the Hughes Will Saga.

So on January 25, 1977, newspaper reporters and television cameramen, drama junkies and Howard Hughes groupies packed the hallway of the Clark County Courthouse in Las Vegas, jockeying for position outside Judge Keith Hayes's courtroom. "Open the doors!" someone called out, followed a few moments later by another, more insistent, voice: "Open the doors!" The doors didn't open. The noise, already oppressive, rose every few minutes at the latest wishful Melvin sighting, causing a collective craning of necks and a stumbling, centipede-like surge forward, or backward, or sideways, depending on where you were standing. "The line of spectators went back from the door of the courtroom to the stairs, down into the lobby, and outside to the street," Harold Rhoden wrote in *High Stakes*. There on the sidewalk he had passed "groups of young girls" with signs, marching like striking office workers. MELVIN, WE BELIEVE YOU, one sign said. WE LOVE YOU, MELVIN, insisted another.

As he walked from the parking lot to the courthouse, Melvin couldn't believe what he was seeing: a parade, and for him! For a moment the feeling that he was being led to the gas chamber lifted, and he smiled and pulled his shoulders back. He was wearing a peculiar outfit for court—Levi's with a big cowboy buckle on his belt and a flowered satin shirt open at the neck—but it sure seemed fine for this. Bonnie, eyeing the braless girls with the signs, hopping up and down and squealing at the sight of their hero, had a different reaction: that she was going to take her husband's place in the gas chamber, because she was about to commit murder. She just couldn't decide if she should start with Melvin with his stupid grin or those girls with their stupid signs. God, she hated Las Vegas.

Inside the courtroom, the doors finally open, the scene was only a little calmer. Journalists loved this kind of scene. They didn't have to do anything to sell it; it had built-in drama and ready-made actors playing for an audience. Thanks to the TV cameras, everyone in the country could feel in themselves the power of judgment that Judge Hayes foolishly thought was his alone.

Hayes, a small, middle-aged man in the middle of radiation treatments for cancer, may have been accustomed to lawyers performing for him, but he had not yet gotten his mind around the idea of the courtroom as a place for mass entertainment. Known as a stern taskmaster on the bench, he nevertheless never really got control of the room, seemingly hypnotized by the circus-like atmosphere that he'd found himself presiding over.

"It was the strangest day in court I believe I've ever experienced," Hayes later remembered in *Melvin and Howard: A Nevada Fairy Tale.* "People lined up early for seats, and at one point a fight broke out between two men who wanted the same seat in the front row. Television and newspaper reporters, that slovenly lot, made themselves at home in my jury box, sketching or taking notes on anyone who came or left. . . . When Dummar came into the courtroom he was stalked by television cameras and people shouted questions at him, and at one point one of the cameramen leaped on my clerk's desk to film the other cameramen filming Melvin."

Melvin sat where he was told and as he swore to tell the truth, he looked out at the reporters and spectators leaning forward in their seats and standing in clusters at the back, and began to realize that he wasn't just giving another deposition. When he performed at church picnics and American Legion halls with the Night Ryders, Melvin always prepared. He believed in preparation, it was one way an entertainer showed his audience that they mattered to him. "I was scared," he says of the moment before the proceedings began, despite his having worked with his lawyers to be ready. He simply hadn't expected such a large audience. "I looked around the room and thought, 'Oh, boy, what am I doing here? How did I get here?'" He instinctively knew that simply answering questions was not going to be enough, not for these people with their pencils and notebooks and cameras and mouths levered open with gum.

That was all that he did, though: answer questions. After Judge Hayes advised him of his rights under the Fifth Amendment of the U.S. Constitution, Melvin admitted that he had lied before to his wife, to his lawyers, to reporters: "I didn't tell the truth to nobody." He said he didn't know where the will came from or who wrote it, but he did know how it got to the Mormon Church headquarters. Through Rhoden's questioning he then began to tell the story that he would stick to ever after. A man he had never seen before came to his gas station on April 27, 1976. The man asked him if he was Melvin Dummar and said something about Howard Hughes's will being found in 1972 near Joseph Smith's house in Salt Lake City. Then the man left, just like that, and Melvin found an envelope on the counter near the gas station's cash register. He explained how later that day he drove into Salt Lake City to the Mormon Church and asked to see President Kimball. "I was going to explain to the president of the church and have a word of prayer with him and tell him the story and kind of let him handle it and advise me, because I could trust him." But the receptionist told him the president wasn't available.

The attorneys contesting the Mormon will took their turns, one by one. They mocked Melvin, yelled at him, brought him to tears, and finally beseeched him in the name of decency to come clean. "You make me sick!" spat

Earl Yoakum, the well-regarded Texas lawyer who represented members of the Hughes family. The crowd gasped and chortled and sometimes was stone-cold quiet, but it didn't make a difference. Melvin stuck to his story; he reiterated that he walked out of President Kimball's office dejected and confused, put the will in a church envelope, "laid it on a guy's desk and left."

Finally, Judge Hayes, a devout Mormon himself, could take no more. "Enough!" he said. He told Melvin to turn around in his seat and face him.

He reminded Melvin that he had taken an oath before God to tell the truth and warned him that the court would seek to criminally prosecute him for perjury if he didn't. Then he asked slowly, in a growling, sonorous voice: "Brother Dummar, I want the truth. Where did the will come from?"

"A man brought it to my station . . ." Dummar began once again, as murmurs of delight rose from the spectators, the murmurs of an audience caught by the impulse to applaud a well-executed dramatic or comedic moment before realizing the scene wasn't over. Judge Hayes quieted the room and continued.

"Do you know who wrote it?" the judge asked.

"No," said Melvin.

Hayes informed Melvin that he thought he was lying. Then he called upon their shared religious faith once again. "Doth it profit a man if he gain the whole world and lose his soul?"

Melvin, wet-eyed again, admitted it did not. He didn't know what else to say to that. People would believe a judge. Melvin says he had thought that telling the truth, even belatedly, would save him, but he was wrong.

"The judge called me a liar, and I just broke down," he remembers. "I just went to pieces. I thought, 'How did I get into this? All I did was stop and help somebody. And it turned into a nightmare.'"

THE INTERVIEW REQUESTS FROM NEWSPAPERS AND MAGAZINES continued. The offers to appear on talk shows included free hotel accommodations and meal allowances. But Melvin wasn't so interested anymore. They were calling him a liar now, a con man, a fool.

"The reporters and TV people just kept coming at me," Melvin says. "At first, [the press] was positive. Then it turned negative. It all went negative. People got a lot of mileage out of me, made jokes about me. Johnny Carson made a lot of jokes about me. Even Bob Hope!"

Melvin didn't see what was so funny. He was growing to hate Harold Rhoden, always puffed up and strutting around, acting better than everybody. He wished Rhoden would drop the whole thing, like he said he was thinking about doing, just to be done with it. He didn't want the money, didn't know what he'd do with it if he had it. He wanted to go back to just being Melvin Dummar. It had been pretty bad when it looked like he was going to get the money: people threatening him, strangers asking for loans, the letters from parents in Africa and India and Mexico with sick children. He had figured it would be a full-time job for him sending money to these people. Now that it looked like he wouldn't be getting any money after all, it was worse. He was being called a liar and a fraud at the grocery store and the post office and when he picked up his kids from school. He went to bed every night with a knot in his stomach that seemed to just get bigger and bigger and bigger.

Reporters who were camped out in Salt Lake City covering the Melvin angle of the Hughes story began to speculate amongst themselves—Did Bonnie write it? Was Melvin's father involved?—and the locals picked up on it. Melvin knew that everyone was looking at him and his family with suspicion. "It was hard for Melvin, people calling him a liar all the time. It really got to him," Bonnie says now. "People still think it. It was out there so much. We just keep to ourselves, even now. I used to wish that all our phones were bugged, that all our lamps were bugged, so people would know."

The negative press couldn't have come at a worse time for the Dummar family. Interstate 15, connecting Salt Lake City to northern Utah, opened in the fall of 1976, overnight turning old Highway 89 into nothing more than a little local street. "We had a lease with an option to buy," Melvin says of Dummar Gas Station, which sat right on Highway 89. "Then they opened the freeway and bypassed us, it was like somebody closed the gate. There's more traffic now, but boy, when they opened that freeway, everybody was on the freeway. I think the day they opened it I had one customer."

In December, just days after the disastrous deposition, the Dummars were evicted from the station and the little house above it on three days' notice. In a matter of weeks, the family that most everyone in the area thought was already rich was, in fact, flat broke and with no prospects. "He couldn't get a job," Bonnie says. "I couldn't get a job."

Melvin had always been willing to do anything, and he'd been good at everything he'd ever done: construction worker, milkman, mine worker, clothes salesman, gas-station operator. He was always on time and always worked late—he never slacked off. But it seemed like none of that mattered anymore. When employers looked at Melvin Dummar, they didn't see a conscientious, hard worker anymore.

"Once we left the station, I couldn't get a job anywhere," Melvin says. "I probably had a hundred different interviews to try and get a job, and nobody would hire me. Even though I'd know that I was qualified. I couldn't even get a job in the oil fields. There were two reactions people would have; either way I was a loser. One, they thought I was a con man and a crook and a liar and everything else they could throw at me. Or they thought, 'Oh, you're gonna be rich. We don't want to hire you and train you and put you to work just to have you quit soon as you get all that money.'"

Ogden and Willard, adjacent to one another, are small, religious Utah towns. The kind of towns where neighbors help each other out. That was what Melvin and Bonnie Dummar had thought about the area when they chose to call it home in 1975. But it didn't turn out that way for them. More than twenty-five years after the Hughes probate trial ended, Melvin and Bonnie still live in the area, but they don't feel a part of it.

As soon as it became public knowledge that Melvin had lied about handling the will, the community where they had lived for two years turned on them, Bonnie says. "Our Mormon Church friends wouldn't let our kids play with theirs anymore," she remembers, her voice laced with bitterness. "They suddenly thought we were bad people. I've never been in the church since then."

"All but a couple people turned their backs on us," Melvin adds. "That's why to this day I haven't gone back to the church. I mean, I'd like to, but everybody still thinks I'm a crook and a liar."

The only people who didn't turn their backs on the Dummars that winter of 1977, it seemed, were the movie people. Universal Studios sent screenwriter Bo Goldman out to Utah to meet with Melvin, and "something just clicked," according to Goldman. He saw something mythical in Melvin's story, but it was a myth that had gone terribly wrong and became something else, something tragic and quintessentially American. Melvin, broke and unemployed, saw his Hughes story in more practical terms: it was a chance to fulfill his dream of being in show business. He signed away his rights to his own story, and then he started calling the film's producers day after day.

"I wanted to play myself," Melvin says, sighing at the memory of it. "I just asked them to give me a chance. They said, No, we want a professional actor. I said, But no one can play me better than me. I kept after them, and they'd just hang up on me." (Melvin would show up on the set anyway and eventually was given a small part as the guy behind a deli counter.)

Even without the lead role, Melvin was enthusiastic about the movie and promised to help the filmmakers any way he could. After having conversations with Goldman and director Jonathan Demme, Melvin says, he was "looking forward more to the movie than the trial."

THE TRIAL, HOWEVER, CAME FIRST. IT BEGAN IN LAS VEGAS ON November 7, 1977.

For Melvin, it couldn't be over soon enough. "Financially, after this whole thing, we were devastated. The attorneys mostly did it on percentage, but we had to sell all our property to pay for the handwriting experts. We didn't have anything left."

They had especially run dry of hope. On the day the trial opened, Bonnie wrote in her diary: "I wish with all my heart that Mel had never stopped to pick up that old man."

Rhoden, however, no longer shared their pessimism. In the nine months since the raucous probate hearing in which Melvin finally came clean about handling the will, Rhoden had grown confident in his case again. He had ink and handwriting evidence that suggested it was highly unlikely anyone but

Howard Hughes could have written the will. He had medical evidence that showed how Hughes could have made such unlikely misspellings and factual errors. He had memos and testimony that made the case that Hughes did leave the Desert Inn and had a compelling reason to go to the Nevada desert. He even had a fifty-three-year-old construction worker named LeVane Forsythe who claimed he had been Hughes's secret personal courier. Forsythe said he had delivered the will to Melvin, and he passed a polygraph exam to that effect.

Rhoden also had another ace in the hole: Dr. Joseph Ford, a dentist who was related by marriage to Kay Glenn, a longtime Hughes employee who had been in charge of Hughes's personal aides. Ford had provided a signed affidavit to Roger Dutson stating that in 1970 he heard Glenn say that Hughes had sneaked out of the Desert Inn many times to go into the desert. Ford specifically recalled Glenn saying that, one time, "something happened out there, and he was picked up and brought back into Las Vegas by someone passing by in a car." When he was called to testify, however, the dentist's memory had changed. He retracted his statement, saying that he couldn't be "positive" about what was said. The best a disgusted Rhoden could get out of Ford was the admission that he had received a phone call from Glenn and that Glenn was upset. On the stand later as a "hostile witness," Glenn denied making any statements about Hughes to Ford or anyone else.

To Rhoden, of course, Ford's original story rang true. Hughes may have been in dire condition both physically and mentally in late 1967, but he still loved making money and he thought he saw a way to score big. At the time, the United States was running short of gold and silver, causing a run on the precious metals that had always backed American currency. Hughes wanted to take advantage of the situation the old-fashioned way: by digging up more of it. He decided to buy up old, inactive silver mines and also scope out pristine acreage that might have wholly undeveloped deposits. The man Hughes put in charge of this effort was a thirty-four-year-old New Yorker named John Meier. Hughes completed his first mining deal, for a series of western Nevada claims, in April 1968, just three months after Melvin says he picked up an old man in the desert. Over the next eighteen months, Hughes would collect more than two hundred claims, spending millions of dollars. What he didn't know was that Meier, in cahoots with many of the sellers, was cheating Hughes. It was eventually discovered that virtually all of the claims were worthless.

After finally being found out and booted from the Hughes empire in 1969, Meier, a man of grandiose self-absorption, unsuccessfully ran for a U.S. Senate seat in New Mexico. Soon thereafter he decamped for Canada and for good reason: He was about to be indicted for income-tax evasion. (In 1978, he would be ordered to pay $8 million to the Summa Corporation, the parent company of the Hughes empire, for defrauding Hughes in connection with the mining properties.)

According to retired FBI agent Gary Magnesen, who briefly interviewed Meier during his 2001 reinvestigation of the will, Rhoden spoke with Meier before the probate trial, and Meier said he could prove that Howard Hughes was in Tonopah in December '67. But he wanted Rhoden to get the income-tax charges against him dropped. Rhoden, of course, could do no such thing, so Meier refused to testify. (He couldn't be compelled to do so in person, as it was a civil suit and he lived in Canada.)

Meier, as the man who was in charge of mining acquisitions for Hughes in 1967–68, would have been the most compelling witness in support of Melvin's story. But he wasn't the only person who claimed to have seen Howard Hughes in Tonopah shortly after Christmas in 1967. So did Eldon Daniel, another Hughes employee, as he was standing in the lobby of Tonopah's Mizpaugh Hotel with Meier on December 29. "Is that who I think it is?" Daniel asked Meier when a rail-thin old man drifted by like an apparition. There was also a local cowboy in a pickup truck who came upon an old man wandering along a dirt road outside of town. The cowboy offered a ride, but the old man refused.

"There are witnesses who say that Howard Hughes was in Tonopah," says Magnesen. "I have documents showing that Howard Hughes was personally inspecting some of the mines he had purchased. It explains why he was on that particular dirt road at that particular time when Melvin found him."

The lawyers contesting the will, however, were hardly willing to concede anything about Melvin's story. One of the lawyers, Phillip Bittle, questioned Melvin's honesty by telling the jury about how Melvin had once given a false name so he could get on *Let's Make a Deal* more often than the rules allowed. Then Bittle and his co-counsel, Earl Yoakum, moved on to the lies Melvin told for nine months about handling the will, until those lies were revealed in his deposition of December 7, 1976. Each lie was combed through carefully and related back to other aspects of his life. Melvin, sitting in the courtroom gripping his hands together, couldn't stand listening to it. He wanted to get back to Utah as soon as his testimony was completed, before the trial's end. "Some days I sat there and clenched my jaw so hard a couple of my teeth broke," he told a reporter.

The trial ended on June 8, 1978, at seven months the longest probate trial in U.S. history. As the jury began its deliberations, Rhoden was feeling confident. He ordered champagne for the celebration he believed inevitable.

Susan McDougal:
The Martyr

The first few weeks that she was in jail, Susan McDougal plotted revenge. She lay on her cot and rolled ideas through her head, calculated
the odds. It was a relief to finally have the time to do it.

"It began with images of torturing and killing Kenneth Starr; that was the
first time it was quiet enough for me to even devise schemes for his torture
and maiming," she remembers. "I would lay there with all of these bitter,
horrible thoughts coursing through me. It felt good. It felt really good."

Throughout the fall of 1996, McDougal tried out all kinds of violent
fantasies as she sat in the Faulkner County Detention Center in Conway,
Arkansas. She turned often to her favorite pastime—the movies—for inspi-
ration. This was nothing new. Before her trial, when a reporter asked her
about Starr, she had barked theatrically that she wanted the special prosecutor dead. "I want his children dead. I want his dog dead. I want his house
burned to the ground," she said, punctuating each desire with an emphatic
finger thrust. The comment hit the front pages of newspapers across the
country, mostly without any mention that it was a quote from the Kevin
Costner–Robert De Niro movie *The Untouchables*. McDougal insists she was
just trying to lighten the reporter's somber mood, but she stands by the sen-

timent nonetheless. "Yeah, I wanted his house to burn down," she says now, more than six years after the whole affair finally ended in 1998. "Oh, yeah."

And why not? Kenneth Starr, the man given the task of investigating President Bill Clinton, had put her through the ringer not just once, but over and over for years. McDougal was an old Arkansas friend of the president, an associate in a suspicious 1970s real-estate deal called Whitewater, and she was standing in the way of Starr's pursuit of Clinton. The experience gave McDougal's lawyer fits. Bobby McDaniel would sit at his desk after negotiations with Starr's Office of the Independent Counsel (OIC), staring at the wall, wondering how to defend his client against a prosecutor who seemed to have his own private rule book.

Susan McDougal.

"I think Susan was being used as a puppet, a pawn, in this grand political struggle," McDaniel says today, carefully enunciating each word. "The tactics they used, if a private lawyer such as myself had used them, I'd have been disbarred and in jail. I know that sounds harsh, but now that it's all over I can express my honest opinion."

When Susan McDougal arrived at the Faulkner County Detention Center on September 9, 1996, she was already a public figure. Most of the other inmates at the jail stared at her with something like awe. They had all seen her on TV. They'd heard her name spoken by news anchors time and again. They couldn't figure out what she was doing there with them. The three male prisoners with whom she'd been transported to the jail had been even more disturbed by her presence. At first, they didn't recognize her. She seemed familiar—pretty in a plain, Southern-belle kind of way, even with the beginnings of middle-aged spread working on the margins. But they figured she was just another prostitute or check kiter as, shackled together at the waist, they headed from a U.S. marshal's holding cell to a waiting van. Then the mob of reporters and cameramen appeared, rushing at them like the Razorbacks' defensive line, all of them shouting: "Susan! Susan! Over here! Susan!" McDougal remembers the waist chains clacking as the prisoners momentarily froze and then jerked in different directions in an instinctive impulse to flee. "What the fuck did you *do*?" one of the prisoners shouted at McDougal in shock and fear.

Sitting in the comfortable, Arkadelphia home of her friend Claudia Riley all these years later, McDougal chuckles at the memory of it. "They thought I was a serial killer," she says, a wide grin on her face. "They were really freaked out. In a situation like that, you hate to say, 'All I did was not testify.'"

Of course, that wasn't all Susan McDougal did. By refusing to testify before Kenneth Starr's grand jury, McDougal had taken on the most powerful prosecutor in the country—one of the most powerful of all time—and fought him to a standstill. She had also put herself on the front lines of what conservative activist Pat Buchanan had called a "cultural war as critical to the kind of nation we will one day be as was the Cold War itself." Her battle with Starr in many ways shaped the American political landscape in the 1990s, providing the very definition of what became known as the "politics of personal destruction."

Starr had struck first, taking McDougal to court on charges of fraudulently obtaining a loan in the 1980s to help Clinton pay off campaign debts and, with then husband Jim McDougal, of giving the future president a sweetheart deal in a real-estate project that went bad. McDougal responded to the charges by clamming up, by retreating in fear to her best friend's house, where she stayed in bed for days at a time.

From the start, the fight hardly seemed fair. Starr, a devout Christian and disciplined workaholic, had graduated at the top of his class from Duke University School of Law and clerked for Chief Justice Warren Burger. He had worked in the Reagan Justice Department and served as the first President Bush's solicitor general before becoming a federal appeals court judge. As independent counsel, appointed by a panel of federal judges, he had virtually unlimited resources.

McDougal, in contrast, was a small-town girl from Arkansas whose worldly experience barely extended beyond attending an undistinguished religious college in Arkadelphia. And she was broke. Her lawyers, McDaniel in Arkansas and later Mark Geragos in Los Angeles, took her case pro bono. Her greatest ally was supposedly the president of the United States, whom she knew through her ex-husband. But she hadn't spoken to Bill Clinton in a decade.

So it came as no surprise when Starr won. McDougal was convicted of fraud in 1996, and, as she awaited formal sentencing on the conviction, was sent to jail for civil contempt of court for refusing to testify before Starr's grand jury. At water coolers across the country she was being reviled as a liar and a slut, amid widespread rumors that she had slept with President Clinton and made some kind of deal with him to keep her mouth shut about their business dealings. Conservative commentators like Buchanan held her up as a symbol of America's—and the White House's—degradation, a victim of moral relativity and liberal arrogance.

"I had just been so pushed to the wall," McDougal says of the crush of emotions she took with her to jail. "I'd had prosecutors threatening me. I had watched my family deteriorate, my mother crying every day. Everywhere I went I was under scrutiny. I was scared to death. I had sold everything I had and borrowed money to defend myself, so I had to depend on other people, even just for food. That was embarrassing and hurtful, and there was a part of me that just wanted to end it. I was just so angry and bitter and hateful."

But instead of ending it, McDougal steeled herself and decided it was time, at last, to talk. Not to Starr and not in court. To the media. That was when something unexpected happened. She became a star.

WHEN SUSAN HENLEY ARRIVED IN ARKADELPHIA FOR THE FIRST time, in 1973, there were still houses downtown that didn't have indoor plumbing. Worse, if Arkadelphians wanted to see a new movie, they had to drive an hour and a half north to Little Rock, the state capital. That alone should have kept the eighteen-year-old away. No one loved movies more than she did. But college in Little Rock was too big a jump for a shy, small-town girl who wanted independence but not too much of it. Arkadelphia and the college there, Ouachita Baptist University, took Susan out of her strict parents' house, which was about forty miles to the southeast of Arkadelphia in Camden, but at the same time it wasn't a whole new world.

Ouachita (pronounced WA-she-tah) was just what Susan was looking for. Her adolescence had revolved around church and books, so she embraced the small, religious college, with its serious-minded, sunny-faced students and conservative, southern ways. There were a lot of ministers-in-training at Ouachita, and they were all proselytizing to the converted, in and out of church. At the same time, it was the 1970s, even in Arkadelphia, and the influence of the wider culture couldn't be entirely beaten back, unlike at the Henley house. In Camden, Jim Henley, a World War II veteran (he met his Belgian wife, Susan's mother, near the front lines), ran a gas station with military precision, and at home expected his seven children and one wife to snap-to with similar rigor, which they did. So, at Ouachita, Susan thought it was great that some of the boys had grown their hair out over their ears and lived to tell about it. She also didn't mind that rock 'n' roll blared indiscriminately from open dormitory windows, sometimes until a few minutes after curfew. What Susan didn't realize, however, was that it wasn't just the students who were pushing, however lightly, at the envelope.

In the summer of 1975, Susan Henley was working as an assistant to a senior faculty member when she met the young political science professor whose office was next door. A secret free-love proponent, the professor immediately hit on her, which she found a little amusing, if disconcerting. "She had an upbeat personality, and her quick-witted repartee hinted at high intelligence," Jim McDougal later remembered of that first encounter with Susan Henley in the The Old Bookstore, an ancient wooden building that housed the school's political-science department. "I asked her out for lunch that day, but she said she had other plans."

Later that week, the twenty-year-old Susan appeared in the doorway of Jim McDougal's office and peered inside. She was trying to keep the panic out of her voice, and succeeded only in giving the impression that she was trying to quietly suffocate herself. The professor she worked for, a notorious taskmaster, was away from campus for the week and he called in every day for his messages at exactly the same time. Susan could hear the phone in his office ringing right now, but she had somehow misplaced the key. Did Professor McDougal, by chance, have an extra key?

Jim McDougal knew an opportunity when he saw one. "Acting out a Ouachita version of the knight-in-shining-armor routine, I accompanied her to [the professor's] office," he wrote in his 1998 political memoir, *Arkansas Mischief*. "Inspecting the door with burglarlike efficiency, I saw it was held by an old-fashioned lock that could be opened by almost any door key. With one quick movement I kicked the lock plate off the door jamb. The door swung open. Susan might have been a bit shocked, maybe even a little frightened, but I got her attention." After Susan answered the phone, Jim asked again if she would join him for lunch. This time, she agreed. Later, the ice broken, she agreed to a date—an afternoon aboard a houseboat with another couple, Jim's colleague and mentor at Ouachita, former Arkansas Lieutenant Governor Bob Riley, and Bob's wife, Claudia.

"Ouachita was a strict place, a very predictable place," Susan says, back in Arkadelphia to visit Claudia Riley nearly thirty years after graduating from the school. "There was no drinking; you had to be in the dorm by nine thirty every night. Very locked-down atmosphere." She sits back in a chair at Claudia's house and lets a smile ease across her lips. "Then I met Jim Mc-Dougal, and life really was different. *Very* different."

Not that she realized that right away. It was just a date, sort of, with a strange—and strangely exhilarating—man. On a nearby lake that weekend, Bob and Claudia Riley were instantly won over by Susan, whom they engaged in a wide-ranging discussion about politics and history, civil rights and Bob's political career. More amazing still, they actually wanted to know her opinion, wanted her to argue when she disagreed—a strange attitude for any adult Arkansan to take toward a young woman. Jim McDougal normally made a point of dominating any social situation, but on this day his thoughts were elsewhere. "A picture lingers in my mind of Susan in her black bathing suit on our first date at DeGray Lake," he remembered years later. When he had her alone for a moment, he looked her over carefully and asked, "Where did you get those curves?" Susan smiled and shrugged, cocking her head. "They just showed up," she said. Jim didn't need to know much more about her than that. He was "smitten."

Susan immediately latched on to the Rileys, but she also unexpectedly found herself drawn to Jim McDougal. In 1975, Jim was considered a catch in Arkansas social circles, even though he didn't look like it. He was a balding, slight, thirty-four-year-old recovering alcoholic whose mouth would pop open like a baby bird's when an attractive coed passed by him on campus. But this odd-looking little man who wore white suits and affected an aristocratic accent was so full of life and fun and intelligence that just thinking about him made colleagues and friends smile. "Jim was at the height of his powers when he and Susan met," Claudia Riley says. "People forget that. They forget what the real Jim McDougal was like."

The real Jim McDougal, along with being a professor at Ouachita, was a burgeoning kingmaker in Arkansas Democratic politics. Jim had grown up in poor, rural Bradford and spent his adolescence working in his father's feed store. But there was a spark in this Arkansas farm boy, and when he was in his early twenties, he bought a suit and moved to Washington, D.C., first to work for Senator John McClellan and then for Congressman Wilbur Mills. He immediately made a name for himself as an astute and efficient political operator, and also as one of the best raconteurs in the capital. He returned to his home state in 1968 to successfully direct J. William Fulbright's U.S. Senate re-election campaign and to make some money by dabbling in real-estate development. He then went to work for Riley, who got Jim onto the Ouachita faculty in 1975 even though Jim didn't have a college degree to his name.

Bob Riley and Jim McDougal were immediate stars on the little Ouachita Baptist campus. Riley, after all, had been governor earlier in the year, when he served out the final ten days of then Senator-elect Dale Bumpers's term. Jim had been Riley's lone staffer in the governor's office, and in the months that followed was frequently mentioned as a possible candidate for political office himself. Susan, who as a child had dreamed of being a member of the Kennedy clan, was awed by all of this. To her twenty-year-old eyes, the movie-loving Susan says now, Jim was "like Peter O'Toole in *My Favorite Year*"—a little bit off, but dashing, larger-than-life, and irresistible. (The later Jim, the Jim McDougal in decline, she likens to Boo Radley from *To Kill a Mockingbird*.)

Ouachita, it could be argued, needed a Peter O'Toole character. Even in the era of student activism, few thought to challenge the school's disciplinarian traditions; eighteen-year-olds did not come to Arkadelphia to rebel. Jim, on the other hand, made a point of smoking in class and of refusing to give final exams. He saw it as his duty to flout the rules, or at least to ignore them. One rule Jim most certainly did not accept was the one that prohibited faculty from having intimate relationships with students.

"This is where I lived when Jim and I started dating; we'd meet right here," Susan says, driving through campus with Claudia Riley and reminiscing about her student days in Arkadelphia. With the car coasting slowly, Susan is looking across a splash of bright green lawn to a boxy redbrick building with concrete front columns. Susan's window is open as she drives, and the wind lifts her hair off her ears and snaps it into the corners of her eyes. Her hair glows orange in the sun, as if it's blushing. It isn't hard to picture a young Susan Henley coming out from between those columns and skipping hurriedly down the steps, breaking into a joyful smile at the sight of her new boyfriend. Jim McDougal, who was late for everything, was never late for a date with Susan Henley.

"We'd play guitar and sing on the lawn there, right in front," Susan continues. "The 1970s was a good time to be at Ouachita. It was very liberal. It was very free. Now it's run by Nazis. In the '70s Bob Riley ran the political-science department, and he was almost a communist."

"He was *not* a communist!" Claudia suddenly erupts, sitting bolt upright in her seat. She'll let Susan idealize the past only so much.

"No, no," Susan corrects herself, touching Claudia's arm. "But he was very liberal. That's what I meant."

Everything Susan says about Bob Riley she means as a compliment, and so saying something about him that gets Claudia's ire up will leave a knot in her stomach for the rest of the day. After all, it was Bob, who died in 1994 at the age of sixty-nine, and Claudia, now Susan's closest friend, who were her parents-away-from-home during her college days. They were also so much more than that. "I'd never felt I fit in anywhere until I met them," Susan says. "Bob and Claudia's house was my first safe place." In her own home, growing up with a clutch of crew-cut, athletic brothers and popular, powdered sisters, she had always felt she was "the weird one." She was cute, and she was funny, but that didn't get you very far in Camden. The local kids, unlike Jim McDougal, didn't have much use for quick-witted repartee.

"My sister was a beauty queen; my brother was a heartthrob," Susan says. "Girls would stand outside the house and squeal like my brother was Fabian. Being popular [in Camden] was kind of like being a celebrity—at least I recognized the similarities years later—because it was such a small town. Everyone knew you, everyone was focused on you, if you were the football star or the homecoming queen or whatever. But I was not the beautiful one; I was the smart one. I remember once my sister saying to me, after I embarrassed her in front of her friends, 'All I ever wanted was for you to be normal!'"

At the Riley house she was, at last, normal. There, it was normal to talk about books and about what was going on in the world. It was normal to come up with your own opinions. It was definitely normal to admire Bob Riley. He wasn't just a brilliant, big-hearted intellectual; he was an honest-to-goodness hero. During World War II, he had fought in the Pacific theater, where he lost virtually all of his sight to a fusillade of shrapnel as he attempted to take out a Japanese pillbox. But Bob Riley didn't view his blinding as a disability. He already knew what Claudia looked like, and that memory was good enough for him. Besides, his mind and his vocal cords still worked, and that was all he really needed. Thirty years after Bob Riley came home from war, Susan, like Claudia, could listen to him talk for hours, and Bob, with his white beard and black eye patch, obliged, expounding on Franklin Roosevelt or the Southern agrarian movement or whatever struck his fancy that day. Usually, Susan and Claudia weren't his only audience. "Bob would dismiss class on nice days, and he would go to their boat down on the lake and hold class out there," Susan says. "And people would come who weren't even in the class. Just to be there, to hear Bob talk. It would go on into the evening. It was the first time I really felt like, 'This is what I want to do. This is what I want to be.'"

That thought still crosses Susan's mind whenever she lets her memory drift back over the years, to The Old Bookstore and Bob Riley on his houseboat, and college kids coming from all corners of the campus to hear him speak. To so many coeds Bob was the image of the perfect grandfather, sitting hunched and cross-legged on the deck of his boat, the wide, curdling sky framing him endlessly. The girls would sit up close, decked out in their sweaters and collared pullovers and stiff, linen skirts that sometimes stuck out like rudders. Boys would be there, too, even couples sitting quietly in the back. This passed as entertainment for college students in Arkadelphia in the middle of the 1970s.

Susan smiles, lost in the memory, as she drives through a back corner of the campus, heading away from the lake. She allows the slope of the landscape to drop the car into the center of town, which replaces a panoramic view of prime Arkansas nothingness with stolid rows of small, sun-beaten houses, shops, and churches. Susan swings the car to the right, and the buildings momentarily become larger, rising up behind the shade of sagging trees.

On a corner, a two-story house has been converted into a restaurant, and Susan taps the brakes. The restaurant's six parking spaces are taken, so Susan parks in the circular driveway. No one will mind; they know her here. As she turns off the car, a college girl in a neon-orange sports bra and bicycle shorts canters past, seemingly naked if not for the garish splash of color. Susan watches the girl slip around the corner and proceed deliberately down the sidewalk. She knows she could never have gotten away with such an outfit in downtown Arkadelphia when she was that age, no matter how liberal Bob Riley's political-science department had been. Now, even with the "Nazis" running the university, it's a normal sight.

"I loved being a student here; it was very freeing," Susan says, smiling at her reflection in the windshield as she climbs out of the car. "I was very, very shy, just enormously shy when I came to Ouachita. Claudia beat it out of me. She told me, 'You have to *enter* a room.' She was always lecturing me on how to be a part of a life bigger than I'd known."

Jim McDougal had known something about living large, too. He was full of stories about the sexual revolution that was taking place in cities like New York and San Francisco and London, and he lectured her on the equality of the sexes. Susan never thought twice about the propriety of dating a professor; Jim told her the old mores were boring and out of date, and he could be awfully convincing. "Don't be small-town," he kept telling her. Loosen up; the world is finally getting interesting.

Any qualms Susan had about such an attitude were easily waylaid. Jim made her laugh so hard she thought she would pass out, and the fact that Bob Riley thought of him as a son only made him exponentially more attractive to her. Bob and Claudia loved Jim and believed he was going to do great things for their state. For his part, Jim wanted nothing more from a day than to impress Bob Riley. Bob could talk until the house fell down around him, and Jim was always determined to top him: to tell better stories, to offer greater insights, to get bigger laughs. And it often worked, even with Susan. "I never heard anyone talk like Jim," Susan says. "He talked like the characters I grew up reading about and wanting to be like. Maybe it was easier for me when I became known from being on TV because Jim always acted like he was famous. He cultivated the persona you have to have. After a while, it seemed normal to be the center of attention, just from being with him."

Jim was also that holiest of holies, an idealist. But not just an idealist—Susan was a mere idealist—Jim was out there doing something about his beliefs. That was the ace in the hole for Jim McDougal. It was impossible for most teenagers to follow a discussion of syndicalism and the economic plight of Arkansas's rural poor with a passionate necking session. But to a certain kind of serious-minded college girl from the South—and Susan was that kind of girl—the words of William Jennings Bryan and Eugene Debs and Noam Chomsky passed from moist lips to sensitive ear like the sweetest of sweet nothings. And Jim could coo all night long about how he was making all those glorious ideals come true.

Susan was hooked, on Jim and on the life he led, and Jim started showing off his beautiful young girlfriend at political parties in Hot Springs and Fayetteville. These soirees were packed with large, red-faced men in tuxedos and gaunt women in dewy, revealing gowns, the kind of people Susan had only seen in the movies. "In one of those early parties I went to with Jim, I actually—I've never told anybody this in my whole life—I actually hid in a closet," Susan remembers. "I was still so shy, and I thought, 'I've got to get out of this; it's just too much input. I can't deal with this.' So I went in the closet and thought, 'I'm just staying here until it winds down. No one's going to miss me. Who would miss me?' Jim was having a big time; people were grabbing him when he walked in the door, yelling 'Jim McDougal!', which is how it always was with Jim. And I'd be thinking, 'I'm getting out of here.'"

Except she didn't, because as much as all the talk and action and new faces scared her, they also thrilled her. She liked living life on the arm of a powerful, important man. "Jim provided the stimulation she'd always craved," Claudia says. "She was hungry for it and just didn't know it." Susan kept going to parties with Jim. She forced herself to chat with the red-faced men and to wear the dewy, revealing outfits that were all the rage. She forced herself to feel sophisticated and comfortable.

Within a year of graduating from Ouachita Baptist University, the shy, churchgoing Susan Henley became Susan McDougal and moved with her new husband to Little Rock. There, in the big city, she found herself living a life she never thought possible. She didn't want to think "small town" anymore. She didn't want to look "small town" anymore. She had a college education, and she wanted to be sophisticated like her husband. She took to this new attitude, if not naturally, then with enthusiasm, hanging out at the Capitol, telling bawdy jokes, and wearing the miniskirts and cleavage-spilling blouses that Jim brought home for her.

That's when Bill Clinton entered the picture.

THE FAULKNER COUNTRY JAIL WASN'T AS BAD AS SUSAN HAD EX-pected from watching prison movies. It was more like *Animal House* than the Big House. The other inmates were mostly hookers and crackheads. The very sight of them should've scared the bejesus out of Susan, but, newly radicalized by her own sense of being betrayed, she wasn't intimidated. They were just *babies*, these convicts, so young and confused. And they were drawn to her. Susan, who had just turned forty, was a full two decades older than many of her fellow prisoners, and she looked even older. Well into her thirties, she had been proud that she could still pass for a college student, but those days were gone now. She had turned fleshy after three years of sitting and fretting in lawyers' offices, listening to men in suits blather on in their indecipherable jargon. Moreover, scoliosis, a degenerative spinal condition that would be severely aggravated by prison life, had begun to push her shoulders forward, giving her a slightly stooped walk. But far more important to the other inmates than her relatively advanced years was the fact that she had been on TV, making her the resident celebrity of the jail. All the inmates, even the psychotics in solitary confinement, knew who Susan was; the video clips of her in handcuffs and leg irons had been shown over and over on CNN and local Arkansas news programs. They all knew that she had personally met the president of the United States. They all knew that she was, somehow, *special*. So a group of the younger women came to her with a Bible one day. They wanted her to read it to them.

"I thought, 'Oh, there is no way.' Because I hated Starr so much for all his hypocrisy about religion," Susan says. "I still had so much rage in me. I had no good thoughts in me. Just anger. But they said they couldn't read it, they couldn't understand the big words, and that kind of got me to focus."

Susan had grown up in church. She had loved Jesus. As an adolescent, inspired by her strict but loving parents, she had dreamed of ministering to the poor, of doing her bit for humanity. The past two decades had dimmed her sense of mission, but these young, banged-up women offering her a Bible reached the missionary in her. "I got on the floor and said, 'How did you guys get here?'" she recalls. "'You're holding these Bibles and you're so young and look so sweet. You don't look like these bad criminals, these mean people.' And that was just the beginning of getting better. Because I had felt so sorry for myself, for so long, when I went to jail. And I got over that really quickly listening to their stories."

Their stories helped Susan put her own in perspective. Yes, her husband had turned out to be a rat, and she had gotten caught up in legal contretemps far beyond her control. But she had friends and a large family that loved her, and she had dedicated lawyers working pro bono on her behalf. That was not the case with any of the other women she met in the Faulkner County Detention Center. Almost without exception, these women had been battered by relatives or guardians or boyfriends. They had no family, no friends, no education. No hope. Most didn't even have $200 for bail; this was jail, not prison, so many of the inmates were awaiting trial for relatively minor offenses. Susan McDougal had spent most of the previous twenty years of her life around politicians and their idealistic, outsized dreams. She'd known Bill Clinton since he was a budding congressional candidate and she was a twenty-year-old college student. Her ex-husband had worked for the legendary Senator J. William Fulbright. Her dearest friend and mentor was the widow of a former governor. But it wasn't until that night that an activist was born.

"I can barely remember who I was before going to jail," Susan says now, her eyes bright with a convert's fervor. "I didn't testify on my own behalf at my trial because I didn't think anybody would listen to me; I didn't think I even had the ability to articulate what I knew and what I didn't know and what had happened to me. I just thought, 'Gosh, they're all just so much smarter than I am.' So I immediately related to these women who thought no one would listen, no one would care. 'I can't do it.' I just thought, 'Boy, this is crazy.' These were women who were making excuses for people who were beating them. For monsters who were molesting them when they were children. They'd say, 'Oh, well, I should have done this or that.' So I decided we were going to start doing something, right there in jail, consciousness-raising things—what should I have done and what should I do now? Really basic things we could do to protect ourselves and be stronger women. So I healed and let go of some of my anger and got better in there."

To her surprise, she also started getting letters—hundreds of them. The image of Susan McDougal, this attractive, middle-aged, slightly dazed-looking suburban wife, handcuffed and in leg irons on her way to jail, had become a TV news staple in coverage of the ongoing Whitewater investigation, and people all over the country had begun to pay attention to her case. One of the ways Susan bonded with her fellow inmates, women with whom she had so little in common, was through sharing her letters, because the other inmates rarely got any mail of their own. As she lay on her cot at night, the other women would call out to her from their cells, astonished at what they were reading. "Susan, you have to read this letter!" one would cry out. "No, you've got to read this one!" came another voice. They were amazed that so many people cared about a convict, a woman in jail, and they were amazed that they knew someone who was so *important*.

Even now, more than six years after winning her freedom, "I think of sitting in prison," Susan says, "looking through letters, all these letters, and saying that this is just like a scene in a movie. And the girls laughing and saying, 'Who's gonna play me? Who's gonna play me?'"

At the time, Susan didn't actually think a movie about her experiences was possible. How could she? She was in jail. She was wearing an orange jumpsuit and had to get permission to eat. But when a radio station sent her a letter asking her to call them collect, she did so—and was stunned to learn that people wanted to hear not just that she was okay, but what she thought about Starr and the whole investigation of the president. She didn't hold back. For the first time in her life, she believed she truly had something to say. "So I started calling collect to lots of radio stations," she says, "and letting them know what I thought about Starr." When the response was positive, she soon was adding to her talking points, weighing in not just on Whitewater and the independent counsel but on jail conditions as well. It made her feel good. She wasn't just some politician's coddled wife getting her comeuppance, legally deserved or not. She had a mission—and she had a platform, a stage, for expressing it. Journalists were calling the jail at all hours, trying to get her on the line. She had never been more popular. She loved the attention. She was happy. "I would put other prisoners on the phone; we would sing to radio stations; we'd just do crazy stuff. So being in jail didn't seem horrible to me," she says. "It seemed safe now. It seemed like someplace I could help people, where I could get better, and where I wasn't under attack."

WHEN SUSAN HENLEY GOT MARRIED, SHE HAD SPENT EIGHTEEN years in tiny, boring Camden and a couple more in only slightly less tiny and boring Arkadelphia. She wanted excitement in her life—and that was what Jim McDougal promised her. There was no doubt that he could provide it. He was the political operator in Arkansas everyone sought out for advice. He was also an increasingly successful real-estate entrepreneur with whom everyone in the state wanted to do business. As soon as she arrived in Little Rock, Susan was meeting important people, like Senator Fulbright, Governor David Pryor, and Attorney General Jim Guy Tucker, who was so handsome he made her eyes hurt. She was tagging along as Jim did important things, whether it was campaigning for his friend Bill Clinton or scouting land for a big real-estate deal. For the first time in her life, Susan went on shopping sprees—big, ridiculous shopping sprees—and she loved it. She appeared in local TV ads for her husband's real-estate developments and got recognized at the mall—and she loved that, too.

When Clinton took up residence in the governor's office in 1979—at thirty-two years old, he was the nation's youngest governor—Susan's already fast-paced life speeded up even more. Clinton asked Jim to join his

Jim and Susan McDougal on their wedding day, 1976.

team, and so Jim put aside his teaching chores and pushed off many of his real-estate deals to Susan and went to work for Governor Clinton. Susan thought she was going to pass out from excitement. She had been tremendously impressed with Clinton during the campaign for governor. She recognized his attempts to connect with people for what they were—a pitch for votes—but she was moved by them nonetheless. "I used to call it 'standing on your tiptoes,'" she says of watching Clinton in action. "You've seen Clinton; he'll raise up on his tiptoes when he's trying to engage you and he'll get in your face and be very engaging and warm and his eyes will be all wet. It was fun to watch; he would just dazzle people and charm people."

By then, the McDougals and the Clintons were old friends. Bill Clinton had met Jim McDougal in 1968 when Clinton, then a bearded college student, volunteered to help out on Senator Fulbright's reelection campaign, which Jim was managing. Despite their seven-year age difference, Jim and Clinton bonded like long-lost brothers, and Jim put the younger man in charge of driving Fulbright to campaign appearances. But on the first day, Clinton's nonstop chatter quickly made the senator's head hurt, and the day ended with

Fulbright marching into Jim's office and warning him to "keep that kid away from me." Still, Jim saw something special in the enthusiastic, constantly talking Clinton and refused to banish him to envelope stuffing. Jim was never jealous of people who could dominate a conversation as completely as he could; it was like finding a kindred spirit, two giants in Lilliput. Clinton was the same way, and over the next half-dozen years they became confidantes. "I never saw Jim with Bill Clinton when Bill didn't practically pick him up off his feet in an embrace," Susan says. "He just loved to see Jim."

Clinton loved to see Susan, too, as it turned out. With her infectious smile and farm-girl curves, Susan surely reminded Clinton of his adolescence, of the naively sexy small-town cheerleaders who were beyond his reach when he was a dorky teen in Hot Springs, Arkansas. Now that he was a rising politician in his home state, Clinton was finding that women, at last, were attracted to him, and he enjoyed it so much that flirting had become second nature. Shortly after Clinton first met Susan, who was then still a Ouachita student, he sent Jim a note, suggesting they get together for dinner and adding: "I hope you bring that long, lanky girl—I liked her."

Clinton's attentions toward that long, lanky girl didn't bother Jim, who respected any man who had an eye for the ladies. In fact, Jim was proud of having a wife who was young and beautiful enough to turn other men's heads. So it only made sense to him, as he threw himself into his new role as Clinton's chief legislative salesman, to start calling on Susan to help him woo state legislators. Making laws, after all, was a dirty business.

In Jim's quest to get things done, his wife's youth and attractiveness became "a marketing tool," Susan admits. Jim would send Susan off to see legislators and other high-powered folks "just to make them feel better," she says. "Jim would say, 'So-and-So is kind of down today, why don't you go say hello.' And I'd go in and sit on their desk and we'd talk and tell jokes and laugh." Legislators knew they would always get a big hug from the twenty-five-year-old Mrs. McDougal, and for some that was worth a vote for some dreary bill they hadn't read. Susan's role was a time-honored one for women in the South—tension release for the men doing the important work—and Susan took it seriously. "Susan, you ought to be able to sell some real estate in that outfit," Clinton's press secretary told her one day as she set off on a mission, sashaying through the governor's office in a sheer, half-unbuttoned blouse and baby-doll skirt.

These missions would sometimes even take her into Clinton's office, where she would help lighten the load for the constantly harried and disorganized young governor. Susan "had a good figure, and in the summer she flaunted it with low-cut dresses," Jim would later write in *Arkansas Mischief.* "If I knew Clinton was grumpy, I'd tell Susan, 'Go in and see Bill. It will make him feel better.'" Nothing more than a few raunchy jokes and a hug were expected of her during these flirting sessions, with either the legislators or the governor, she says. The rumors about an affair with Clinton, she insists, were false. But Susan admits Jim wouldn't have minded if more did happen.

"It was the '70s and people thought different then," she says. "I wanted to not be small town; I wanted to be sophisticated. In Jim's world, that meant you didn't have small-minded mores."

That was what it meant in Bill Clinton's world, too. With the frenetic Rhodes scholar filling his staff with his own generation's best and brightest (Jim, at thirty-eight, was the oldest member of Clinton's inner circle), the governor's mansion took on the mood of a frat house, especially when his wife, Hillary, was away. A pinball machine was brought in, and plenty of beer for after-hours relaxation. There were even late-night parties in the basement, with a gorgeous secretary banging her thigh against the pinball machine while half-drunk men on the staff watched raptly, daring each other to sidle up to her. There were always pretty women around the governor's mansion, and it was never clear if they worked there or not. Yet Jim didn't worry about all the whispering going on about Clinton sleeping with any-thing in high heels. He knew star quality when he saw it, and he saw it (and himself) in the governor. He believed that people like Clinton, men so com-fortable on TV and so relatable to those watching, were bulletproof in this new age they were entering. The young governor was going places, no mat-ter what he did with women who weren't his wife, and Jim wanted to go along. To this end, he even planned ahead, something he was typically loath to do. Before the governor's race got under way in earnest in 1978, Jim had brought Clinton into his latest real-estate project, a fifty/fifty partnership between the McDougals and the Clintons that would buy, subdivide, and sell two hundred and thirty acres of pristine land in the Ozarks for vacation and retirement homes. Jim brought it up one evening when he and Susan ran into the Clintons at the Black-Eyed Pea, a favorite restaurant in Little Rock. Susan, a budding marketing maven, already had a slogan for the development, which they called Whitewater: "More than a place to live, it's a *way* to live . . . quiet, peaceful, serene, simple and honest."

SUSAN IS CONVINCED THAT IT BURNED KENNETH STARR UP THAT she was getting so comfortable in jail. And so famous. "He wanted the attention. He was doing it for the attention, so he could then become a senator or Supreme Court justice," she says. "He loved being stopped in his driveway or taking out his trash by a TV reporter. Every time I was on the radio, I was threatening that."

After three months in the local jail, Susan, with no warning, was moved to another facility—and then another and another. The independent counsel would encourage her, through her lawyer, to start talking, and when she refused, she'd find herself being hustled off to a new, even more unpleasant home. Over the next eighteen months—when she was in prison solely for contempt of court—she was treated more like Hannibal Lecter than someone who was refusing to testify before a grand jury. She was moved around to seven different jails and federal prisons, and at one point spent nearly two months, twenty-three hours a day, in a soundproof plexiglass pod that caused her to suffer severe sensory deprivation. She even did a tour of duty at the most notorious women's prison in America, Sybil Brand in Los Angeles, where she was housed on "Murderers' Row." There, she was forced to wear the red prison outfit that was supposed to be reserved for killers.

Even more than other prisons, Sybil Brand reveled in its own neglect, the grime having become almost like a polish, the toilets proudly stopped up, the walls and ceilings flaking as if it were constantly lightly snowing inside the cells. An army of roaches and rats prowled the cell blocks here, giving inmates the sense of being in a world in which everything but them was constantly moving, usually just out of their field of vision but always palpable. "Cockroaches would fall on your face in the night, and if you didn't grab up your tray right when they pushed it through, the rats ran to it," Susan remembers. Prisoners had a tendency to unconsciously shake themselves, over and over, like dogs emerging from a lake. In 1997, the ACLU filed a lawsuit alleging that Susan was being subjected to "barbaric conditions" on Starr's orders in an effort to get her to testify. A week after the lawsuit was filed, Susan was moved to a better-maintained prison. (Sybil Brand was eventually shut down.) "Her confinement included punishment which can only be deemed 'cruel and unusual,'" veteran White House journalist Helen Thomas wrote in the introduction to *The Woman Who Wouldn't Talk*, Susan's Whitewater memoir.

"I have no respect at all for Kenneth Starr or the techniques he used," adds Bobby McDaniel. "It was the most abusive use of governmental power that can be imagined."

From the independent counsel's perspective, the treatment that Thomas described as "cruel and unusual" was simply an incentive for Susan to cooperate. There was no reason for the OIC to think it wouldn't work. On her first day in a federal prison in Texas, Susan watched in horror as a woman tore a pay phone off the wall and beat another inmate with it. Even Susan's underwear wasn't safe: it consistently disappeared in the prison laundry— keepsakes for the male prisoners who did the washing. Susan was a celebrity, after all. Despite all this, she didn't complain. Instead of breaking her down, the independent counsel was building a better, stronger woman. In prison, Susan McDougal was suddenly a larger-than-life version of herself, a famous heroine, and she liked it. Time and again she became the jailhouse leader, standing up for the rights of herself and her fellow inmates for causes ranging from privacy while bathing to the necessity of clean drinking water. Speaking out, she discovered, was empowering. And the audience, her fellow inmates, was almost always adoring. She became a mother hen to the inmates in the various jails and prisons she found herself in. She peppered them with questions on how they got there, offering up advice on how to reshape their lives in more positive terms, making up aerobic exercise classes she could lead to make them feel better about themselves. In the worst situation of her life, Susan found that she was happy. Actually happy. Danielle Dickinson, Susan's older sister, remembers with awe the time Susan called from prison to sing "Happy Birthday" to her.

"There it was, my birthday, and I was being sung to by Susan and a bunch of inmates—*murderers*," she says, still disbelieving. Susan laughs as her sister tells the story, but Danielle's face is pained as she relates it. "She would call me from prison and tell me how wonderful she was doing, how much fun she was having," Danielle says. "And I'm on my knees after she's come off the phone, just sick at the thought of her in prison. I cannot tell you. She was always laughing. I don't know how she did it."

No one could understand it, certainly no one on the outside. Journalist Judy Bachrach asked Susan about being made to wear the red uniform—"the color used to designate convicted child killers and other violent types"— when she was at Sybil Brand, and about a former inmate's claim that Susan was singled out for punishment by the guards. Susan's response made Bachrach blanch. While some saw the guards' treatment of her as unfair, Susan saw it as being recognized as someone special. She was on the news all the time, she pointed out, so who could blame the guards for being jealous? "And I thought the prison outfits were so beautiful," she added, referring to the red uniforms reserved for the worst of the worst. "They were sixty percent cotton, and you know that's hard to come by."

Some reporters, encountering a response like this, might have suspected that Susan McDougal had gone round the bend while behind bars. But in fact Susan had never been saner. She *was* powerful in prison—powerful in a way she had never been before. The other inmates saw it; they came to her as if to a sage. When Susan talks about those days now, she can't help but smile— the dreamy kind of smile one gets when recalling a singular triumph, the smile of deep and honest pride. "I think they felt first that they could approach me because I had been on television. Television is so funny; it makes people think that they know you," she says. "So I was approachable. If I had just been some educated white girl who'd come in there, how would they have approached me? How would they have known they could even speak to me? They probably wouldn't have. But because I'd been on television I was like their next-door neighbor. When I walked though the door the first time, they all yelled, 'Susan! Susan!' I was like, '*Susan?* What is that?' Then it kept going because I was educated and different. One night, we were playing this game—I would make up whatever games I wanted to make up—and one night it was 'What is the worst thing a man has ever done to you?' We went down the cell block, hearing terrible things, and we got to the end and they said, 'Okay, what is the worst thing a man has done to you, Susan?' And I wasn't even going to play; I just wanted to get them all talking. After hearing all their stories, I said, 'Oh, I don't think I can do it.' And they started yelling, 'You've got to do it, you've got to do it.' So I said, 'Okay, once, when I was married, I decided that to be a good wife I had to wash and iron my husband's white shirts—they were very expensive shirts. I was really young, and he wanted me to take them to the cleaners, and I said to myself, 'No, I want to show him how great I am at this,' and I burned the cuffs. When he found out he got mad about it, and that really hurt my feelings because I had tried so hard. So I locked the door to the bedroom and said just leave me alone. He said to open the door, and I wouldn't, and he said, 'Open the door,' and I wouldn't. So he kicked it, and the door fell down. And I said to the girls, 'I thought at that moment, I might have to divorce him.' Well, they just exploded with laughter. They thought it was the funniest story they had ever heard. It just showed the difference in who we were. But they loved the fact that I was so innocent. I didn't know what crack cocaine was when I went to jail. I had never heard of it. I had heard of powder cocaine, but I had never heard of crack cocaine. They loved the fact that I knew nothing about crime. That I had no idea how to make crack cocaine, and they would tell me, you mix this and this, and I would say, 'No way, *household* items?' All of that they just loved. They loved being able to be part of a life they had never known and for me to tell them stories about that."

IN THE EARLY DAYS, BEFORE EVERYTHING WENT BAD, BILL CLIN-
ton came around all the time. As he was preparing to run for attorney gen-

eral, and then governor, he would hang out at the McDougals' little house in Little Rock, talking about all the things he and Jim were going to do for their state and for the country. The talk was infectious, a natural high. Susan discovered she always had a smile on her face when she realized Bill Clinton was coming through the front door.

"Jim and Bill Clinton could talk about their ideals until you wanted to parade in the streets and yell, 'Hey, we've got to do this,'" Susan says. "It was very noble, when we would just be sitting around talking, and it would be from the heart. I loved that."

She believed they could do it all, too. Bill and Jim could do anything they set their minds to. She saw that Clinton was vain, just like her husband, but she admired him enormously. It wasn't until she met Jim McDougal that she had ever seriously conceived of a life different than the one she knew growing up. But Bill Clinton, who was born in an even smaller town and in unenviable conditions, seemed to know from the time he could walk that he had places to go.

"Years later," she says, "I would tell women in jail, 'Don't ever think you can't do anything because of your background. Look at Bill Clinton. His father was dead; his stepfather was an alcoholic who beat his mother. There was never any money; he never had new clothes. His mother worked as a hairdresser for a time. And he's president of the United States! So don't ever give up.' Now, I recognize Bill Clinton has talents, intellect, that you either have or you don't. But, at the very least, the very least you can do, I would tell women, is you can be a good person."

Of course, Jim McDougal had many of those same talents that Clinton had, and the same ambitions. After two years of working for Governor Clinton, he decided it was time to step forward and put those talents to use. So in 1982 he quit his government job and decided to run for Congress. He told Susan of his decision an hour before he made it official at a press conference. He and Clinton, who was running for governor again, often campaigned together.

Susan was never happier than during that campaign. She believed in the things Jim was saying. She believed Arkansas could be transformed. She gave coffee klatches for Little Rock's ladies-who-lunch, and she beamed from the back of makeshift stages set up in campgrounds along the base of the Ouachita Mountain range. She was on her feet fourteen hours a day, shaking hands, revving up crowds, giving pep talks to volunteers, and when she would finally collapse into bed at night it was with the most satisfying bone-weariness she had ever felt. "Believe it or not—this is embarrassing—I used to cry at Jim's speeches," she says more than twenty years after the campaign. "I would listen and I would think, 'He's just got to win. He's got to.'"

He didn't. Despite a barnstorming campaign unseen in the district since Franklin Roosevelt's time, Jim polled only 34 percent of the vote against popular eight-term Republican Congressman John Paul Hammerschmidt. It was the first significant defeat in Jim's career, and it would prove to be the start of a destructive trend. Not long after the election, Jim's health began to give out in fits—"a dark shade seemed to come over my eyes," he would later say of the episodes that periodically gripped him—and in the years ahead he would be diagnosed with manic depression and a heart condition. But he didn't know any of that yet. He only knew that there was so much to accomplish, that he still had to be the big man—someone Bob Riley could be proud of, someone Bill Clinton could be impressed by.

After the election defeat, Jim continued to obsessively build his real-estate business and take on new ventures, often seemingly by whim. In a newly deregulated environment that now allowed savings-and-loan institutions to expand their investments beyond home mortgages, Jim decided to buy both a bank and an S&L in small Arkansas towns, Madison Bank & Trust and Madison Guaranty. He had big plans. He would use the bank and the S&L to get some fun back in his life, to do big things. That was what he had promised Susan at the very beginning, after all. He was going to be the man everyone in Arkansas—at least every thinking man—wanted to be.

"He had made it very clear from the start that ours was not going to be a mom-and-pop sort of marriage," Susan says. "He didn't want to have children. He said we were going to have fun. It was going to be a great, fun marriage doing a bunch of fun things and we should feel free."

Jim didn't want to be a typical banker. He wanted to be a populist banker, the one man in the community everybody turned to for help. "We kept payments low by doing our own financing," Susan says of the basic business plan. "That was unheard of. We didn't check your credit; you just gave us the money, and you made your payments. If you didn't make your payments, we'd resell [the property]." This idealistic, low-maintenance approach fit perfectly with how Jim liked to think of himself, but as interest rates rose it didn't help his bottom line. That was where the savings and loan came in. Since S&Ls were now allowed to invest in most anything, Jim decided that Madison Guaranty would invest in real estate—his.

None of this really registered with Susan. She was too busy living large and not thinking much. That was what Jim wanted his wife to do. After all, she was the wife of a banker now, and even a populist banker had to look prosperous. Still in her twenties, Susan found that she took to it quite easily, even naturally. She drove around in a Jaguar. She gave sales pitches for real-estate properties, using words like *easy* and *beautiful*. She pulled on hot pants and rode a white horse for a local TV ad promoting one of the developments. She laughed high and loud and often, just like Jim did, just like Bill Clinton did. One day, she walked into the lobby of Madison Bank & Trust and bellowed, apropos of nothing, "*I own this fucking place!*" And with that, it was official. Susan Henley, the voracious reader, the churchgoing girl from Camden, the idealist, was gone. Susan McDougal had taken over. This new, improved Susan lived in a different kind of dream; she *was* a dream: the wild-haired wife of the Important Man. The successful businesswoman on the move. Strangers recognized her in the grocery store: *Aren't you the girl in that TV commercial?* Life, Susan McDougal thought, was perfect. She woke up in the morning and turned over in bed, languorously, and thought exactly that: Life is perfect. She even believed it for a while—even when she and her husband stopped sleeping together. Even when Jim started screaming at her, in front of everyone at the bank, in order to cover his own mistakes. Even when her father's voice started sneaking back into her head. *Discipline*, it said, that dreaded word.

"Oh, yeah, it's easy to lose your way," Susan says now. "I first lost my way with this moral relativity with Jim. That rules don't apply to you or that the rules are stupid. Or that you're bigger than the rules. Or you're better than the rules. I think that's where I first lost my moral compass."

Jim never heard that inner voice; he never had the time. Like each enthusiasm that came before it, Jim threw himself into his new career as a banker, and he appeared to be enjoying himself immensely. He remodeled the bank building to give it a sleek, prosperous new look. He went on a hiring spree for customer-service reps, loan officers, and sales staff. He came up with creative marketing campaigns that brought in a rush of new depositors. None of which changed the fact that he didn't know a single thing about how to run a bank or an S&L. The savings and loan, in particular, opened up too many possibilities, too many ways in which, say, a cash-flow problem with one of his real-estate projects could be temporarily solved. "After Jim got involved in the bank and the savings and loan, when he started doing these huge real-estate projects where he was building roads and parks and all of that, it was very hard to know what he had in his mind," Susan says. "It was something new every day. He was great on the front end; he wanted to know every single detail. He would give orders: 'Don't do this one thing unless you call me.' But once his attention drifted, he didn't want to hear it again. He was the same way with me, with our marriage. When he decided he wanted to marry me, he was not going to be stopped. But once his attention drifted, he couldn't care less."

It certainly didn't surprise Susan that Jim's good spirits and enthusiasm didn't last once the thrill of being a bank owner wore off. Increasingly, Jim's undiagnosed manic depression jerked him up and down. He was restless, irritable, and even morbidly fatalistic—a spiraling mood Susan could never quite put her finger on.

Whatever the problem was, by the spring of 1985, Susan could no longer ignore the deterioration of her marriage. She and Jim had been living as roommates, surly roommates, for some time, and Susan finally decided to get out. She told Jim that they needed to separate, that she wanted to go to Dallas for the summer and get her head together. Jim seemed surprised that she had beaten him to the punch; he agreed immediately to the separation. Susan found an apartment in Dallas and spent the summer lying around the pool and watching TV, daydreaming about the life she wished she had, the life she would've had if she'd never met Jim McDougal. She lost herself in movies, especially a new favorite, the Michael Keaton domestic comedy *Mr. Mom*. She watched it over and over. "It just represents normal life to me, or what normal life should be," she says of the movie. "I had to buy the tape because I was renting it so much." At the end of the summer, Susan packed up her daydreams of normalcy and briefly returned to Arkansas to formally work out her separation from Jim. She fell into a new relationship with a man named Pat Harris who once worked for Madison. Within a few months, she left Arkansas again, this time with her new boyfriend. They headed for Los Angeles, where he planned to go to law school, and she landed a job as personal assistant to Nancy Mehta, the wife of renowned international conductor Zubin Mehta.

At the time, it seemed like she got out just in time. When Susan left for Dallas, Madison was growing rapidly, and Jim was being hailed as Arkansas's newest financial wizard; his face even graced the cover of Arkansas's top business journal. By the following spring, bank examiners had announced that Madison Guaranty was teetering on the brink of ruin. Three years later, at the height of the national S&L crisis, Madison collapsed and was taken over by federal regulators. The government would spend $60 million bailing it out.

BILL CLINTON'S ELECTION AS PRESIDENT IN 1992 WOULD DESTROY his good friend Jim McDougal. The campaign had brought forth all sorts of corruption accusations, and, with the appointment of an independent counsel, every business transaction in which Clinton had even peripherally been involved over the years was getting a good long look, including Madison and Whitewater. It didn't matter that a jury in 1989 had cleared Jim McDougal of wrongdoing—if not stupidity—in the collapse of his S&L. The Office of the Independent Counsel dusted off the Madison case file and looked for new ways to approach the same material. The investigators asked Susan to come in and answer some questions.

Susan didn't have any problem with the independent counsel asking questions and looking into her past. "I wanted to cooperate," she says, re-membering her introduction to the OIC. "But in the first meeting I had with them I told them that I didn't know of anything that the Clintons had done that was illegal. I mean, I would've been glad to tell them, but I just didn't know of anything." That didn't get the reaction she expected. One of the lawyers patted a large stack of files on the table and told her it was evidence of criminal wrongdoing—hers. Susan was shocked. She thought she was coming in simply to answer some questions. She stuck to her story, her hands starting to shake, and then the OIC lawyers marched out of the room.

It didn't take her long to figure out what was coming, and in August 1995, a year after Starr had been appointed independent counsel, it did. Jim, Susan, and Jim Guy Tucker, now Arkansas's sitting governor, were indicted on multiple fraud charges. The Office of the Independent Counsel charged that Whitewater was a sweetheart deal for the Clintons, that the McDougals brought them into the deal solely to curry favor with Bill Clinton, then a ris-ing political star in the state. When the lots didn't sell, according to the OIC, the McDougals defrauded their own savings and loan and the federal gov-ernment to staunch the losses, and also to help Clinton pay off campaign debts.

The biggest PR hole in the independent counsel's case was the fact that the Clintons had lost about $50,000 on Whitewater—a fact the president and first lady reiterated to the press at every opportunity. The problem was, their partners lost three times what the Clintons lost, even though the two couples were fifty-fifty partners. Jim and Susan's explanation for this was a simple one: Jim was embarrassed that Whitewater was failing—he had told the Clintons it was a sure thing—and he didn't want to face them about it. So he took on more and more of Whitewater's debt himself.

In March 1996, Jim, Susan, and Tucker, who had represented Jim Mc-Dougal and Madison when he was in private law practice, went on trial. Even though it had been six months since the indictments had been handed down, Susan was still in a state of shock. She couldn't believe she was sitting in court—at the defense table. She had been nothing more than Jim's "flunky" at Madison, in charge only of making the promotional commercials, she said.

She did what he told her to do, signed what he told her to sign. And didn't ask questions. She wasn't even there during the S&L's death throes, having moved in 1985 to Los Angeles, where she went to work for Nancy Mehta. Not that that was of any help to her. Susan's escape to the West Coast had become another liability, for trouble seemed to follow Susan these days. After three years as Mehta's assistant, Susan left the job on bad terms with her employer. When Susan became media fodder during the Whitewater investigation, the Mehtas jumped on the bandwagon, bringing a theft charge against her for allegedly writing unauthorized checks totaling $200,000. All of a sudden, Susan had *two* trials to worry about.

First up was the Arkansas case. The OIC's chief witness in the Little Rock fraud trial was former municipal-court judge David Hale, who owned a lending company accused of misrepresenting loans it was making so it could get matching funds from the Small Business Administration. In 1992, authorities raided Hale's business and found that he had been stealing millions of dollars by writing fraudulent loans and putting the money in his pocket. Hale agreed to testify against Jim, Susan, Bill Clinton, and others in exchange for a reduced sentence. He claimed that Clinton, then Arkansas's governor, pressured him in 1986 to give a $300,000 SBA loan to Susan as an illegal way to pay off some of Clinton's campaign debts. There was a problem with the accusation—none of the $300,000 went to Clinton—but Hale had an explanation for that. He said he was shopping at a popular indoor mall in Little Rock some months after making the loan when he saw the governor of Arkansas stamping toward him. "Do you know what that fucking bitch Susan McDougal did?" Clinton yelled, his face red and his whole body vibrating with rage. "She spent all the money! The bitch took all the money!" The prosecution's case, at least against Susan, rested almost solely on Hale's testimony.

What did the president of the United States have to say about such an accusation? Neither Susan nor Jim had spoken with Clinton for years. As Jim's fortunes declined in the late '80s, facing health problems and then charges over the collapse of Madison, Bill simply drifted away from his friend. So the defendants considered the president a wildcard witness, even though they were the ones who called him to testify. But Clinton, in videotaped testimony on April 28, 1996, backed up his former Whitewater partners, who insisted the loan had been legitimate and had nothing to do with the Clintons. Testifying from the White House, Clinton said he had never pressured Hale to make a loan to Susan or to anybody and that he did not conspire with Hale or the McDougals or Tucker. Hale, he said, was simply lying.

Hale certainly had reason to lie. "The Feds were coming to look at [Hale's] books," Sam Heuer, Jim McDougal's attorney, told the jury. "He knew he was in trouble. He knew that Jim McDougal was a friend of Bill Clinton. He was trying to come up with a story that would sell so he could move to have his time cut. That's what's going on."

Susan's defense was even simpler: she didn't know anything about anything—a strategy that reporters privately took to calling "the bimbo defense." She applied for the $300,000 loan, supposedly for marketing work she was doing related to a property development, because Jim told her to apply for it. She trusted Jim; he told her the loan was for a deal that would go toward her divorce settlement.

Susan felt completely out of her depth as she sat at the defense table and watched Bobby McDaniel fight on her behalf. Her strategy was to simply keep quiet and let Jim and the lawyers explain things. "I had no confidence," she says of her state of mind at the time. "I had so relied on Jim my whole adult life for decision making. I didn't know the details of the loan or anything. Jim kept telling me, 'I'm going to explain it. There's no wrongdoing here.'"

Jim did explain it—and buried both of them with the explanation. Cocksure as always, he started out by playing to the crowd, intent on getting the Arkansas gallery, as well as the jury, behind him. He received a satisfying laugh when OIC prosecutor Ray Jahn asked him if he were a lawyer and he responded, "No, sir. Thank God." Later, Jahn asked Jim to explain a document, and Jim drawled, "It seems to me a rather straightforward memo. I'm sure it would confuse a government lawyer." But Jahn wasn't willing to play the fool. He came prepared, and when he caught his witness in contradictory statements, Jim began to falter and, eventually, flail. During his three days of testimony, he told the jury that Susan was intimately involved in the running of Madison. When asked about the $300,000 SBA loan to Susan, he responded as if Jahn were setting a trap. "I have no awareness of how that was prepared," he said. Susan sat just a few feet away from her ex-husband, her jaw slack, unable to believe what was coming out of his mouth.

Suddenly, President Clinton's opponents believed all their suspicions were confirmed. Jim Guy Tucker, Jim McDougal, and Susan McDougal—the governor of Arkansas and two of the president's former business associates—were each convicted of multiple counts of fraud. "At five P.M. today, the cover-up began to unravel," announced Tony Blankley, spokesman for Republican House Speaker Newt Gingrich, on May 28, 1996. Kenneth Starr was the star of the moment. He had stood before the White House and yelled *Stop!* This round, bespectacled, seemingly retiring man had no fear of Bill Clinton's vaunted political war machine.

What Starr—and Blankley—didn't realize was that the independent counsel was about to meet his match.

SUSAN McDOUGAL LIKES THE TIDINESS OF MOVIE LIVES. "WE ALL grow up with movies where you get saved in the end if you're innocent," Susan says. "That didn't happen here. They convicted me with David Hale's lies."

The jury verdicts were so shocking to Susan that she spent days after the trial curled up in a fetal position at Claudia Riley's house, unable to get out of bed. She kept expecting to wake up and find that none of it had happened, and when reality stubbornly remained unchanged each morning, she would begin to cry.

Kenneth Starr had her—as well as Jim McDougal and Jim Guy Tucker—right where he wanted her. The independent counsel was pursuing a bottom-up strategy that he expected would take him, step by step, to Bill and Hillary Clinton. The first to flip had been Hale. But the problem with Hale was that, as *Salon* magazine put it, he was "a tainted witness" who had allegedly taken "money and legal help from anti-Clinton activists with ties to Starr himself." The OIC needed a better witness, and they turned to Jim and Susan.

Susan stuck with her story: she knew of nothing the Clintons had done that was illegal. Jim, however, wasn't so sure anymore.

Jim was straightforward about the reason he was willing to change his story and become a witness for the independent counsel. He was facing the possibility of decades behind bars for his multiple convictions, and he was angry and hurt that his old friend in the White House was not coming to his aid. "There was not one word of sympathy or friendship toward me or Susan," he told *The New Yorker* in 1996. "There's no reason to do anything for the Clintons, for they're not going to do a damn thing for us."

Almost immediately, "he just started making up stories" to implicate the Clintons, Susan says. "He just started telling flat-out lies. He knew it and I knew it." Despite this, and despite the fact that Jim had implicated her in his own wrongdoing at trial, Susan couldn't cut him out of her life. In the run-up to his sentencing hearing, FBI agents and OIC lawyers visited Jim daily in Arkadelphia, where he was living in a trailer on Claudia Riley's propety, and Jim regaled them with stories of Arkansas political chicanery. "He would come up to the house after his meetings with the FBI," remembers Susan, who was staying with Claudia Riley after the trial, "and he would say, 'How does this sound? Let me try this out on you. How about if we say this? . . .'"

"His story for the day," affirms Claudia. Claudia and her late husband had been close with Jim since the late 1960s, when Bob was being urged to climb down from the ivory tower and run for statewide office and Jim was a young idealist desperate to learn at Bob's knee. Claudia shakes her head at the thoughts piling up inside her and pauses, to ensure that her emotions don't overtake her. "Jim became an alien," she says matter-of-factly. "If there's one thing you could be assured of, it was that Jim's word was his bond. Not anymore."

Susan was terrified. At first, she thought that if she held her ground, her ex-husband would back down and retract the stories he was telling the independent counsel. But her refusal to play along didn't cause Jim to re-evaluate; in fact, it seemed to make him bolder.

One of the lies, Susan says, related directly to the loan that brought about her conviction. "They wanted to know when the plot was hatched to borrow the money for Clinton, and Jim said, 'I think I'm going to tell them that the day I went down to the Legislature'—and he had this specific date—'Bill and I were standing there in the hall talking, and that was when he said he needed some money for the campaign. Doesn't that sound good?' That's what he would do: he would take what they wanted and plug it into real events so all the surrounding details would be true. But what was really ludicrous was the whole idea that Bill Clinton would need Jim or me to borrow $300,000 at that point in his life. He was the governor. He had Tyson Foods; he had all the big-money people in the state. We didn't have the money, so he'd ask us to borrow it? It's just ludicrous."

One day, Susan had finally had enough. "I said to him, 'You know you're scheming against the president of the United States. Let's just get into reality here, Jim. They've got all the money in the world. They've got all the attorneys in the world. You're making this stuff up. You're going to get on the stand, and [the president's lawyers] aren't going to be able to show that most of this is just bull that you're coming up with?' And he looked at me just as serious as death and said, 'They're giving me the documents.'"

Even now, all these years later, just thinking about that statement makes Susan McDougal stop and take a deep breath. She lets out a weary sigh, as if she's annoyed she hasn't been able to erase her memory of the moment, and sinks into her chair.

Back in 1996, when she and Jim were awaiting sentencing on their separate fraud convictions, that statement threw her into a panic. When Jim left Claudia Riley's house that day, Susan burst into tears. "That's when I became one hundred percent certain that the independent counsel knew that Jim McDougal was weaving those crazy stories," she says. "He showed me the documents."

Susan says the independent counsel gave Jim documents from his failed savings and loan, where paperwork under his chaotic leadership was often incomplete and misleading, and "he'd weave his stories around them, whatever they wanted. I knew I could never contradict him now. He started showing me the stuff. What they were doing was, instead of him giving the story and the independent counsel going out and finding the proof, they gave him the documents and Jim weaved the story around it. That scared me. I thought, 'If I ever testify against him, I'm dead. I have no corroborating documents. I have no faculty like he has for remembering everything that happened. There's no way I can stand up against all this preparation they're doing day after day after day down there, where he's making up all this stuff and they've got documents and I'm going to go in there [to court] and say he's lying? Who's ever going to believe that?' I got really scared at that point. I'm either going to go with him and lie and probably save my life or I can go against this huge operation they've got, where they've got all this money, all these attorneys. And I've got nothing. Yeah, I was scared to death."

It didn't help her state of mind to see how thorough the independent counsel was being. The selling of Jim McDougal went on for weeks, for hours at a time, and it involved even Kenneth Starr himself. "I would see them arrive down there at the trailer, and they would open the door for Starr and he would step out of this big car and he would have gifts in his hand. And I would think, 'You are so corrupt. You know all this is made up.' But I don't think they cared. I think it was a holy war. In Starr's mind, his religion was so important and he was so much better than the Clintons it did not matter who he ruined."

To her, Starr had become a chubby Darth Vader: ruthless, evil, and impossible to defeat. So when Jim kept telling her that the independent counsel's office wanted to talk to her, that they had a great deal for her, she agreed to hear them out. In the summer of 1996, with her sentencing hearing looming, Susan, Claudia Riley, and her attorney, Bobby McDaniel, met via Speakerphone with the OIC's Ray Jahn. Jahn asked for a proffer—a written statement of what she would testify to—and reiterated that if it were acceptable, he would recommend probation rather than jail time for her.

"Exactly what is it you want from her?" McDaniel asked.

Jahn's answer: "She knows who this investigation is about. And she knows what we want."

McDaniel still gets angry when he thinks about that response. "It was clear that this wasn't about the pursuit of justice," he says. "It was about the pursuit of the Clintons. The only way Susan could have avoided jail would be if she perjured herself." In the topsy-turvy world Susan found herself in, she would be rewarded for lying, and possibly charged with perjury for telling the truth. "They had David Hale to say X-Y-Z, and now they had Jim McDougal," says McDaniel. "If the OIC thought Susan's testimony was perjury—and they obviously thought that anybody who had anything exculpatory to say about the Clintons was lying—they could've gotten the grand jury to indict her for perjury. She was in a catch-22 of the worst kind."

Susan's family and friends couldn't take it anymore. They begged her to cooperate, to give the independent counsel what it wanted. Only Pat Harris, her former boyfriend and now one of her lawyers, warned her about doing what it would take to make Starr happy. "I told her that if she lied, she would have to tell that lie for the rest of her life," he says.

Susan expected Claudia to be in Pat's camp, but Claudia, too, was suffering at seeing her friend's predicament. "At one point I said to her, 'Susan, give them what they want, don't go to prison,'" Claudia says. "I didn't understand Whitewater, and I said, 'Tell them something. Just tell them something.'"

Susan couldn't believe that Claudia, of all people, was caving on her, too. Taken aback, she blurted, "What would Bob Riley do?"

That, Claudia says, got her attention. Her late husband never took the easy way out of anything in his life. "There was a textbook in courage," she says. "I said to Susan, 'Why, he would have been burned at the stake before he lied.' And that was that."

In late August 1996, Susan decided not to lie. In fact, she would not testify at all. "Mark Twain said it takes two to tell the truth," she says now, repeating one of her favorite quotes. "One to tell it and one to hear it."

The independent counsel responded by asking for a thirteen-year prison sentence for her fraud conviction, far stiffer than they were asking for anyone else, despite the fact that by the OIC's own admission Susan was a secondary figure in the Whitewater and Madison cases. (Starr personally appealed for leniency for Jim McDougal, who was sentenced to three years in prison.) The request for a thirteen-year sentence was the last straw for Susan. It had become personal. She immediately barred her lawyers from even talking to the independent counsel. Her hatred for Kenneth Starr was heading for all-time highs. "I remember he would come out during the trial at these press briefings and say these things," she says. "Once he said, 'I stopped at a red light on my way to the court and sang a hymn.' I thought, 'I may have to physically intervene.' It was galling that he could be ruining my life, ruining other people's lives, and use the guise of his Christianity to say, 'Oh, I'm such a nice guy.' It's the hypocrisy I couldn't stand more than anything else."

It comes up time and again from those involved with Susan's defense: that Starr's team didn't act like professionals but more like religious zealots on a mission from God. "They felt like the end justified the means; they felt so self-righteous and holier-than-thou, so much better than the Clintons," says McDaniel. "They were willing to do anything they could."

In Susan's mind, her refusal to testify before Starr's grand jury never had anything to do with Bill Clinton. It had to do with being able to live with herself. It had to do with her need to stand up for what she thought was right and to fight the bad guy.

"You know *Broadcast News?*" she asks. "It's one of my favorite movies. Albert Brooks says in the movie, 'Do you think Satan's going to come back with a pitchfork and horns? No, he's going to be this amiable, bumbling, nice guy, and everybody's going to like him.' That's Kenneth Starr!" When she's told that *New York Times* columnist Maureen Dowd once used the very same movie analogy to describe Bill Clinton, Susan shrieks. *"Really?"* she exclaims, leaning forward. Then she cocks her head and ponders the implications. Bill Clinton, after all, is the man millions of Americans thought she was keeping quiet for. She still thinks fondly of Clinton, and she sure loves his idealism. But she can almost understand Dowd's point. Almost.

"Well, to some people, I guess it would depend on your viewpoint, on where you're coming from," she says. "But when someone talks to me about Republican politics or a conservative viewpoint, I always say, 'You're not going to change my mind on this, because I think I can tell you that they tried to kill me.'"

Susan McDougal does not mean that figuratively. She is convinced that the Office of the Independent Counsel tried to destroy her mind and her body to gain her cooperation. Beginning in 1994, she had offered to cooperate with the OIC time and time again, but they weren't satisfied with what she had to say. "They wanted the Clintons," she says, "and they just wanted me to make something up."

SUSAN SOMETIMES WONDERS WHY SHE DIDN'T SAVOR PRISON more. She had found peace and satisfaction there; she believed she was helping people, helping herself. For years as Jim McDougal's wife, searching for the next exciting thing, she had kept moving to avoid thinking about what she was doing with her life. It was the new ethos, and she had gone along, convinced that if she was laughing a lot she must be happy. Then, in prison, because there was nothing else to do, Susan had taken the time to just sit still and reflect. She was still filled with rage, the rage of a woman who had been

McDougal being released from jail, 1998.

treated unjustly, but the conclusions she reached while sitting in her cell surprised even her. "I promised myself I would never be the same again," she says. "I was going to stop living this life of things. I had a bottle of shampoo and a black comb and sometimes a clean uniform. And life was good."

Once she was out of prison, she wanted to continue this new stripped-down approach to living. "I had come to appreciate a simpler life, and I was ready to live it, without reporters or courts or Kenneth Starr," she says.

That wasn't going to happen just yet, though.

In early 1998, Jim McDougal had a fatal heart attack before he could testify in open court for Starr. Jim had done everything Starr had asked of him, and yet he still couldn't avoid what he had so desperately feared: dying in prison.

With Jim McDougal gone, Starr now needed Susan more than ever. The balance of power, however, had begun to shift, though Starr didn't know it yet. The independent counsel had enjoyed wide popularity during the early years of his investigation because, as British polemicist Christopher Hitchens wrote in *The Observer*, "Clinton could change his mind on any issue, but he couldn't change the fact that he was a scumbag." People tended to believe the worst about the president, and the president seemed determined to prove them right. But as the Monica Lewinsky sex scandal began to unfold and Clinton's poll numbers for trustworthiness fell through the floor, a funny thing happened: his approval ratings for job performance began to move up.

The debate about the president's various scandals and Starr's investigation resonated for almost everybody in the country, because what Americans believed about Bill Clinton and Kenneth Starr couldn't be separated from what they believed about themselves—and often didn't want to admit. Did they forgive Clinton his transgressions—the sexual and intellectual profligacy, the lying, the knee-jerk hypocrisy—because of the booming economy or because they had to forgive themselves for many of the same sins? Did they forgive the president for any "minor" personal peccadilloes as long as, in *The New Yorker*'s phrase, he remained the country's "Entertainer-in-Chief"? A baby boomer, an attention junkie, a media animal, Clinton seemed to be a natural stand-in for Americans' own unease with themselves at the end of the twentieth century, a stand-in for the unexpected breakdown of their own self-discipline and impulse control in a time of unprecedented prosperity.

It was only natural, then, that to many Americans, Starr would become the bad guy. As Whitewater led nowhere—at least nowhere near the White House—Starr began to look increasingly desperate and brutal in his tactics. The independent counsel's investigation of Clinton's affair with Lewinsky was a turning point. In the end, the only one in the whole mess who didn't look sneaky and mean, the only one who had sacrificed for more than their own self-interest, was Susan McDougal.

This public reevaluation of Susan was coming about just as she was being released from prison after twenty-one months and as she was going on trial for allegedly stealing some $200,000 from Nancy Mehta. The conductor's wife, a former starlet, quickly saw the writing on the wall. "This girl is a very, very charming person," Mehta told a *Vanity Fair* writer during the theft trial. "Oh, she will make you believe *everything*. Everything and anything. I have seen grown men swept away by this girl. I have *seen* it."

In 1998, all of America seemed to be swept away by Susan McDougal, and she hit all the right notes as she threatened to expose Starr right after she and her new lawyer, Mark Geragos, were done with Mehta. Susan, wrote Judy Bachrach during the 1998 trial, "sees herself as a genuine heroine in America. Clearly others do as well. This didn't simplify the jury-selection process at the Mehta trial. With each passing day the judge grew more frustrated, the prosecutor more livid, the pool of potential jurors ever more shallow. One by one, citizens expressed their deepest feelings about Kenneth Starr. To them, McDougal seems innocent by comparison. 'The sainted Susan McDougal!' bellowed the prosecutor after yet another excused potential juror took his leave (having mouthed 'Good luck' to the defendant)."

Susan wasn't a saint, but she was lucky in her adversaries: first the pursed-lipped, *tsk-tsk*ing Starr and then the aristocratic, piggish Mehta, a woman who, the trial would show, treated her Borzoi dog better than she treated her employees. In Susan's opinion, Mehta was simply crackers: a rich, spoiled, middle-aged woman so desperate for attention and so accustomed to getting everything she wanted that she had to try to punish Susan for choosing to leave her employ. It didn't work. Susan was acquitted of the theft charges, despite a circuslike atmosphere that pervaded the proceedings.

The Mehta prosecution team simply could never overcome the mushrooming marquee value of the Susan McDougal name. After acquitting Susan, the entire jury held a press conference to vilify the prosecutor for bringing such a threadbare case to trial in the first place. When Susan came down the courthouse steps after the jury verdict, it seemed like every reporter in the world converged on her. Most seemed to be congratulating her as much as they were asking her questions.

The independent counsel was not ready to let that be the end of it, however. Susan had served her time and been released from prison (she got an early release in part because of health problems stemming from her scoliosis), but she still had not testified for Starr. So the OIC tried to extract another pound of flesh, this time trying Susan for criminal (rather than civil) contempt of court and obstruction of justice for her refusal to testify. But by then it was simply too late. When most Americans got their first good look at Susan McDougal, some three years before, she was wearing handcuffs and leg irons. The image resisted complexity. People across the country who saw video of her shuffling along in chains knew who she was without being told. She was a criminal. But Susan had become determined to have the final word on the subject; it was *her* reputation, after all. And when the letters started to arrive, hundreds of them, she stopped worrying about what Kenneth Starr had to say. She was no longer that shy, insecure young woman who did what she was told. She was Susan McDougal, TV star. And if there was one thing she now knew, it was that once the public was in your corner, you could never lose. Some of the jurors from the Mehta trial even traveled to Little Rock to show their support for Susan. "I'm going to kick his butt up between his shoulder blades," she told reporters of her upcoming court fight with the independent counsel.

That's exactly what she did. Even though it was undeniable that she had refused to testify before Starr's grand jury, she was acquitted on the obstruction charge and the jury hung on the contempt charges—an outcome that was widely viewed as a major blow to the independent counsel's credibility. When the judge read the not-guilty verdict on the obstruction charge, the courtroom's gallery burst into cheers and whoops. Susan pumped her fists like an athlete who'd just made the big play. "They had an unlimited budget, could threaten people with all kinds of things, and we won," Susan says. "That said something." When Starr finally brought his impeachment report before Congress a few months later, it was focused almost entirely on the Lewinsky affair, not Whitewater. On the day he left office, Bill Clinton pardoned Susan.

FOR YEARS DURING HER COURT BATTLES, SUSAN McDOUGAL sought out the cameras and microphones to tell her story. She had become famous for her provocative statements and aggressiveness, once telling reporters that, no, she wasn't scared of Kenneth Starr, "he better be scared of me." A cottage industry sprang up around her. Local entrepreneurs around the country made tidy little profits from "Free Susan McDougal" T-shirts and bumper stickers; journalists built their careers on tracking her legal battles; her lawyer, Mark Geragos, used the notoriety of being her attorney to become Los Angeles's top celebrity lawyer and a TV talking head. Susan herself was a favorite of radio jocks across the country and had a standing invitation to appear on *Larry King Live*. As she emerged from prison and her courtroom battles, she was at the height of her fame, well known to radio and TV audiences around the country for her Clint Eastwood imitation when she publicly challenged Kenneth Starr. And to her surprise, she found she wanted no more of it.

When she got out of prison, she says, "People were saying, 'You're going to do this, you're going to do that. You're going to do TV shows, you're going to do a movie and a book.' And I said, 'No. I'm just going to go home.'"

Which was exactly what she did. She moved back to Camden to live in the house where she grew up. After years of trying to get away from small-town life and small-town mores, she now decided she needed them. "I get hugged a lot" in Camden, she says. "My mother says, 'You've got to go to the grocery store with Susan; people just walk up and hug her.' It's very comforting to be in a secure environment. Big places are a little scary."

Almost anyplace other than Camden, where she is still Jim Henley's daughter, is now a big place because it has people who know her only from TV. In Los Angeles during the Mehta trial, grown men asked for her autograph. Heads turned in unison when she entered restaurants. Even though she had beat her drum as loudly as possible and in as many media venues as possible, Susan couldn't understand the fascination. "It wasn't like I was an astronaut; it's not like I became famous because of some great accomplishment where I could say, 'Gee, look what I've done,'" she says.

Dozens of offers came her way in the weeks and months after her final court showdown with Starr, offers for talk shows and speeches and even a movie about her life. The producers of *Celebrity Boxing* wanted to pit Susan against Paula Jones, the former Arkansas secretary who had accused Clinton of exposing himself to her. Jones had already agreed to be on the TV show, no questions asked. Susan refused.

With a loud sigh, Susan shakes her head at the thought of it. "There are people in Arkansas who have the opinion that Paula Jones needs that attention and that fame," she says. "She misses that attention. Even though it was so negative. That's why she shows up in the audience every time Clinton is in the state, appearing at the library site or whatever. She's there. I can understand it. It can be hypnotizing. Reporters are very good at making you feel like you're the only person in the world."

Susan first felt that hypnotic pull when Jim McDougal ran for Congress. "My God, it was the happiest I'd ever been with him," she says. "Because he was talking about things that meant something. And I was a part of it. He'd say, 'If I go to Congress, these are things that are important to me; these are the things that we have to do. We are living in the poorest state in the nation, and it would be so easy to fix this, this, and this. Why aren't we doing it?' I'd think, 'God, that's great!' But it was because I felt a common goal, not just because we had reporters and people around. Just fame itself is uninteresting. But to be famous or working with a famous person whose goals or whose ideas I love, that's wonderful. Bob Riley, when he was governor, he could just leave me spellbound."

For most of her life, that was what Susan had wanted more than anything else, to be left spellbound and to leave a few people feeling that way, too. "It was like being in a movie," she says of being around Bob Riley and Jim McDougal in those early days, and she immediately became addicted to it. It filled the emptiness; it blotted out the existential angst that is the burden of being human. Susan has seen and felt the power of media attention and public striving, and still does. "There are people who were involved in Whitewater who still call me and want to talk about Whitewater," she says. "They still want to do something about it. 'Could we go to Congress? Do you think we can go to Congress and protest?' they say. And I'm like, 'I don't know, there's a lot going on right now, we have this war in Iraq.' There are people who just can't let it go, who still want to talk about it, still want to be a part of that media whirlwind; it's very alluring. People in Little Rock, in Arkadelphia, felt a loss when the national media left. People lead these lives of going to work, paying the bills; they don't have a lot of recognition. And suddenly someone wants their opinions, is interested in what they have to say. The independent counsel was very complimentary to people, telling them they were a really important part of this national story. I can see very easily how people can say, 'Boy, that's me' and love to be a part of it. In fact, I did see it. I don't have to guess at it. Some people are just devastated that it all went away."

In her own way, Susan was devastated, too. After her release from prison and after the final two trials, she quickly felt ordinary again, adrift. She had expected to feel a huge wave of relief when she got out of prison and put Kenneth Starr behind her; she expected to enjoy just shopping in a grocery store again or hanging around the house. Just being away from all the hubbub she'd experienced with reporters and lawyers and fellow inmates around her all the time. But she almost immediately found herself chafing at the fact that her days had no purpose. "I got out of jail, and I was really hurting," she says. "I missed prison. I missed the feeling that each moment was important. I wasn't sleeping at night. I was walking the floor. I was having bad dreams—bad, bad nightmares. I was really wondering, 'How am I going to cope?' Because going out in public was hard. Especially since people recognized me. I would think, 'What should I say? What should I do?' I have nothing to say to people anymore."

The answer came to her in a dream. She would go back to prison. The next morning, "I called the sheriff at Conway and asked if I could come back up there [to the Faulkner Detention Center]. And they said yes. And when I got there and they let me in, I felt so good, so at home. When I was in prison and I was talking to the women, I sort of promised myself I wouldn't forget. And when I got out and life was so easy, I started kind of feeling guilty. Because I wasn't doing anything, even though it had just been three months, four months or so. So when I went back to the jail that day, just to talk to the women there, I thought, 'This is it. This is what I want to do. There are a lot of jails; this could be some really easy therapy.' So when all the speaking offers started coming in to Mark Geragos, because no one knew how to find me they'd call him, he would say to me that it would be great if I would go and speak to these people—a lawyer group or whatever—and I would think, 'There's a jail there.' And I would start to get pumped up. I would try to do that first, go to the local jail, so I could hear the girls' stories and try to get back to that feeling of what it is to be powerless. How it felt to have nothing. How it felt to see people in terrible pain and not be able to do anything for them. Then if I went from that to speaking to all these powerful people—like prosecutors, judges, district attorneys, political people—I would say, 'I'm going to talk to you like I did on the concrete floor from the jail I just came from, that's how we're going to talk today.' And I would be going from people where there's a complete disconnect with society to these powerful people who feel very part of their community. It was wonderful to see them respond to what I was saying."

Susan had found her postprison cause: the plight of women in jail, the unacceptable living conditions in many jails across the country. She began writing a memoir, so she could spread the word about jail conditions to a wide audience. She began accepting speaking engagements, for little more than traveling expenses, just so she could check out local jails across the country.

Once again, her celebrity came in handy. "I would call up and say, 'This is Susan McDougal. I'd like to come down to the jail and see it.' And they'd say, 'Oh, let me get you the PR guy,' and—*bam!*—he'd call me and I'd be in. I'd walk in with the sheriff, and I'd say, 'I'd really like to have some time alone with the girls,' and they'd say, 'Oh, yeah, sure, that's fine.' I would get not only access but I would get left with them. Not stripped searched. No questions like, 'Do you have illegal drugs with you? Do you have sharp objects with you?' Just walking in and being left with the women. And that was strictly fame or infamy or whatever you wanted to call it. And I was so grateful, so I started doing that more and more. This was long before I wrote the book. This is what I was doing: going to jails and then talking to people in the community about looking at the situation there, what was needed. Then when the book came along, I'd go speak about Whitewater or Starr and sign books, and then I'd go to the jails. I started calling radio stations, and they'd send a radio reporter along and he'd chronicle the walk-through. And I thought, 'This is great.' They would see that there were women who needed medical attention or women who were in lockdown cells twenty-three hours a day—or twenty-four hours a day for some of the mentally ill inmates— and I could talk about that with the reporter who was there. The press has really helped me with jail conditions. When I was in jail, I had this forum; I'd call TV and radio stations collect. A lot of people came to the jails; Larry King came. You talk about a jail getting a little nervous when Larry King comes with his cameras. Food gets better; people who need them get doctors. They don't want me going on camera, going, 'Oh, by the way, there's a pregnant woman over there who's been having blood spotting for two weeks, and we can't get her a doctor.' So suddenly problems disappeared. The press was a huge tool, whether they wanted to be or not, for what I wanted to do. I remember in Austin [Texas], two television stations came, filmed Susan Mc-Dougal arriving at the jail; it was just amazing. They walked through with us, with the sheriff and the head of public relations and four or five dignitaries. I was thinking, 'This is the best thing about being infamous'—I refuse to say I'm famous. It was an amazing, amazing gift. The thing I most wanted to do I was able to do because of being splashed on television in an orange suit for two years. I was trying to think of the best thing that came from all that, and that was it."

The next best thing, though she'd never officially give it such high standing, might have been a phone call she received in the spring of 2003. Her memoir was on every best-seller list in the country, and she was on the TV and radio talk circuit, for the first time since the high-water days of the independent counsel. "This voice said, 'Susan, this is Bill Clinton'—because I hadn't talked to him for years," she recalls, her eyes widening into O's. "And he said, 'I've read your book, and I just want to say I'm so sorry. I didn't know; I didn't know what you went through, and I just want to say I'm so sorry.' I told him it was OK. We've always had a very jocular relationship. Everything's always been very light and ha-ha. And he was not like that at all when he called. And I said to him, 'Oh, let's not talk about that, because it really ended up being a good thing in the end. Let's just not talk about that.' And he said, 'No, I really don't think I've been a good friend to you. I just have to keep saying to you how very, very sorry I am.'"

Susan sits back in her chair, her eyes misty, her cheeks red, her mouth open in astonishment. She didn't need to hear Bill Clinton say that; she would have enjoyed running into him in Little Rock at some event or other even if he didn't mention the book at all. But she likes that he called. "It was very kind of him to call; he didn't have to do that," she says. "He told me he had a nightmare about prison after reading the book, and I told him I had had nightmares myself about prison for a couple months after getting out. I understood completely."

So Susan McDougal chose celebrity over the quiet life, after all, and she did it for her own unique reasons. She did it to quiet the voice in her head that told her she wasn't doing anything with her life, that she was wasting her time being selfish. She did it because she liked the attention when it was as much about what she was doing as it was about her, the famous—or infamous—Susan McDougal. She did it because it was, for the first time since getting out of prison, what felt truly right. "When life is easy I start feeling uncomfortable, because I promised myself I wouldn't forget," she says. "I take volunteers with me when I go to jails, people who want to help women in jail. And the first time they go they say, 'This is horrible. This is just terrible.' And I was saying to somebody last night, 'It's not so bad; I just don't even think of it really as bad anymore.' But it is. There aren't any windows, and there are concrete floors. Maybe this is just what I was supposed to do. You've heard me say I don't regret a day. I don't. Because if you can get happy by going to a jail, that's just a great thing, isn't it?"

Melvin in the Spotlight

OGDEN, UTAH
June 8, 1978

Melvin Dummar was a happy man. He stomped his feet and beamed, holding his arms out as if to embrace the whole world.

The Howard Hughes probate trial had ended just hours earlier, but Melvin wasn't thinking about that. He wasn't thinking that a call could come at any moment that would change his life forever. He was singing, and he was strumming his guitar, and people were enjoying it. He looked over his shoulder at his bandmates, still beaming, and they nodded back at him, one after the other. That was all he had ever wanted. The respect of musicians. And people looking up at him, moving to the music, clapping their hands, and smiling.

It was after ten, but it didn't seem late. Melvin leaned down and grasped the hand of the girl who'd been reaching out for him all night, reaching out and calling his name. They'd been desperate for him all night, these girls, and Melvin should have known not to give in. Sure enough, this one moment of weakness—barely fingertips against fingertips—brought the rest of them surging forward, all the more brazen because tonight there were TV cameras. Chairs were knocked over, irritated boyfriends sloughed off with the jerk of shoulders.

The boyfriends did have good reason to be annoyed. This was not how you were supposed to act at a church dance. And Melvin Dummar might have a decent voice, *maybe*, but he sure as hell was no Elvis Presley. He was a three-dollar-an-hour beer deliveryman. Tonight, though, it didn't matter.

"Girls were flopping all over him. They were going, 'Oh, Mel! Oh, Mel!'" remembers Chuck Paul, Melvin's drummer. "You know how girls are with celebrities."

Except these weren't exactly girls. Most were middle-aged, or at least close to it. Thirty- and forty-something women who were married and had children and PTA meetings and a beer every night if their religion allowed it. It took something more than a nice cowlick to get these "girls" to scream.

Like $156 million. This was the day Melvin was going to cash in, and everybody knew it. Everyone who knew Melvin was nervous, jumpy, excited. Bonnie had had a lump in her throat for weeks, and right now she felt like she was going to choke on it. But Melvin did his best not to think about it. He just went about his life like it was any other day. His lawyer in Nevada had ordered champagne for the celebration he expected. Melvin could have been in Nevada himself, sweating it out in a courthouse corridor. But he'd committed to the gig weeks ago, and he was a man of his word. Besides, he didn't want to face those lawyers again.

Paul understood, or thought he did. The little Ogden clubs had always been enough for him, and he thought they should be for Melvin, too. But Paul knew that Melvin saw bigger things for himself, and tonight was only going to make him think even bigger. "It was a big church dance in Riverdale. Channel 2 and Channel 5 were there," Paul remembers. "When they shine those cameras, it's bright. It really disrupted the dance. Some people liked it, because it's TV, but a lot of people didn't like it at all. They knew it wasn't for them, it was for Mel. The TV people'd get Mel to go out on the dance floor and dance with his wife, then he'd come back up on stage and do a number. They pulled him out to dance with his wife again and again, then a reporter went over and told him the will had been denied. Mel didn't get his guitar or anything. He just walked out."

Someone told Melvin it took the jury just eleven hours to find the will a forgery, but Melvin didn't know if that was supposed to mean something. He and Bonnie saw that all the reporters wanted to have at them, so they walked into the parking lot and sat on the hood of a car "while they took pictures and tossed questions at us. Was I disappointed? No. What will I do with my life? Just keep on living, I guess." The reporters surrounding him wanted something more than that, though. They wanted to see the anguish and anger one would expect from a man who'd just lost a hundred and fifty million dollars. They would be disappointed. "I wasn't happy about the verdict," he says, but it had been a long road to this point. "I knew I was never going to see anything from that will. I already knew that."

Rhoden wasn't surprised to hear that Melvin had been singing at a dance when the jury's decision was announced. He figured Hughes, wherever he was, wasn't surprised, either. That was the kind of man Melvin was. That was why Hughes left him all that money in the first place. Hughes "lived a sad, vacant life, and he had few dreams," Rhoden said in *Melvin and Howard: A Nevada Fairy Tale*. "There was no romance. When one of the hundreds of movies he watched came to a love scene, he called in an aide and asked him to fast-forward it, to push it past the 'mushy parts.' To think that such a man could suddenly, in his death, take control of his legacy, to find in himself a pocket of sentiment, lends a credence to life and human nature itself, doesn't it? Don't you want to believe that Howard Hughes—a frightening, enigmatic symbol of corporate greed and the weakness of the human spirit—could salvage his soul with a simple act of kindness like this? Believe it! Somehow it makes his whole life easier to understand, easier to accept."

Melvin, sitting on the hood of that car with Bonnie, answering reporters' questions, still thought about his soul sometimes. He had given up the church, but he still wondered if all this had been some kind of test. Would all that money have changed him? Would he have become like Howard Hughes, locked away somewhere fine, a prisoner in his own head? Melvin found himself smiling as the reporters asked their questions, and Bonnie, seeing it, started to smile, too. She knew what he was thinking. "Go on," she finally told him, and Melvin lifted himself off the car, excused himself, and headed back inside to finish the set.

Gerry Cooney:
The Contender

In real life, truly happy endings are rare. One that starts with being knocked out in front of 16,000 people has to be unique. But that's when Gerry Cooney's life began turning around.

On June 15, 1987, Cooney fought Michael Spinks in Atlantic City, New Jersey. It was an important bout, one covered by the national sports media. Five years after being beaten by Larry Holmes in a heavyweight championship match—his only professional loss in twenty-nine fights—Cooney, at age thirty, was still boxing's "Great White Hope," a six-foot, six-inch lantern-jawed Irishman with a left hook that sent most opponents sprawling. Spinks was a spindly boxer who'd somehow managed to beat Holmes, Cooney's conqueror, two times in a row. He was undefeated, but most boxing observers, Cooney included, thought Spinks just hadn't faced anyone yet who could punch hard enough to slow him down. So they were matched in what the fight's promoters billed as The War at the Shore, and Cooney, getting paid $2.5 million for his night's work, climbed into the ring hung over, a condition he'd grown used to since he started drinking in junior high.

"Hey, I drank right up to the day of the fight," Cooney says. "I'd tell you I was goin' through a period when I couldn't stand myself, but I'd felt that way my whole life. The thing I believed, though, was that Michael Spinks did not belong in the same ring with me no matter what shape I was in."

Judgment clouded and reflexes slowed by liquor and a lifetime of wracking self-doubt, Cooney plodded after Spinks for four rounds, while his opponent danced away and waited for the right moment. That came in round five, when Spinks stopped dancing and started punching Cooney, who was thirty pounds heavier and five inches taller. In that fifth round, Spinks landed 84 of 101 punches, Cooney just 5 of 26. Halfway through the round, Spinks knocked Cooney down with a right. Cooney got up. Spinks knocked him down again. Cooney got up for the second time. Spinks hit him with a half-dozen more punches, all hard shots to the head. The referee stopped the fight. The resulting headline in *Sports Illustrated* read: "Say Good Night, Gerry."

But in his dressing room after the fight, Cooney said something to himself instead. At the absolute worst moment in a life full of awful ones, he was somehow able to condense all the problems, all the pain, into a single, simple question.

"I was just wiped out, and all of a sudden, like electricity, it hits me," he says. "I thought to myself, 'Hey, who's in charge here? Who runs your life? Is it your father who beat you up all the time? Is it the booze? Or is it going to be you?' I'd kept going for years by bein' somebody famous, gettin' attention that would let me forget for a while that I just couldn't stand myself. In the time I was famous, I had no joy from it, just the fear of it being taken away. I thought the fame was the only good thing about me. Well, that night I knew I had to get serious about changing my life, because if Michael Spinks could beat me, if the talent could have slipped away from me that much, then it was time to be scared. Because the fame thing as a fighter was not going to last much longer."

The next morning, Cooney says, "I still had the who's-in-charge idea. I watched some TV, and there was a guy on the show talking about how he drank and acted crazy and would make his wife stand by the fireplace while he shot a cup off her head. And I could identify. So I got the number of a place I thought I could go for help to stop drinking."

The counselors there told Cooney he might not have to be committed into a full-scale program. If he tried to stop drinking and couldn't, he should call them back. He quit for about four months, "but I got destructive about myself when I started to feel good, to feel healthy. So I drank again for two more months, and then I stopped on April 21, 1988. You bet I remember that date. I looked in the mirror that day, asked the who's-in-charge question again, and answered myself back that I was gonna be. Me."

As an immediate result, Cooney says, "I found out how vulnerable I was. I didn't have booze to hide behind. I wasn't fightin' and everybody figured I'd retired after Spinks, so I didn't have all the attention that helped me hide from my problems, either."

He grins, just a crooked little smile, amused at the irony: "But ol' Michael Spinks got me goin' toward better things when he knocked me on my ass. Funny thing, bro, don't you think?"

AT FIVE-THIRTY ON A MUGGY TUESDAY SUMMER MORNING nearly sixteen years to the day after Michael Spinks flattened him, Gerry Cooney slips quietly from his house in a pleasant New Jersey suburb. He closes the door gently, trying not to wake his wife and two small children. Then Cooney drives through the dark streets, heading for a nearby health club.

"We got to be there by six, bro," he explains in his heavy, engaging accent. He sounds like Sylvester Stallone in the *Rocky* movies, but he doesn't look like him. Where Stallone was short and bulky, Cooney is tall and surprisingly lean, carrying most of his weight in his shoulders and chest. His legs are storklike. He says he weighs 225 pounds, about fifteen less than during his career. Cooney's wearing shorts, a black Spartan Gym T-shirt, and, on his balding head, a bright red do-rag with white polka dots. The effect is piratical. But the smile that's perpetually plastered on his face keeps Cooney from looking menacing.

"What I'm doing this morning is workin' with a couple guys for a fundraiser we got comin' up," he explains. "A friend named Carol Pizzuto called me, said a local day-care center for old people needed some help real bad. So

Gerry and Jennifer Cooney with their children, Jackson and Sarah, 2001.

I'm doin' this thing I sometimes do five, six times a year, training a couple politicians and firemen and people like that. I spar with 'em a couple mornings each week for maybe four, five weeks, teach 'em some things about fightin', and then we have this charity show. I go a couple rounds with some of 'em, a couple of 'em take other beginners on. People buy tickets; we have a pretty good time; the money goes to a good cause."

As Cooney relates this, he frequently takes his eyes completely off the still-dark road to look directly at his passenger. Turns loom at nervously frequent intervals, because Cooney does not drive slowly. Every time a collision seems inevitable, he turns his attention back to the road at what must surely be the last split second. It's obvious, after a while, that he enjoys making his passenger nervous. There's no sense of malice involved, just one guy joshing another. Cooney's having a little fun.

"Think I oughta be a race-car driver?" he chuckles. "They don't get hit in the head as much as fighters, I guess. Ah, don't worry. I'm just breakin' your balls a little. We'll get there okay."

In the parking lot of the health club, Cooney extracts two bulky equipment bags from his car. They're crammed with sixteen-ounce sparring gloves, headgear, wrapping tape for hands, foul protectors, and jump ropes. Everything stinks of soaked-in, ancient sweat. The bags are both heavy, but Cooney hefts them with the ease of a child toting balloons.

When Cooney enters a long, low room just after six A.M., three people are waiting for him. One, Carol Pizzuto, is dressed in a business suit. The other two are men, one perhaps fifty and the other probably in his late twenties, both clad in clumsy-looking gear: mismatched shorts and T-shirts, low-slung sports shoes that would look more at home on pristine tennis courts. "This is Dan Puntillo; he's the head guy for a kids' program called Middle Earth," Cooney says, nodding at the older man. "I'll be breakin' his balls pretty good at the show in a couple days. Other guy's Terry Hudnett. He's a fireman, thinks he's pretty tough. He's fightin' some stranger who might know what he's doing. I got to teach him how to take care of himself."

While Pizzuto helps Hudnett and Puntillo tug on boxing gloves and set-tle headgear on straight, Cooney moves to another corner of the room and begins wrapping his hands with long, grimy strips of elastic tape. He does this with casual precision while calling over to Hudnett and Puntillo that they better get that headgear on *right*, 'cause they're gonna need it. Then Cooney pulls on his own gloves, pops in a plastic mouthpiece, and motions for Hudnett to move into the center of the room with him. Pizzuto starts a timer that will buzz when ten seconds are left in the traditional three-minute round, and clang loudly at round's end. Cooney and Hudnett circle each other for a moment. Then, snakelike, Cooney snaps out a right hand that smacks against Hudnett's headgear. His left, the fist that pounded down some of the most famous heavyweights in modern boxing history, digs into the fireman's belly. Hudnett does his best to fight back, but his swings are slow in comparison. Cooney never seems to be where his sparring partner's gloves end up.

"Keep the punches short," he growls, the words muffled a little by his mouthpiece. "Shorter! Quicker!" Hudnett tries, and a few times his gloves brush briefly against Cooney's shoulder or waist. Mostly, there's the *thwack* of Cooney's gloves bouncing off Hudnett's head and midsection. The fireman's sweat flies in a fine, salty spray. Hudnett is a good-sized man, easily six feet and 180 pounds. Cooney dwarfs him. When the bell sounds at the end of three minutes, Hudnett is breathing hard. Cooney pulls out his mouthpiece, grins, and yells, "Hey, bro, it's harder than it looks."

Then it's Puntillo's turn while Hudnett catches his breath. Cooney, not even slightly winded, flattens a nostril with a finger, leans over a large plastic trash can, snorts out a clot of mucus, and is ready to go again. He stalks the older man, too, but there's a difference. This time as Cooney punches he expels loud puffs of air from his mouth—*"Whuff! Whuff!"*—and the noise gives the impression he's hitting harder than he really is.

"Gerry's easier on Dan because he'll be boxing him that night," Pizzuto whispers. "But Terry's going to have to fight somebody we don't know, and he might be good. So Gerry's pushing him harder. He wants Terry to be ready for whatever happens."

Hudnett, his face reddened from Cooney's punches, says he didn't know what he was getting into when he was asked if he wanted to help raise money for the adult day-care program. "My boss told me it was for a good cause, that I'd train three times a week for a month." He doesn't mind Cooney

Gerry Cooney—FIST founder and
contented husband and father.

whacking him around. "It's real clear he cares about us learning how to do this right. I just can't imagine what it would be like for him to hit me as hard as he really could."

An hour later, Cooney has sparred three rounds with Puntillo and four with Hudnett. Once, concerned that the fireman wasn't remembering to properly tuck his elbows in to defend against body blows, Cooney unleashed a shot to Hudnett's midsection that was hard enough to send him staggering, doubled over, across the entire long room. Even Puntillo, treated more gently, has a small nick under his left eye. With the boxing over, Cooney yanks off his own headgear and throws his sweaty arms around his two pupils.

"You guys are doin' good!" he enthuses. "Terry, you got to keep those elbows *in*, bro, 'cause whoever you go against next week might hit a lot harder than me. Dan, what they gonna say to you at work when you come in with blood on you?"

"Ah, it's fun," Puntillo replies, beaming. "Thank you." He's been punched hard enough by the famous Gerry Cooney to have a cut as a souvenir, and he's very, very proud of it.

"Can you believe these rat bastards?" Cooney asks, beaming himself. "I hit 'em, cut 'em open, and they tell me thank you. They crazy or what?" While Hudnett and Puntillo leave for another part of the club, where they'll pound punching bags for an additional forty-five minutes, Cooney blots a little sweat from his forehead and gives an interview to a young reporter from a local newspaper. She arrived toward the end of the sparring, and, seeing the sweat and blood, appeared to be contemplating flight. Approaching her, Cooney bends from the waist so he won't tower over her. His voice is softer, without any trace of the comradely taunting directed toward Puntillo and Hudnett.

"Don't worry about me hurtin' 'em," he says. "People like Terry know they're tough guys, but bein' a tough guy doesn't mean you're a good fighter. I got to break 'em down a little so they'll listen to what they're supposed to do."

Why would *anyone* want to be a fighter, the young reporter wants to know, her voice a little shaky.

Cooney's eyes widen. It's a question he's eager to answer. "See, if you learn to fight, you end up knowin' you can do just about anything," he says. "You learn about what your body can do. It could help anybody be a better person. Now, the professional fight business isn't always a good thing, but the science of fightin' is."

A few minutes later, after the reporter has left, Cooney is reflective as he stows boxing gear back into the bags.

"Time was, I hated fightin'," he says. "I liked the reputation it got for me, but I didn't like *doin'* it, you know? One of the best things in my life now is understanding how I can use the good parts of fightin' to help other people, make 'em happy, without letting the bad stuff into it."

Back in the car, driving home, Cooney adds, "Hey, in the beginning at fourteen, fifteen, I was scared to death of fightin'. But it helped me express my anger. It made me into somebody. When I was sixteen, won some amateur tournaments, I saw my picture on the back page of the New York *Daily News*. For the first time in my life I thought, 'Hey, I'm somebody important. I matter. Shit. What do you know?'"

Cooney reminisces the same way he fought: full speed ahead, keep things simple, leave the fancy stuff to somebody else. Plain words do just fine. During his years in therapy, he says, he learned the best way to get over his past was to first confront it, then use it for motivation rather than self-castigation.

"Where I came from was bad, bro," he says of his childhood in a Long Island suburb. "When I was a kid I was just stunted emotionally. When I was home I'd hide in the basement, 'cause if my father was pissed off and drinkin' he'd hunt for me to beat me up, and he was pissed off and drunk all the time. He'd take me to church at seven in the morning, then take me back home into the garage and beat me up. I'd think, 'What's goin' on here? God who?' and he just did this all the time. Here are the things I learned from my father: I was no good. I was a failure. I wasn't gonna amount to anything. Also, don't trust anybody. Don't tell anybody your business. Those things, he said to me over and over, plus *Bam! Bam!* There, I told you 'bout my whole life as a kid."

Cooney had several siblings, but they were just as eager to avoid Tony Cooney's wrath as Gerry. Accordingly, they were only too pleased to scatter while Dad, an ironworker during the day, was beating their brother. They had no comfort or protection to offer him. Cooney adds his mother "was great, but it was the tradition then that the mother stood back and let the father do whatever he did. And I sure wasn't gonna tell anybody about it, like a teacher at school. You just *didn't*."

"You know," Cooney adds, as he pulls into his driveway, "after I got my head straight I finally figured out that what my father was sayin' to me was what he really thought about himself."

GERRY AND JENNIFER COONEY MARRIED IN 1994. THEY HAVE TWO children, Jackson, six, and Sarah, two. At seven thirty in the morning, the kids rush to greet their father as he returns from instructing Puntillo and Hudnett at the health club. Shrieking, they climb him like a piece of playground equipment, not even waiting for Cooney to sit down.

"I know how, from therapy, either you grow up and do the same things to your kids that were done to you or you go the other way, mostly," Cooney says with some difficulty, because toes and fingers and elbows keep getting stuck in his eyes, ears, and mouth as Jackson and Sarah clamber about. "My wife had a healthy family. She's a little more reserved with our kids than me. I like the kids to stretch out. If they get a little worked up, it's okay, you know? They're just bein' kids, is all."

Jennifer Cooney, emerging from the kitchen, where she's been trying to make Jackson eat his breakfast before he goes off to school, tells her son to stop playing with Daddy and get back to the table. If anything, Jackson starts wriggling more madly across his father's shoulders, while Cooney guffaws and ruffles his son's hair. Mom emits a sigh that's equal parts affection and exasperation.

"He doesn't understand what normal families are like," she says, nodding at her husband. "I was telling him once about my family going to the beach, my father playing in the water with us, and he thought that was just amazing. He had no idea that's what most families do. And with our kids, it's always kissy-huggy, always. They say in every family one parent says 'yes' and the other one has to say 'no.' Well, I'm the 'no' parent. He lets the kids do anything."

"Hey," Cooney says, suddenly better able to talk because Jackson and Sarah have jumped down to grab toys off the floor in the den. "I love wakin' up with my kids in the morning. I like life. And now, because I do things normally myself, I can understand how people really live. I tell you, I'm lucky, and here's why. I can go out during the day, do some things, and people still make a fuss over me, like 'Hey, I'm talkin' to Gerry Cooney, can you *believe* it?' That part of fame I still got. Yet after that I come home and my wife, who really loves me, is tellin' me to put down the kids and take out the garbage. Real life is what it is. And I'm smilin' while I'm hauling out that garbage."

Smiling wasn't part of Cooney's childhood until he started boxing. School offered no escape from his problems at home: "I never applied myself. Why bother? I was gonna be a loser anyway." He went to class because his father couldn't get at him there. By junior high, Cooney was already drinking on the sly. He felt alienated from his classmates. They all laughed more than he did. He was positive every one of them was going to go on to college, while he'd barely graduate from high school, get some shit job, and be the loser his father always told him he was.

Then Cooney's older brother Tom started boxing at a local gym. Cooney, hit so often himself, thought it would be a change to do the hitting. One day he tagged along after Tom. "It was '72, and I was fifteen and a half," he remembers. "They put me in with a little guy who knocked me around the friggin' gym. I threw the gloves off. But four months later I went back again, and don't ask me why. Remembering it now, I think it took some courage. My father told me I was a quitter, but I wasn't. 'Cause I went back, right?"

And when he went back to the gym, Cooney gradually discovered something thrilling. He wasn't the quickest kid in the ring, and others mastered the skills of boxing quicker—how to slip punches, how to throw crisp, picture-perfect jabs. But Cooney could take out anybody with one left hook. When he really let loose, hit as hard as he could, the other kid went down and stayed down. When he started boxing in amateur tournaments, he won them. There were ribbons and trophies to take home. His father wasn't impressed.

"My old man built a boxing ring in the backyard and had my mother keep time for the rounds," Cooney says. "He'd hit me as hard as he could. I'd feel bad when I hit him back, 'cause he was my father, you know?"

At least Cooney was succeeding at something. Getting his picture on the back cover of the *New York Daily News* helped him look other kids in the eye. "When I got in a ring, I was better than anybody else. At school, they couldn't look down on me, 'cause I had something goin' too." Boxing success didn't prevent him from drinking; already, he depended on that escape from reality too much. He liked the extra attention he now got from girls. Weaknesses for liquor and women would plague him throughout his career.

Eventually, Cooney twice won New York Golden Gloves championships in front of sellout crowds at Madison Square Garden. He boxed in amateur tournaments in England, Scotland, and Wales as part of an American squad. Then came the 1976 Olympic Trials. Cooney would have been one of the favorites to make the U.S. team, but he says he never tried out. His father had terminal cancer, and the son he beat so savagely didn't want to leave him. "Besides," Cooney says, "I still had mostly low self-esteem. I didn't think that I deserved to go to the Olympics, that if I made the team my country would feel ashamed somebody like me was representing America in such an important competition."

Tony Cooney died soon afterward. The last time he saw his son Gerry, he couldn't hit him, but he could still hurt him. "I said I'd take him for his chemo," Cooney says. "He said he'd rather crawl to the hospital on his hands and knees before he'd let somebody like me take him. That's the truth. I'm sorry. And I loved him, you know?"

Cooney decided it was time to turn pro. "I didn't really have anybody at home to help me, to advise me," he says. "I knew you got managers and they got you fights." Cooney ended up with Dennis Rappaport and Mike Jones as his co-managers. They impressed him because they already managed Howard Davis, a lightweight who'd won an Olympic gold medal.

"But those two were not veteran boxing managers," explains Pete Alfano, a former sportswriter at *Newsday* who covered Cooney's early career. "They were real-estate guys who got lucky enough to get their hooks into someone who became such a visible heavyweight contender."

In February 1977, Cooney won his first professional fight by a first-round knockout. He had six more fights that year and won them all. In 1978 he fought eight more times, again without a loss. 1979 found him fighting and winning seven times. None of his twenty-two opponents was particularly skilled, but that didn't stop Cooney from quickly becoming a star in his violent sport. He was good-looking, he was powerful, and he was white. That last one was the most important.

"The term 'Great White Hope' goes back a long way in boxing," Alfano says. "The general theme is that there are mostly minority fighters, blacks and Hispanics. If a white fighter has great skills, if he can be champion—especially heavyweight champion—then the belief among boxing promoters is that white fans will really pay to see him. He can generate enormous amounts of money."

Ever since white heavyweight champion Rocky Marciano retired undefeated more than twenty years earlier, the boxing division had been dominated by blacks—Floyd Patterson, Sonny Liston, Muhammad Ali, Joe Frazier, and George Foreman—with a brief one-fight title reign by Sweden's Ingemar Johansson. Every few years, a white contender like Jerry Quarry or Duane Bobick would briefly surface, only to be pounded into ignominy by a high-caliber black opponent. Cooney, hulking and pale-skinned, became the latest intriguing prospect.

"I hated that, just hated that," he says. "I never cared nothin' about race. I wanted to be the heavyweight champ, period. But there was no way I could stop people thinking of me that way."

Cooney's fights were characterized by his absolute dominance of opponents. He attacked mercilessly. "If he had any of his father's traits, I suspect they were put on display in the ring," says Alfano. "He wanted to tear people apart."

In 1980, Cooney was finally matched against well-known fighters who had been ranked at the upper levels of the heavyweight division, with *had been* the key attribute. Both Jimmy Young and Ron Lyle had fought, and lost, to the legendary Muhammad Ali for the heavyweight title. Past their primes, they were knocked out by the much younger Cooney. Those were his only two fights that year. Managers Jones and Rappaport might not have known much about boxing techniques, but they did know how to keep the paying public eager to see their young fighter.

"It was smart of them in a way," says Steve Farhood, a former editor of *Ring* magazine who's now a boxing analyst for the Showtime cable network. "They fed him a couple of big names who didn't have much left. No way were they going to risk putting him in against somebody younger who might be as good."

Then in May 1981, Cooney was matched against Ken Norton in Madison Square Garden. Norton, eleven years older than the twenty-four-year-old Cooney, was still considered dangerous. In three fights with Muhammad Ali, he'd gone the full distance each time and even won their first bout. Norton had also recently gone fifteen rounds with current champ Larry Holmes, losing a close decision. But this time there was less a fight than a massacre. The referee stopped the bout just fifty-four seconds into the first round, with Norton squatting helplessly against the ropes while Cooney pounded him remorselessly. In the final moments, Cooney landed four hooks. "Fortunately, none hit [Norton] perfectly or this might be an obituary," Thomas Boswell of the *Washington Post* wrote the next day. Twenty-three years later, veteran journalist Alfano says, "They had to pull him off Norton. I saw more savagery there than I have ever seen."

Cooney remembers the Norton fight for another reason. "I knocked out Ken Norton in fifty-four seconds and afterwards somebody gave me cocaine for the first time," he says. "You know why I liked it? Because, on cocaine, I could then drink three times the amount of booze. I regret having done that. It cut short my career. It was just a way not to think, not to feel, and because I was becoming this famous fighter, people made it easy for me to do it."

THOSE WHO KNEW COONEY BACK IN HIS GLORY DAYS AS A FIGHTER— '80 and '81, when he was undefeated and on the cover of every prominent sports publication—agree that he clearly disliked how he was making his reputation and living.

"Boxing was a job for Cooney," Alfano says. "It was very obvious. He would go in the ring and do what he had to do as quickly as possible."

Yet a little more than two decades later, the walls of Cooney's den are literally lined with mementos of his career: framed action photos, posters from bouts, and magazine covers. Most of these are from two fights, the fifty-four-second annihilation of Norton and the 1982 megabout against Larry Holmes. For a man who once hated the sport to decorate his home with reminders of it seems odd, but Cooney has an explanation.

"I didn't have any of this stuff around for the longest time," he says, playfully wrestling with Sarah while Jackson, voluably irked, is marched off by his mother to finish breakfast. "My mom passed away a couple of years ago, and she had this stuff in her basement. I guess enough time had passed for me to kinda enjoy seeing it again. I mean, I did all this stuff, bro. Might as well remember it."

Therapy and distance from actually fighting combined to make him appreciate the good parts of the sport without blinding him to its evils. "I was told once that a fighter is a whore and his manager is a pimp, and that's basically true," Cooney muses. "You do good for a while, win some money fights, and your manager and the promoters love you. Fightin's just your whole life, but the minute you lose your edge the manager's gone, the promoters don't know you, you got no education and no idea what to do next, and nobody cares. It's just wrong, it's friggin' *evil*. Everybody knows that's how it is except the fighters, but nobody's gonna go out and protect them. Except I am. Me and my foundation."

During the course of this and several subsequent conversations, Cooney talks endlessly about Fighters' Initiative and Support Training (FIST), a nonprofit organization he, Jennifer, and several friends founded in the late

'90s. When the topic is FIST, Cooney's already wide smile gets wider. He can't sit down when FIST is the subject. He has to jump to his feet, get his long arms waving to emphasize what he's saying. Now, in his den, he hops up to start explaining, and little Sarah Cooney, seeing Daddy's arm extended like a tree limb, swings from it as he talks.

"Part of the problem for fighters starts with the money," Cooney says. "I got out all right financially, but I was lucky. Everybody who fights thinks he's gonna be Mike Tyson, couple million a fight, but one or two do that and the rest average maybe ten bucks per round for their whole careers. There isn't much money for most fighters, but their managers and the promoters never explain this to them. And there's no pension plan, no retirement benefits. So you spend what you make, and when you're not makin' any more, that's it. You're not trained for any other job; maybe you got health problems or deals with drugs or alcohol. Meanwhile, you got kids to support, families to feed. And your managers, the ones who were supposed to care about you, have moved on to the next fighters, the ones who can make 'em money *now*. So FIST, my foundation, we find the old fighters who are broke, no job, scared, all these things, and we help 'em. Money, sure, we get that from donations and events we put on. But we also get 'em into job trainin', back in school if they wanna go, help 'em get into rehab if they need it. We're still growin', still startin' out. I guess in six years we've helped maybe three hundred guys. A lot more need help. But we're tryin'."

Cooney's not a figurehead at FIST. Most of the fighters the group's helped so far have come from the New York/New Jersey area, and, often, it's Cooney who sits down with them, talks fighter to fighter, gets across the idea that "it's not a hand *out*, it's a hand *up*."

"We find the guys who need help through the gyms," explains Joe Sano, a labor leader and old friend of Cooney's who is president of the FIST board. "Gerry has credibility with these guys that, initially, a social worker wouldn't. He knows what they're feeling, because in so many ways he felt it himself."

FIST keeps the identities of its clients confidential, but Cooney says fight fans would be amazed at some of the prominent names on the list.

"A former world champ with ten kids who lost his job as a bus driver," Cooney says. "Another guy who fought for the heavyweight title, put on a great show before he lost. You can fall fast and a long way. In fact, pretty often the more famous you became, the less you were able to take care of yourself. I'm your good example."

After beating Norton in 1981, Cooney says, he experienced the full effects of fame. It was a foregone conclusion that this new Great White Hope would fight for a heavyweight title; with the two major boxing organizations refusing to recognize each other's champion, the question was which Cooney would try for. Mike Weaver was champion of the World Boxing Association, but he had lost an earlier bout to World Boxing Council champ Larry Holmes. Holmes had a recent successful defense against a pathetic, aging Muhammad Ali. Weaver would clearly be easier for Cooney to beat, but the best money would come against Holmes, recognized by most fans as the legitimate champ. If comanagers Rappaport and Jones had chosen Cooney's previous opponents with care, at least he fought often enough to keep his reflexes sharp and gradually improve his fighting skills. Now they were even more anxious not to risk the millions of dollars that loomed with a Holmes fight. While his comanagers plotted, Cooney was inactive as a fighter, which meant he could be, and was, extremely active as an abuser of alcohol and drugs. It would be fourteen months after defeating Norton before Cooney got into the ring again, and Alfano believes the long delay is proof comanagers Rappaport and Jones believed deep down that their fighter was just one more overhyped white heavyweight.

"Not letting Cooney have a tune-up fight between Norton and Holmes is very telling," says Pete Alfano. "They wouldn't even risk putting him in the ring with a handpicked tomato can [boxing's term for an opponent who is so bad, he's a pushover]. What if the other guy got lucky with a punch and knocked Gerry out? Rappaport and Jones weren't going to risk their big payday. They really didn't have faith in Cooney, I think."

As his managers took their time, Cooney enjoyed the attention of sycophants, old pals who hoped some of Gerry's shine might rub off on them and women who would do literally anything for attention from a famous athlete.

When Cooney wanted beer, someone would quickly fetch it for him. Cocaine? No problem. Everything from doing his laundry to getting his car repaired was handled by somebody else.

"Normal people learn because they have to how to handle life's usual little problems," Cooney says. "You get famous real young, like I did, and you don't get that experience. Fame lets you put off doing that. The little problems don't exist for you, so you never learn how to handle 'em, and then when the fame is gone and other people your age have already learned how to get through life, you still don't know how to deal with the littlest shit, a job interview or goin' to a restaurant and waitin' in line for a table. How can you possibly handle a big problem? Answer is, you can't. The things that helped give you self-esteem—gettin' your ass kissed, people runnin' to do everything for you, the shit that made you feel like you were *special*—turns out to be what nails your ass afterwards. Because being protected from life's problems is not being protected at all. 'Course, I didn't know that after the Norton fight and before Holmes."

JACKSON COONEY GOES TO A PRIVATE SCHOOL ABOUT TWO MILES from his home. His father takes great pleasure in driving him there in the morning, always stopping on the way to pick up a neighborhood girl Jackson's age. After driving to the neighbor's house, Cooney greets the child and her mother with loud compliments on how nice they look, and he won't move out of the driveway until both children have their seat belts on. Maybe Cooney likes to drive a little recklessly with grownup passengers, but he's little-old-lady careful with kids on board.

Many of the parents pulling up to the school simply drop their children off; teachers and school staff are clustered in the parking lot to make sure everybody gets to the right room. But Cooney takes Jackson inside. The goodbye between father and son is extended, with lots of hugs and reminders from Dad to listen to the teachers and do what they say. Then Cooney's on the move, roaming halls and going up and down staircases, calling out to everyone he passes. If he already knows them, they're hailed by name, and, if he doesn't, he still shouts out a cheery greeting. School isn't quite in session yet; there's excited buzzing from the kids in the various classrooms. Cooney's voice bounces off the walls. He *likes* being here at the school.

"The teachers know if they need anythin', they just gotta ask me," he enthuses. "I want my kids to have that good self-esteem, you know, and it doesn't just come from home. The teachers here are good to my son, so I'll do anything for 'em I can."

Driving around his New Jersey neighborhood, Cooney is constantly reaching for his beeping cell phone. Everybody, it seems, has the number, from FIST board members reporting on ticket sales to upcoming events to a policeman from a nearby town announcing that a wallet Cooney recently lost has been turned in at the station.

"What?" Cooney blurts into the phone. "What's the name of the guy that found it? You got his number? Can I call him? People are *good*, you know?"

The policeman on the phone with Cooney says he'll just jump in a car and bring Cooney the wallet. No need for Gerry to have to drive all the way to the station. Ten minutes later, the cop hands over the wallet, and Cooney hasn't had to make a side trip. He's pleased, more so by his wallet being returned than the fact a policeman made a special trip on his behalf, though Cooney certainly thanked him profusely for doing so.

"It's something that he doesn't get," Jennifer Cooney says. "He's had his ass kissed so long, he sometimes doesn't understand that he still gets treated specially, that other people often aren't treated that way."

IN THE LAST FEW MONTHS BEFORE JUNE 11, 1982, WHEN HE FInally got into the ring with Larry Holmes, Gerry Cooney was one of the most famous men in America. It's impossible, more than two decades later, for many people to realize how much attention that fight attracted. Cooney's face was plastered on the cover of *Sports Illustrated*, but he was also a cover boy for *Time*. The money involved was incredible, about $10 million to be divided equally between the two fighters. (Ten years earlier, Ali and Frazier split $5 million for their first bout.) Holmes, who had been champion for several years, was offended that his relatively unproven challenger would get half. But the fact was that more fans would pay their cable operators thirty-five to fifty dollars to see Cooney than the bland Holmes, who, though impressively skilled, had the misfortune to follow the bombastic, media-savvy Ali as the sport's dominant heavyweight. Lacking a charismatic champion to sell tickets and pay-per-view cable TV "buys," the "Great White Hope" factor was not only present but also heavily exploited by promoter Don King, who gained his first boxing notoriety by promoting the Ali–Foreman "Rumble in the Jungle" in Zaire in 1974. A streetwise former con from Cleveland, the African-American King made certain he controlled the heavyweight championship by insisting managers of challengers sell him a piece of their fighter before King would arrange a title match. That way, every new champ would belong at least in part to Don King.

"Rappaport and Jones were not about to let go of a percentage of their meal ticket," Alfano remembers. "The only reason King made an exception and let Cooney fight Holmes was that he would make so much money. Plus, like many other boxing people, King really believed Cooney would prove to be another overrated white hope. So Holmes would knock him out early, keeping King's hold on the title safe, and meanwhile there would be that large cable TV payday."

Cooney was the focus of all the prefight hype, so much so that when a multicity tour was scheduled to promote the bout Cooney went on it but Holmes was left out. At each stop—Dallas, Phoenix, Los Angeles, a half-dozen other cities—local media would be invited to come watch Cooney spar in a local gym, then answer their questions about the Holmes fight. While Holmes, away from the spotlight, was training in earnest, Cooney's work was sometimes heavier on entertainment than actual sweat. Alfano, who was assigned by *Newsday* to go along on the entire trip, remembers that Cooney was unhappy with the underlying theme of the tour.

"There remained this whole concept of the fight as a confrontation between black and white for supremacy," says Alfano. "I remember once, in his hotel room in Dallas, Gerry got a call from a fan who made racial remarks about Holmes, and Cooney got off the line just shaking his head. He hated

In 1981, Cooney scored his most famous victory,
a first-round knockout over Ken Norton.

the thought of essentially fighting for white America. Another time, in Las Vegas, Alan King the comedian had a party at Caesar's Palace, and there was quite an honor roll of guests, all famous people if not quite the A-list from Hollywood. Cooney arrived and was immediately the center of attention. A sort of reception line of other, somehow lesser, celebrities was set up for him. One of these people was a very famous member of the media, I won't say who, and he said, 'Gerry, you've got to do this for us,' and the implication was very clear that he meant for white Americans. All of this did not get past Cooney, who himself was not in any way racist."

Cooney says he *was* thrown off balance by the white-versus-black atmosphere: "I didn't have anything against black guys. He was the champ and I wanted to be champ, that was all it was for me. But the big thing was, I wanted to be champ so bad, because I thought if I didn't do that I'd be letting down anybody who'd ever cheered for me, and it would prove my old man was right about me, besides."

Many famous athletes routinely dismiss their adoring followers, even disdain them. Not Cooney, who was so desperate for approval that he felt intense obligation to anyone who claimed to support him. On the prebout tour, Alfano recalls, "he was sort of a Bunyanesque character, this gentle giant stopping anything he was doing to talk and sign autographs for anyone who recognized him and rushed over. Never, in private, did he in any way mock them. If Gerry Cooney had beaten Holmes and become champ, maybe afterwards he would have done too much drinking and partying and that would have had its effect, but while he had the crown he would have been the ultimate people's champion, someone who cared about them as much as they cared about him."

More than twenty years later, Cooney is still offended by the suggestion that fans who emotionally attach themselves to athletes don't have their priorities straight. Obsession with sports and the athletes who perform at the highest professional levels is, in Cooney's estimation, healthy.

"People got it tough in so many ways," he says, his usual grin disappearing. "A guy who's workin' two jobs to keep his family comfortable turns on *Monday Night Football*, and if his favorite team, say the Jets, wins, he'll have a little better day tomorrow. I don't like it when somebody says it's wrong, the attention sports gets, the way athletes get turned into heroes. I say if fans are using athletes to help get through their own lives, God bless 'em. Sports give hardworking people a way to think for a little while about something other than their own troubles. Tell me why that's bad."

But in 1982, Cooney's desperation not to let down his fans only added to the prefight pressure on him. So, while he was touring and supposedly training for the fight of his life, he fell back on his ultimate emotional armor. At the end of long days promoting the fight, there was liquor, and there were women. Alfano says, "We knew that he liked to party. But I never on this tour saw Cooney drunk, and I even went back to his room with him sometimes at night to talk. If he was doing some things, he was very good at not being obvious about it."

By the time Cooney climbed into the makeshift boxing ring in the parking lot of Caesars Palace on the night of June 11, he hadn't had a fight in thirteen months. He'd had that long to drink, to use drugs, and to worry that he was going to fail and let everyone down. Without telling his trainer or co-managers, he'd decided that it wouldn't be enough to win by his usual early-round knockout. He wanted a victory that would erase any doubts about him.

"I remember that I got it in my head all the writers were saying I couldn't last a whole fight, fifteen rounds," he says now. "The knock on me was I had to get a guy out of there quick or I'd probably wear out and fall on my face. So I thought, 'Okay, I guess I have to prove I can go the distance,' and that was what I was thinkin' about when the bell finally rang."

TWENTY-TWO YEARS AFTER HE FOUGHT LARRY HOLMES, GERRY Cooney still sees much of life as a chance to compete. He used to lay his psyche on the line in the boxing ring. Now, in a healthier but still obsessive way, he's transferred his symbolic battles to the golf course.

"Ah, I love golf," he says on the way to a nine-hole course near his home. "This is my sixth year playin'. Last year, I made a hole in one and an eagle on a par four. That was more exciting for me than some of my biggest wins in fights. It's because I'm playing golf for myself, not to impress anybody else. I can laugh my way through bad shots and still enjoy the good ones."

Not that Cooney always plays for the fun of it. He likes opponents who agree to small wagers, as little as a dollar, since "all of us need to constantly keep puttin' ourselves out there, challenging ourselves. That's because when we do, we're gonna feel things. Some of them won't be great, but I believe every feelin', every experience, helps. It's when you don't let yourself feel that you get bitter. It wasn't until I stopped drinking fifteen years ago that I understood I was drinking so I wouldn't have to feel. But now, I got *golf.*"

Everybody in the course shop knows Cooney. Much of that has to do with Cooney's ubiquitousness at charitable events. If he's not putting on a fund-raiser of his own, he's gladly appearing at someone else's. But some of it results from Cooney simply getting out in public places like schools or golf courses and loudly making friends with everyone he can. In the corridors of his son's school, a place largely populated by women and children, his genial shout-outs are G-rated. At the clubbier golf course, seeing mostly familiar faces of grown men, Cooney switches to chummy obscenities. From the golf pro who gives him lessons to playing partner Dominick Bratti, a lawyer who serves on the FIST board, everyone is addressed as "you rat bastard." When his golf ball doesn't fly in the direction Cooney wants, it's a rat bastard, too. His cursing isn't meant to be offensive, and it obviously isn't to the beaming recipients of Cooney's words. When Gerry Cooney calls you a rat bastard, it means you're his buddy, and, particularly in his home state of New Jersey, that still counts for something.

On this particular day, Cooney's got some afternoon meetings scheduled. A couple local businesses haven't kicked in for tickets to FIST's next charity event, and Cooney figures the best way to get them to cooperate is to find the guys in charge and break their balls a little bit. He's not looking for five-figure donations. FIST's annual budget for 2004 is around $275,000. A few minutes spent joshing with Gerry Cooney ought to strike a small Jersey business owner as worth a hundred bucks, Cooney reasons.

But first, there's golf. Bratti is a rank beginner, and Cooney is encouraging. When the lawyer manages to send his ball even a few dozen yards straight ahead instead of to the side, Cooney bellows, "You got all a *that* one, you rat bastard!" When Bratti manages two good shots in a row, Cooney loudly wonders if his ol' pal isn't settin' the ex-fighter up so he'll make, and lose, a big bet.

Cooney's own game is wildly erratic. He's left-handed all the way, and short, controlled swings are not his forte. He zooms his battery-powered golf cart around the course the same way he races his car around New Jersey streets, avoiding trees and sand traps at the very last minute, cutting such sharp turns that the cart sometimes wobbles on the very edges of its wheels. Cooney cackles happily when the cart nearly turns over. Getting close to the edge is part of the fun.

Cooney's pedal-to-the-metal approach results in spectacular shots followed by abysmal ones. On the first hole, a 324-yard par four, his drive lands within five yards of the green. From there, it takes Cooney another four strokes to get his ball into the hole. He loudly castigates himself for the bogey and wheels his cart up to the second tee. He skulls a couple of shots again. On the third hole he manages a par, and by then he's in a rhythm, hollering advice to Bratti across the fairway, waving to pals playing on adjacent holes, chattering on his cell phone as he maniacally maneuvers his golf cart after one of his prodigious shots that hasn't gone anywhere near where he was aiming.

The only problem with the great time Cooney's having is that none of the other golfers ahead of him are playing at an equally accelerated pace. He's impatient to hit his ball, drive to it, and hit it again, but these other guys actually want to take a little time between shots. It's slowing Cooney down. He has hopes of playing at least nine holes before he has to get back to FIST business. There's also this other guy, playing all by himself, who's in the same boat. He's right behind Cooney and playing the way Cooney likes to play, keeping on the move, tapping his foot impatiently while waiting for his turn on tee or green. The fellow is older but still trim, with neat iron-gray hair and mustache. After communicating with him for a few holes via broad gestures, Cooney turns to Bratti and suggests, "Let's let this guy join us. He's in a hurry, too." Then he waves the man over, shaking hands and explaining, "I'm Gerry, and this guy's Dom," before getting distracted again by his cell phone.

A medallion clanking off his golf bag identifies the man as a retired Marine named Bob Catullo. His ramrod-straight posture is evidence of rigid self-discipline. But his nearness to Gerry Cooney has his knees knocking a little. He doesn't say anything, though. He stands apart from Cooney and Bratti, and when all three have hit their drives he walks off after his ball without joining in their banter. Cooney, deep in conversation with Bratti about some sort of FIST news he's just received on his cell phone, doesn't notice.

"Are you with the media?" Catullo eventually asks someone who's riding around the course with Cooney and Bratti. "Are you writing about Gerry

Cooney? Of course, I recognize him. Who in New Jersey doesn't know Gerry Cooney? I don't want to be pushy with him. He's probably out here to get away from fans. He won't remember me, but I played nine holes of golf with him at an event years ago. He was so great then."

Catullo won't be coaxed into talking with Cooney between shots, repeating that he doesn't want to bother him. Cooney, finally off the phone, notices Catullo's reticence. He furtively asks Bratti what their playing partner's name is—"Bob" is all the lawyer can remember—but Cooney is then told by his other companion that the man says he once played golf with Cooney at some charity event. That's all Cooney needs to hear.

"Hey," he bellows at Catullo as they prepare to putt, "we've played before, right? What's your name?"

The grizzled ex-Marine literally capers. "I'm Bob, Mr. Cooney."

"Shit, I already know your first name. I meant, what's your last name?"

That's all the encouragement Catullo needs. For the next hour, he's in lockstep at Cooney's side, laughing at the ex-fighter's jokes and telling a few of his own. Cooney loudly informs anyone within earshot—which, at Cooney's volume, includes almost every golfer on the course—that Bob Catullo is a real rat bastard who knows more good jokes than just about anybody he's ever met. When the jokes run out, Cooney entertains with stories about other famous people. Catullo listens carefully, making sure to remember it all. It's easy to imagine him repeating the tales to friends who'll be incredulous that Bob, this guy *right here*, palled around with Gerry Cooney!

"I know a lotta people," Cooney tells Catullo, Bratti, and a few other golfers gathered near the eighth tee. "Like, one time I went to a party of Elton John's. He's at the piano, sees me, and starts playin' 'When Irish Eyes Are Smilin'.' When my mother was in the hospital, he sent her the biggest bouquet of flowers. Elton John's the only man I ever kissed on the lips." Cooney pauses, demonstrating the timing of a master comic. "Of course," he adds slyly, "I didn't give him no tongue." Everybody cracks up. Cooney laughs, too. It's a sunny day, he's playing golf, and there's absolutely no doubt who's the most popular kid on the playground.

When their round is finally over, Cooney and Catullo part like old pals. Afterward, in his car on the way to the FIST meetings, Cooney is told he just did a very nice thing, going out of his way to make someone so happy.

"Shit, I live on that," he replies. "The way he believed I'm worth somethin' helps remind me that I am."

It also reminds him of the Holmes fight. Cooney says he was convinced, as he got in the ring, that if he didn't win, all the fans who had believed in him would despise him for the rest of his life. "No way I woulda thought I could lose to Holmes and twenty-somethin' years later people'd still wanna be seen with me. I mean, if I'd known . . ." His voice trails off for a moment.

"You know I nearly beat Holmes, don't you?" Cooney asks. "In spite of everythin', I came so, so close."

GERRY COONEY REMEMBERS HIS BOUT WITH LARRY HOLMES DIFferently from how most of those who were there remember it.

The fight lasted thirteen entertaining rounds out of a scheduled fifteen. Almost as soon as the bell rang for the first round, there were indications Cooney was just another in the long, overhyped line of Great White Hopes. He shuffled after Holmes, pawing out ineffectual jabs and hooks while the champion simply observed, trying to time Cooney's punches. Just thirty seconds into the second round, Holmes smashed a right hand against Cooney's jaw and knocked him down.

"There was this awful sense at ringside that it was true, that Cooney was just another bum," Alfano recalls. "We thought, 'We've been scammed; this guy is nothing. The public had been gypped again.' But then he got up and, for quite a while, made a very respectable showing. While he couldn't dominate Holmes, he landed some good body shots and won a few rounds, though not as many as the champion."

In Cooney's memory, Holmes caught him with an early, lucky shot, "but I got up and I was takin' it to him. Holmes was a great fighter, don't get me wrong. I'm glad that after the fight we got to be friends. All people remember is that I lost, but the truth is I was gettin' to him and if I'd had my head on straight, hadn't had that idea I had to go the full fifteen, I woulda been champ."

Stories about the fight filed by some of the most respected boxing writers of the era largely disagree. Dave Anderson wrote in the *New York Times* that "from the beginning, Holmes jabbed (Cooney) almost at will . . . eventually the challenger landed some good punches, but Larry Holmes never appeared dazed." William Nack wrote in *Sports Illustrated* that "Holmes was hitting him at will." In the ninth, Cooney hit Holmes low, and the referee ordered the three judges scoring the fight to deduct two points from Cooney. In the tenth there was another low blow, and Cooney was penalized a third point.

"Those shots weren't that bad," Cooney says now. "Hey, he was pullin' my head down with his forearm every time I got in close. Referee didn't take any points for that."

The bout was hard fought, with both fighters absorbing punishing blows. By the thirteenth round, Cooney looked exhausted. But Holmes, a canny veteran, had plenty of energy left. He began pounding Cooney with lefts and rights. Cooney later told William Nack that, as the champion pummeled him, Cooney's thoughts somehow drifted to the film *Raging Bull,* which starred Robert De Niro as fighter Jake La Motta. In that film, standing helpless before a similar onslaught by middleweight champion Sugar Ray Robinson, La Motta shouts, "Go on, hit me! You can't hurt me!" to demonstrate to his opponent that he wasn't going to quit. Cooney staggered defiantly in front of Holmes in real life, not able to defend himself but not willing to quit. "It was very foolish, a stupid thing to do, but I wanted to show him," Cooney told Nack afterward. "Show him I had guts, I guess."

Finally, Cooney staggered back into the ropes. His glove brushed the canvas. Under boxing rules, that constituted a knockdown. The referee gave him a mandatory count of eight and let the fight continue. But before Holmes could hit Cooney again, Victor Valle, the challenger's trainer who was working in his corner, jumped in the ring and threw his arms around Cooney. This meant, technically, that Holmes won on a disqualification rather than a knockout.

Cooney had a bad cut over one eye. His face was lumpy from Holmes's blows. He needed to go to a hospital for stitches, but before he went he asked to be handed the ring microphone. Then, speaking to the 32,000 in attendance at ringside and the millions watching closed-circuit broadcasts in theaters or on cable TV at home, he said he was sorry for letting them down. He was crying as he spoke.

"Think about that," says Farhood, who was covering the fight as editor of *Ring* magazine. "That's his first reaction, to think about everybody else. He's fought his heart out, given everything he had, even had the right to maybe feel pretty good he'd done as well as he did. But he's crying because he thinks people have a right to be disappointed in him."

Alfano was with Cooney at the hospital as the defeated fighter waited to get stitches for his cut. "With the nurses, he tried to put some spin on it," Alfano recalls. "He would say, 'I got myself into some mess tonight.' But riding back to the hotel, he was depressed. He kept apologizing for losing, saying he had disappointed everyone. It was pointed out he'd put up a great fight, that he'd acquitted himself very honorably, but you couldn't say anything to change his mind. There was nothing from him about how he might have been winning until one of his managers came in with the judges' scorecards and yelled, 'Look!' Without the three points deducted for low blows, two of the judges would have had Cooney winning, and the other would have had it about even. Had the fight not been stopped, there would have been a few more rounds where Cooney might have made up the difference on those scorecards. I'd had Holmes comfortably ahead, and most of the other press did, too. If the fight had gone the distance and Cooney had been given the decision, there would have been race riots all over the country. This happens sometimes in boxing, that the judges' scorecards don't reflect the fight everyone else saw."

Now, Cooney admits, "I think about that Holmes fight all the time. If we'd fought again, I would have been champ. There was no rematch because Holmes didn't want one."

Alfano says there was a different reason Holmes–Cooney II never took place. "Cooney had acquitted himself well enough by taking Holmes to the thirteenth, and if he'd returned to the ring in a credible amount of time, if he'd won a few fights and worked himself back up to the head of the line, he would have been perceived as a very worthy challenger. The chance was still there. The one loss to Holmes didn't have to end it. But Rappaport and Jones, his co-managers, did."

Don King had let Cooney have one shot at Holmes because the fight brought in millions and because the promoter believed Cooney would be a pushover. But Cooney had shown a lot of heart and considerable ability. Holmes was getting older. King wasn't about to give a second chance to a fighter who wouldn't be contractually obligated to him if he did win the heavyweight title.

"It comes back to the politics of boxing," Alfano says. "King managed Holmes, a clear conflict of interest in any sport other than boxing. Jones and Rappaport would not give up a piece of Cooney to King as part of a deal for a rematch, and King wouldn't give a rematch without one. So Cooney, while Holmes was champ and King controlled the division, was never going to get another title shot."

Cooney, millions of dollars richer but without the championship he wanted so much, found himself with nothing to do. He says he asked for fights, but his managers, probably hoping King would be forced by public demand to grant a rematch at some point, told him nobody was offering them. Cooney had no financial pressure to fight. He was one of the rare boxers whose money was actually in the bank where it was supposed to be. "My two managers didn't trust each other," he says. "They watched every penny so the other guy wouldn't steal it. Meanwhile, I'd lost to Holmes, and my managers didn't care enough about me or maybe didn't understand me well enough to keep me busy, just get me some fight to keep me occupied. I had all this time, and I didn't use it wisely, bro. I guess I got bitter."

When Cooney wasn't drunk or high, he fixated on the loss to Holmes. While he blamed himself for letting down his fans, he also convinced himself that the real fault lay with others. The referee took points from Cooney for low blows but not from Holmes for holding. The media had played with Cooney's head, making him decide he had to go the full fifteen rounds instead of just overwhelming Holmes with a barrage of early punches. Hey, two of the three judges thought Cooney was winning!

"See, if you're famous and you fail at something, your reaction is to look for somebody or something else to blame it on," Cooney says now. "And, when you do that, you don't grow up. The ass kissers tell you you're perfect, you can do no wrong. So famous people don't learn from their mistakes. *Un-*famous people, they're the ones who have to learn how to do that. They're luckier than famous people that way."

GERRY COONEY MAY BE A CELEBRITY IN MOST OF NEW JERSEY, BUT not in the Chili's where he stops for lunch after his morning golf. The place is packed, and loud with the conversations of young men and women taking their breaks from work. Most of the people at adjacent tables weren't old enough to be in elementary school when Cooney lost to Holmes. Certainly, the waiter standing by Cooney's table wasn't even born in 1982. "You guys ready to order?" he asks in a bored monotone, eyes on some pretty girls a few tables away.

"Yeah," Cooney says, leaning toward the kid, trying to make eye contact. "I think we want some chicken wings to start." He waits for the kid to look at him—five seconds, ten. Then he adds, "An' make 'em all *left* wings, wouldja?" The waiter walks off instead of reacting. Cooney is clearly disappointed. He's not bothered the youngster had no idea who he was. Some people do; some don't. The problem is that there wasn't any contact between them. Cooney is a man who thrives on *connection*. "I don't think he got the joke," Cooney says mournfully. "Maybe it was too loud for him to hear me or somethin'."

He makes distracted small talk until the kid returns to the table bearing a plate of bright-orange chicken wings. Raising his voice, making sure he can be heard, Cooney grins and inquires, "Now, they all left wings like I asked you?"

The waiter is immediately confused. "I don't know how to tell," he replies earnestly. "What's the difference?"

Now Cooney's worried the kid is upset. "Hey, not a problem," he says reassuringly. "It's a joke, you know? I'm just breakin' your balls here. We're havin' fun."

The waiter looks doubtful. "I can take them back."

"Nah!" Cooney says. "They look great! You're doin' a great job!" The kid hurries off, nervously looking back over his shoulder. Cooney digs into the chicken wings.

"Only left wings, that's a pretty good joke," he mutters.

COONEY MADE FEW JOKES FOR ALMOST TWO YEARS AFTER HE LOST to Holmes. He had no fights at all. "I was disappointed, depressed," he says. "I'd let my fans down. I'd sit and think maybe my father was right. I really was a loser. I had money to sit home and live on, except I really had no home. I was living in hotels. My managers couldn't get me fights, but they sure did fight with each other. I was in the middle. I'd hoped they were with me 'cause they cared about me, but after Holmes when I was all shook up, they just bitched about money. I realized they only cared about the money, not me."

So Cooney numbed himself with drugs and liquor. He says he spent most of the two years drinking heavily on a daily basis. "My past had overcome me," he says. "The one thing I'd always been able to do was relate to people, just get out and talk and mingle, you know, but now I didn't even go out much."

Finally, in September 1984, Cooney fought again. He dispatched Philipp Brown, "some guy who was twenty-six and oh," in four rounds. Three months later, Cooney fought again, knocking out George Chaplin in the second round. Some boxing writers had considered Chaplin an up-and-comer. Cooney was back in the title picture if he wanted it, particularly since Holmes had split away from Don King. But liquor and depression had pretty much conquered Cooney. He wouldn't fight again for seventeen months. He spent that time aimlessly wandering around. "I didn't have a wife, didn't have any daily responsibilities," he says. "I couldn't come up with a reason to spend my days doing useful things. I had the time and money to disappear and feel bad about myself. I worked out some, I traveled a little, you can say I dated women 'cause that sounds better. I spent money. What I was doing, of course, was putting off the normal growing-up process in life by avoiding it all."

Cooney pauses, then grins.

"Hey, I think that's the real definition of fame," he says. "It lets you avoid for too long things you're gonna have to deal with at some point. Fame is *avoiding*, not *getting*, which is what most people believe it is."

Cooney avoided everything until 1986, when he suddenly had new incentive to get back in the ring. In September 1985, Larry Holmes finally lost the heavyweight title, and to the unlikeliest of challengers. Michael Spinks was an overblown light-heavyweight who put on thirty pounds to move up to the higher, more lucrative heavyweight class. Smaller than Holmes, Spinks had ducked and backpedaled and thrown punches from awkward angles until, at the end of fifteen rounds, the judges awarded him a narrow victory by decision. Holmes was expected to easily win the rematch in April 1986, but Spinks won another close contest. Holmes, disgusted, announced he was retiring. Spinks was considered an accidental champion, a good fighter who got lucky. Since Don King didn't control Spinks, Gerry Cooney was suddenly a viable contender again. A month after Spinks beat Holmes for the second time, Cooney got back into the ring and knocked out Eddie Gregg, who was regarded as a decent though not first-rate fighter, in the first round.

It wasn't the best of times for heavyweight boxing. Holmes claimed he was retired. Three different organizations claimed to recognize the "real" champion. Don King, anxious to regain control of the division, collaborated with cable TV's HBO to stage a tournament to consolidate the three titles. Spinks chose not to enter, so he was stripped of any official recognition. No matter, Spinks simply declared himself "the People's Champion" and signed to fight Cooney in Atlantic City.

Maybe if he'd trained hard and focused on the fight, Cooney could have won. In retrospect, he thinks he made certain he didn't have a chance. "Deep inside, I didn't think I deserved any success," he says. "I found the certain way to destroy myself. I was drinkin' a bottle of scotch a day when I was training for Spinks. I believe my managers knew it, but they didn't want to pull me out and get me straightened out because that would get the fight called off and they'd lose that money. I was a sick kid.'"

He was sicker when Spinks got through with him. "That was it, the absolute bottom," Cooney says. "After lettin' him beat me, if I was still a celebrity, it was as a celebrity joke. Right afterwards I finally asked myself who was in charge of my life, and that was the moment it started to turn around."

Cooney quit drinking but recognized that wasn't enough. He went into therapy and finally confronted his problems: "The doctor said, 'Look inside yourself and tell me what you see there.' I looked, and I saw this big empty black hole. And the doctor told me I needed to think how to fill that hole up."

Cooney spent a good part of the next few years in therapy. The hardest admission, he says, is that "I was bein' my father. The very thing I hated about him was how he wouldn't face his problems. For him, booze pushed everything away. And that's what I was having it do to me. Okay. Not gonna happen anymore. And then there was the next thing: my father wasn't the one making me drink; I was the one doin' that. Okay some more. I was thirty-two, thirty-three, still pretty young. I was getting my brain back together, and here's the next question. Do I fight anymore?"

Cooney had enough money in the bank to live comfortably, if not extravagantly. A fireplug-shaped fighter named Mike Tyson had become the universally recognized heavyweight champion. One of his victims was Michael Spinks, who Tyson blasted out in the first round. But after his dismal showing against Spinks, Cooney couldn't challenge Tyson without at least a few bouts in between to prove himself all over again to boxing fans. He chose to retire instead.

"I decided it was time to turn the page, but fighters got a hard time knowing what to do next," Cooney says. "I'd fought for the heavyweight championship. How do you follow that crowd roar, thousands of people callin' your name? How do you give up people wantin' your autograph, offering you anything you want? So you get tempted to try it one more time, and then one more time after that. Drugs and booze aren't the only things that can make you crazy. Being famous for a while can be just as bad."

Cooney walked away from being an active fighter but not from boxing. He would stay in therapy from 1988 through 1992—"I call it 'the black hole time'"—but he didn't want to sit around all day in his house. So he began promoting fights himself, putting together matches that featured top names in the sport, including former heavyweight champion George Foreman, who, after a ten-year retirement, was making a comeback in his early forties.

"Boxing people still remembered me," Cooney says. "I signed guys for fights and treated them fair. It was interestin'. Then in '89, two years after I was in against Spinks, Foreman, who knows more about marketing than anybody you ever met, says to me that it's silly for me to be tryin' to find him somebody to fight. We oughta fight each other, he says, 'cause that'd draw the most money of all."

The more Cooney thought about it, the more intrigued he became. For the first time since he started boxing as a teenager, he was sober. Maybe it would make a dramatic difference in how well he could perform in the ring. True, he was thirty-three and hadn't fought in two and a half years, but Foreman was forty-one. The massive Foreman, one of the most feared fighters of his generation, had generated amazing publicity for his comeback effort, winning nineteen bouts in a row. If Cooney beat him, maybe he'd be in position to fight for the title again!

"So I worked *hard,*" Cooney says, grinning. "I hired Gil Clancy, one of the best trainers in the business. He spent four months with me. We worked on stayin' balanced, all this stuff I never thought that much about before."

Cooney fought Foreman on January 15, 1990, in the same Atlantic City ring where he'd lost to Michael Spinks in 1987. The first round was all Cooney. Confident and clear headed, he pounded Foreman with lefts and had the former champion in serious trouble.

"But the rat bastard got through it," he says, laughing. "I thought I'd take him out in the next round, but I got caught by a shot myself, and they hadda stop it. I lost. And it was a great moment for me. You know why? For the first time in my life, I could turn the page. I'd kept straight, I'd worked hard, did my very best, and, guess what? I didn't win. I thought, 'Well, it's the end of one chapter, but I've still got the whole rest of my life.' And that's when I knew it was gonna be all right for me."

Recovering alcoholics can best avoid the temptation to drink again by keeping busy. Finally retired as a fighter, Cooney looked for rewarding ways to use his time. An advantage was that he didn't need to earn a weekly paycheck. The money he'd made in the ring spared him from that. But he still wanted to do *something*. Sitting around his house all day would lead to boredom, and boredom could lead back to drugs and alcohol. His first option was the most obvious. Particularly in New Jersey and New York City, Cooney's name still meant something, "so I did appearances." Stores paid him to cut ribbons at their openings. Youth groups wanted him to make speeches. He signed autographs, posed for pictures, and enjoyed learning that fans still *liked* him even after he'd lost some fights. That knowledge helped sustain him through the frustrations of his new life. He didn't have the gofers who'd been so much a part of his boxing retinue. If he was out of groceries, he had to go to the store himself. Since his picture wasn't in the papers all the time, the maître d's at restaurants didn't automatically seat him if other people were waiting ahead of him.

Then, for the first time in his life, he took a job. "I started a boxing program in the Hamptons for Omni Health and Fitness," he recalls. "I didn't have to, you understand, but it just seemed interestin'. I'd teach, word got around, and their membership started to pick up. It was a regular job, three nights a week, and I hadda plan the rest of my schedule around work. Never had to do *that* before. I had one student who was a sixty-four-year-old woman. *Sports Illustrated* heard about that and came out and did a piece."

As he tried, and mostly enjoyed, living what he calls "a regular life," Cooney found himself thinking how lucky he was compared to most other retired fighters. He'd finished his career without mental or physical impairment. He'd earned enough money in the ring that, with wise investments, he wouldn't ever have to worry about making a living. But in the gyms where he would still sometimes go to work out, he always noticed the sad old pugs, the broken-down ones with haunted eyes who, past their primes, were ignored by managers and promoters and still hung around because they had no place else to go.

"I'd always worked with charities, even during my bad times, and now that I wasn't fighting anymore I thought it would be good for me if I really found ways to help others," Cooney says. "I had learned I could love the good parts of boxing without having to love the bad parts, which mostly involved using fighters until they broke down, then throwin' them away. So here I was sober, retired, time to do whatever I wanted, and what I found I wanted was to help these guys, these old fighters nobody seemed to care about anymore."

Cooney's first attempt took him to Washington, D.C. His fame was still sufficiently intact to get him appointments with senators and congressmen. He hired a lawyer "who charged me about fifty thousand dollars," and asked at these meetings for the legislators to work with him to craft and pass laws protecting fighters—"things that would help 'em reconnect with real life after their careers." Though all the elected officials Cooney met with expressed interest, no one offered specific help. Everyone wanted to pose for photos with him that could be reproduced in the newsletters they sent to voters in their home states and districts. Cooney went back to New York feeling frustrated. "I spent fifty thousand dollars to learn I was just one fish in a real big sea," he says. Though he didn't forget about the fighters he wanted to help, he put the idea aside for a while. Besides, he'd met someone who proved able to teach him a whole lot more about having a normal life.

JENNIFER RICHARDS COONEY IS A PLEASANT-LOOKING WOMAN WHO seems to think very carefully before she says anything. She looks directly into the eyes of whomever she's talking to—not glaring, but measuring. Somebody in the Cooney family has to be the cautious one, and it's certainly not going to be her impulsive, outgoing husband.

"Sometimes I think he does too much," she says. "He says yes to everybody. You just can't do something for every single charity. But he loves it. His big weakness is that he has a hard time saying no, even to telemarketers. They call, and if he answers the phone he listens to everything they have to say. I tell him, 'Give me that phone!' But he doesn't want to hurt their feelings."

Jen Cooney says she didn't know anything about boxing when she met her future husband in 1992. "It was a blind date," she remembers. "I'd graduated from college and got a job at an accounting firm in New York City. A guy working there knew Gerry. We met for lunch. I made the guy who knew Gerry come, too, and even made him bring a girl. I didn't think I'd have anything to talk to Gerry about. But we hit it off. Gerry's very sweet. I've noticed that now with a lot of fighters I've met through FIST. You think of them as brutes, tough guys. But so many of them are just sweet and gentle. They left all their aggression in the ring, I guess."

Cooney told Jennifer a little about his past. He had a son from a previous relationship. And there were, of course, his past problems with drugs and alcohol. She remembers him telling her that he was "still getting his brains back."

"All this was new to me," Jennifer says. "I wasn't familiar with alcohol abuse and drug addiction. My family was very, very normal. But right away I realized I'd never met someone who was working so hard to become a better person. Even after a while, though, I didn't know how bad it had been for him. He didn't want to talk about some things. We were married two years before I knew he had half sisters. And boxing was still pulling at him. He was getting calls to fight Holmes again. It took a while for him to open completely up."

During their courtship, Jennifer had to adjust to her new boyfriend's celebrity. "It got weird for me," she recalls. "People would come up to him for autographs, which he always signed. We were in the Hamptons once, walking around, and Gerry says, 'There's Billy Joel, let's say hi.' I mean, I love music, my family's musical, this is Billy Joel, and *he's* acting excited to see Gerry. No wonder Gerry didn't have much sense of how regular people live and do things."

Gradually, Jennifer began to understand how Cooney's self-image still depended a great deal on being a celebrity. Those autograph requests were as important to him as they were to his fans.

"We took our honeymoon in '94 in Europe, and after a couple days he got very quiet, very strange," she remembers. "It was like pulling teeth, but I finally got him to tell me he felt strange because nobody recognized him. It's changed some since, as he learns to relax more, as he gets more confident as a person. We just got back from a trip to Florida, and I said, 'Well, nobody recognized you there,' and he said, 'Yeah, isn't that great?' I thought, 'Wow!' He's letting go a little more of the celebrity thing, because he finally feels so comfortable about himself. That makes me very, very proud of him, since I know it hasn't been easy."

Part of the process, Jennifer and many of Cooney's friends believe, has been FIST. He was discouraged by the failure of his first attempts in Washington, D.C., to get something done to protect fighters. But he kept all of the paperwork from that effort, and Jennifer found the material in a box when the Cooneys were packing to move to a new house shortly after their marriage.

"I looked at them and said, 'Gerry, this seems important. Why didn't you tell me about it?'" she says. He told me about going to Washington, about all the red tape, and how he had tried his best but couldn't get anything done. I said, 'Well, this needs to be resurrected,'" and he started thinking about it again."

Cooney kicked around a few ideas, and by 1997 thought he'd come up with a new approach. He called Joe Sano, a labor consultant he'd known for almost twenty years, and suggested they get together. When they met, Cooney told Sano that he wanted to found a retirement home for old fighters.

"My mother was active in the teachers' union, and sat on a board for a teachers' retirement home," Sano says. "It got closed down, and I remembered that. So I said, 'Gerry, that's not the way to go.' But he was right that used-up fighters needed something, so we talked more and decided the best way to help fighters would be to give them ways to stay in the community where they had friends. That meant job counseling, help with health issues.

And that, of course, meant putting together a nonprofit organization to provide those kinds of services."

Some of the money Cooney had earned with his own sweat and blood in the ring paid the incorporation fees for Fighters' Initiative for Support and Training. That was the easy part. The newly formed FIST was a work in progress. Everybody agreed on goals, but nobody was sure how to go about achieving them. How would money be raised? How would they find the fighters who needed help?

"The early days were very raw," recalls Farhood, the former *Ring* magazine editor. "Gerry had called and asked me to help. I was glad to, but we weren't very well-organized. Jen Cooney was sort of the staff. It was frustrating in the beginning."

Gradually, though, a coherent strategy emerged. Cooney contacted old boxing pals who'd also come through their careers relatively well: Vito Antofuermo, Chuck Wepner, Emile Griffith, and even Larry Holmes. The retired fighters could still be star attractions at fund-raising dinners and golf tournaments. Cooney began putting together charity shows where he'd train, then box, local politicians and celebrities. The money that started flowing was hardly a deluge, but the few thousands built into tens of thousands, and finally in 1999 FIST had enough money to start seeking out fighters who needed end-of-career assistance.

"We go into the gyms where fighters train," Sano explains. "We talk to people there. That's how we hear about who needs help. Now, we have five caseworkers in New York City—registered nurses and social workers. See, we reach out to these fighters where they are. FIST has now been finding them, helping them, for five years, and levels of trust are still being developed with the people who need our assistance. It's hard to admit you can't handle your own life. People have pride, and we respect that."

Jennifer Cooney believes FIST helps her husband as much as it does its fighter-clients: "It's allowed Gerry to find his niche in life. He's helping others, which is something he loves and needs to do. This is a hard time for nonprofits. There isn't as much money available out there. But we're able to find enough to help a significant number of fighters. And that makes Gerry so happy."

"I THINK A LOT OF PEOPLE WHO GET FAMOUS AREN'T REALLY equipped for success," Gerry Cooney says, leaning back on the couch in his den. Jennifer's busy elsewhere in the house, Jackson's at school, and Sarah has pretty much collapsed after wearing herself out clambering all over Daddy. Cooney is feeling reflective. Despite everything, his life is finally turning out so well, and he wants to find the right words to articulate why.

"You see it all the time, these so-called celebrities sabotaging their success, and it's because they're afraid of it," he continues. "They wonder, deep down, if they deserve it, and for a lot of them the answer's no. That was me, for sure. And too many famous people are ready to quit when the first problem comes along that they gotta handle for themselves. Everybody gets knocked down. People with normal lives know you just get up and move on. But if you don't have that regular structure in your life, the problems other people can deal with are things you just can't comprehend. I'm not sayin' everybody ought to feel sorry for famous people who can't handle it. But I *am* sayin' there's a reason so many of 'em can't."

At forty-seven, Cooney doesn't exude any sense of middle-aged ennui. He's got plans, lots of them. FIST is only going to get bigger and better. The word's getting out about it in the boxing community, he believes. Just hearing about FIST might inspire some current fighters to start thinking about, even planning for, life after retirement from the ring. Right there, that's a big thing. And Cooney wants someday to write a book about his own life and all he's learned from the bad and good parts of it. But he thinks that step "is a little premature right now. We finally got FIST goin' good, I've got all these events for it, and I need to put my time into that."

Then there's the other thing, the one Jennifer Cooney says she absolutely won't allow. Gerry Cooney would like to have his own gym, a place where he could train pro fighters, not only to teach the guys all the tricks of the trade but also to counsel them about getting their educations, about having plans in place for when the day comes that they can't fight anymore.

"Whenever we drive past an empty store or building, I see him looking at it, and I tell him, 'No, we're not opening a gym,'" Jennifer says. "He doesn't want to do it for the money. Money is not his be all and end all. He's happy with what he's got. He just likes being part of the boxing *thing*. And he does have a gift for training fighters."

Months apart, Gerry and Jennifer Cooney tell the same story. A few years ago, after hearing stories about FIST's boxing events, a thirty-three-year-old, overweight stockbroker approached Cooney. Jeffrey Mansfield wanted to learn to box. He thought it was a way he could get in shape. Cooney got the paunchy guy in the ring and decided he had potential. They worked together for months, and then the stockbroker entered himself in the New York Golden Gloves, one of the most prestigious amateur boxing tournaments in the world. He won the heavyweight division.

"That makes Gerry think he could take some professional boxer and take him to a championship," Jennifer says. "He'd love that. Maybe he should have a chance to try. But what worries me is that whenever he trains someone, he gets in the ring with them himself. I really don't like that. He's been hit enough in his life."

Cooney still looks like he could make a boxing comeback. If that possibility has occurred to him, he hasn't mentioned it yet. But it's hard for fighters not to feel the tug of the ring, even after they've been away from it for years. During the spring of 2004, Cooney's old foe George Foreman announced that, at age fifty-five, he'd decided to get back into training and return for one last fight, just to prove that a man his age could do it. According to reports, Foreman was looking around for the right opponent. Jennifer Cooney says he shouldn't bother calling New Jersey.

"Gerry's not going to do anything like that," she says firmly. "I think he's a level-headed guy. He respects his body and his health and his reputation." She pauses. Like her husband, Jennifer Cooney knows how to time a punch line. "Besides," she adds after just the right interval, "he knows I'd kill him."

EVEN WITH SOBRIETY, FIST, AND A FAMILY HE LOVES, COONEY'S life isn't quite perfect. He doesn't see his teenaged son as often as he'd like. It bothers him that he and his siblings aren't closer.

"Anybody who saw any of my family would automatically ask them 'How's Gerry?'" he says. "Some of them felt like it was a way of saying they didn't count, only me. Me, my brothers, and my sisters—all of us grew up with my father to deal with, and we all found our different hiding places. And as much as you may care for other people, they have to look at themselves and make their own lives right, eventually."

Cooney mourns some of the happiness he might have had during his boxing heyday. "I know if I beat Holmes, I'd probably be dead by now, because I just would have been out of control," he says. "But I still was famous, and I was on the cover of *Sports Illustrated* and *Time* magazine. And yet there was no enjoyment for me in it. I wish I'd had the tools to cope back then. I think about that a lot. And I think about this: I was fighting Ron Lyle in the Nassau Coliseum, and a friend says, 'When you knock this guy out, why not imagine you can reach out and touch the crowd?'" I knocked him out and I tried it, feeling like I was right out there with them, and it was a thrill. I was sharing their excitement. But I still could only allow myself to feel that way for about ten minutes, because I started wondering if I'd ever have a chance to be happy again. I got good times now, but I can't get that lost time back."

Cooney admits he still likes being recognized. Autograph seekers are always going to be welcome. But he has a healthy attitude toward fame, he believes, because he's learned to enjoy it without depending on it.

"I don't need somebody else's opinion to reassure me I'm okay," he says. "It's like the Hall of Fame, the one for boxing. They got one, but I don't care about whether I'm ever voted into it. Being in a hall of fame is a way for other people to say you were important. It doesn't make it automatic that you'll believe it, too. What you think about yourself, what you honestly think of yourself, is what makes the difference between being happy or unhappy. Fame is what other people think of you."

Cooney pauses, shakes his head, looks around his den at the fight photos and then down at the toys scattered on the floor. "I want the words to express this right," he says. "I finally have what I always wanted, the chance to do good things and enjoy a great family. I was pretty famous. It took me gettin' past that to finally figure out that the best things are simple. Like my wife tellin' me to take out the garbage.

"Take *that,* famous guy."

Melvin in the Big Time

For once, Melvin Dummar's timing was perfect. Reno was booming in the summer of '81: new restaurants seemed to be opening every week; new casinos were going up at a breakneck pace. The new Las Vegas at last. Just look around! The first hour Melvin was there, Tony Bennett swept right by him, looking like he'd stepped out of a liquor ad. Beautiful women wearing next to nothing were just walking down the street in the middle of the day. Valet and hotel clerks had to be raking it in. High rollers from New York or wherever were literally giving money away; you just had to be standing there when they came by. In only a few years, the whole place had gone upscale.

"Reno was hot and heavy then," remembers Mel Shields, the longtime Reno correspondent for the *Sacramento Bee*. "On an average night you could catch Red Skelton at the Nugget, or go see Tony Bennett or Mitzi Gaynor or Sammy Davis, or Cher or Charo. At the Harrah's Reno you could see B. B. King, Kenny Rogers, Pat Collins, and topless revues—all for a two-drink minimum."

So they came. People from San Francisco, San Jose, Sacramento, and the rest of northern California regularly decamped to Reno for the weekend. Until the December snow made coming over the pass treacherous, the casinos and lounges were packed. The two-drink minimums were a joke; no-body stopped at two drinks. A woman sitting alone in a lounge, even the middle-aged matrons in town only for Kenny Rogers's engagement, could see a dozen drinks sent her way in half an hour.

"They were trying to get that Vegas kind of thing going on," says Mark Brenenstall, who spent twenty years as a dealer in Reno casinos. "They brought in name acts; things got rockin' for a while."

Melvin was one of those name acts. The movie about his life, *Melvin and Howard*, had made him famous all over again. Rumor had it that the Sahara, one of the biggest hotel-casinos in Reno, was paying him more than it had paid anyone who had ever played the Gilded Cage. It wasn't one of the big lounges, but Sonny Turner of the Platters played there. Wayland Flowers and Madam, Pinky Lee, Rusty Warren—they all played there. The Gilded Cage was a nice little venue.

Melvin broke into a big grin the first time he stepped into the lounge. It held maybe two hundred, two hundred fifty, people, and had large glass windows that looked out on the bar and casino. Red-velvet booths sat against the wall, and small round tables stood down by the stage. Back when he was getting death threats every day, Melvin would have looked at that wide stage sweeping across the room and thought that it made him a sitting duck for anyone out to get him. Oh, he knew there were still kooks out there; not too long back Melvin had gotten a letter stating that if he didn't send $15,000 right away, he was going to end up in a mental institution. (That one really scared Bonnie, and she could only whisper why: "*Voodoo*.") But Melvin didn't let the kooks bother him anymore. You had to take the bad with the good.

And good had finally come out of all the Howard Hughes mess. Melvin was getting his chance to be a singer, and that was all he had ever asked. The Sahara was even giving him a big push. In August it sent a press release to reporters throughout the region that announced itself as the "Last Will and Testament of Melvin E. Dummar." It started out almost like a real will, stating "I, Melvin E. Dummar, a former milkman, TV game show contestant, gas-station owner and frozen-fish salesman residing in Willard, Utah, declare that this is my Will."

None of it made any sense, but in "Article II" it at least got to the point: "I invite you and a guest to the premiere stage performance of Melvin E. Dummar and Revival on Tuesday, September 22, 1981, in the Gilded Cage Cabaret of Del Webb's Sahara Reno at 8:30 P.M. Immediately following will be a press party in room 2012 of the Sahara Reno. The spirit of Howard Hughes will be there."

Who could pass that up? The whole thing had been the brainchild of a man named John Elizondo, a part-time drummer, movie extra, and schemer whom Melvin had met on the set of *Melvin and Howard*. Shortly before the movie opened, Elizondo called Melvin from California and asked him if he had an audition tape. Melvin said he didn't, so Elizondo came out to Utah, and he and Melvin recorded one of Melvin's original songs, "Santa's Souped-up Sleigh." They sent it to an agent Elizondo knew in Las Vegas, and all of a sudden they had a two-week gig in Reno all set, with a tour afterward to places like Lake Tahoe and Atlantic City. Melvin cried for an hour when he found out. About a month later, Melvin left his job delivering beer in Utah and headed to Las Vegas to work out the details and put a band together.

Melvin had wanted the Night Ryders to come out to Reno with him, but the other band members decided against it. Melvin begged: this was their chance to play some big rooms, maybe even land a record deal, he told them. But the others, particularly the band's de facto leader, Chuck Paul, didn't want to do it. "I'm a religious man," Paul told Melvin. "Vegas and Reno are the kinds of places that are going to tear your morals down. You'd have to leave your job and you'd be away from your family, and there's always the danger of doing things you shouldn't be doing."

Melvin couldn't argue with Paul there. He had a wife and kids, too. But he had to take the risk. Paul thought Mel should be happy playing around town with the Ryders, just like Paul was, but Melvin wanted more than that. Besides, he and Bonnie had been in debt ever since the trial, and he'd had trouble finding good work. Now the movie was giving them another chance. Maybe a last chance.

The day Melvin and Elizondo arrived in Las Vegas, they met with Elizondo's agent, who made one thing clear: the act had to revolve around

Melvin's notoriety. Melvin had to tell jokes about forging a will, and he had to write lyrics about Howard Hughes. Melvin didn't much like the idea, but he figured if that was how he had to start out in the business, he would do it.

Melvin and Elizondo immediately started auditioning girls for backup singers. The girls were not aware of this—they were shopping—but few would have been offended. The Fashion Show Mall in Las Vegas was ahead of its time. It was more like a movie scene than a shopping mall, paced at the speed of actual life but with a mood and an attitude—even a continuous soundtrack!—that were pure Hollywood. All day long women undulated through the gleaming concourse in their designer outfits, sexy and confident, necklines cut way down past their sternums. Lost in the creative act, the regulars gazed at the window displays as they tried on expressions they'd seen Meryl Streep master in *The French Lieutenant's Woman*: haughty boredom, haughty surprise, haughty thoughtfulness. There was, after all, an audience. With the latest fashions inspired by *Charlie's Angels* and other "Jiggle TV" shows, the Fashion Show Mall had an unusual demographic: high-school boys, standing around every afternoon watching, outnumbered the girls as much as two to one.

Stacey and Sari Rudich weren't far removed from high school themselves when they joined the Fashion Show cast. They were all of eighteen, twins, long and willowy—what the locals still called a tall drink of water—and full of adolescent energy. They had been stage assistants that summer for Carlton & Company, a local magic act, but the show had closed and they needed a new gig. So they wandered through the mall, flipping their blond Farrah Fawcett locks in unison, their gleaming white teeth flashing. Melvin and his drummer turned on their heels and ran after them.

"I think he asked us if we ever sang and that he wanted to meet with us," remembers Sari Rudich. The girls didn't know who Melvin Dummar was, but that didn't matter. "We were into the whole showbiz thing. We would do anything," she says. "He had us come in and sing a song with the keyboard player. We grew up singing and doing vocal training, but at that point I don't think we'd ever been in a band. We both wanted to do it because it seemed like it would be fun. He's a really nice man, Melvin."

Melvin Dummar and the
Rudich sisters, Reno, 1981.

The twins sang a Pointer Sisters song, which didn't really fit the country vibe Melvin and his new band had going, but that didn't matter. The twins were quickly hired—there had really never been any doubt—and Melvin and John Elizondo let them in on the act's concept: Melvin, the luckless do-gooder who had picked up a hurt, desperate Howard Hughes on the side of the highway and paid a heavy price for it.

"It sounded like a crazy story," says Sari. "When they mentioned it, I re-membered hearing something about it, and it was just hard to believe." But she and Stacey were quickly won over. "It was crazy until you sat with Melvin and got to know him. He's a very nice, humble man. And what he had to go through—who would ask for it?"

In a way, Melvin's story made it all the more exciting for the twins. They weren't just performing, which was all the two had ever wanted to do. They were also helping right a wrong by telling the real story in song. Every day in rehearsal, the girls were excited—they were on a mission. They were almost as excited as Melvin. He and Elizondo were working feverishly, writing new songs, rewriting lyrics to famous songs, planning costumes and patter and introductions. Melvin hated going to bed at night; sleep just took time away from working on the act.

One might assume that it was the new surroundings and opportunities that inspired Melvin, but really that was the only way he knew how to work—all out. He was thirty-six years old and he'd worked hard all his life, building houses, filling bags with magnesium, delivering milk, running a gas station, delivering beer. He loved hard, too—maybe harder than anyone had ever loved. He almost went crazy loving his first wife, chasing after her from California to Nevada and back, begging her to stay with him. But as much as he had loved Linda, and as much as he now loved Bonnie—a woman much more suited to him—he adored music even more. He was so excited about this opportunity that he sometimes felt he was about to hyperventilate; he was excited even though it occasionally ate at him that he had to incorporate this Howard Hughes concept into the act. "I didn't think I needed to do that Hughes stuff so much, but everyone else did," he says. "I wanted to do my own material. The songs that didn't have nothing to do with Howard Hughes."

When he was complaining about it one day, Elizondo took him aside and set him straight. There were always going to be people who could sing well, Elizondo told him. That was boring. You needed a "gimmick"; that was how you got famous today. Melvin's gimmick was that he wanted to be famous . . . and rich.

That was good enough for Melvin. He had just needed to be told why. Now he took to his gimmick with all he had. "I decided it was okay," he remembers. "Everybody had to have a gimmick. So I was having fun. I liked some of the songs where we changed the lyrics around. We decided to do songs like Buck Owens's 'They're Gonna Put Me in the Movies' ["Act Naturally"]. And we changed the lyrics to 'The Wreck of the Old 97.'" Melvin wrote and rewrote lyrics for "The Wreck of the Old 97" on notebook paper in his hotel room and, when he was out eating at a diner, on napkins. The adulterated song ended up being one of his favorites, and he would launch into it at the beginning of rehearsal with a grin:

> *I was drivin' through the desert doing sixty miles per hour*
> *When this old man waved me down*
> *I said, "Where you goin'," he said "Las Vegas"*
> *"Well, jump in and I'll drive you into town."*
> *Now hear my warning, if you're driving through the desert*
> *Never stop and give anyone a ride.*
> *Cuz if they're rich, and they leave you in their will*
> *It's guaranteed to screw up your life, like mine.*

Things could get maudlin at times, when Melvin's lyrics hinted at his bitterness, but that was unintentional. What he wanted was to be over-the-top. He wanted the audience to have a rollicking good time. Along those lines, Melvin wrote an original song about Hughes, "Thank You, Howard," that would close every show.

Of course, Melvin, busy writing songs and comedy patter, couldn't do everything on his own. Elizondo had hired a handful of veteran lounge musicians as a backup band, and Melvin let two of them—he knew them only as Freddy and Vic—handle the arrangements. The Rudich twins, meanwhile, took charge of their own choreography and outfits, and started to get some buzz going in the casino in the run-up to opening night.

Mark Brenenstall, a dealer whose table looked into the Gilded Cage lounge, watched the girls walk past every night after rehearsal, giggling with each other, everything swaying just like it was supposed to. "They couldn't sing that well, but they could get up and shake around," he recalls. "They wore these short dresses that were low-cut. Melvin sang 'Dang Me,' but changed the lyrics, and the girls would sing in the background, 'Whip me, beat me, just don't mistreat me,' and slap themselves on their behinds. I remember that part very well."

Stacey and Sari may have been newcomers to casino lounge performing, but they had grown up in Las Vegas—they understood what worked. They decided that when they made their entrance onto the Gilded Cage stage every night, aggressively blond, wet-eyed, and smiling, they would be wearing the kind of fitted, pseudosheer outer-space pajamas that the TV show *Buck Rogers in the 24th Century* had made popular, except with the addition of serious décolletage and ending with tassels just below the crotch. The outfit, ultimately, was all about movement: the girls would lean forward in unison in baby-doll pose and then throw themselves backward in full earthquake shimmy, breasts flying apart like billiard balls exploding on break.

Twenty-three years later, Sari Rudich remembers it only too clearly. "When you're eighteen, you're kind of in la-la land," she says today. "They had us doing little dance movements. I think we provided the outfits, some kind of spandexy, disco-y kind of thing. Thanks for bringing back that memory."

However memorable the girls' outfits were, Melvin was unquestionably the star. Everybody knew Melvin back in Utah, and he figured it was the same everywhere else, too. "He was a big celebrity in Ogden," says Jeff Neiloson, an Ogden native who had moved to Reno in 1980 to work in the casinos. "He had been in a movie."

Melvin looked enough like Paul Le Mat, who starred in *Melvin and Howard*, that many people thought Melvin had played himself in the movie. Even though he hadn't, Melvin still was a movie star, of sorts. *Melvin and Howard* was about his life, after all. And that had been enough to get booking agents thinking when John Elizondo called them up and told them about the real Melvin Dummar.

The initial release of *Melvin and Howard* in September 1980 had brought disappointing box-office returns, but the Oscars six months later helped kick-start some new hype. (The movie won two Academy Awards, one for best original screenplay and one for best supporting actress for Mary Steenburgen, who played Linda.) Critics had loved the movie and were happy to say so again. Pauline Kael, the grande dame of American film criticism, called it "an almost flawless act of sympathetic imagination." To *Time* magazine, it was "just about as good as American films get."

The director, Jonathan Demme, claimed the movie was a tribute to Melvin and other hardworking people like him. "I have tremendous respect for how hard it is to keep it together in this country," Demme told the *Washington Post*. "I love people who work . . . I'm as impressed by Melvin as I am by Howard. Melvin is my idea of a superhero. To me, hard workers are the greatest heroes."

Despite those words, Demme's *Melvin and Howard* was a film much more about the dangers of unrealistic or misguided dreams than about the value of hard work. His allegory takes flight when Linda appears on the fictional game show *Easy Street*, where she tap dances to the Rolling Stones' "Satisfaction" and is awarded the big cash prize—"The Golden Gate"—as the audience's favorite. But it's a pity prize. Linda has a determined, hopeful smile stuck rigidly to her face throughout the performance, but her tap dancing is so intensely bad that the audience feels that its cheers and applause are the least it can do for her.

Unlike Linda, Melvin doesn't get it. When Linda wins *Easy Street*'s top prize, Melvin sees it as proof that their luck has finally changed, and he rushes out and buys an expensive new car. When he refuses to return it, Linda calls a cab and tells him she's leaving him. Melvin jumps in front of her, and makes her take a good hard look at his new toy.

MELVIN: See this car? That's not just a car, you know. That's *our* car. I used to see cars like that go by on the highway from Reno to Vegas and from Vegas to Reno all the time when I was working with my dad. They went by so fast you could hardly even see them. I used to want one. Now I've got one. Understand?

LINDA: We are poor, Melvin. Poor!

MELVIN: We're not poor. Broke, maybe, but we're not poor. We won The Golden Gate!

LINDA: *I* won The Golden Gate.

MELVIN: Don't go. I don't want you to go.

LINDA: *C'est la vie*, Melvin.

MELVIN: What's that?

LINDA: It's French. I used to dream I'd be a French interpreter.

MELVIN: You don't speak French.
LINDA: I told you it was a dream.

Melvin and Bonnie went to the movie's premiere in September 1980, and they went again when the film came to Utah, but Melvin had mixed feelings about it. "I wished that I'd had more control over it," he says today. "A lot of good parts I think they left out." The movie took Melvin's side of the debate about the will, presenting his encounter in the desert as undisputed fact, but it grated on him how they got the scene all wrong, starting with having Hughes out in the desert riding a motorcycle. Plus, Jason Robards looked much healthier, and was much chattier, than the old man Melvin had picked up. "He didn't do half the things they had him doing," Melvin says.

There was also the problem of how Melvin was portrayed. Melvin instinctively chafed at the depiction of himself as the kind of working-class naif who figures out what his dreams are by watching TV game shows. He chafed even more at the idea that he was too enamored of status symbols to live within his means. "Oh, no. Repossessed again," Steenburgen, as Linda, sighs in her very first scene in the movie, waking up to the noise of her husband's motorcycle being taken away. Frustrated with the movie, Melvin turned his wrath on Le Mat, who played Melvin. "I think Paul Le Mat is a terrible actor," he says of the *American Graffiti* star. "He's terrible in everything I've ever seen him in. Jonathan Demme is a good director, but the movie made me look dumb. It made me look like a dumb hillbilly hick."

At the time the movie came out, Melvin figured that might be why nobody called him about being an actor in any other movies, and he struggled with what he should do next. That was when he got the call from Elizondo about making an audition tape and putting a group together. Could he sing as well as the Melvin in the movie? Better, he said. So maybe you should come on out to Las Vegas. Melvin couldn't believe his luck.

Now there would be no more amateur nights for Melvin, and no more church dances for sixty bucks. Hughes had bequeathed him something after all: notoriety. It would be all right with him that he didn't get Hughes's money, if he ended up getting a music career out of it. To Melvin, that seemed like a fair tradeoff. After all, he wasn't asking to have it handed to him on a silver platter, like with the Hughes will. He was willing to work for success. He wanted to be good. He wanted people to come see him because they liked the music, not just because they'd heard about his strange story or seen the movie. All he had ever wanted was a fair chance.

Could Melvin Dummar, a thirty-six-year-old beer deliveryman, be a singing star? He didn't see why not. He knew he had a nice voice. He felt comfortable up on stage. And anything he wasn't too good at he was willing to work on, however long it took. He was determined to make the most of this chance. One night, Melvin poured his excitement and happiness into writing and he came up with an original song that he would give a featured place in the show.

"George Washington had an all-American dream," Melvin sang in "All-American Dreamer." "So did John F. Kennedy. So did Martin Luther King. So did Melvin Dummar. And mine was to be an entertainer. My dream is being fulfilled."

THE SHOW STARTED RIGHT ON TIME ON OPENING NIGHT, TUESDAY, September 22, in the Gilded Cage Cabaret. Melvin insisted on it.

Several men were still standing at the back, probably waiting for their dates to return from the ladies' room, when the air above their heads suddenly erupted in a swirl of sound that startled even Melvin, who knew—or should have known—it was coming. One man in the audience busted out laughing when he recognized the entrance music—"If I Were a Rich Man"—and the rest of the crowd, most of whom were press, joined in with appreciative chortles. The reporters were there to have some fun—and then have a few free drinks at the afterparty in Melvin's honor—and they were ready to be entertained. Next came the emcee, his voice booming in waves through the sound system, shouting like a preacher gone amuck: "I believe . . . I *believe*, ladies and gentlemen . . . I *believe* in Melvin! *Hallelujah!*" And they were off.

Melvin stepped forward, concentrating on just putting one foot in front of the other until he was in his spot on stage. He was nervous, of course. He was scared. But somehow he was confident, too. He beamed into the lights as the applause came toward him. Melvin had his suit, a white tuxedo with shiny satin collars. He had his hair, a perfect coif, like a beautiful shiny shell. He had the twins moving forward behind him as if out of a dream, and his band kicking into high gear. It was all exactly how he had imagined it would be. Except for one thing: His foot hurt. A lot.

A few weeks before opening night, Melvin had broken his foot dodging a car as he crossed a street. He had told the doctor, quite specifically, that he needed his foot healed by September 22, but the doctor wouldn't commit to Melvin's timetable. And sure enough, when opening night arrived, Melvin still had the cast on. "I just didn't want to go out there on stage with my foot in a cast," he says. "So a couple hours before the show, I didn't tell anybody, I tore the cast off my foot."

The foot was so swollen that Melvin could barely get his shoe on. "I got it on, and it was just super tight. If I moved around, anytime I would put any pressure on the one foot, it would just shoot pain right up my back. I would have been better off to just leave the cast on." Then in the opening number at least his face wouldn't have periodically frozen into a mask of shock whenever he accidentally leaned the wrong way. "People must have thought, 'What the heck's wrong with him?'" Melvin says now, shaking his head as if he wish he knew.

It made for an inauspicious start. Melvin launched into "Let's Twist Again," but he left the twisting to the twins; he settled for grimacing. It only got worse from there.

"Dummar is entertaining in the lounge at Sahara Reno, his first professional engagement," Mel Shields wrote that night for the *Sacramento Bee*. "The evening is one of the most embarrassing anyone should have either to perform through or sit through. Whoever had the idea to so exploit this man, Dummar himself or someone else, should be ashamed."

Twenty-three years later, Shields is convinced he didn't do the show justice in his review, and he's glad for that. "It's hard for me to tell you how bad this show was," he says. A friend of Shields's from another paper sat in front of him, he remembers, "and after about ten minutes he turned around and said, 'Jesus *Christ!*' I nodded my agreement. Then about ten minutes later, he turned around again and said again, 'Jesus *Christ!*' He did that throughout the show. About every ten minutes or so. We've laughed about it ever since, because it just kept bowling him over how bad it was."

There were times when Melvin seemed to realize the same thing. About halfway through the show, he did an Elvis impression—"wriggling [his] hips like an engine with a busted piston," Shields reported in the *Bee*—and when he was done he grinned sheepishly and said, "Thank you. That was really terrible." Next came the Hank Williams classic "Kawliga." Melvin pointed out that Williams's son had recently rerecorded the song. "He did a terrible job on it," Melvin said, "and I'll do a terrible job tonight." He was as good as his word.

Sensing that his audience was losing patience, Melvin searched his brain for anything he could do to stop the bleeding, even patter they had tried and rejected in rehearsal. He joked that he was working on a Rockefeller will, "if anyone wants a piece of that." Then he offered up another joke.

"It was a bad joke. I think it was racist, if I recall," Shields says.

After that Melvin asked for questions. With the movie still out there in dollar theaters, Melvin figured the press would want to revisit the probate trial or the night he picked up Hughes in the desert, but no one asked any questions. After a long silence, Melvin said, "Surely someone's got a question; you're press." There was only one: "Why'd you tell that joke?" someone called out.

Melvin laughed at himself along with the rest of the audience, then said: "If there are no more questions, I'll sing another song." Elizondo, sitting behind his drum set, called out to the audience, "Ask another question!" Melvin gave Elizondo a look, like the crack wasn't in the script, or things were going so badly he should have known to drop the joke. "He was joking throughout the show, but I don't mean to suggest that he thought it was a joke," says Shields. "I don't think he did."

So Melvin pushed on, through the altered lyrics of "The Wreck of the Old 97," Roger Miller's "Dang Me," and Buck Owens's "Act Naturally," which he played straight (and got a pretty good hand for doing so). By the time he got to "Thank You, Howard," which he had never performed publicly before, he had cast off the attempts for humor altogether and, consciously or not, was going for straight pathos.

"Yes, I remember how it all began," he sang. "Back in 1967. I picked you up, drove you into town. Only you know what went down." Melvin looked up and squinted into the lights, like he was trying to divine the reaction he would get from the song, then jumped into the chorus:

Thank you, Howard
For leaving me something.
All I got was frustration, and I'll never be the same
But I thank you just the same.

"Some people claim that I wrote your will," Melvin continued (with the twins piping in: *"Ooo-wah-ooo"*). "All I ever wrote was these lyrics. (*Ooo-wah-ooo.*) I wish you'd come back for just one day. Save my name from all these critics!"

To the audience of journalists, it went without saying that even Howard Hughes, materializing over the proceedings with flapping angel wings, couldn't have saved Melvin from the critics.

"He couldn't hold a tune. The songs were terrible. He had no stage presence at all," says Shields. "I hate to be so negative, I really do, because he did seem to be a genuinely nice guy. But he just didn't have any performing talent. I wouldn't say he was a god-awful singer; he was just nothing, really. Weak voice, no sense of rhythm, no presence. Only sincerity. Sincerity counted for something, but not when you're asking people to pay to see you perform."

Melvin could find solace in the knowledge that not everyone in the audience was disappointed in the show. Bonnie was on her feet applauding as Melvin finished up his last song and dipped awkwardly into a bow.

"Most of the show went well," she wrote in her diary a few days later. "Mel covered his mistakes well. The thing he was worried most about was the behavior of the two new guys in the group, Freddy and Vic. They kept changing the way the songs were played, and Mel would lose his timing. But it went real good. I heard some good comments from media in the audience. It was attended by all reporters and they had a press party afterward and it was real nice; they had a buffet bar and an ice sculpture. I stayed till Saturday."

While Bonnie was admiring the ice sculpture, Shields was pounding out his review and, this being before faxes (let alone e-mail), drove it to Greyhound Express to send it over the hill to Sacramento. It was, he says, the most aggressively negative review he'd ever written and ever would. He got home at two in the morning and went to bed with a knot in his stomach.

The next day, subscribers to the *Bee* were reading about the disaster that had just befallen Reno. "Melvin Dummar is a nice man," the review stated up front. "That much is clear from the outset. But Melvin Dummar has no performing talent . . . Somebody surely should have seen the poor man needed help and provided it. But no. Instead, we have a worse-than-average band and two sisters, twins, who sing so far off key it's difficult to believe they have one good ear between them. They're beautiful girls but the good looks don't make up for the lack of talent in this case." Shields reminded Sacramentonians just why Melvin Dummar's name might sound familiar, and then he listed all the ways Melvin had tried to trade on that tenuous claim to celebrity. "If somebody thought this was [good-natured] spoofing," he wrote, "somebody missed; it's just bad."

Daily Variety, the show-business bible, soon followed with a similar evisceration: "Dummar's own songs are amateurish, but touching, however not in the way he intended," the review said. "He sings about Hughes leaving him nothing but frustration and about the fact he'll never live it down. He comes off ultimately pitiful, a man used and abused, just one who doesn't know any better."

CRITICS TYPICALLY LOVE TO GIVE BAD REVIEWS; NOTHING IS MORE fun to write about than show-business train wrecks. Not so in this case.

"Melvin came across on stage as a very nice man, and that's why I got sadder and sadder watching it," Shields remembers. "I know I wasn't the only one who thought that way. He had obviously been told he could be a big star, which certainly wasn't going to happen."

The critical reaction came as a shock to Melvin and Bonnie. The band members pretty much kept their distance after opening night, but the twins closed ranks with Melvin. "For what it was it was cute," Sari says. "I don't think he ever claimed to be the best singer in the world. He wasn't bad; he had a nice voice. It was a cute little show. His performing meant a lot to him. Just no one wanted to take it for what it was."

There's something to be said for getting the worst out of the way at the beginning, and Melvin Dummar and Revival had every reason to think that that would be the case for them. The Sahara did too, and it reiterated its support to Melvin, even providing Bonnie with comps to play her favorite game, The Whirlwind of Money. Bonnie could be found regularly in the glassed-in, three-foot-square box. The game was pleasingly simple: paper money would fly around, and you'd have a certain amount of time to grab as much as you could and shove it through a slot. Whatever you got through the slot you got to keep, and it didn't take long for Bonnie to get pretty good at it. But Bonnie's success didn't rub off on Revival. In fact, she got a larger audience at the Whirlwind of Money than Revival did in the Gilded Cage. They quickly became the invisible band.

For the next two weeks, the Gilded Cage Cabaret took on an eerie, *Twilight Zone* feel. The band would launch into its set, complete with the emcee roaring, boxing-announcer style in his rolling baritone, "I believe Mellll-vvvvin," often with no one but the band in the house—while visible through the open door was a bustling, noisy casino so crowded that people had to turn sideways to get past one another. It wasn't that the press had done its job with vicious efficiency. The word on the street about Melvin Dummar and Revival wasn't toxic; then at least people would have popped in to see it because they'd heard how bad it was. There simply was *no* word on the show. Nobody gave it a first, let alone a second, thought.

"I saw him play every night," says Brenenstall, whose shift started at six P.M. and went until two in the morning. "No one would come to the show, so they opened the curtains that hung over the glass windows and put speakers above the bar to try to get people to go in. He was so bad no one came. There were times when there were one or two people in there; there were times no one was in there for the show."

The sight of a band playing in an empty room can be a strangely powerful lure. It's almost like seeing a disfigured man on the street; you know it's rude to stare, but you just can't help it. So now and again, as Melvin belted out a song or chuckled through his stage patter to row after row of empty seats, someone would appear at the entrance and lean against the door frame for a few minutes or blink balefully through the window.

"A lot of people were kind of amused by them. They wanted to know who they were and why they were playing here," says Brenenstall. "People thought they were funny, and it was clear Melvin thought he should be taken more seriously."

Melvin doesn't remember playing to empty seats, except for the red-eye performance. "We'd do three shows a night, and the one they had us come in and do at three o'clock in the morning there was hardly anybody there; maybe four, five people. That was like a dress rehearsal. We'd do like an eight to nine show, and we had a good crowd then; and then we'd play again from eleven thirty to twelve thirty, and there were a few less people. But the three o'clock we were playing to nobody because the only people there were either drunks or professional gamblers."

Berenstall does give Melvin credit: "Even when no one was in there, he was giving it his all. I'll say this much: it didn't matter if there were two hundred people there or two people there, he never phoned it in."

Two hundred people, two people: to Melvin, that was semantics. He was being paid to perform, to be a part of the entertainment environment at the Sahara, one of the biggest and most popular casinos in Reno, and so he performed. He never had any doubt he was getting better with every performance. As his foot healed, his timing got sharper, his delivery clearer. When they weren't playing he wanted to be rehearsing, and when he wasn't rehearsing he wanted to be up in his room writing new songs or lyrics. He was willing to work as hard as he possibly could, because that was how you became a success in life. You got up in the morning, you prepared, you went to work on time, and you didn't slack off. He knew that if you did that, good things would come.

After the first night, however, no one but Melvin wanted to even be there anymore. The band members didn't see this gig as a launching pad to a new career in music, like Melvin did. They had music careers already, and the fact that they were here playing behind this bumpkin meant their careers were on a steep downward arc. They had never played to completely empty houses before. They had never seen a half-drunk tourist snicker at them as he stood in the doorway. They were there for the paycheck. When they weren't playing, they wanted to eat and drink and get laid, and any one of those took precedence over the show. It wasn't long—a matter of just a few days, actually—before the two-week engagement had tipped over into a two-week bacchanal for them.

It didn't help that Melvin was uncomfortable in the leadership role that, for the first time in his life, was his to play. A vain and fastidious man, dedicated instinctively to the ethic of hard work, he was singularly ill-suited to dealing with the unpredictable temperaments of musicians. It also didn't help that he was entirely incapable of keeping track of what was going on around him—or understanding any motivations different from his own.

"I always wanted the band to be dressed neat, not looking like a bunch of hillbilly idiots," Melvin says. "But the bass player and the piano player— Freddy and Vic—they were buddies, and they'd go out and buy their booze and their drugs. They didn't want to rehearse. They didn't care what they sounded like, because they were too busy boozing all the time."

Melvin tried to just ignore them, and for the first few nights that worked all right. But then, for the featured evening performance about a week into the run, "the bass player came out with his pant-legs rolled up above his knees, and he was so drunk he could hardly stand up," Melvin remembers. "So he went over and sat down on one of the amps, and when I was trying to sing he was in the background going, '*Yodelee-yodeleee, yodeleeheee-he-he.*' I just stopped right in the middle of the song and I told him to get off the stage. It was horrible. That was the worst, when I had to fire Freddy and Vic right on the stage. That was embarrassing. I don't like being made fun of. I was taking it seriously."

Even that kind of drama didn't bring anyone in to see the show. "These two guys were thrown out of the casino and we were told not to let them back in," says Jeff Neiloson, who was working as a valet at the Sahara during Revival's two-week engagement. "I didn't know what happened, but the word was out by then. I wouldn't pay to see them. No one would."

The next morning, Melvin and John Elizondo quickly auditioned and hired two local musicians to finish out the engagement. Seeing the enthusiasm of the new musicians, even if they weren't very good, made Melvin feel like he shouldn't have waited so long to fire Freddy and Vic. "There was a line out the door of musicians wanting to join," Melvin says. "We picked two new guys, rehearsed a few of the songs, and went on stage that night. And they were better than the guys we got rid of. The whole show got better because of it."

By this time, however, the Gilded Cage had been all but shuttered for more than a week, and Melvin Dummar and Revival was about to go out of business. Melvin never saw it coming. "We were scheduled to go from the Sahara to Stockton's in Elko; we were supposed to open there," Melvin says. "John didn't tell me anything was wrong until like the day before. There was like a week in between, and he wouldn't tell me nothing. And I think it was the day before we were supposed to open in Elko and I was packing, and I called them and said, 'Well, are you ready to go to Elko?' And John said, 'Oh, no, that gig is cancelled.' And I said, 'Since when?' And he said, 'Oh, for a week or so.'" Melvin shakes his head at the memory, still befuddled by it. "They just decided to cancel it."

Faced with the abrupt end of the tour before it even started, Melvin crumbled. He had viewed the Reno gig as a learning experience, a work in progress—a success in spite of all the problems. He was confident that by the time they got to Atlantic City, which was supposed to be the last stop on their tour, they would be sharp enough to get the attention of record labels or big-time promoters. He'd had it all planned out in his head. Suddenly, all those plans were dust.

"I thought I'd finally got a break in life, and it ended up blowing up on me," he says. "I couldn't believe it."

Now he didn't know what to do—everything had gone to heck. He wanted to talk to Elizondo's agent himself, and to the local promoters, but he didn't know them; he hadn't handled any of that. That was all Elizondo's thing. Melvin didn't even have their phone numbers. It was simply over, and there was nothing he could do about it. By the time he got back to Utah, unemployed again, back at square one, he was gripped by a depression unlike anything he had ever experienced before. It would last, in varying degrees of seriousness, for the next ten years.

"It was like I was dead; I was just existing in life," he says. "I just quit. I was so depressed. I totally went to pieces. I almost contemplated suicide after that."

He made a few attempts to get his music career started again. HBO called and asked him to perform the song "I'm Gonna Sit Right Down and Write Myself a Letter (and Make Believe It Came from You)" for a comedy special in Toronto, but that turned out to be another disaster. "I was supposed to come out and break into song," Melvin says. Instead, he froze up. "I couldn't do it. I felt like somebody had me in a stranglehold. I heard people in the audience calling me. I heard one guy say, 'I heard this guy was pretty good; he can't even talk.' And of course that just made it worse. The song came out horrible. I talked it through. It was probably the worst I ever did. I don't understand it. I did it great in rehearsal."

Melvin had similar problems on *Good Morning America* and *The John Davidson Show* and *Late Night with David Letterman*. And then the offers stopped coming.

"That almost killed Melvin," Bonnie says. "I was worried about him after that for a long, long time."

"From about '81 until just a few years ago, it was like I was lost," Melvin says, shaking his head at the picture of himself in his mind. "It was like I almost lost my will. Like I just lost my will to live. For about ten years, I didn't sing. I didn't write songs. I didn't listen to the radio."

"Or smile," says Bonnie.

"Yeah," he admits. "I guess it affected me."

 The Next Generation

Kelly Clarkson heard about the terror alert being raised to orange as she was staring at herself in the mirror. She didn't say anything, but her expression turned sour. It was an orange day. The terror alert was orange, and her face was orange. She fixated on her soft, shapeless mouth, and the powdered pimple over her lip, a darker shade of orange than the rest of her. It was the first time the terror alert had reached this level since the 9/11 anniversary five months before. The makeup girl was saying something about people stocking up on bottled water and duct tape and plastic sheeting, and Kelly's head suddenly swiveled until she located her own half-empty bottle of Poland Spring. Everyone knew water was the best way to keep your complexion clear, and obviously she wasn't drinking enough.

"Can I get some more water?" she said to no one in particular. "I could really use some more water."

A few minutes later, a fresh bottle of Poland Spring in her hand, Kelly, twenty-one years old and ready for action, was back out on the beach. It was hot even though it was midwinter, which was what she loved about Florida. That was when she noticed she was wearing a black one-piece swimsuit with an ankle-length purple shawl wrapped around her waist. Kelly hardly paid attention anymore when outfits were pulled off her and others put on, but now she stopped dead and checked herself out with a sigh. She may as well have been draped in a chador. This was not a coincidence.

All around her, college-age women kicked through the sand wearing tiny multicolored bikinis, or white crop tops and booty shorts. One sleek blonde standing near the bandshell mindlessly snapped her thong over and over. Still, everyone was looking at Kelly. The old men who had retired to Miami for the wet heat were looking. The little girls with knobby knees and open mouths were looking. The creepy groupies who had followed Kelly from place to place for weeks were looking. She had wanted this her whole, short life. *Constant* attention. "Me and my friend Amber Gibson, when I was little, used to make up dances every hour," she told a reporter earlier in the day. "And we'd be, like, 'OK, Mom, you have to watch,' and we'd drag people into the living room to be our audience. I never thought about whether they liked it; I just wanted them to watch."

Now *everyone* was watching, and it was starting to freak her out. So Kelly headed for a friendly face: a gorgeous young man with a pile of curly hair exploding from his head like a mushroom cloud. A year ago, this strutting twenty-four-year-old stud from Pennsylvania never would have given Kelly a look. He was too pretty for her—too cool. ("I was a dork growing up. I had Coke-bottle glasses and braces," Kelly liked to tell people.) Kelly and the pretty young man, Justin Guarini, had met nine months before on the set of an amateur musical talent contest called *American Idol*. The singing contest, a toss-off for the Fox network during the dog days of summer, unexpectedly became the biggest TV phenomenon of 2002, and Kelly went on to win the thing. Guarini had to settle for second place. Just like that, Kelly Clarkson, a guffawing waitress and dreamer from tiny Burleson, Texas, a girl who willingly admitted she had never had a boyfriend, was the "American Idol." Now all these bouncy babes were here on a Miami beach in February because of her. She and gorgeous Justin Guarini were the stars of a movie, *From Justin to Kelly: The Rise of Two American Idols,* and the babes were extras. *Extras* as in, not really necessary, which was how Kelly liked to think of them. More important, they all wanted to be with *her.* It was like she'd been dropped into an alternative-reality high school where the beautiful, stupid girls sought approval from the talented, dorky ones.

Kelly was still getting used to being a celebrity, and she was still loving it. "Things do get funny sometimes," she said as she waited for a scene to be set up. "I love being in the tabloids."

She even took what they had to say seriously. Like that she was chubby. She didn't dispute it, not at all. Stuck in that not-yet-charted place between ordinary and celebrity life, Kelly almost looked like two different people stitched together at the neck. There was that fabulous head, with its perfect, designer-spritzed hair and that glowing smile known to millions. And attached to it there was this everyday, heretofore unseen-by-the-masses body, with its graceless, adolescent stride, its thick arms, and its sweetly tubby tummy. She had just told an *Us* reporter that she wouldn't "starve to be a star," but that was a reflex answer. She knew something had to be done.

IT USED TO BE YOU HAD NO CHOICE BUT TO GO TO HOLLYWOOD TO fulfill the kind of dreams Kelly Clarkson had. You had to send off your photo to hundreds of agents, stand around at endless "cattle calls." You had to have *ambition.* Not anymore. Forty years after cultural historian Daniel Boorstin defined the essence of media-age celebrity as someone known for his or her "well-knownness" (he used Zsa Zsa Gabor as the quintessential example), this new breed of celebrity was now almost all that was left. And they could be found everywhere. Star hunters now traveled America holding auditions, looking for the next American Idol or Survivor or whatever. If you wanted it, you just had to stand in line and hope you got lucky.

The term *superstar,* argued pop-culture critic Neal Gabler, had to be invented in the latter part of the twentieth century if only to assert a celebrity hierarchy, separating those who deserved the spotlight by the old standards of achievement from those who merely, well, *had* the spotlight. The result was that talent, at least what we had long considered to be talent, was becoming superfluous. Americans didn't need it anymore. "Metaphor has left art and gone into current events," film director Mike Nichols said in a 1994 *Vanity Fair* interview, which Gabler cited in his seminal book *Life: The Movie*. "Who in the fuck is going to compete? Where is there a hero who can fall from greater heights than Michael Jackson? Where is there more naked rivalry than between Tonya Harding and Nancy Kerrigan? What couple can you write about that is a stronger metaphor about relations between the sexes than the Bobbitts?"

Of course, the fact that the mention of Nancy Kerrigan and the Bobbitts draws blank stares today, just a handful of years after they dominated headlines, was exactly the reason Kelly Clarkson knew she had to do something. There was a lot of competition out there. Record labels, under constant pressure from a Napster generation that seemed to seek out entirely new stimuli daily, were discovering, debuting, and discarding singers at an unprecedented pace. So-called reality TV had become a true phenomenon, spinning out shows faster than audiences could keep up with them. Kelly had to focus on the task at hand—staying in front of the public—to the exclusion of all else. It was a fluke, really, that she didn't miss the whole terror-alert thing altogether. "I hate watching the news," she said as she waited for her next scene to start. "All it is, is bad. You turn it on and every station it's, like, 'Oh, good, we blew that up,' or something."

Who had the time to watch the news? After the first season of *Idol* went off the air, Kelly and the other finalists went on tour, some two dozen cities in as many days. Then she was in the recording studio. Now the movie. It was exhausting, but she realized she was one of the lucky ones. People were getting really desperate for the kind of fame she had stumbled into. Wannabe Kelly Clarksons were flocking to reality-show auditions by the tens of thousands, and they were willing to do *anything* to have the cameras trained on them. One of *From Justin to Kelly*'s competitors at the box office in the spring of 2003 was going to be "the first reality feature film," *The Real Cancun*. The movie's "stars"—mostly blank-eyed college students on spring break—

participated in wet T-shirt and "hot body" contests, and then headed back to their hotel rooms to have sex as the cameras continued to roll. Plenty of social commentators lamented what they were seeing, but it seemed there was no turning back. "Television has turned everything into a contest, from courtship to adoption," Anna Quindlen wrote in *Newsweek* magazine. "In a voyeuristic world, fame becomes a ubiquitous career goal."

Nobody was immune. A doctor left his successful practice to be a scheming cad on *Big Brother 2*. A struggling NFL quarterback spent his off-season not in the weight room but in the studio, awkwardly seducing prospective TV-order brides on *The Bachelor*. *Girls Gone Wild* videos hit store shelves on a regular schedule because an endless wave of college women, the chosen ones of the most affluent and entitled generation in history, were thrilled to flash their breasts in public at the sight of a camera. "Sure, they're doing it because they're insecure and desperate for attention and fame," *Entertainment Weekly* columnist Joel Stein pointed out, "but who isn't?"

You had to be desperate now to get on TV, and so desperation was losing its social stigma. Even an heiress, Paris Hilton of the hotel empire, was willing to humiliate herself to be a TV star.

Reality-show producers wanted to see that kind of desperation in their stars. They didn't want you to look too cool—then viewers wouldn't be able to relate to you. After getting started chiefly with legitimate talent contests, the reality genre had quickly devolved to the point that shows were edited to play up the participants' deficiencies, heightening the circus-freak perception of celebrity and increasing the need for a continuous assembly line of new discoveries willing to work for nothing. Pop star Jessica Simpson, Kelly Clarkson's chief competition for the "Wholesome Britney Spears" niche, surely couldn't have expected to be depicted as a whiny, demanding moron when, in the aftermath of *American Idol*'s success, she agreed to have the first year of her marriage to fellow singer Nick Lachey filmed. But that was what she got. "If you need a quick pick-me-up or really want to feel better about yourself, watch Jessica Simpson and her equally brain-dead husband's reality show on MTV. . . . They're both vapid, shallow, pretentious, and as dumb as a box of wet cotton balls," wrote a "fan" in an Internet chat group shortly after *Newlyweds: Nick and Jessica* debuted in the summer of 2003. Another viewer told the *New York Post* that the show was fun to watch not because Simpson was sexy and talented but because she was "dumb as a stick."

Such criticisms of its star were fine with MTV, which saw ratings for the series exceed even its best expectations. Though Simpson didn't seem to mind (it made her name one of the most recognized in America), the ridicule she received worried Irene Cara, who had experienced similar media highs and lows in her career. Getting into the spotlight is "that double-edged sword," she says. "It can make you feel great or it can make you feel like the lowest form of life on earth. It's made me be very careful about who I'm dealing with, knowing everything about them. You have to know that there are always people out to bring you down. Even if they're making you money, it doesn't always mean they're good for you."

American Idol, she believed, was dangerous. It made music-industry success seem so easy that anyone could do it, literally anyone who could hold a tune. Cara sighs at the thought of it, what the Fox show has wrought. "That poor, stupid girl," she says of Kelly Clarkson. "I hope she has someone she can trust. I hope she knows what she's dealing with. Maybe she'll do fine, I don't know."

The possibilities in the entertainment business now, even to Cara, sometimes did seem endless. After *American Idol* scored huge ratings and became the water-cooler topic of the moment, NBC quickly launched its own talent show. Its twist was to hook the show to a well-known franchise it owned: the movie *Fame.* One of the first people NBC called about being a judge was Cara, who turned them down flat. "Why would I want to do that?" she asks with a dismissive sneer. "It's ridiculous. That's not how you develop talent. I told them to stop calling. They kept calling me."

Even without her participation, though, the *Fame* talent show put Cara's name back into the mainstream mix. After all, for a generation of Americans, the show's theme song was irretrievably linked to her. Calls started coming in from radio stations, and Cara, working on her comeback CD, took advantage of the opportunity to promote herself. She was delighted to discover that people remembered her—and remembered her fondly. It made her truly believe that she could have her second chance and that it could be so much better the second time around. Even after being burned by celebrity, Cara found the attention intoxicating. She believed she was in a better frame of mind for it twenty years down the road.

"I am now finding out the positives of my celebrity, and it's been a lovely discovery, the impact I had," she says. "People from all over the world, they're very open and eager to tell me what I mean to them. When I was on the radio in New York, one lady called in and she said, 'Irene, I'm just thrilled to hear you and speak with you, and I'm now just so thrilled to be able to experience you again, this time with my daughter.' What a lovely thing to say to me at eight fifteen in the morning in New York. That's been a revelation to me. I never really realized, after all these years."

None of which means she made the wrong decision when reality TV came calling. The *Fame* talent show played it pretty straight, like *American Idol*, but Cara's suspicion of the genre was warranted. After the first blast of *Idol* copycats in 2003, real talent contests soon became passé. By 2004, the first breakout star of *American Idol*'s third season wasn't the eventual winner but a no-talent dweeb named William Hung who was so bad he became the focus of a mean-spirited "rejects" episode. Hung, whose horrific, tuneless version of Ricky Martin's "She Bangs" was lampooned on late-night talk shows and on the Internet, nabbed a record contract, and the quickie CD he put out made it onto *Billboard*'s Top 40. Throughout Hung's brief run in the spotlight, it was never entirely clear if he was in on the joke; like Melvin Dummar, he was thrilled simply to have a camera pointed at him. The next logical step, therefore, was *Superstar USA*, a truly vicious show on the WB network that, turning *American Idol* on its head, purposely chose the most awful performers, but didn't tell the contestants that that was why they were being advanced. "It's *definitely* mean," the show's creator, Mike Fleiss, told reporters. "But these people want to be stars, so we're giving them what they want, just not for the reason they think."

It was the inevitable evolution from *American Idol*, which despite its claims was never really about creating pop stars as much as it was about perpetuating its own existence. The success of contestants like Kelly Clarkson, whose debut album went platinum, was merely a glorious bonus. "I think that it's an interesting little way of creating, I don't want to say stars, but creating people who can be within the record business at this time when nobody is buying records," a *Rolling Stone* critic told the Associated Press. "But this is not the way of creating lasting stars."

Nobody knew that better than Kelly, who had spent six fruitless months in Los Angeles trying to make it as a performer before returning to Texas and stumbling on an *American Idol* audition. She had a stock answer when asked about the possibility of all this attention going away, of meeting her sixteenth minute: "If, God forbid, something happened and I couldn't sing anymore, I'd just go on with my life," she insisted. "I just want to be happy. I was happy being a waitress. I don't have to be a singer or an actress or whatever to be happy."

On that bright February day in Miami, the extras didn't look like they believed her. Walking to and from the set, they fell in step with her or at least close to her. There was status to walking with Kelly Clarkson, and some of the extras noticeably squared their shoulders. They weren't just fans running up to her for a quick snapshot; they *knew* her. Kelly took comfort in the knowledge that all these beautiful women wanted to be around her, but she also took it as a challenge. Out on the beach, watching all the bikini girls who wanted to be the next Britney Spears or Christina Aguilera—or the next *Kelly Clarkson*—she understood exactly what she had to do: get herself in shape. "I need to get my booty into the gym," she said laughing, turning away from the women who preened in their bikinis and mock-covering her naughty bits with crooked arms and buckled knees.

She would do exactly that. Two months after wrapping *From Justin to Kelly*, Kelly kicked off a publicity blitz for her debut CD by wearing a revealing black cat suit for a national television performance, and to the naked eye she looked like someone who had been spending a lot of time in the gym. The performance, complete with writhing background dancers and a splash of gorgelike cleavage from Kelly, caused a firestorm of outrage in Internet chat groups devoted to the singer. Kelly's original fans, the ones who had latched on to her early in the run of *American Idol,* had wanted nothing more than a pleasant, talented, normal-looking girl to get the spotlight for once. "She got some really bad advice," one fan wrote. "She looked like a slut." Even the weekly alternative paper for Fort Worth, near Kelly's hometown, weighed in, giving some words a tweak to make sure everyone got its point: "Last year's American Idol, Kelly Clarkson, came across as the small-town girl that she is—a cute little Burleson gal with a big voice and girl-next-door demeanor . . . Then she went to Californica [*sic*] to make a movie and a c.d., and apparently succumbed to an image makeover by demonic El-Lay [*sic*] advisors."

Through it all, Kelly remained unapologetic. She was doing what she had to do—what she wanted to do—to keep the public's attention. "People always say, 'Oh, I'm sick [of it] because it's not about voices; it's about body and everything.' Well, that's what people are buying, so it's not always the artist's fault all the time," she said. "People have said to me, 'Please, don't change. Never change.' People *always* change. Life is all about growing and finding out about yourself and broadening who you are. I'm always going to be trying new things and not limiting myself."

Kelly did have a point. She was twenty-one years old now and had been a cute little Burleson gal her whole life. She had wanted fame for as long as she could remember and suddenly she had it. But now she was figuring out that she wanted more than that. If she was going to have a career beyond 2003, she needed to move beyond her *American Idol* persona—a fact that soon would be brought home when the saccharine-sweet *From Justin to Kelly* bombed at the box office and Justin Guarini's label dumped him. The innocent act clearly had a shelf life. Maybe a sweaty El-Lay or two with the likes of Justin Timberlake or Enrique Iglesias was exactly what she needed to bring some meaning to those love songs she was singing. Maybe getting out there and *living* life—after so many years of dreaming about it—would actually make her a better artist. The question she had to ask herself was: Should there be a camera crew present? After all, Jessica Simpson's marriage had been picked up for a second season.

# Melvin and Bonnie

April 2003

Melvin and Bonnie Dummar are sitting in the living room of their manufactured home in Brigham City, Utah, looking at each other and giggling. They are doing something they almost never do: talking about the old days. Talking about when they fell in love, some thirty years ago.

"I thought she was real cute; she had long, pretty hair." Melvin says.

After Melvin's second divorce from Linda, he moved into the apartment complex in southern California that Bonnie lived in. Their young daughters soon became friends, but Melvin admired Bonnie from a distance. "I lived there a couple of years, and I'd see her every once in a while," Melvin says. "I figured she was either married or had a boyfriend. Every time I'd see her she'd be with some guy."

"Hey, that sounds kind of bad," Bonnie protests.

He smiles. "Well, I didn't know what was going on."

"I had all my brothers over there to watch over me."

"Finally, one day her daughter comes over, she was ten or eleven at the time," Melvin continues. "She said, 'Can my Mommy borrow your truck to help us move?' And I said, 'What's the matter with your dad? Don't you have a van or a truck or something?' And she said, 'Oh I don't have a dad.' And I said, 'What are you talking about?' So I went over there to see what was going on. It's been downhill ever since." Melvin giggles at that, and Bonnie joins in, releasing an eruptive *ack-ack* report that could bring down a Scud.

"Little did I know what he was going to drag me into," she adds, wiping a tear from her eye.

Melvin is fifty-eight years old, a couple years older than Bonnie. As he sits in the living room he helped build himself, he says, "I'm not doing too bad now." For the past decade or so, he can say he's been in charge of his own life, for the most part. Every couple of weeks, he packs the two freezers he's got in the back of his pickup with fresh meats, checks the motor that keeps the freezers humming in hundred-plus-degree weather, and heads off to a string of rural Utah and Nevada towns that are so far from anything that a trip to a real grocery store might be a day-long excursion for residents.

"I have my own business where I sell meat," he says. "In fact, that's where I make most of my money. I have a meat route. It's my own deal. I have suppliers who pack it for me, and I go out and retail it. I sell it to anybody who wants to buy it. Stores, restaurants. Mainly individuals. Home delivery. I usually do quite well." It's the perfect kind of setup for him, he admits.

"He doesn't like to bow to a boss," Bonnie says. "But he will allow me to bow to a boss for twenty-two years so he can have health insurance."

"After twenty-two years, you should own the place," he teases.

Bonnie works at Mervyn's department store in Ogden, "folding, stocking, whatever needs to be done," she says. By now, she can barely remember having ever done anything else.

"Bonnie never worked at the dairy, like they showed in the movie," Melvin says. "They got that part wrong."

Melvin and Bonnie don't seem like the kind of people Hollywood makes movies about. When he's not delivering meat, Melvin works for a liquidation company because, as his brother Ray once put it, "he's been broke so many times he ought to be an expert." He prefers being in the truck.

"When I been doing a job for the liquidation company, my customers wonder where the heck I've been for a few months." He laughs to himself. "Four, five, six months sometimes. And then I show up, and they say, 'Where have you been?' I have regular customers. I've had most of them for as long as I've been doing this, and so I go back and they're just so tickled to see me. The old ladies want to hug me."

"He comes home smelling like perfume," Bonnie says with another *ack-ack* laugh.

"Where I deliver to is out in the middle of Nevada. Not too many people are familiar with towns like Austin and Eureka and a town called Ball Mountain Mine. Hadley and Carver. Tonopah. The stores don't have a lot of competition. If they are lucky they have one supermarket in the town, and a lot of the time their selection is not that great. I usually have more customers than I can handle. I wish I had a bigger truck."

Melvin will be gone for four or five days on a "meat run," and sometimes he stops in Gabbs and spends a night with his brother Ray. Bonnie tries to work at Mervyn's those days he's gone. Melvin says it's hard being away from home, but it suits him.

"I like the idea of where I'm in control," he says. "If I worked a little harder I could probably make twice as much money. But I don't know, I guess I'm kinda moving toward semiretirement."

Ordinary lives. Simple lives. Some people might even say boring lives. But, oh, that spring of 1976. It was the bicentennial year. Anything seemed possible, and almost anything was. A former peanut farmer from Georgia was elected president, and Melvin Dummar—Melvin Dummar!—a gas station operator from Willard, Utah, came so very close to becoming rich because he had apparently picked up billionaire Howard Hughes in the desert one night, not far from where he delivers meat today. Hughes died in '76, and a will surfaced that named Melvin as a beneficiary. That was why they made a movie about him.

Melvin didn't get to play himself in the movie like he had wanted to. He did get to be in the film and have a couple lines, though. It wasn't much, but he thought it might be the start of a whole new career. He still doesn't understand why it wasn't.

"I liked Jonathan Demme, except he sure doesn't keep his word," Melvin says of *Melvin and Howard*'s director. "We did several shows together on the publicity tour for the movie. We traveled around together, to Seattle and Chicago and New York and Boston and Denver. Just about everywhere we went, the question would come up, because I did that little bit part in the movie, people would ask, 'Well, are you going to get Melvin into the movies, into your next movie?' And Jonathan Demme would say, 'Oh, yeah, he did such a great job, I'm gonna have him do some more acting.' And I haven't heard a word from him since then. Not a word. And I know of several movies he's directed."

Of course, it never had to be movies. Melvin's always wanted to be a game-show host, too. He knows he would be perfect for that. He knows all of the shows. And then there's singing, his first love. He's heard they've got an *American Idol*–type show for people over thirty-five, "and I've thought about that. Except I'd want to do my own material. I don't want to copy nobody."

It hasn't helped his show-business ambitions that so many people still think he's a fraud, even right here in Brigham City. "When we bought this property in 1996, these neighbors over here threw eggs at our bus and they wrote 'Go home, go away' on it," Bonnie says matter-of-factly. "The woman who lived in the second house over leaned over her fence one day and said we were trashing up the neighborhood. And these guys here on the other side built about a year after us. Mel decided he'd go over and say hi, and the first thing that came out of the guy's mouth when he saw Mel was, 'Dummar, what are you doing over here?'"

"We just keep to ourselves. Mind our own business," Melvin says.

History has been just as ungenerous as their neighbors. The 1979 book *Empire: The Life, Legend, and Madness of Howard Hughes* stated plainly that the will that named Melvin as a beneficiary was "an elaborate hoax that would make Clifford Irving's 'autobiography' of Hughes pale into insignificance." Irving was the writer who tried in the early '70s to fraudulently pass off his own work of fiction as an as-told-to autobiography of the billionaire. A later book, 1997's *The Money: The Battle for Howard Hughes's Billions,* also

Melvin and Bonnie Dummar at home, 2003.

took for granted that the Mormon will was a hoax. "One of the many fake wills that surfaced [after Hughes's death]," the authors wrote, "had such an ingenious scenario behind it that it was made into a popular movie, *Melvin and Howard,* which still surfaces on TV." Never mind that, in point of fact, it was because the scenario was not ingenious, but so simple and illogical, that so many people found it hard to believe.

In 1983, Hughes's multibillion-dollar estate was settled among twenty-two cousins. The Howard Hughes Medical Institute was given control of Hughes Aircraft, which the institute sold to General Motors two years later for $5 billion. Summa Corp., Hughes's parent company, was given title to most of Hughes's hotel and casino holdings in Las Vegas. Melvin got nothing but his celebrity, and that didn't last long.

But people *had* been fascinated with Melvin for a while, and that counted for something. Melvin certainly fascinated Harold Rhoden, the lawyer who tried the case in support of the will—so much so that Rhoden felt compelled to draw a portrait of Melvin during a break in court proceedings one day. The press, equally fascinated, got a hold of the sketch and made copies.

"They crowded around Dummar in the lobby, requesting his autograph [on the drawing]," Rhoden recalled after the trial. "I remember vividly the boyish pleasure he took in this. This, if nothing else, will fulfill at least some of his dreams, I thought."

All these years later, the original, coffee-stained sketch, in a simple black frame, hangs in a prominent place in the Dummars' living room. It's a dark, moody portrait, full of shadow and sharp angles, suggesting nothing so much as an aching, unidentifiable void. Bonnie points it out proudly to visitors. A look, wide-eyed and excited, fills her face when she shows it off.

Melvin stands in the back of the room, watching his wife describe the drawing. Maybe he understands her attraction to it. Maybe the sketch somehow proves, in the face of so much contradictory evidence, that she did not make a mistake by marrying him. He looks down at his feet. No, he doesn't think like that. It's something else, a glitch in his memory, something in himself—anger, he supposes, or fear. Fear that all those people who called him names knew something that he doesn't.

"I've read a lot of books about Howard Hughes, and wherever Melvin is mentioned it's in a negative way," says Gary Magnesen, the retired FBI agent who has reinvestigated the Mormon will case. "They say he was a fool. That he was a fraud. There's no evidence of that, but they kind of feed off each other. One guy writes it, and another picks it up. They just say he's an idiot, a fool, and move on. I thought he was a kook, based on what I read. But now, I think he's a decent guy. He's not an educated man, and he tries to do the best he can. He's an honest man. I believe that."

Magnesen's scenario might not be very dramatic, but he believes it's the truth. "I contend that Hughes's aides perjured themselves during the trial," he says. "During the trial there was a lot of testimony from them that Hughes never left his suite at the Desert Inn in Las Vegas. [The will's proponents] didn't have the money to hire investigators like the other side did. There was a lot of investigation that was not done by their side. There was a witness, a cowboy, who saw Howard Hughes wandering on a dirt road toward an abandoned mine that night. Another witness, Eldon Daniel, said he saw Hughes at the Mizpaugh Hotel in Tonopah. Daniel was a maintenance engineer at the [Hughes-owned] Frontier Hotel in Las Vegas. He said to John Meier, 'Is that who I think it is?' And Meier said yes.

"In a civil trial it's a preponderance of evidence that you have to prove," Magnesen continues. "And I believe the preponderance of evidence really shows that Hughes was out there for a couple of days looking at mines he wanted to buy, and he disappeared. My theory is that he felt pretty spunky and got in the car on his own and drove to another area and started walking. A cowboy saw him and rolled down the window and asked him if he needed help. He said no. He was carrying a walking stick and a paper bag. I found one juror [from the probate trial], and he said the first vote was split four/four. He said the handwriting testimony was discounted on both sides, so basically it came down to that the jury didn't think Hughes ever left the Desert Inn. I asked him, 'What about Eldon Daniel, who said he saw Hughes at the Mizpaugh Hotel? What about the cowboy who said he saw him?' And he didn't even recall that testimony. The reason is that it wasn't very good testimony. Daniel got beat up and was suddenly very reluctant to testify. When they got him on the stand, it was like pulling teeth getting any answers out of him about anything."

Magnesen sighs. It's a complex case, impossible to sum up easily. "Melvin took two polygraph tests," he says. "The first one, he flunked every question, including that his name was Melvin Dummar and that he lived in Utah. He's a fairly emotional type, and I think he was so pumped up there was no way to do it. After the trial, a television station in Salt Lake convinced him to take another polygraph, and the pressure was off, and he passed that one. It was administered by the same person who did the first one. I believe, in all likelihood, the will was legitimate. If I'd been on a jury, with the burden being a preponderance of evidence, I would have said the will was legitimate. And I am a hundred percent sure that Melvin is telling the truth, that he did pick up Howard Hughes in the desert."

Melvin received a call from John Meier in the summer of 2003, thanks to Magnesen's investigative work, and that was nice. "He told me a couple things I wish he would have said thirty years ago," Melvin says of the former Hughes executive. "He said he was with Hughes out there; he took him out there himself. He said on that same road where I found him, if you follow it to the end, that was the first mining claim that Hughes bought some twenty or so days later." Meier was still keeping a low profile, though. He's not coming forward, as if that would do any good now. "He said he's still hiding out in Canada for tax evasion," Melvin says.

Still, after all these years, and all the abuse he's taken, just getting a call like that put Melvin in a good mood. Bonnie, however, isn't so easily won over.

"I've said this before: I wish Mel had never picked up that old man," she says. "He ruined our lives."

"It's not his fault," Melvin tells her, reflexively protective of the man who—by his own design or not—put Melvin's name out into the world. Melvin wrote "Thank You, Howard" as a gimmick, but it came from the heart. For Melvin, at least, it was still the thought that counted. Sure, because of Howard Hughes he'd gone broke, lost his friends, and seen his reputation destroyed. But being up there on that stage in Reno, belting out his song, it was almost as if it was all part of Hughes's plan.

Melvin tries to think only about the good parts of that Reno gig now. For years afterward, he didn't sing at all, didn't even listen to music. His disappointment was too deep. But music eventually came back to him, and he's grateful for that, too. In 2001 Melvin was diagnosed with lymphoma. He's in remission now and he's back working every day, back on his route, but for a while he wasn't sure he was going to make it. Melvin doesn't like needles, and there are a lot of needles involved in cancer treatment. So that first time in the hospital, the nurse sang to him so he wouldn't notice she was putting a needle in his arm, and Melvin sang along. "There he was in the hospital, singing with the nurse at the top of his lungs," says Bonnie.

Music may have helped save his life, he doesn't know. Either way, he's glad he's singing again. He vividly remembers the day music came back to him, a couple of years before the cancer diagnosis. It just spilled out one day, without any effort, like it had never been gone.

"It was six or seven years ago, and I was on the road all the time, selling meat and seafood, driving," he says. "I felt so bad I was gone from home so much of the time, and it was our anniversary. So I just turned around and headed back home. I bought Bonnie a rose somewhere and drove back. She thought I was going to be gone for a week. I bought her a rose and I wrote her this song as I was driving home, it's called 'I Found a Rose,' and I sang it to her when I got there. Not long after that we went on a cruise, and they had a talent show. That's the first time I sang 'I Found a Rose' in front of other people. It did my heart good. I heard a lot of comments," he says, his face flushing with pride. "I was walking through the room afterwards, over to Bonnie, and I heard one woman say, 'Why don't you write a love song for me?' All the women were cryin', and all the men were mad."

Bonnie sighs. Then she sits up stock-straight and says, "I sure wish I could get ahold of somebody and get them to record that song for the radio."

Epilogue

I n November 2003, a cold afternoon rain hammers against the wide front
windows of Wooster Projects, a funky art gallery on West Fourteenth
Street in New York City. In a few hours, invited guests will arrive for a special preview of the gallery's new photo exhibit: *Nat Finkelstein: Then and
Now*. The burly Finkelstein, now seventy-one, salt-and-pepper mustache
bristling, prowls inside like a restless grizzly, adjusting display angles and using a fingernail to remove minuscule specks of dust from shiny frames. He
knows every little detail better be just right; the prices for many of these prints
of his photographs *start* at $1,750, and go all the way up to $20,000 for a few
collages. Most of the (relatively) cheaper items are shots of young women in
various stages of explicit undress. They are also recent, photographed in
2003. All along one long wall are 1965–66 shots of Andy Warhol, alone or
posed with his bizarre sidekicks: Edie Sedgwick, Nico, Ultra Violet, Baby
Jane Holzer. There's one of Bob Dylan doing a screen test for a Warhol film.
Lou Reed and the original Velvet Underground pose in several others.
There's no denying Finkelstein's exceptional photographer's eye. Each of
these pictures offers considerable nuance to anyone pausing to study it care-

fully: the way Dylan's hair seems to wobble in black-and-white splendor, the hint of desperation in Edie Sedgwick's heavily mascaraed eyes.

As Finkelstein prowls, he tells the story of how he met Warhol in early 1965. Back in New York after a year spent in the South photographing civil rights marches, Finkelstein hooked up with a girl at a party for author Tom Wolfe. She asked him to go with her to a second bash at Andy Warhol's place. When they got there, they ended up making love on a couch right in the middle of the party. Nobody paid any attention, Finkelstein remembers, except for someone who stole the girl's purse while she was otherwise occupied.

"Two days later, I went back," Finkelstein remembers. "Andy wanted to be famous, so he wanted me to shoot him so he could get his picture in all the big papers and magazines. Okay, I would."

Finkelstein ended up spending the better part of two years trailing Warhol and his followers around New York City. He never became friends with any of the others.

"Besides Andy, none of them liked me, really," Finkelstein says. "I was the interloper. They were all completely uninterested in current events, the historical things. Here I was, coming straight from the antiwar demonstrations, the civil rights movement, all the culturally shattering things, and I find myself among people whose only interest was in getting their names and pictures in the newspaper."

Finkelstein starts to elaborate, but there's a commotion outside. People are running and sliding on the wet sidewalk in front of Wooster Projects, jabbering loudly enough for their voices to be heard through the closed door.

"Shit," Finkelstein grunts. Reflexively, he pulls out a small camera.

Then there's a sudden glare like a flash of lightning, but it just keeps radiating, and then lighting stanchions and boom-microphone cranes are rolled into place by a film crew. Someone's shooting a scene for a TV show, and the cameras under the microphones are pointed at—Yes! It's Sarah Jessica Parker and Cynthia Nixon, clip-clopping down the wet sidewalk in impossibly high-heeled shoes, smiling and chattering as though it wasn't raining on them. *Sex and the City* is taping one of its final episodes! Cops hold back gawkers, while, after the take ends, assistants blot rain from the faces of the actresses, taking special care not to muss their hair. Somebody with a bull-horn announces that everyone can watch if they stand well away from the cameras and keep absolutely quiet. Obediently, the onlookers shuffle to the side and pipe down. Many, though, yank out cell phones and frantically whisper to friends to get over here *right now*; it's just amazing!

"Shit," Finkelstein mutters again, and he's off, hustling out the door and right up to some HBO flunky who says firmly, "Sir, you're not allowed to go past me and take photos."

"Excuse me," Finkelstein says quite politely, and slams by the guy, hopping to the side of the two actresses and snapping away while they go right on with their scene, oblivious to his presence. The flunky looks on helplessly. Ninety seconds later, they're done shooting and so is Finkelstein. He lopes back into the gallery, rain dripping off his mustache. Outside, assistants rush over to Parker and Nixon, holding umbrellas over the actresses' heads while they themselves get wet. Parker and Nixon stand a few feet apart, both looking straight ahead, not acknowledging each other or the crowd waving frantically from the spot a dozen yards away where everyone was herded. Soon, two Lincoln Town Cars purr up to the curb. Parker gets into one and Nixon into the other, even though there would have been plenty of room in one backseat for both. The vehicles glide off, a crew starts loading the microphones and lights into trucks, and the crowd disperses. It's all over in just about twenty minutes.

"Well," Finkelstein says, tucking the camera in his pocket. "How about a drink?"

In a nearby bar, sipping a Campari and soda, Finkelstein talks a while about his own checkered career—there was a fourteen-year interruption beginning in the early 1970s when Finkelstein got busted for marijuana in Texas and fled the country until a judge finally threw out the case—before he gets back to his time with Warhol.

"Andy always liked me, though everybody else with him wanted me out of the way," Finkelstein recalls. "He and I finally split up over a book deal. In late '66 I got the idea for a book called *The Andy Warhol Index,* with photos and things, and sold it to Christopher Cerf at Random House. Andy and I had a handshake deal for a fifty/fifty split. Then, just before we sign the contracts, Andy's lawyers say Andy's decided on ninety/ten in his favor. See, he was that way. He cared about money even though he might pretend he didn't. We eventually compromised on seventy/thirty, but that was it for me. I'd had enough of that scene."

Finkelstein finishes his drink, sighs, and rubs his forehead when he's asked to talk about the specific moment when Warhol made his famous prediction. Finally he says, "Now, the fifteen minutes of fame thing, that one, I don't mind he took. I threw it to him."

He's asked to explain.

"Okay," Finkelstein says, leaning forward. "I wanted to photograph this odd guy in very normal surroundings. So I took Andy into a street where kids were playing. When I got ready to shoot, the kids ran in front of the camera and started jumping up and down. A butcher came hustling over still in his white apron with blood on it. They all wanted to be in the picture as badly as Andy did, and Andy wanted to [be in it] one hell of a lot."

Then, Finkelstein says, came the moment, though not the way we've all believed for so long.

"Andy's looking at them, and he says to me, 'Gee whiz, Nat, everybody wants to be famous,'" Finkelstein says, leaning his bulk forward across the table. "I say back, 'Yeah, for about fifteen minutes, Andy.' He took that line. My quote became Andy Warhol's famous words. It doesn't matter to me. I'm more upset about the time he let somebody steal a whole roll of my negatives."

But it's upsetting for anyone—meaning just about everyone—who has spent the last almost-forty years thinking Andy Warhol said it. Warhol, the cool, weird icon we saw on TV all the time and read about in the papers. Warhol, who knew about being famous because he was famous himself. The prophecy that defined our Age of Celebrity just doesn't sound right coming from somebody who *wasn't*.

Why is Finkelstein telling this version of the story now? Maybe he's making it up and Warhol really did say "Everyone will be famous for fifteen minutes." We can still believe that. Most people will. Fame is all about ordinary people projecting their desires onto others, and facts don't have to play any part in it.

Back in the bar, Nat Finkelstein's got a couple of drinks under his belt and he's waxing philosophic. He's gotten a lot of mileage and money out of his two years with Warhol, and he's spent time, he says, pondering the meaning of it all. Believe him about who really said the fifteen minutes thing or don't. He was there, not you.

"I'm disgusted with the way things have turned out," grumbles Finkelstein. "Something I originally said has come true in a terrible way. America is totally obsessed with celebrity. Why should celebrity matter? Paris Hilton, some dumb young slut, dominates the news."

Nat Finkelstein has never met Gerry Cooney or Susan McDougal or Maury Wills. He wouldn't know Jim Wright or Mick Foley if he fell over them. Irene Cara he might remember as a sexy kid songstress, and Melvin Dummar as the goofball who claimed he picked up Howard Hughes in the desert. But he wouldn't be predisposed to like them. Finkelstein's personal experiences at the creation of modern-day "fifteen minutes" culture soured him on it. He split from Warhol & Co. at the height of their celebrity, and so wasn't on hand to see which ones learned hard, valuable lessons from their moments of fame and came out the other side as stronger human beings. Sometimes the ride leaves its participants better for the experience rather than bitter. But Finkelstein has a point: sluts can get famous, too.

With the kickoff of his show approaching, the burly old man gets up and stretches.

"Modern American culture is a combination of Andy Warhol and *People* magazine," Nat Finkelstein concludes. "Anybody who isn't famous wants to live vicariously through someone who is. People grow up thinking it's their right to be famous. They want their fifteen minutes of it. I said it. I just wish it wasn't so true."

Then he walks through the rain back to the gallery, where he will sell his photos of famous people for thousands of dollars.

Acknowledgments

Thanks, above all, to our editor at Tarcher, Sara Carder, for her keen eye and insight, and to Andrea Ahles Koos for outstanding research assistance. Also at Tarcher, we very much appreciate the contributions of Joel Fotinos, Ken Siman, and Katie Grinch. We'd also like to thank Guy Clifton of the *Reno Gazette Journal* for his help in tracking down pertinent information. We appreciate the cooperation and candor of Irene Cara, Gerry Cooney, Melvin Dummar, Mick Foley, Susan McDougal, Maury Wills, and Jim Wright. The following also generously gave us their time and observations: Pete Alfano, Chanda Bailey, Buzzie Bavasi, Carrol Beringer, David Bonior, Bobby Bragan, Dominick Bratti, Mark Brenenstall, Gabrielle Brooks, Bob Catullo, Iris Chang, Jennifer Cooney, Bonnie Dummar, Steve Farhood, Colette Foley, Terry Funk, Darcy Dummar Hidalgo, Terry Hudnett, Tom Loeffler, Sari Rudich Lopez, Gary Magnesen, Audrey Martell, Shirley Mendive, Jeff Neiloson, Tom Nunziato, Chuck Paul, Carol Pizzuto, Reina Poindexter, Dan Puntillo, Claudia Riley, Joe Sano, Rick Scaia, Mel Shields, Jennifer Suitor, Jenise La Vel Super, Matt Wrbican, Betty Wright, and, of course, Nat Finkelstein, who was there with Andy Warhol when it all began.

References

Introduction, Epilogue

Interviews of Nat Finkelstein and Iris Chang conducted by Jeff Guinn.
Interview of Kelly Clarkson conducted by Douglas Perry for the *Fort Worth Star-Telegram*.

Melvin Dummar

Interviews conducted by Douglas Perry:
Mark Brenenstall
Bonnie Dummar
Melvin Dummar
Darcy Dummar Hidalgo
Sari Rudich Lopez
Gary Magnesen
Shirley Mendive
Jeff Neiloson

Chuck Paul

Mel Shields

Noah Dietrich, Arnold Dummar, Keith Hayes, and Harold Rhoden, all of whom are deceased, are quoted from:

"Melvin and Howard: A Nevada Fairy Tale," by Jim Sloan, excerpted in *Literary Las Vegas: The Best Writing About America's Most Fabulous City,* edited by Mike Tronnes. Henry Holt & Company, 1995.

Harold Rhoden is also quoted from:
High Stakes: The Gamble for the Howard Hughes Will, by Harold Rhoden. Crown Publishers, Inc., 1980.

Additional Sources
Empire: The Life, Legend, and Madness of Howard Hughes, by Donald L. Bartlett and James B. Steele. W. W. Norton & Company, 1979.
High Stakes: The Gamble for the Howard Hughes Will, by Harold Rhoden. Crown Publishers, Inc., 1980.
The Money: The Battle for Howard Hughes's Billions, by James R. Phelan and Lewis Chester. Random House, 1997.

Maury Wills

Interviews conducted by Jeff Guinn:
Buzzie Bavasi
Carrol Beringer
Bobby Bragan
Maury Wills

Additional Sources
On the Run: The Never Dull and Often Shocking Life of Maury Wills, by Maury Wills and Mike Celizic. Publishing Group West, 1992.

You Can't Hit the Ball with the Bat on Your Shoulder, by Bobby Bragan and Jeff Guinn. The Summit Group, 1990.

Irene Cara

Interviews conducted by Douglas Perry:
Chanda Bailey
Irene Cara
Audrey Martell
Tom Nunziato
Reina Poindexter
Jenise La Vel Super

Additional Sources
The Associated Press
Billboard
Cosmopolitan
The New Yorker
People
Rolling Stone
United Press International
Variety
The Washington Post

Thinking Tuna Fish, Talking Death: Essays on the Pornography of Power, by Robert Scheer. Hill & Wang, 1988.

Jim Wright

Interviews conducted by Jeff Guinn:
David Bonior
Tom Loeffler
Betty Wright
Jim Wright
Interviews with Ben Procter and John M. Barry conducted for the *Fort Worth Star-Telegram*.

Additional Sources
The Ambition and the Power: The Fall of Jim Wright, by John M. Barry. Penguin, 1989.
Balance of Power: Presidents and Congress from the Era of McCarthy to the Age of Gingrich, by Jim Wright. Turner Publishing, 1996.

Mick Foley

Interviews conducted by Jeff Guinn:
Colette Foley
Mick Foley
Terry Funk
Rick Scaia

Additional Sources
Foley Is Good: And the Real World Is Faker Than Wrestling, by Mick Foley. ReganBooks, 2001.
Have a Nice Day! A Tale of Blood and Sweatsocks, by Mick Foley. ReganBooks, 1999.
Tietam Brown, by Mick Foley. Knopf, 2003.

Susan McDougal*

Interviews conducted by Douglas Perry:
Danielle Dickinson
Pat Harris
Bobby McDaniel
Susan McDougal
Claudia Riley

Additional Sources
Arkansas Times
The Observer
Salon
Vanity Fair

"Majority Report of the Special Committee to Investigate Whitewater Development Corporation and Related Matters."
"Whitewater: A Perspective from Little Rock and Washington." (Congressional testimony by Kenneth Starr, November 11, 1996)

Arkansas Mischief: The Birth of a National Scandal, by Jim McDougal and Curtis Wilkie. Henry Holt & Company, 1998.
Blood Sport: The President and His Adversaries, by James B. Stewart. Simon & Schuster, 1996.
The Woman Who Wouldn't Talk, by Susan McDougal with Pat Harris. Carroll & Graf, 2003.

*Portions of this chapter originally appeared in the *Fort Worth Star-Telegram.*

Gerry Cooney

Interviews conducted by Jeff Guinn:
Pete Alfano
Dominick Bratti
Bob Catullo
Gerry Cooney
Jennifer Cooney
Steve Farhood
Terry Hudnett
Carol Pizzuto
Dan Puntillo
Joe Sano

Additional sources
Sports Illustrated
The Washington Post

Kelly Clarkson

Interview of Irene Cara conducted by Douglas Perry.
Interview of Kelly Clarkson conducted by Douglas Perry for the *Fort Worth Star-Telegram.*

Additional sources
The Associated Press
Entertainment Weekly
Fort Worth Weekly
Newsweek
New York Post
Us

Life: The Movie, by Neal Gabler. Vintage Books, 1998.